Victims and Victimization: A Reader

Victims and Victimization: A Reader

Brian Williams and Hannah Goodman Chong

 Open University Press

Open University Press
McGraw-Hill Education
McGraw-Hill House
Shoppenhangers Road
Maidenhead
Berkshire
England
SL6 2QL

email: enquiries@openup.co.uk
world wide web: www.openup.co.uk

and Two Penn Plaza, New York, NY 10121-2289, USA

First published 2009

A catalogue record of this book is available from the British
Library

ISBN-13: 978 0 335 22527 9 (pb)
ISBN-13: 978 0 335 22526 2 (hb)

ISBN-10: 0 335 22527 6 (pb)
ISBN-10: 0 335 22526 8 (hb)

Library of Congress Cataloguing-in-Publication Data
CIP data applied for

Typeset by RefineCatch Limited, Bungay, Suffolk
Printed in the UK by Bell and Bain Ltd, Glasgow

Fictitious names of companies, products, people, characters and/or
data that may be used herein (in case studies or in examples) are not
intended to represent any real individual, company, product or event.

Mixed Sources

Product group from well-managed
forests and other controlled sources
www.fsc.org   Cert no. TT-COC-002769
© 1996 Forest Stewardship Council

FSC

The *McGraw-Hill* Companies

Contents

About the writers

Professor Brian Williams qualified as a social worker in 1980 and began his career working as a probation officer. Brian began undertaking research into services to victims in the mid-1990s, including studies on the implementation of probation work with victims or prisoners under the *Victim's Charter*, police work with the victims of volume crime, and restorative justice services in prisons and the community. His most recent book was *Victims of Crime and Community Justice* (2005) and he co-edited the *British Journal of Community Justice*.

Hannah Goodman Chong is a research fellow in the Community and Criminal Justice Division of De Montfort University. She has previous experience working with the Victims and Witnesses Action Group in Leicester; Leicester Witness Cocoon; Victim Support Enfield; North East London and Leicestershire & Rutland Probation Services. She was formerly Book Review Editor for the *International Review of Victimology*, and has co-written chapters on victimology, many of them with Brian Williams.

Professor Joanna Shapland is Professor of Criminal Justice and Director of the Centre for Criminological Research at the University of Sheffield, UK. She is also the Executive Editor of the *International Review of Victimology* and was formerly Editor of the *British Journal of Criminology*. She has written widely on victimology and is currently evaluating restorative justice schemes for the Ministry of Justice.

Basia Spalek is Senior Lecturer in Criminology and Criminal Justice at the University of Birmingham. Her research interests include British Muslim communities, crime, victimization and community safety issues, also equality and diversity within the public sector, and communities, identities and crime. Recent publications include: *Islam, Crime and Criminal Justice* (2002)

Crime Victims: Theory, Policy and Practice (2006), *Communities, Identities and Crime* (2008) and *Ethnicity and Crime: A Reader* (2008).

Professor Sandra Walklate is currently Eleanor Rathbone Chair of Sociology at the University of Liverpool, having held posts previously at Manchester Metropolitan University, Keele University, the University of Salford and Liverpool John Moores. She has written extensively on policing, gender and crime, and criminal victimization, with her most recent work being focused on the impact of the fear of terrorism on people's everyday lives. Her, most recent publications include an edited collection (with G. Mythen) entitled, *Beyond the Risk Society: Critical Reflections on Risk and Human Security*, published in 2006 by McGraw-Hill/Open University Press and a single-authored book entitled *Imagining the Victim of Crime* published in 2007 also by McGraw-Hill/Open University Press. She is editor of the *Handbook of Victims and Victimology* (2007).

Publisher's acknowledgements

The editors and publisher wish to thank the following for permission to use copyright material:

Von Hentig, H. (1948/1967) *The Criminal and His Victim: Studies in the Sociobiology of Crime*. Yale, CT: Yale University Press/Archon Books.

Hindelang, M.J., Gottfredson, M.R. and Garofolo, J. (1978) *Victims of Personal Crime: An Empirical Foundation for a Theory of Personal Victimization*. Cambridge, MA: Ballinger.

Boswell, G. (2005) 'Child victims', *British Journal of Community Justice*, 3(2). Reproduced with kind permission.

Bowling, B. (1998) *Violent Racism: Victimization, Policing and Social Context*. Oxford: Clarendon.

Garland, J. and Chakraborti, N. (2006) 'Recognising and responding to victims of rural racism', *International Review of Victimology*, 13(1).

Jordan, J. (2001) 'Women, rape and the police reporting process', *British Journal of Criminology,* 41.

Williams, C. (1993) 'Vulnerable victims? A current awareness of the victimisation of people with learning difficulties', *Disability, Handicap and Society*, 8(2). Reproduced with permission of the Taylor & Francis Group.

Ammar, N.H. (2001) 'Restorative justice in Islam: theory and practice', in Hadley, M.L. (ed.) *The Spiritual Roots of Restorative Justice*. New York: State University of New York Press. Reprinted by permission of the State University of New York Press © 2001, State University of New York. All rights reserved.

Umbreit, M.S. (1997) 'Humanistic mediation: a transformative journey of peacemaking', *Mediation Quarterly*, 14(3). Reprinted with permission of John Wiley & Sons.

Box, S. (1983) *Power, Crime, and Mystification*. London: Routledge. Reproduced by permission of Taylor & Francis Books UK.

Braithwaite, J. (2002) *Restorative Justice and Responsive Regulation*. Oxford: Oxford University Press. Reproduced by permission of Oxford University Press.

Kauzlarich, D., Matthews, R.A. and Miller, W.J. (2001) 'Toward a victimology of state crime', *Critical Criminology*, 10(3).

Alvazzi del Frate, A. (2003) 'The voice of victims of crime: estimating the true level of conventional crime', *Forum on Crime and Society*, 3(1).

Ashworth, A. (2002) 'Responsibilities, rights and restorative justice', *British Journal of Criminology*, 42.

Erez, E. and Rogers, L. (1999) 'Victim impact statements and sentencing outcomes and processes', *British Journal of Criminology*, 39(2).

Shapland, J. (1988) 'Fiefs and peasants: accomplishing change for victims in the criminal justice system', in Maguire, M. and Pointing, J. (eds) *Victims of crime: A new deal?* Milton Keynes: Open University Press.

Goodey, J. (2004) 'Promoting "good practice" in sex trafficking cases', *International Review of Victimology*, 11(1).

Howarth, G. and Rock, P. (2000) 'Aftermath and the construction of victimisation: 'the other victims of crime', *Howard Journal of Criminal Justice*, 39(1). Reproduced with permission of Blackwell Publishing.

O'Donnell, I. and Edgar, K. (1998) 'Routine victimisation in prisons', *Howard Journal of Criminal Justice*, 37(3). Reproduced with permission of Blackwell Publishing.

Dedication and introduction

This reader is dedicated to the memory of Brian Williams who began work on it in 2006. Brian was Professor of Victimology at De Montfort University. He wrote extensively on the subject but also gave his personal time to work as a victim support trainer and volunteer.

Brian tragically passed away in 2007 and is missed by his many colleagues who benefited from his kindness and willingness to share his extensive knowledge of the field.

This book was at that stage in its infancy, with Brian working on selecting many articles and chapters that he thought would help introduce the reader to a topic which he found so fascinating.

Many people have contributed to this book in order that the work that Brian had started would be completed and would help and be of interest to future students of victimology. Thanks must go to Sandra Walklate who provided additional guidance and support to me, and also to Basia Spalek, Joanna Shapland, and again to Sandra Walklate for writing introductions to chapters.

This reader contains a selection of articles and chapters that have been chosen in order to introduce the reader to the subject of victimology. The readings span the historical development of the subject from the earliest writings to later pieces and demonstrate how victimologists have expanded the general awareness of who can be a victim of crime, what it takes to be identified as such, and also the impact of crime on victims.

The selected readings exemplify the development of the field of victimology, from the early writings through to the greater understanding of the extent and impact of victimization as highlighted by feminists and other anti-oppressive activists and academics. This reader goes on to identify areas that have often been neglected by criminologists and victimologists including the effects of white-collar crime on victims, as well as areas which have become more topical in a world post 9/11. The reader concludes with two chapters which return to the theoretical underpinnings of victimology before going on to look at some of the current key issues that victimologists are pondering, including methodologies for determining the extent of victimization.

These articles offer the reader an opportunity to examine the original writings which have helped form and shape the discipline of victimology. They have been selected in order to offer an introduction to a broad range of issues and offer the opportunity to access the work of a wide variety of authors. Some of these contributions are considered victimological classics, others are not so well known, but all offer the reader a chance to expand their knowledge of the field.

Victimology is a relatively new discipline, generally regarded as having begun with the publication of Hans von Hentig's *The Criminal and His Victim,* in 1948. Part 1 represents some of the early writings in the field. The introduction puts them in the context of the period and outlines the critique of the victim-blaming approach embodied in much of this work, which was developed by feminist writers in the 1980s.

In direct contrast, Part 2 illustrates the challenges to these ways of approaching the study of victimology, posed first by feminist writers and subsequently, by anti-racist and disability researchers. This section is designed both to show how victimological methods developed as a result of this debate, and how the insights of hate-crime activists and the practitioner victims movement on anti-oppressive practice influenced thinking about victims and the study of victimology. Readings in this section span victimological writing from North America, Europe and Australasia.

Part 3 addresses the influence of religion upon work with, and research on, victims. This section highlights the contribution of groups such as the Mennonites in the USA, the Quakers in Great Britain and Islam in Europe and beyond, to thinking about services for, and the study of, victims of crime, including the development of restorative justice practice.

This is a new area for victimology and is important because of the contributions made by academics and practitioners writing from different religious backgrounds. Basia Spalek also includes a selection of references that may be useful for someone wanting to read further into the subject in her insightful introduction to this chapter.

Part 4 addresses the relatively neglected area, at least until recently, of victimological work on victims of corporate and state crime. It includes work by Braithwaite illustrating the range of possible approaches to these issues. In her introduction to the topic, Sandra Walklate reflects on how this strand of victimology has raised questions regarding who is seen as a victim and who as a criminal. This chapter highlights the importance of placing victims of corporate crime on the victimological agenda by discussing the scale of harm that they experience. This raises interesting discussions, for example those highlighted in the selections from Braithwaite about possible responses to this, including the use of restorative justice.

Part 5 addresses significant theoretical and conceptual issues such as the role and limitations of victim surveys. This covers topics such as the close links that exist within victimology between research and practical work such as support work with victims of crime. Pieces in this chapter question key theoretical issues, such as how societies respond to victims of crime in terms of allowing their involvement in the criminal justice process. Joanna Shapland introduces the chapter by highlighting some important changes that have been made to how victims are treated by the criminal justice system but points out that these changes have been made for the benefit of the system, and not necessarily simply to aid the victims.

Part 6 demonstrates the range of mainstream writing on victimology and the health of the discipline. This section covers issues such as victim involvement with (and satisfaction with) restorative justice, police work with victims, probation work with victims, victims' needs and dissatisfactions with the criminal justice system, arrangements for supporting victims in different jurisdictions and so on. The readings included in this chapter discuss survey data exploring the extent of victimization, and policy implications that flow from data gathered from victimization surveys. Emerging issues from the last few years are discussed, including the treatment of victims of human trafficking, and the impact of crime on the families of offenders. These groups of people, while being seriously affected by their experiences, struggle to be seen as victims in many cases.

Overall, the articles and chapters that have been chosen should introduce the reader to the history of victimology, and the key debates going on within the field at present. The reader should be able to gather an understanding of the practical needs of victims of crime, the current responses to these needs, and following on from this the gaps that need to be tackled in the future. Readings have been chosen that will allow those new to the field of victimology to understand how the subject has developed over the last 60 years, and from here be able to continue studying, researching, identifying and meeting the needs of victims of crime in the future.

Reference

Von Hentig, H. (1948/1967) *The Criminal and His Victim*, Evanston, IL: Archon.

Series editor's introduction

This is the fourth collection of readings to be published as part of the McGraw-Hill/Open University Press series, *Readings in Criminology and Criminal Justice*. The purpose of this series is to offer a student-friendly approach to the issues and debates that are central to the contemporary discipline of criminology. Despite the proliferation of textbooks claiming to offer a wide coverage of criminology and the criminal justice system, it is inevitable that such books frequently do not do justice to the needs of the undergraduate curriculum beyond Year 1. The intention of this series is to fill this gap. Indeed the changing nature of the criminology undergraduate market in and of itself makes its own claims for more readily available material and a wider variety of material beyond the standard textbook. In particular the modular system of curriculum delivery means that in order to deliver a course of an appropriate standard, tutors require available, easily accessible, and student-friendly material to support their courses. In the modular system collections of readings that address the core features of the criminology curriculum provide an essential starting point for students and tutors alike, especially in the light of the increasing number of journals and other outlets which may not be that easily accessible or subscribed to by all libraries, electronic developments notwithstanding. Lack of availability of a wider range of both historical and contemporary material has a detrimental effect on the discipline and the student experience. The intention of this series is not only to fill this gap, and as a result do better justice to the debates in the discipline, but to also provide the opportunity for the nominated editors, and the series itself, to make a mark on the discipline, by both stretching and contributing to its boundaries. This collection, offered by Hannah Goodman Chong and Brian Williams, achieves both of these aims.

Concerns and debates relating to criminal victimization have a shorter history that those relating to criminology per se but nevertheless those debates reflect parallel concerns. Historically victimology has asked such questions as 'what makes a victim?' and in more contemporary times has asked, 'what kinds of lifestyles contribute to becoming a victim?' But whatever question is asked about the nature of criminal victimization and its causes as a discipline it is a meeting place for policy makers, academics, practitioners and politicians, in much the same way that criminology is. As concerns about the nature of criminal victimization have risen up each of these respective agendas, so the academic curriculum has reflected and contributed to these concerns. The collection of readings presented here taps into this multi-faceted and multi-layered agenda.

In Part 1 we are given a flavour of the origins of victimology. Both of these extracts are considered to be classics within the literature and presented here they provide the reader with a very valuable insight into the way in which concerns about victims of crime were addressed and afford the opportunity to consider the extent to which these early concerns still operate within contemporary debates. One key feature of these readings is their implied focus on the nature and extent of vulnerability to victimization. Dimensions of vulnerability are the focus of the second selection of readings ranging from the structural vulnerabilities of ethnicity, age, gender through to the sometimes more hidden vulnerabilities associated with questions of disability. The issue of vulnerability is developed further in the next two sections of readings, the first of which considers the role of religion and religious beliefs, the second of which addresses the role of the state. Space is given to thinking about the role of religion and religious beliefs and the potentially different ways that such beliefs contribute to not only an individual's identity but in this context to the way in which such beliefs might offer an opportunity of dealing with and/or responding to criminal victimization in the extracts offered in Part 3 whereas the role of the state in *creating* criminal victimization is the focus of the readings in Part 4. In the last two selections of readings we are given a flavour to how academics and policy makers have endeavoured to make sense and respond to this vulnerability. The readings in Part 5 consider the problems and possibilities generated for policy change by how we think, measure, and define criminal victimization whereas the readings in Part 6 encourage us to consider what kinds of policies actually work for whom.

So as can be seen this collection of readings captures the complexity of victimology and the complex nature of the people who come together with the focus of the crime victim at the heart of their concerns. These readings are also a strong reflection of Goodman Chong and Williams's commitment to the kind of victimology that is not just about academic agenda setting but also about making a difference to people's lives. This was the particular forte of the work of Brian Williams and I hope that he, wherever he is, and his family, feel that we have done justice to his spirit and to his concerns for the victim of crime.

Professor Sandra Walklate
Eleanor Rathbone Chair of Sociology
University of Liverpool
August 2008

Part 1

The development
of the discipline

by Brian Williams

At the time that this chapter introduction was written, Brian was planning to translate an article by Mendelsohn published in 1956 from French into English. Unfortunately this is no longer possible. However, the chapter introduction has been left as far as possible as Brian had written it in order to capture how he planned to introduce victimological history to the reader.

It is generally agreed that victimology as a discipline began with the publication of Hans von Hentig's *The Criminal and His Victim* in 1948. In one sense, re-reading it nowadays, von Hentig's book is a vivid example of how far the discipline has come: much of it seems dated, even archaic, and many of his ideas are quaint or offensive to the contemporary reader. And yet, he made a remarkable contribution to criminology by emphasizing and demonstrating the importance of the victim in the 'doer-sufferer entanglement' (von Hentig, 1948, 1967: 448) – what Mendelsohn (1956: 99) later called the 'penal couple' of the victim and the offender. He asserted that studying offenders without taking any interest in victims is futile, leading to incomplete understanding or to incorrect conclusions. While criminologists have not fully taken this insight on, it has become increasingly difficult to ignore. Indeed, the overlaps between the two groups and the extent to which offending can be better understood when one understands the offender's prior experiences of victimization have informed much recent victimological research and writing (Boswell, 2000; Rumgay, 2004) and patterns of victim behaviour have been studied by criminologists interested in repeat victimization (Gill and Pease, 1998; Titus and Gover, 2001). These issues were raised in *The Criminal and His Victim* (see for example the discussion of John Dillinger's early history). Von Hentig was also one of the first to draw attention to 'the collective victim, the community' (von Hentig, 1948/1967: 442) in the case of electoral fraud and corporate crime. Sutherland's ground-breaking *White-collar Crime* was not published until 1949.

Von Hentig was also one of the first criminologists to draw attention to the ineffectiveness of imprisonment.[1]

Many writers have argued that von Hentig's work laid down the basis for a pernicious tendency which has become known as 'victim blaming': by studying the connections between offending and victimization (rather than, for example, the social causes of victimization) he individualized the issue and made it easier for criminal justice professionals, the media and people in general to blame victims for their plight (Walklate, 1989). The title of the section of his book reproduced here, 'The contribution of the victim to the genesis of crime', demonstrates this, and the detailed typology developed on pages 420–38 bears it out in detail. However, von Hentig's great contribution was to take the criminological profession to task for having neglected to study victims; he provided an example of how this could be done, producing compellingly readable work which demonstrated the possibility of taking a more rounded view.

Sadly, he also perpetuated another regrettable criminological tradition, by giving academic respectability to speculation and prejudice. Just as some of the so called positivist writers such as Lombroso dressed up their own ideas as scientific facts in their search for cause-and-effect relationships, so did von Hentig.[2] It is difficult, 60 years later, to differentiate between what was conventional wisdom at the time, and what was peculiar to von Hentig himself. It certainly seems likely that he collected 'true crime' stories which confirmed his prejudices: many of the references in the book are to literature of this kind[3] (although many others refer to respectable scientific sources). In his chapter on mental disorders, for example (von Hentig, 1948/1967), he asserts that epileptics are particularly likely to commit unprovoked assaults, arson, murder or suicide before, during and after seizures and that they commonly make false confessions to crimes. The only evidence given for the latter statement is an anecdote whose source is not mentioned and, in a footnote, a reference to a story told by Basil Thomson in a book entitled, *The Story of Scotland Yard*. No evidence at all is provided for the earlier claims, apart from references in footnotes to the work of the neurologist Kraepelin. At times sweeping statements are made without any evidence at all: 'That old men are at once the most lucrative and most moderate clients is a professional tenet among prostitutes' (von Hentig, 1948/1967: 409). How does von Hentig know this? He provides no references. However, this example also illustrates another aspect of his writing, alluded to earlier. His style is extremely vivid and lively, unlike that of much academic writing (in the 1940s or since) and it repays close attention. The references to 'hearse-chasers', 'jack-rollers', 'suckers', fences and pawnbrokers and to criminal slang seem positively gleeful at times. Some of the comments made in passing by von Hentig have subsequently justified deeper study: in the same section on older victims as the one quoted in the previous paragraph he points out how little is known about the causes of many older people's deaths and suggests that there are often younger relatives who stand to gain from such deaths. It was not until decades later that elder abuse including financial abuse was systematically researched (Glendenning, 1999).

Later in the extract reproduced in this book he comments briefly on the discriminatory sentencing of black offenders, an issue which continues to merit detailed study today, and he notes that the statistics in relation to murder victims in southern US states demonstrate judicial failure to value black people's lives equally. He also argues (in a footnote on p. 445) that racial discrimination may contribute to high rates of recorded crime by black people. Elsewhere in the book, however, he expresses crude racist views, and quotes those of other writers with apparent approval: the extract, for example, contains references to the 'vanity [and] cupidity of Negroes' (p. 426). His article on 'The criminality of the colored woman' (von Hentig, 1942/2005), however, eschews such prejudice, and imaginatively deconstructs the crime statistics to suggest that many factors other than race itself combined to explain the apparently high levels of criminality among black American women in the 1930s, including unemployment, disease, poverty, poor diet, overcrowded housing, and the differential age distribution of black and white women.

Von Hentig's research methods have, however, been much criticized. His book was essentially based upon desk research and his own experience. Although he explains his assumptions and methods when using statistics, his methodology can only be guessed at in other parts of his work. Although he pioneered the academic study of victims of crime, he did not interview any victims, which makes it seem likely that he perpetuated a number of other myths apart from that of the victim's contribution to crimes.

The Criminal and His Victim merits study today for a range of reasons. It is of great historical interest, which would be the case whatever its weaknesses because it was the first full-length study of victims of crime to be published. It also challenged conventional criminological assumptions about the place of the victim. It is also important *because of* its weaknesses: the positivist attempt to create a typology of victims was clearly linked to the victim-blaming tendency and it has been enormously influential. The argument that 'the collusion between perpetrator and victim is a fundamental fact of criminology' (von Hentig, 1948/1967: 436) is made with great brio. Because von Hentig's study was the first, others emulated it. On its own, it might not have had much influence, but it represented the beginning of an academic tradition which has helped to justify some of the political and judicial manifestations of victim blaming. The judge who introduced the notion of 'contributory negligence' may not even have been aware of von Hentig's concept of the 'wanton victim' (p. 427)[4] but he was nevertheless probably influenced by it (Walklate, 1989).

Michael Hindelang, Michael Gottfredson and James Garofolo display a more nuanced understanding of the relationships between victims and offenders than earlier writers, and they write in an empirical tradition which acknowledges the need for assertions to be backed up by evidence. While they, like the earlier victimological writers, failed to speak directly to victims, they drew upon evidence from a wider range of sources, including secondary analysis of a large statistical database, the Law Enforcement Administration's central surveys of personal, household and business victimization. Their book is written in a much more measured style than either von Hentig's or Mendelsohn's work, but they also contributed to the discourse of the blame-worthy victim by perpetuating the notion of the 'victim-precipitated' crime (first propagated by Wolfgang in 1958). Like von Hentig they were interested in the 'personal characteristics associated with risks of victimization'. Their stat-istical analyses showed that these were 'rather stable across cities' (Hindelang et al., 1978: 3). Younger people, males and single people had consistently higher rates of victimization than older people, females and those who were married. They reasoned that this must have to do with victims' lifestyles, and that there was likely to be a correlation between victims' age, gender and marital status and 'being in places and situations with high *opportunities for criminal victimization*' (p. 121). In addition, certain conditions such as the proximity of offender and victim and an offender sufficiently motivated to com-mit an offence are required. The likelihood of these coinciding, they hypothesize, is related to lifestyles.

Notes

1   See von Hentig (1941) and the discussion on pp. 446–8 of *The Criminal and His Victim*.
2   Like von Hentig, Lombroso pioneered the idea of scientific study in an area previously characterized by unscientific assumptions. He introduced scientific measurement as a way of developing a typology of criminals – but his attempts at using anthropometry and craniometry (measuring human bodies and skulls in a search for correlations with characteristics such as offending behaviour) turned out to be a blind alley (see Garland, 2002).
3   See for example the references to Collins, *New York Murders*, Mackaye, *Dramatic Crimes of 1927*, and Nelson, *Prison Days and Nights* on a single page (von Hentig, 1948/1967: p. 64).
4   Elsewhere, von Hentig writes of 'a living tempter, called the victim' (p. 450) and of 'a nefarious symbiosis . . . between doer and sufferer' (Foreword).

Recommended further reading

Mendelsohn, B. (1956) 'Une nouvelle branche de la science bio-psych-sociale: la victimologie', *Revue Internationale de Criminologie et de Police Technique*, 95–109. The journal has since changed its name to the *Revue Internationale de Criminologie et de Police Technique et Scientifique* and is now published by Polymedia Meichtry SA.

1.1

The criminal and his victim: studies in the sociobiology of crime
by Hans von Hentig

General classes of victims

The young

The weak specimen, in the animal kingdom and in mankind, is the most likely to be victim of an attack. Some such as the young and the old are feeble in body; some belong to the weaker sex, others are feeble in mind. The failing may consist in the excessive strength of some vital urge which tends to blunt the ordinary mechanisms of caution and forethought.

Youth is the most dangerous period of life.[1] Young creatures under natural conditions are the ideal prey, weak and easy to catch and savory.[2] Many survive because an older protective group, the parents, lend them their physical strength and experience. They are kept in the sheltered zone of a nest, den, and so forth. The perilous task of search for food is spared them. They are not released from this sphere of paternal care until by growth, play and imitation, they have attained an adequate faculty of self-protection: the adult stage.

The protective instincts of parents may be lacking or reverted. Human society has therefore set up rules in support of them. By violating such duties the parents commit an offense. Yet laws cannot regulate the variety of relationships linking parents and children. In modern industrial civilization the adolescent often becomes an active and decisive partner in the family unit. His departure may break the economic equilibrium. There is the offense of cruelty to children, but no "cruelty to parents"—the widowed mother for instance. The runaway breaks the "social contract" of mutual aid in a family community as much as does the father who neglects the youngster or turns him out. Many of our legal notions still reflect the closely knit agricultural family group, but the father has largely lost the economic power of boss, foreman, and teacher rolled into one.

Children do not own property and thus should be largely exempted as victims of property crimes. They can, however, be interposed heirs, and their elimination may switch an inheritance in a given direction.[3] Children often are insured; their death may bring money.[4] The child may be in the murderer's way for other reasons. In a Hamburg case a woman whose husband had not been heard of for ten years wanted her lover to return to her; he had left because she had a 12-year-old boy who was troublesome. The mother drowned the boy to win him back.[5]

Since the practices of birth control and abortion have gained ground the old crime of infanticide has become rather rare. The victims were mostly illegitimate children.

Our statutes have raised the 10-year age of consent to 14, 16, 18, and 21 years in the various states. In a case of carnal knowledge the woman is always a victim, since even the consenting female is presumed to be incapable of consenting. It is obvious that in many instances the legal notion conflicts with the factual situation; in practice it is up to the "victim" whether she will make use of her victim powers or not. All our statistics on rape are unreliable; recent trials in which noted movie stars and producers have been involved show that blackmail is rampant.[6]

It is not only among grown females living in states with a high consent age that the seducee-seducer type is met; it is astonishing how many younger girls and even children are victims more in law than in fact. F. Leppmann, one of the most experienced medicolegal experts, has pointed out the facts that some very small girls do not make any resistance, do not try to escape, and show "semicompliance", a mixture of curiosity and fear, bodily intactness, and mental challenge. Without this prerequisite many cases of statutory rape, Leppmann says, would not materialize.[7]

In my own investigation of a large number of incest cases I found that the incestuous relationships in nearly half the cases had a duration of a year or more, the best evidence that the alleged factor of compulsion must have been absent in many instances.[8]

The female

Female sex is another form of weakness recognized by law—numerous rules of our criminal code embody the legal fiction of an ordinarily weaker and a stronger sex. The groups of crimes against chastity and against family and children are meant to be a protective device against the superior physical force or the neglect of the male. As we look more closely into the situation it is apparent that there are many victims of greater male strength; but women do not easily become victims of this inequality except as special circumstances supervene. Wherever we study European murder statistics the high rate of female victims in the vocational group of personal services is remarkable.[9] What happens is first corruption and, when pregnancy has resulted, physical removal of the eventual claimant. The maid or servant comes from the poorer strata of population.

On the other hand many older women are murdered because they are supposed to be wealthy and, in their narrow stinginess, possessors of cash or valuables. By greed of gain they have acquired what needy people consider to be riches; the same avidity renders them blind to the possibility of new gain and to all individuals who throw bait to their greediness, thus forcing a tempted swindler to the length of murder if he is to profit. We shall meet this victim in the psychological classification.

It is legally incorrect to speak of a "victim" when both perpetrator and "victim" are involved in a criminal enterprise, but psychologically in certain forms of crime there is a sort of victim status. This is demonstrated by the much higher risk rate of one of the associates; the hazardous part is mostly played by the younger partner. Such relationships are for instance the fence-burglar, or the prostitute-pimp or the boss-slugger or -killer combinations. Burglar, pimp, and killer are regularly younger; they are the "exploited" and this is true even in the case of the bully who receives money but in turn has other heavy duties to perform. Some old criminals become "pawnshop owners" or fences because they thereby reach a higher level of profit and security. It is one of the advantages of the pickpocket and similar criminal attackers to get money at full value instead of the 60–80% deductions of the fence.[10] Fence, prostitute, and gang boss can at any moment get rid of the compromising associate by delivering him in some devious way to the police. The high conviction rate of the young group, the low rate of the older group evidence a psychological and factual victim situation.

The old

The aging human being is handicapped in many ways. Of the life-preserving instincts, self-preservation, coinciding largely with the acquisitive impulse, is stimulated. The weaker an individual grows physically the more he will tend to strengthen other supporting strong points around him: the more or less artificial security granted by property, the safety-giving institutions of society, paid guards, and so forth. It is a mildly or openly fearful attitude, and whoever can overcome the distrust or relieve the chronic apprehension of the senile can approach him for better and for worse.[11]

Although the sex instinct seems irritated in old age, it is my belief that it is not by reason of a real stimulation but by a deficiency of the controlling brakes. The inhibitions are slurred. But regardless of whether toxic products of disintegration operate on the mechanism of the impulses or their inhibitors, a belated career of sex delinquency may and often does result. A highly profitable career may be opened to the criminal, with a perfect victim—perfect because of the social status to be lost and therefore to be considered; because of the perhaps very great economic power of the aged man; and because of his blind infatuation for some object of his senile predilections.[12] That old men are at once the most lucrative and most moderate clients is a professional tenet among prostitutes.

It is true that one should stick to the legal definition of the victim. Yet old and young alike can become "victims" in the form of decoyed associates. They come to be, first, victims of the stronger mind, then perpetrators under the law, and when caught and sentenced, "victims" again. One frequent form of being thus victimized is to join a gang or an immoral association. Under the guise of a protecting assemblage these groups lead boys and girls deeper, more thoughtlessly, and more insidiously into delinquency. If young creatures are thus above all self-harming—victims of their biological and mental incompleteness and subject to the leadership of an older or stronger mind— in old age the relationship is reversed. The younger man is now the stronger and the older associate becomes the victim, or better, the living tool. The mere tool quality is not recognized in law except in cases of complete irresponsibility. East has reported the following history of a patient:

> He [an old man] was arrested with another man for stealing two dozens of camisoles. He had a clean record until ten months before, when he was arrested for loitering in company with the same man; he was then discharged. His wife considered, and with reason, that he was a tool of the younger prisoner, for he lacked any initiative himself and was only fit to carry out the simplest instructions. And his part in the offense appeared to have been limited to carrying the cardboard boxes containing the stolen articles through the streets.[13]

Leaving aside such secondary problems as that of the senile doctor playing an unsuspecting role in a murder scheme,[14] two forms of death have not been paid sufficient attention: the mass death of old and decrepit people hospitalized in private homes[15] and the large number of deaths by fire.[16] In the first case the situation presents an incentive to get rid of the old patient, since a lump sum is paid so that the old man be cared for for the "rest of his life". The danger lies in the fluidity of this period; a reduction of the interval promises profit and infirmity renders the diagnosis of cause of death difficult. As to the second category, approximately 15,000 deaths are caused by fire every year in the United States.[17] This figure does not include deaths from injury or exposure to fire. Too many people, in this writer's opinion, are burned by exploding oil burners, or while burning weeds or leaves in the barnyard, or are said to have fallen asleep while smoking and thus ignited their bedding. That a woman of 72 should pour benzine over her body, touch a match to the fluid and commit suicide[18] can only be accepted after very careful investigation. In all such fires babies and old people are the main sufferers.

The elder generation holds most positions of accumulated wealth and wealth-giving power. At the same time it is physically weak and mentally feeble. Its rate is high in accidents and suicides, and although statistics do not openly say so, in victims of homicide. In the combination of wealth and weakness lies the danger.[19] Old people are the ideal victims of predatory attacks. Since the aged section of the population is ever increasing, crime will be directed against it with new vigor and in new forms. It is probable that, like youth and the female sex, old age will be in need of new protective devices—protection from its own infirmities.[20] Law will reduce that perilous unlimited self-determination which, at great age, often becomes a self-wrong or a wrong to the family group.

The mentally defective and other mentally deranged

The feeble-minded,[21] the insane, the drug addict, and the alcoholic form another large class of potential and actual victims. The English Mental Deficiency Act of 1913, section 1, defines the varieties of amentia:

> The following classes of persons who are mentally defective shall be deemed to be defective within the meaning of this Act:
>
> *Idiots:* That is to say persons so deeply defective in mind from birth or an early age as to be unable to guard themselves against common physical dangers;
> *Imbeciles:* That is to say persons in whose case there exists from birth or from an early age a mental defectiveness not amounting to idiocy yet so pronounced that they are incapable of managing themselves or their affairs, or, in the case of children, of being taught to do so;
> *Feebleminded persons:* That is to say persons in whose case there exists from birth or from an early age mental defectiveness not amounting to imbecility yet so pronounced that they require care, supervision and control for their own protection or for the protection of others, or in the case of children, that they by reason of such defectiveness appear to be permanently incapable of receiving proper benefit from the instruction in ordinary schools;
> *Moral imbeciles:* That is to say persons who from an early age display some permanent mental defect coupled with strong vicious or criminal propensities on which punishment has had little or no deterent effect.[22]

In all four categories the normal play of motivating forces is upset; benefit does not attract, danger does not turn away. The danger may be physical, may come from human beings or from human institutions. It has justly been maintained that certain high-grade defectives 'may be more dangerous than the professional criminal, who has at least some regard for his own safety'.[23] Their very imperviousness to the warning sensations of danger renders the feeble-minded imprudent. The fearless are imagination-proof and thus good victims.

[. . .]

Immigrants, minorities, dull normals

Three other groups of typical victims may be mentioned. An artificial disadvantage is imposed on the immigrant, the minority race, and the large class of what the psychological testers call the "dull normals". This handicap extends from the social sphere to everyday conflicts. All are easily and frequently victimized.

We have already considered the immigrant status, or the situation of being a foreigner, from the point of view of criminality. There is a tendency all over the world to make the foreigner bear blame for others.[24] Their different appearance,[25] their poverty, the life in slums, the disturbed balance of sexes, their competitive efficiency, all render them suspect. In America for a long time the idea prevailed that these aliens must be highly criminal, till careful statistical studies gave evidence of their low delinquency. In European countries foreigners coming from the West—the United States and the Dominions—are supposed by contrast to be rich people; they are regarded as wealthy—noncriminal, but good victims.[26] Immigrants from the East, again, are poor, highly competitive, and thus received with distrust.

Immigration means more than a change of country or continent. It is a temporary reduction to an extreme degree of helplessness in vital human relations. Leaving aside the linguistic difficulties, all psychological ties have to be redisposed which connect the human being with other men and protect him from them. Through many costly mistakes and blunders and through many years of painful experience a new and safe equilibrium is established.

The inexperienced, poor, sometimes dull immigrant is an easy prey to all kinds of swindlers.[27] Fraud would not have happened in the narrow and closely knit world he came from; the former social situation, rigid but highly protective at the same time, has not prepared him for the competitive new surroundings, and since the immigrant thinks that the new life is superior he confuses technical progress with moral superiority. He therefore arrives full of expectations, hopes, and idealized prospects, his ingrained peasant suspiciousness dismantled and disarmed by his belief in a new and a better world.

[. . .]

Racial minorities do not receive the same protection of the law as is given to the dominating class. This attitude makes it easier to victimize them. Minority groups, with justification, fear exploitation and abuse. They can be approached with less suspicion by members of their own group; that is why Italians prey on Italians, Negroes on Negroes, Filipinos on their countrymen.[28]

The delinquency of certain races even bears a special character; thus modern techniques have deprived gypsies[29] and Negroes of the profit of their time-honored skills.[30] Defenseless victims of this catastrophe, they resort to minor forms of property delinquency.

One is not allowed to speak of delinquents as "victims" of criminal justice, with one exception. If the treatment of many law-enforcing agencies is grossly discriminatory, concept and term are justified. No crime is more difficult to judge than murder when mere statistical methods are used and details are lacking. Discrimination however is demonstrated in the following figures:

Murder Indictments by Race of Offender and Victim[31]
Richmond, Virginia 1930–39
(Per cent of total convicted)

Sentence	Negro–Negro	Negro–White	White–White	Total
Life, or death	5.7	100.0	26.7	10.5
20 years to life	22.0	–	20.0	21.1
10 to 19 years	30.5	–	6.7	27.1
Under 10 years	41.8	–	46.6	41.3

All the few Negro-white murder indictments ended in a life sentence; when a Negro killed a Negro the penalties were lighter than when a white killed a white.[32] In Richmond there was about the same number of nollepros and acquittals in slayings of Negroes by Negroes and whites by whites. In five North Carolina counties, however, mentioned by the same author, the percentage of these releases was 18.6 in all cases in which Negroes killed Negroes and 31.1 when white killed white.[33] The value of these figures is greatly accented by the fact that many killings will have left the prosecution at an earlier stage of the judicial procedure and cannot be considered any more. We know that the justifiable category of homicide falls heavily on the colored victim.

The large group of "dull normals" seems born to be victimized in many ways. The success of countless swindlers can only be explained by the folly of their victims, not by their own universal brilliance. Insane and feeble-minded girls are protected against seduction; simple-minded females are not. The physiological stupidity which is just above a mental age of 11 years and 2 months and just above an intelligence quotient of 70 is the great hunting ground for all types of criminals.

It is not without significance that the class stratification within a prison sets apart the simple-minded and rustic persons who are despised as eternal suckers.[34] The vocabulary of the prison is full of terms disdainful of the fool and his delusive ways of life. The words "yokel", "clown", "lout", "bumpkin", "apple-knocker", "hoosegow" designate an ignoramus, an awkward and easily imposed-upon country fellow. From the terms "sucker" and "yap"[35] it may reasonably be concluded that the dull normal types are recognized as close to certain infantile levels. A sociology of epithets remains to be written.[36]

Psychological types of victim

The depressed

Our legal categories look very simple: one is injured, the other guilty. But psychologically things are not so easy. For instance:

a. The injury may be desired, in some cases even lustfully longed for.
b. The injury may be the price of a greater gain.
c. The detrimental result may be brought about partly by the concurrent effort of the victim.
d. The detrimental result would not have followed without the actual instigation or provocation of the victim.

The law assumes that the perpetrator is always the directing agent at the back of any move. It takes for granted that the "doer" is always, and during the whole process which ends in the criminal outcome, active, the "sufferer" always inactive. It is characteristic of our legalistic thinking that the notion of provocation has been allowed to enter into our criminal codes, only in a very limited way. Individual variations are discounted. "There must also be a reasonable proportion between the mode of resentment and the provocation":[37] this is the law—full of majesty but devoid of finesse.

The reciprocal operation of affinities between doer and sufferer can be measured in degrees of strength. It ranges from complete indifference to conscious impulsion. The following scale may be set up:

Attitudes of the victim

1. apathetic, lethargic
2. submitting, conniving, passively submitting
3. cooperative, contributory
4. provocative, instigative, soliciting.

However, in the present state of our knowledge it appears more practical to form a tentative classification following broad psychological symptoms. The first and probably most important of these categories is the apathetic type.

The so-called combative propensity consists of fighting qualities and traits which enter into play as long as physical contest does not seem hopeless. The most courageous savage would beat a hasty retreat from a spirit in which he believed or from a volcanic eruption. Human beings are thus equipped with a "radar" of fear. It is the imagination of danger and therefore an instinct of highest biological value.

Among all maladies there is no graver and more dangerous disease than a disturbance of the instinct of self-preservation. We may omit the disorders of the instinct of nutrition, which may be pathologically reduced, suppressed or increased. More interesting to us here is the instinct of bodily integrity; without it the individual, deprived of warning outposts, would be easily surprised and overwhelmed by dangers or enemies. The ailment may consist of analgesia, the absence of sensibility to pain, or of indifference to harm or injury in prospect. It reaches its culminating point in weariness of life and the innate tendency to self-destruction.[38]

Such depressions are met in most psychoses: of course in the manic-depressive insanity, but also in dementia praecox in all its shades, in alcoholism, general paralysis, epilepsy, and senile dementia. In addition there are numerous individuals who cannot be labeled clinically insane but who suffer from a low vital tonicity, are mildly depressed—not suicidal, but indifferent to peril and defense, unsuspecting, careless, "fearless",[39] from simple unconcern. The laziness which many criminal anthropologists thought to have found in the criminal is more "indolence"—that is, the refusal to be moved by pain, present or future.[40] If some groups of delinquents seem to belong to the human type of low vital tone, it must be said that these depressed individuals are the most likely to be detected and arrested. That persons endowed with a weak instinct of self-preservation are often victimized cannot be doubted. Sometimes they present themselves as adequate victims not only to the criminal but to the state itself by false confession.[41]

The depression may be chronic[42] or temporary and physiological. A victim function is sometimes assumed by one of the associates in a crime who is persuaded to participate. Slowed down physically by the depression, he is the first to be caught. Such was the case with the widower William Jones whose story is told by Ferrier.[43]

[. . .]

The acquisitive

The acquisitive specimen of humanity is another excellent victim. The greedy can be hooked by all sorts of devices which hold out a bait to their cupidity. The excessive desire of gain eclipses intelligence, business experience, and inner impediments. "Bankers", says a swindler, "are very good prospects. They engage in a lot of speculative business and anyone who speculates is a good prospect".[44] "The 'sucker', as a rule", writes a competent police officer, "believes in his own superior intelligence and knows that certain things are possible. He has heard of others who have made large sums through similar operations. He will therefore listen very readily to the smooth proposals of the buncos".[45]

The assertion of a former convict is doubtless correct that it is impossible to beat an honest man in a confidence game.[46] The idea that if "there were no larceny in a man and he were not trying to get something for nothing and rob a fellow-man it would be impossible to beat him at any real con-racket"[47] has been shared, in part at least, by the New York judiciary. The Court of Appeals some years ago enunciated the general theory that where a person parts with his money for an unlawful or dishonest purpose, even though tricked into so doing by false pretenses, a prosecution for the crime of larceny could not be maintained.[48] However, at the next session the legislature amended the penal code to invalidate this stand.

The acquisitive victim may be lured away from the moral supports of his home and his usual surroundings[49]—from a cautious wife, perhaps—to be murdered, as happened in the famous Troppmann case (1869).[50] Often another factor is added: a wave of avarice is sweeping the country,[51] or the attacker makes his approaches in a confidence-inspiring disguise. For many people devoutness is an effective cover.[52] "Pickpockets sometimes dress as clergymen; pretend to be short-sighted and carry a book in hand. . . ."[53] Book and glasses represent intellectual accomplishment, allergy to material things, and estrangement from worldly things.

The so-called white slave traffic does not consist of archvillains and drugged girls carried to waiting automobiles and shipped forcibly to foreign countries. "Young girls," writes an expert, "are sometimes beguiled into going abroad, but in other than very exceptional instances, the only influence used is the persuasion of an oily tongue and imaginary pictures of pleasure, beautiful clothes, applause, happiness, and wealth—base and lying appeals to vanity and cupidity."[54] The victim is eager for high wages and for a good time. The inducible breeds the inducer.

[. . .]

The wanton

Our laws presuppose the leading part of the male in all unlawful sex relations. Legally speaking, rape can only be committed by the male and "any man, who, by means of temptation, deceptions, arts, flattery or a promise of marriage, seduces any unmarried female" is guilty of seduction. A male person cannot be abducted and there is no female pimp in American or European law.

Psychologists disagree with this unconditional view. "While in the major-ity of cases", writes Hollander, "the man is at fault, there is a certain class of women whose seduction is a literal impossibility. There may be a first offence, but a seduction never. There is a numerous class in which the woman is more than compliant, or even enacts the active rôle in the so-called seduction".[55] We thus arrive at the category of the wanton victim. It is a type well known in fact[56] but obscured and dimmed by the rough generalizations of our laws and social conventions. Often a sensual or wanton disposition requires other concurrent factors to become activated. Weather conditions, loneliness, alcohol, and certain critical phases are "process-accelerators" of this sort. They are closely interrelated; alcohol, for instance, eases the discomfort of the menstrual period or the menopause.[57]

Leppmann in his studies on sex criminals has pointed out the relation of night work to sexual irritability.[58] He is thinking of the male perpetrator, but his conclusions apply to the female as well, especially if the marriage is disharmonious or both are busy on day and night shifts so that the couple no longer meets or is exhausted when united. The tired individual suffers from a partial paralysis of inhibitions. This fact explains many of the undesired results of the "share-the-car" system during the industrial boom of wartime. Regardless of legalistic distinctions, both men and women were probably victims of overexertion and that special form of spatial temptation, overcrowding.

Karpman has related the story of a "diminutive male psychopath" who was corrupted by elderly women.[59] Regardless of whether this patient has overdrawn the passivity of his own role, it is certain that such cases are not exceptional.[60]

The lonesome and the heartbroken

Is another grouping, that of the lonesome victim, justified? I believe it is.

Loneliness has three main effects. First, the desire for companionship is one of the fundamental urges of animals and men; it fades away only in old age and in some forms of insanity. To seek isolation is even regarded as a pathological symptom and viewed with suspicion. Confinement is isolation and felt deeply as suffering, sometimes so deeply that death is risked to break out and escape the intolerable sting of this segregation. Loneliness therefore creates the longing for forcing a way out of this blockade, and also creates optical illusions as far as the wished object goes. Anything is better than the solitude of a lonesome life.

The critical faculties are weakened under these circumstances: "Some women believe that all men are fine, hearty, upstanding fellows, shrewd, intelligent and dependable . . ." writes Ferrier.[61] When one of Karpman's patients was strongly attracted by a woman he would not call good-looking he justified himself as follows: "I was more attracted to her for the reason that I had not been around women for some time, as I had just gotten out of prison and almost any woman looks good to a man who has been locked up for some time".[62] This is probably the explanation of the reduced value of widowers in the marriage market.[63] In any case, the lonesome human being, just because of his bereavements, is an easy prey to the "blockade-runner".

A third factor is of a merely practical nature. The groups to which we belong are protective. We cannot disappear without being missed and investigated. No one would have missed Mrs. Crippen for herself, but she was a member of the Music Hall Ladies' Guild and, as treasurer, for obvious reasons clearly in view.[64]

"Mass murderers" are criminals who by the inadvertence of doctors and crime-investigating agencies, and because of the social and familial position of their victims, remain undetected for an unusually long time, and are thus enabled to continue their activities.

[. . .]

Babbitt Sinclair Lewis has depicted the figure of a tormenting wife who in a moment of excitement and self-humiliation admits her wickedness and threatens to kill herself.[65] But she goes on deviling and he shoots her. She represents the type of person who seems to want to destroy herself, whether directly, by suicide, or indirectly, by forcing the hand of some other desperate person. "Life was a plot against her", says Lewis, "and she exposed it furiously".[66] She does the same with the men around her. It is a different case with delusional enemies and persecutors. Anyone may by chance become the victim of a sufferer from paranoia or dementia paranoides.

[. . .]

Blocked, exempted, and fighting victims

It would not be hard to distinguish other categories: the gambling type,[67] the seductible,[68] and the competitive category of victims.[69] Since a classification to serve its pedagogical purpose must not be too broad, we will limit ourselves to one final type. One may call him the blocked victim, by which is meant an individual who has been so enmeshed in a losing situation that defensive moves have become impossible or more injurious than the injury at criminal hands. Such is the case of the defaulting banker, swindled in the hope of saving himself. It is a self-imposed helplessness and an ideal condition from the point of view of the criminal.

The strategy of blackmail rests solidly on the foundation of a defenseless victim. The "badgergame"[70] is the prototype of this eternally successful procedure, and we would be wrong in assuming that the husband is always a phoney. The sums the police extort from criminals are enormous; millions of dollars are extorted by the criminal from the fence and by cashiers from bank presidents. Crime in countless cases brings one risk: it has to pay to someone, in money or information. The fix is the penalty of failure. The criminal in paying feels deeply his imperfection and his victim quality. The result of jumping the bond is financially in the same line.

A man who is irreproachable and unapproachable and who cannot be reached through friends, employers, and so forth may be otherwise blackmailed into silence on being victimized. "His private life will be looked over for some weakness whereby he can be handled."[71]

One of the most lucrative rackets is called the "muzzle". Details are given by Sutherland's professional thief. The victims are homosexuals. "Arrests are so rare that when one does occur it is a matter of much discussion among thieves . . . The muzzle is one of the few rackets in which a go back (second attempt) can be successfully staged."[72] We may add that "muzzle" has little to do with "mouse", as stated in the glossary of the professional thief.[73] The muzzle is on the victim.

It is relatively safe to commit a robbery under circumstances which do not allow the victim to report the affair. This may be a situation of unlawful intimacy,[74] or just a prisoner who is held up by a fellow prisoner and cannot complain because he was illegally in possession of money.[75]

The vast field of fraud, that form of crime in which the greatest sums are turned over and passed on to criminal elements in our midst, is the habitat of the blocked or "frozen" victim. Two requirements have to be realized: the sucker must have sufficient money and the willingness to use dishonest methods to make more money.[76] This fundamental trait protects the criminal against the victim himself [. . .]

Notes

1   Hans von Hentig, "DIe biologischen Grundlagen der Jugendkriminalität," *Monatsschrift für Kriminalpsychologie*, XIX, 713.

2   The terms "greenhorn" (in German *Grünschnabel*) and "gull" (derived from "yellow"—see the German word *Gelbschnabel* and the French *bec-jaune*) both denote one easily cheated, a dupe. The "pigeon" means one who is an easy prey and an inexperienced, unsuspecting, amusingly simple creature. We need only look at older crooks robbing younger delinquents of their loot, by shooting dice and compelling them to do more stealing, to see that the victim element and delinquency are closely interwoven. See the story of James Martin in Shaw's *Brothers in Crime*, p. 235. Youth, of course, may be a protective element—in poison murders, for instance, when sudden death will regularly arouse suspicion. A lack of finesse along this line ended Dr. Palmer's successful career. Kingston, *Law-Breakers*, p. 40.

3   As in the Swope murder case. E. H. Smith, *op. cit.*, pp. 175 ff.

4   See the Billik case, *idem*, pp. 128 ff.

5   Elssmann case. Wosnik, *Beiträge zur Hamburgischen Kriminalgeschichte*, I, 116 ff.

6   The change of a "benefactor" into a malefactor was demonstrated by the Charlie Chaplin trial in March and April, 1944.

7   Leppmann, "Der Sittlichkeitsverbrecher," *Zeitschrift für gerichtliche Medizin*, 1906, p. 26. Leppmann gives examples of how the cracking of

ambiguous jokes, certain dancing techniques, even certain immoral mores of crowds which girls have joined, contribute to the criminal outcome. *Idem*, pp. 28–29.

8 Von Hentig and Viernstein, *op. cit.*, pp. 203–207. See case No. 23, p. 124. On belated rape information as a weapon to achieve revenge, extortion, and exculpation from other slips and from jealousy see Georg Nordhausen in *Handwörterbuch der Kriminologie*, II, 230.

9 The problem is obscured in the United States by the interference of racial factors. Of 100 females ten years old and over gainfully employed in domestic service,

> 19.8 were native white females
> 62.6 were Negro females

Sex ratio and age distribution, having their peak between 15 and 29 years, add more weight to the unfavorable balance. *Abstract of the 15th Census of the United States, 1930*, p. 331; and *Population by Relationship to Head of Household and Age*, 16th Census, 1940, Series P-19, No. 3, July 15, 1943 (Washington, 1943), pp. 2, 3, 4.

10 On fences see Sutherland, *Professional Thief*, pp. 145–147; and Spenser, *Limey Breaks In*, p. 180, where the author admits that he would not have been so busy pulling jobs if the fence had not urged him on, even by scouting places to break into. For a description of another fence in operation see pp. 221 ff.

11 There is a strange sort of senile bias which sometimes favors the access of a murderer. See the Swope case in Kansas City (E. H. Smith, *op. cit.*, p. 177), and the Rice case in New York (Lawes, *Meet the Murderer*, pp. 143–146).

12 One murder case had the following background. I quote the report: "The Merkli—she was a 55-year-old pawnbroker—soon was charmed with the (22-year-old) defendant because he bore a resemblance to a defunct former lover. She demonstrated her liking by loaning pretty highly on his pawns, in spite of her usual stinginess." Wosnik, *op. cit.*, II, 132.

13 East, *Forensic Psychiatry*, p. 220.

14 In the famous murder case of Dr. Palmer the murderer had found an old colleague who supported his diagnoses and signed the death certificates. "The chief practitioner of the town," says one report, "was an octogenarian of great local repute but failing mentality, . . ." After poisoning his wife, Palmer "to render his position ironclad, called a further opinion in the form of another octogenarian practitioner . . . who without making any examination of the body had no hesitation in adding his signature to the document." Douthwaite, *op. cit.*, pp. 92, 101–102.

15 Two such cases are reported by E. H. Smith (*op. cit.*, pp. 265, 296 ff.). In the case of the baby-farmer Elisabeth Wiese (Hamburg, 1903) at

least four children of illegitimate mothers were adopted on payment of a sum. The children vanished, allegedly adopted by parents in England or Austria. Wosnik, *op. cit.*, I, 41 ff.

16 Much attention has been paid to property loss through fire but little to loss of life. It has been maintained by competent investigators that professional firebugs can be procured for fees, usually a percentage of the insurance collected. Fees from life insurance should not be overlooked as a possibility.

17 *Twenty-fifth Annual Report of the State Fire Marshal, State of Iowa* (1938), p. 23.

18 *Idem*, p. 20.

19 A typical instance is the case of the murdered 84-year-old millionaire Rice. The old man had a butler-secretary-nurse called Jones. The millionaire was described as "cooking his own food, while Mr. Jones ate in a restaurant." Edmund Pearson, *Five Murders*, p. 209. Jones confessed, "I told him [a man who was eager to have a new will made in his favor] that Mr. Rice was in the habit of waking up suddenly and was not exactly conscious of what he was doing and that he would sign any paper I would put before him." *Idem*, pp. 232–233.

20 It is the old problem of the "willing victim". Are we allowed to prevent an individual by force from committing suicide? Whether an abortion committed on a patient, moreover, leaves that woman a "victim" is hard to decide. Here again there is conflict between the legal presumption and the factual situation.

21 We are concerned here not so much with the individual of defective I.Q. as with morally, emotionally, and volitionally defective persons who become included in this category as soon as the I.Q. or M.R. (Mental Ratio) falls below the age of nine. Social inefficiency or fitness for being a victim depends much more on temperamental defects than on defective intelligence.

22 East, *Forensic Psychiatry*, p. 29. On the definition of the Royal Commissioners see *idem*, p. 91.

23 *Idem*, p. 86.

24 In a discussion of defectives in G. County, Ind., one report says: "Considerable degeneracy was found among the feeble-minded. Degenerate mountain folks from North Carolina have come into the county. Descendants of the English convicts, who poured into Georgia when England opened her prisons and sent her convicts over here to the colonies, are also found." Quoted by Newell Leroy Sims in *The Rural Community, Ancient and Modern* (New York, Charles Scribner's Sons, 1920), pp. 574–575.

25 In fathoming the "Middletown spirit" the Lynds run into the tenet that "only foreigners and long-haired troublemakers are radicals" and that "most foreigners are 'inferior.'" Robert S. and Helen Merrell Lynd,

Middletown in Transition (New York, Harcourt, Brace & Co., 1937), pp. 414, 407. "In Italy a drunkard is called a Frenchman, a beggar a Spaniard, a card-sharper a Greek." Ellis, *The Criminal*, p. 168.

26 In order to take in the cardsharper's gang which was lying in wait for him, the master crook described by Netley Lucas played two easy-victim roles at the same time. He ". . . was young and spoke like a colonial, though his speech even on arrival was somewhat thick and there was no doubt that he was in a state which would render a thorough plucking an easy matter." Lucas, *op. cit.*, p. 51. Speaking of two confidence men spenser writes: "They were well dressed and fairly well spoken, but no Englishman of the better class would have been deceived by them. They therefore confined themselves to 'working' Colonials and Americans." *Op. cit.*, p. 240. "These thieves prey largely upon Americans and Colonials . . ." Ferrier, *Crooke and Crime*, p. 140.

27 See the Polish immigrant woman who did not know the difference between bills. She was a middle-grade imbecile. "She has very often passed $5 for $1." Thomas and Znaniecki, *The Polish Peasant in Europe and America*, II, 1660.

28 MacDonald, *Crime Is a Business*, pp. 2–3.

29 Horse trading has been ruined by the automobile. On the gypsy's ability to do smith's work and his increasing "unemployment" see Block, *Zigeuner. Ihr Leben und ihre Seele*, pp. 102 ff.

30 Von Hentig, *The Criminality of the Colored Woman*, pp. 251–252.

31 Computed from figures from Guy B. Johnson, *The Negro and Crime*, Annals of the American Academy of Political and Social Science (Philadelphia, 1941), p. 99. Our data rest on Johnson's nonreduced data and differ from his computations.

32 There was only one case among 220 indictments in which a white killed a Negro. *Ibid.*

33 *Ibid.* The North Carolina figures—330 cases—embrace three rural and two urban counties.

34 "This third, or lowest class, includes practically all the abnormal sex offenders, the dull, backward, and provincial persons, the lower range of the feeble-minded, some of the known stool pigeons, the persons who show a marked lack of physical courage, the confirmed 'suckers,' the extremely pious, the habitual braggarts, and some sexual perverts." Clemmer, *The Prison Community*, p. 108.

35 A yelping young dog. The corresponding German word is *Pinscher*, which means a tiny ratcatcher. It is certainly good psychology on the part of Scotland Yard to send to the race courses officers dressed as farmers. Ferrier, *op. cit.*, p. 150. These countrified detectives are the most likely to attract swindlers.

36 Another group of epithets originated from the corruptness of the medieval servant class, "knave" in English for instance meaning in a general

way a rascal, and the German terms *Halunke* and *Knote* both signifying a low type of servant. The English "cornstalk" for an Australian means rustic and slow; see the German *langstielig*.

37 Sears and Weihofen, *May's Law of Crimes*, pp. 272–273. "Thus it is believed that while drunkenness may explain the sudden passion, which normally would not have existed in a sober man, yet the drunken man should not be permitted to assert that certain conduct was a provocation unless it would have been recognized as such if the defendant had been sober." *Idem*, p. 57.

38 It starts with carelessness and proceeds to a readiness to hurt oneself, or self-mutilation. It is to be found in a depressive phase, alcoholic intoxication, epilepsy, and imbecility.

39 On the fear of consequences see the able argument in Bernard Hollander's *Psychology of Misconduct*, pp. 114 ff.

40 Ellis, *op. cit.*, p. 143: "It is not without reason that French criminals call themselves *pègres* (from *pigritia*), the idle."

41 Altavilla, *Psicologia giudiziaria*, pp. 251 ff. Or they commit crimes in order to be executed. Of a patient who attempted to cut a boy's throat with a razor East writes: "I found him to be deeply depressed, unconcerned with his position or the fate of the boy. . . . He said he had been depressed for a long time, and wished to die, but was afraid to commit suicide, so he made up his mind to commit murder in order to be hanged." *Forensic Psychiatry*, p. 35. See also von Hentig, "Gerichtliche Verurteilungen als Mittel des Selbstmordes und der Selbstverstümmelung," *Archiv für Kriminal-Anthropologie*, LIV, 54 ff.

42 In a paper published in the *American Journal of Criminal Law and Criminology*, 1940, p. 304, I have drawn attention to the most peculiar Peltzer murder case (Brussels, 1881) and the depressed victim, who indifferently walked into the trap the murderer had set for him.

43 "A case which caused . . . public interest was that of William Jones, David Hood, William Rae, and Peter Robinson, four notorious burglars. Probably 50 per cent of the burials in North London occur at Finchley, and as Jones had lost his wife, she was buried in one of the Finchley cemeteries and his three pals attended her funeral with him. After the interment they adjourned to a public house near the cemetery, and had several drinks to 'drown their sorrow.' Hood, addressing Jones, said:

'It's all very well for you, Jones, putting the old woman under the sod, but what about us three? Your pleasure has cost us a day's pay. Don't you think we had better make a good day of it—"do a job," get a day's pay, and so "kill two birds with the one stone"?'

The others agreed. During the burglary they were disturbed, and had to run across a field; of the four, Hood and the mourning widower Jones were the first to be arrested." *Op cit.*, pp. 50–52.

44   Sutherland, *Professional Thief*, p. 70. "We try to find someone who is living beyond his means, who has social ambitions, or whose wife has social ambitions which are beyond their income. The banker who is speculating is probably short in his accounts already, and a chance at big profit will generally appeal to him as a way out of his difficulties."

45   MacDonald, *op. cit.*, p. 1, "Professional men, reputable businessmen, and even bankers are their victims. Police executives have also been listed as victims, yet these men seldom succumb virtuously, for while the operations may appear to be those of a legitimate business enterprise, the victim is seldom deceived on this point and really knows that he is in some manner gaining an unfair advantage." *Idem*, pp. 1–2.

46   Sutherland, *op. cit.*, p. 69. In an interesting piece of rationalization another swindler writes: "These suckers ought to be trimmed. It is a hard thing to say, but they are a dishonest lot and the worst double-crossers in the world." *Ibid.*

47   "A confidence game will fail absolutely unless the sucker has got larceny in his soul." *Ibid.* MacDonald adds, quoting a bunco: "An honest person will not allow himself to be a party to any scheme in order to gain sudden riches. A man must have larceny in his mind to become a perfect victim." *Op. cit.*, pp. 1–2.

48   Train, *True Stories of Crime*, p. 114.

49   In the Peltzer case, in order to lure the lawyer Bernays away from home a certain Vaughan, who represented himself as a big businessman, held out the bait of a substantial profit: ". . . the business was urgent . . ." he wrote, "could not the lawyer himself make the journey from Antwerp to Brussels, where Vaughan had just rented a house at 159 rue de la Loi, quite close to the station where Bernays would arrive?" The unknown client added that he would place his carriage at the disposal of the lawyer in case he should care to take advantage of his visit to Brussels to attend to other business there.

"For a lawyer to visit a client, especially a client whom he has never seen, is against all legal etiquette, but Vaughan had such good reasons for this disregard of custom that . . ." Bernays accepted and was murdered. Harry Gerard, *The Peltzer Case* (New York, Charles Scribner's Sons, 1928), p. 36.

50   The murderer induced his friend to leave his home town and go with him to the eastern border of France. "There was, he confided, in an old and apparently abandoned château at Herrenfluch, Alsace, a room in which good friends of his own had installed the last word in up-to-date machinery for the manufacture of spurious coin; machinery that turned out its products with such verisimilitude that after a long term of operations the authorities were not even aware that base coin was in circulation." Douthwaite, *op. cit.*, p. 131.

51   Note the background of the Troppmann case: "At this time France was

undergoing a phase of industrial transition. Revelation of the power of steam in its relation to manufacture and transport had shown possibilities of *making* to those who for uncounted generations had realized only the possibility of *growing*. Steam was turning the farmer into the manufacturer and transforming the hind into the artisan. If the husbandman still held pride of place, many were lured from their holdings by the prospect of easier money and softer living. Inevitable, also, with the new ease with which fortunes were made, that the thirst for wealth should break out like an angry rash upon the face of the country." *Idem*, p. 126.

52 Ferrier reports of a fraud: "He was of the oily, plausible variety of human, and preached at street corners in London. His wife and his relatives were rather pleased at his eloquent preaching and his influence for good. Whenever he preached at formal meetings he invariably attracted a large audience. He learned that the widow had money invested in New Zealand Stock, and, while commending its reliability, he laughed at the small percentage and told her that if she would entrust her £1000 to him he would reinvest it at 15 per cent instead of a paltry 4 per cent." After having paid interest at the rate of 15% for 6 months out of her capital he absconded. *Op. cit.*, p. 128.

53 *Idem*, p. 41.

54 *Idem*, p. 159.

55 Hollander, *op. cit.*, p. 129.

56 "One of my patients was a woman of . . . very good family, for whom at least half a dozen men committed suicide. She was a prepossessing woman, so fascinating and enchanting, and with such expensive tastes, that men, to keep in her favour, committed frauds and defalcations, and when discovered were so overcome with shame and remorse that they made an end to their existence." *Idem*, p. 131.

57 See the situation and the medical findings in Winifred Duke (ed.), *Trial of Field and Gray* (Edinburgh, William Hodge & Co., 1939), p. 7.

58 *Op. cit.*, p. 25, Case 31.

59 Karpman, *op. cit.*, pp. 594, 602, 668. See the tragic story in Evalyn Walsh McLean, *Father Struck it Rich* (Boston, Little, Brown & Co.), 1936, pp. 212–214.

60 My studies ("Eigenartige Formen der Zuhälterei," *Zeitschrift für Sexualwissenschaft*, 1927, No. 4) have shown that in a large number of cases the prostitute selects a younger man as her "protector." The law starts from the assumption that the girl is pushed into her way of life by the brutal exploiter. Later inquiries have confirmed my position (see Van der Laan, "Das Zuhältertum in Mannheim," *Monatsschrift für Kriminalpsychologie*, 1933, pp. 457 ff.).

61 Ferrier, *op. cit.*, p. 118. On the dangerous bravado spirit engendered by long-suffered loneliness see Zorbaugh, *op. cit.*, p. 81.

62 Karpman, *op. cit.*, p. 21.
63 "The widower is usually disconsolate and miserable, and is considered everybody's matrimonial walk-over, as all women, dark or fair, fat or thin, appear lovely to him." Ferrier, *op. cit.*, p. 125. This observation would not apply to all countries and all widowers.
64 E. H. Smith, *op. cit.*, pp. 162 ff.
65 *Babbitt*, chap. X, p. 136: "I've been a bad woman! I'm terribly sorry! I'll kill myself! I'll do anything! . . ."
66 *Idem*, p. 132.
67 "The artistic card-sharper is clever and plays a straight game until he senses the right opportunity for setting and then springing his trap. There have always been dupes, they exist in hundreds of thousands to-day, and the world continues to turn them out in mass production." Ferrier, *op. cit.*, p. 28. It need not be stressed that gambling can be done without cards in any suitable situation.
68 A reciprocally stimulating quality in criminal and victim alike, to some degree. "Susceptibility to suggestion is one of the most common factors of misconduct." Hollander, *op. cit.*, p. 40. Not only does the possession or view of a weapon act as if by suggestion (see *idem*, p. 80), but a good victim acts as a suggestion on a perpetrator, and an inventive criminal maneuvers a suggestible victim into any trap.
69 "Father's business life," wrote one of Karpman's patients, "seemed to be a constant battle with his competitors. . . . he was often involved financially, principally because he trusted everybody [he was an immigrant]. . . . About 1910 he became the victim of the 'cut-throat' methods of a few large competitors who wanted to force the smaller firms out of business, and who would stop at nothing to accomplish this end. They cut prices, damaged stock, and even resorted to stealing. Father had several expensive rugs stolen from his place. The result of such methods was that he was forced to the wall." Karpman, *op. cit.*, p. 747.
70 See Sutherland, *Professional Thief*, p. 81; Karpman, *op. cit.*, pp. 690–691; Ferrier, *op. cit.*, p. 171. It is played on women, too, and the menace is especially serious if there is an elderly husband of jealous disposition. Photographs taken in compromising postures are used increasingly. Ferrier, *op. cit.*, p. 172; Karpman, *op. cit.*, p. 689.
71 Sutherland, *op. cit.*, p. 104.
72 *Idem*, pp. 78–79.
73 *Idem*, p. 240.
74 "I too would walk out of the park linked arm in arm with some rich and crapulous burgher, take him to a quiet spot, and knock him down and take his wallet . . . And I was supported by a feeling of moral justification. These old men seemed placed by their practices beyond the pale of moral justification." Benney, *op. cit.*, p. 259.

75 "In the quarry one day while the inmates were at work one man approached another with a drawn knife. . . . He approached a man who carried money and, at the point of the knife, forced him behind a large rock and robbed him. The man who was robbed could not tell officials because he was not supposed to have the several dollars which were taken from his person." Clemmer, *op. cit.*, p. 159.
76 Sutherland, *op. cit.*, p. 57.

1.2

Toward a theory of personal criminal victimization[1]
by Michael J. Hindelang

Introduction

To this point, our work with the victimization survey data – and the work of most of those who have used the data – has been almost wholly empirical and methodological. On the basis of what is now known about victimization experiences, it is time to attempt to move beyond the data in order to postulate a theoretical model to help to account for these phenomena. Owing largely to the recency of victimization data and the complexity of victimization experiences, the theoretical model proposed in this chapter is a tentative, first step in constructing a theory of personal victimization. Although the theoretical model proposed here is, by and large, grounded in data about victims of crime, for many of the *explanatory mechanisms* that are postulated no data are currently available. Nonetheless, what is proposed in this model appears to be compatible with what is known about victims of personal crime from victimization surveys and other data.

Our theoretical model of the likelihood that an individual will suffer a personal victimization depends heavily on the concept of *lifestyle*. Briefly, lifestyle refers to routine daily activities, both vocational activities (work, school, keeping house, etc.) and leisure activities. What is offered is a theoretical model that postulates the antecedents of lifestyle and the mechanisms that link lifestyle with victimization. The findings that have been presented both in the earlier chapters and in other criminological research are then discussed within the context of the model.

The basic model is shown in Figure 1.2.1. We postulate that role expectations and social structure impose constraints to which persons must adapt if they are to function smoothly in society.[2] Role expectations and structural constraints for any individual depend upon that individual's constellation of demographic characteristics. The use of dashed lines in connection with demographic characteristics in Figure 1.2.1 is meant to indicate

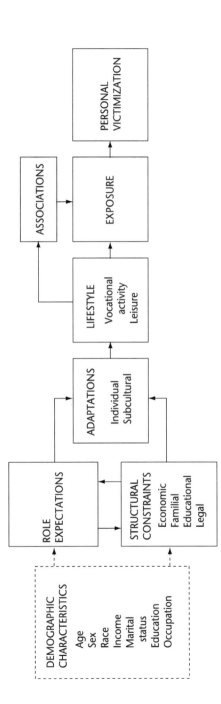

Figure 1.2.1 A Lifestyle/Exposure Model of Personal Victimization

that these characteristics do not cause role expectations and social structural constraints.

Role expectations as used here refers to cultural norms that are associated with achieved and ascribed statuses of individuals and that define preferred and anticipated behaviors. The role expectations with which we are concerned are those that pertain to central statuses of individuals – central in the sense of having a diffuse influence on the person occupying the status.[3] For example, role expectations vary dramatically with the age of the person; what is expected and/or deemed appropriate behavior for a child is generally not what is expected of an adult. Similarly, traditional American childrearing practices involve implicit and explicit definitions of role expectations – the differential propriety of dress, manner, expression of emotion, choice of play objects, etc. – depending on the sex of the child. Also, with respect to marital status, there are different role expectations for married versus unmarried persons; the former are generally expected to spend more time at home and in general to lead a more settled existence.

The other source of constraints identified in Figure 1.2.1 is the social structure. The *structural constraints* originating from this source can be defined as limitations on behavioral options that result from the particular arrangements existing within various institutional orders, such as the economic, familial, educational, and legal orders. For example, economic factors impose stringent limitations on the range of choices that individuals have with respect to such fundamentals as area of residence, nature of leisure activities, mode of transportation, and access to educational opportunities; to some extent racial barriers, particularly with regard to area of residence, are economically based. In addition, in the United States, the decline of the extended family structure has had an impact on the behavioral choices of family members. For example, parents must assume at-home responsibilities – including child supervision, cooking, and cleaning – that in former times were shared with grandparents and other relatives in the household.

No attempt is made to assign priorities to these institutional orders; they are certainly interdependent, and most people, at various times in their lives, are simultaneously constrained by several of them. By way of illustration, adolescents under a certain age are constrained by both legal and educational institutions. That is, the structure of the educational system (e.g., school calendar and class times) as well as legal requirements (e.g., compulsory attendance laws and child labor laws) limit the behavioral options of adolescents.

Note that in Figure 1.2.1, role expectations and structural constraints are reciprocally related. In recent years, for example, sex role expectations have been modified so that there has been some convergence in the role expectations for males and females. This change, in turn, has been translated into structural changes, particularly in the family and, to a lesser extent, in the economic realm. One might argue that role expectations and structural constraints are indistinguishable, that social structure is simply a composite of social roles. However, we believe the two are analytically distinct; for example, the expectations associated with the role of parent may be quite different in a social structure characterized by detached nuclear families than in one characterized by an extended family structure of communal childrearing.

As pointed out earlier and as illustrated in Figure 1.2.1, members of society adapt to role expectations and structural constraints. Such *adaptations* occur on both the individual and group levels. Each person learns skills and attitudes that allow him or her to operate with some individuality within the constraints imposed by role expectations and social structure. Among the skills and attitudes that an individual acquires in adapting to role expectations and structural constraints, of particular interest in connection with personal victimization are attitudes and beliefs about crime, including fear of crime. Once learned, these attitudes and beliefs are often incorporated into the routine activities of the individual, frequently as limitations on behavior.

Role expectations and structural constraints have similar effects for people with the same demographic characteristics. Thus, *shared* adaptations also emerge and can even be incorporated as norms among subgroups of society. Such group adaptations are postulated in Cohen's (1995) description of the 'delinquent subculture' and Wolfgang and Ferracuti's (1967) 'subculture of violence' theory.

Individuals adapt to structural constraints and role expectations in ways that result in regularities in behavioral patterns. What is important for our purposes is that these include such routine activities as working outside of the home, going to school, or keeping house, as well as typical leisure time pursuits. These daily routines constitute *lifestyle* as we use the term here.

Our usage of lifestyle is similar to Havighurst's (1961: 333): 'a characteristic way of distributing one's time, one's interest, and one's talent among the common social roles of adult life – those of worker, parent, spouse, home-maker, citizen, friend, club or association member, and user of leisure time'. Our definition differs from Havighurst's in that ours is not limited to adults; furthermore, our emphasis is heavily on *routine* activities.

In our model, lifestyle differences result from differences in role expectations, structural constraints, and individual and subcultural adaptations. Variations in lifestyles are related differentially to probabilities of being in particular places at particular times and coming into contact with persons who have particular characteristics; because criminal victimization is not randomly distributed across time and space and because offenders in personal crimes are not representative of the general population – but rather there are high-risk times, places, and people – this implies that lifestyle differences are associated with differences in *exposure* to situations that have a high victimization risk.

In the course of vocational and leisure pursuits, individuals spend a disproportionate amount of their time with others who have similar lifestyles. One reason why vocation – whether it be keeping house, going to school, or being employed – is so central to lifestyle is that it structures a large portion of daily activities. To the extent that these vocational activities are carried out as formal roles within institutional structures, the nature of an individual's interactions with others has a greater degree of predictability. That is, formal roles generally define socially acceptable daily routines that structure the lifestyles of those involved.

As shown in Figure 1.2.1, the major linkage between lifestyle and exposure to high victimization risk situations is direct. There is, however, another indirect link, which operates through associations. *Associations* refer to more or less sustained personal relationships among individuals that evolve as a result of similar lifestyles and hence similar interests shared by these individuals. Because offenders disproportionately have particular characteristics, association with people having these characteristics serves to increase exposure to personal victimization.

Personal victimization, the final element in the model, follows probabilistically from exposure to high victimization risk situations. Below, we will give additional attention, primarily in the form of a series of propositions, to the model and how it helps to explain variations in the likelihood of personal victimization. Before doing so, however, it is necessary to discuss more fully the key component in our model, lifestyle.

Lifestyle

Such diverse phenomena as life expectancy, morbidity, automobile accidents, suicide, and criminal victimization are all closely associated with demographic characteristics. For example, the life expectancy for women is about eight years longer than that for men and the life expectancy for whites is about seven years longer than for blacks (U.S. Bureau of the Census, 1974: 58). Blacks have higher infant and maternal death rates than do whites (U.S. Bureau of the Census, 1974b: 60). Younger drivers are more likely than middle-aged drivers to be involved in automobile accidents. Persons who have never married or who are separated, widowed, or divorced have suicide rates that are substantially higher than those for married persons (Gibbs, 1966). Males have higher suicide rates than females particularly in older age groups (U.S. Bureau of the Census, 1974b: 63). As we have shown throughout this book, demographic characteristics are also related to differential probabilities of personal victimization.

In terms of our model, these relationships between demographic variables and these diverse consequences, particularly personal victimization, can be attributed to differences in lifestyle. This is because various constellations of demographic characteristics are associated with role expectations and structural constraints that, mediated through individual and subcultural adaptations, channel lifestyles. For example, the lifestyles of young drivers can help account for their relatively high accident rates. They have less driving experience and relatively immature judgment; they are more likely to socialize in groups and to be influenced by group pressures to drive recklessly, drag race, and so on. Younger persons are typically more mobile and active than older persons and hence have a greater *exposure* to risks of automobile accidents. Similar inferences about differential lifestyles can be suggested to account for the relationship of demographic variables to the other consequences noted above: men are more likely than women to be exposed to the health hazards related to occupation; because of the relative economic constraints impinging on blacks and whites, blacks are more likely to live under conditions conducive to ill-health and are less able economically to take advantage of preventive medical care; unattached persons (single, divorced, widowed, or separated) may tend to spend more time alone and to have fewer dependents who rely upon them for nurturance and support.

It should not be surprising that lifestyle is closely tied to the most fundamental aspects of human existence: how long we live, how well we live, and how we die. The antecedents of lifestyle not only affect life chances in the long run, but also affect short-term life experiences. As conceptualized in our model, variations in lifestyles are attributable to the ways in which persons with various constellations of demographic characteristics adapt to role expectations and structural constraints. Our attention will now turn briefly to some examples of how lifestyle can be traced back to demographic characteristics in our model.

Age

Perhaps the clearest example of a demographic variable that dramatically affects lifestyle is age. Role expectations vary as a function of age. In addition, a variety of structural constraints – kinship, economic, educational, and legal – differentially impinge upon individuals according to age. In infancy and early childhood, the child's existence is highly structured according to parental expectations; that is, such things as when the child is fed, the stimuli within the child's environment, where the child is permitted to play, and with whom the child comes into contact are all largely under parental control. However, as the child approaches school age and begins to associate increasingly with others outside of the immediate family, parental control is less influential in restricting the extrafamilial exposure of the child – where the child is, with whom she or he comes into contact, and generally how the child's time is spent outside of the home.

During the years in which the child is completing her or his education, the child's lifestyle begins to shift dramatically. The waking hours spent outside of the home are largely structured by the activities involved in travelling to school, participating in curricular and extracurricular activities, and returning from school. As the child moves into adolescence, there is increasing autonomy; a greater proportion of time is spent in association with peers, and, by late adolescence, the activities of the child are by and large no longer within the institutional control of family or school. During early adulthood, lifestyles become increasingly determined by adaptations to the constraints of educational and occupational (economic) structures. For those pursuing neither occupational nor educational careers, there is considerably less institutional structure. The occupation of the person – that is, the role that the individual assumes within the economic structure – will have a substantial impact on that person's lifestyle throughout adulthood. This impact manifests itself with respect to where, when, and with whom time is spent. Of course, throughout the occupational career, age itself will also have an impact on lifestyles, especially in terms of time spent outside of the home, restrictions imposed by childrearing, and leisure time activities. As retirement years are reached, individuals begin to experience another dramatic shift in daily activities: mobility decreases, the number of interpersonal contacts decreases, and the experiential world of the individual becomes constricted generally. One of the important *adaptations* that occurs as age increases is a shift in attitudes, including an increased fear of crime. This increased fear contributes to limitations of activities, mobility, and contacts with strangers. By virtue of adaptations to role expectations and structural constraints that vary as a function of age, age itself an important indicator of lifestyle.

Parenthetically, it is important to note that throughout the life cycle, individuals are more likely to associate with and to come into contact with those occupying similar age-linked roles than with those occupying different roles: students with students, workers with workers, homemakers with homemakers, and retired persons with retired persons.

Sex

Despite the growing movement toward sexual equality in all institutional spheres and away from sex role differentiation, there remain structural constraints and differences in sex role expectations. Adaptations to these make sex an important indicator of lifestyle. Traditionally, the sex role socialization of females has been different from that of males. Because of sex role differentiation, sex is related to daily activities such as where time is spent, the number of interpersonal contacts, and the likelihood of encountering strangers. For example, females spend a greater proportion of their time inside the home because as adolescents they are more closely supervised than males, and as adults they are more likely than males to assume house-keeping responsibilities. Although sex is a major indicator of lifestyle, it is a weaker indicator for the youngest and oldest members of society. That is, in pre-adolescent and postretirement age groups, the lifestyles of males and females are less differentiated than in the intervening years, during which sex-linked differences in structural constraints and role expectations are more pronounced. For example, after retirement, both men and women are likely to be less mobile, to spend more time at home, and to have fewer contacts with persons outside of their primary groups; at this point in the life cycle (and in preadolescence as well), the role expectations and structural constraints associated with age tend to take precedence over those associated with sex.

Marital status

Another variable that is closely tied to lifestyles through the processes shown in our model is marital status. Among adults, the lifestyles of those who are married can be expected to differ in several important respects from those who are not married. The common living arrangements associated with marriage (or cohabitation) introduce a form of structure that is less prominent in the lives of 'unattached' persons. For example, married persons would be expected to spend proportionately more time within the home than would single persons; this is especially true of those who have children. Marital and familial ties result in an increased number of at-home responsibilities. In addition, leisure time spent out of the home is likely to be in the company of partners or with other persons of similar marital and familial statuses. Also, because the marital bond brings together two extended family networks, the likelihood of spending time with family members increases. On the other hand, single persons are likely to spend their time outside of the home more often unaccompanied or in the company of other single persons. The transition from an 'unattached' to an 'attached' status (e.g., single to married) generally implies a dramatic shift in lifestyle; this transition involves a shift in role expectations and structural constraints to which individuals must adapt. Thus, marital status is another indicator of where, when, and with whom individuals routinely spend their time.

Family income and race

Family income is closely associated with life chances and life experiences because it is reflective of one's position in the economic structure, which is one of the most important constraints on behavioral options. As family income increases, so too does the flexibility to adjust one's lifestyle to one's wishes. This flexibility includes the ability to select the area in which to live, the mode of transportation that will be used in daily activities, the proportion of time spent in private surroundings versus public places, and the very nature of leisure time activities. It is important to note that the choices provided to those with sufficient family income often result in an income-linked segregation in housing, transportation, privacy, and many leisure time activities. Thus, patterns of *association* are also income-linked: those living in suburbs are likely to be of at least moderate income; those relying primarily on public modes of intracity transportation are likely to be less affluent; members of country clubs are likely to be relatively wealthy. Thus, those of similar family incomes tend to cluster in particular residential, recreational, and other social settings.

Like family income, race is closely tied with life chances and life experiences. Some of the importance of race as an indicator of lifestyle derives from its association with family income. However, whites and blacks of the same socioeconomic stratum live in quite different worlds. For example, non-economic structural constraints associated with race result in segregated housing patterns, and thus blacks tend to live in more economically heterogeneous areas than do whites (Taeuber, 1968; Erbe, 1975). Such housing patterns have particularly strong implications for patterns of associations among blacks versus whites; among the latter, patterns of association will be more income-segregated than among the former. These differences are apparent throughout the life cycle, especially in the educational and recreational realms. For example, attending private schools and belonging to private clubs are much more common among whites than among blacks.

Our attention will now turn to an examination of some of the major victimization findings and to a discussion of ways in which patterns of victimization can be related to variations in lifestyles. Our discussion will draw on the analyses presented both in earlier chapters and in Hindelang (1976). In order to assist the reader, references to the tables in which particular findings are presented will be given as those findings are discussed. In addition, to the extent that the data are available, our discussion below will draw upon relevant findings of prior research.

Victimization and lifestyle: a set of propositions

For a personal victimization to occur, several conditions must be met. First, the prime actors – the offender and the victim – must have occasion to intersect in time and space. Second, some source of dispute or claim must arise between the actors in which the victim is perceived by the offender as an appropriate object of the victimization. Third, the offender must be willing and able to threaten or use force (or stealth) in order to achieve the desired end. Fourth, the circumstances must be such that the offender views it as advantageous to use or threaten force (or stealth) to achieve the desired end. The probability of these conditions being met is related to the life circumstances of members of society.

Lifestyle is the central component in our theoretical model. In our view, the centrality of lifestyle derives primarily from its close association with *exposure* to victimization risk situations. Victimization is not a phenomenon that is uniformly distributed; it occurs disproportionately in particular times and places; it occurs disproportionately by offenders with particular demographic characteristics; it occurs disproportionately under certain circumstances (e.g., according to whether or not the person is alone); it occurs disproportionately according to the prior relationship between the potential victim and the potential offender; and so forth. Because different lifestyles imply different probabilities that individuals will be in particular places, at particular times, under particular circumstances, interacting with particular kinds of persons, lifestyle affects the probability of victimization. In the following discussion, we will suggest ways in which particular lifestyles have implications for exposure to personal victimization in light of the empirical properties of these victimizations. Although the format we will use involves the statement of a single proposition followed by a discussion of its theoretical and empirical tenability, it should be stressed at the outset that these propositions are interdependent. Therefore, for each proposition, the phrase 'other things being equal' is implied.

Proposition 1: *The probability of suffering a personal victimization is directly related to the amount of time that a person spends in public places (e.g., on the street, in parks, etc.), and particularly in public places at night.*
[. . .]

Proposition 2: *The probability of being in public places, particularly at night, varies as a function of lifestyle.*
[. . .]

Proposition 3: *Social contacts and interactions occur disproportionately among individuals who share similar lifestyle.*
[. . .]

Proposition 4: *An individual's chances of personal victimization are dependent upon the extent to which the individual shares demographic characteristics with offenders.*
[. . .]

Proposition 5: *The proportion of time that an individual spends among nonfamily members varies as a function of lifestyle.*[4]
[. . .]

Proposition 6: *The probability of personal victimization, particularly personal theft, increases as a function of the proportion of time that an individual spends among nonfamily members.*
[. . .]

Proposition 7: *Variations in lifestyle are associated with variations in the ability of individuals to isolate themselves from persons with offender characteristics.*
[. . .]

Proposition 8: *Variations in lifestyle are associated with variations in the convenience, the desirability, and vincibility of the person as a target for personal victimizations.*

[. . .]

A note on victim precipitation

One aspect of personal victimization that has had a prominent place in American criminological literature on aggressive crimes is that of victim precipitation. According to Wolfgang (1958: 252):

> The term *victim-precipitated* is applied to those criminal homicides in which the victim is a direct, positive precipitator in the crime. The role of the victim is characterized by his having been the first in the homicide drama to use physical force directed against his subsequent slayer. The *victim-precipitated* cases are those in which the victim was the first to show and use a deadly weapon, to strike a blow in an altercation – in short, the first to commence the interplay or resort to physical violence.

A similar notion is embodied in Toch's typology of violent activity, which 'is intended as a catalogue of ways of relating to people which carry a high probability of degenerating into contact of an aggressive nature' (Toch, 1969: 135).

Compatible with these conceptions of victim precipitation is the notion that individuals and subcultural groups may subscribe to a set of values that result in an increased willingness to exhibit defiant or aggressive reactions to a wide range of stimuli. Wolfgang (1958: 188) has pointed out that 'the significance of a jostle, a slightly derogatory remark, or the appearance of a weapon in the hand of an adversary are stimuli differentially perceived and interpreted . . .'. These differential perceptions and interpretations can be expected to vary as a function of race, sex, age, and socioeconomic status. Wolfgang and Ferracuti's (1967) subculture of violence thesis postulates that such propensities are disproportionately found among young, black, lower-class males. In connection with assaultive crimes, such propensities on the part of the victim may serve to precipitate an event that might otherwise have not occurred or to escalate the level of violence in an event that otherwise would have been less violent.

Although the victimization survey results contain no information on victimizations that may have been victim-precipitated, the data presented elsewhere do indicate that the rate of injury to victims is substantially greater for those victims who used a physical force self-protective measure than for those victims who did not. . . . The victimization results in the eight cities show that males were more likely than females and younger persons more likely than older persons to use physical force self-protective measures; however, no race effects were found (Hindelang, 1976: 260). Regardless of the tenability of the subculture of violence thesis, it seems reasonable to postulate that the propensity to precipitate or escalate violent victimization is not uniformly distributed among members of society.

Although a notion such as propensity to precipitate or escalate is implicitly subsumed in our model as a possible individual and/or subcultural adaptation to role expectation and structural constraints, we have not discussed this particular adaptation in our general presentation of the model. Because such a propensity is only one of a variety of possible specific adaptations, we believed that to have displayed it in the model in Figure 1.2.1 would have given to it undue prominence, perhaps to the exclusion of other important adaptations that are less widely discussed in the literature. In addition, propensity to precipitate or escalate – although it has been discussed and investigated by Normandeau (1968: 286–92) in connection with robbery – does not, we believe, have applicability to the vast majority of theft-motivated offenses. It should be stressed that although some adaptations, such as propensity to precipitate, result in an increased likelihood of victimization, our model is equally concerned with common adaptations that decrease the likelihood of victimization. For example, adaptations to the role expectations of parenthood and the constraints of family structure lead to a lifestyle that involves spending more time with family members in the home and therefore decreases the exposure to high risk victimization situations.

Interdependence of propositions

In this presentation of the lifestyle/exposure model of personal victimization, we have refrained from using the phrase 'other things being equal.' It should be clear, however, from the propositions themselves, that we have been generally discussing zero-order effects. This in no way implies, of course, that the propositions are independent in their effects on the likelihood of personal victimization. For example, the most desirable targets for theft-motivated crimes, as discussed in Proposition 8 (e.g., the affluent) may simultaneously be the individuals who are least likely to spend time in public places (Proposition 2). Predictions about victimization risks can be derived from a given proposition only when the other propositions are taken into account. Obviously, it would be easier to test this theoretical model if the propositions were independent of each other. This is especially true in light of the fact that many of the data required to operationalize the propositions adequately are not readily available. Unfortunately, the phenomenon of personal victimization, as is the case with most social phenomena, is sufficiently complex to preclude univariate explanations or multivariate explanations in which the critical dimensions are assumed to be orthogonal.

Some expectations from the model

In the course of discussing the individual propositions, we pointed to readily available research findings that are compatible with our lifestyle/exposure model. In addition, there are important expectations that can be derived from this model for which data are not as readily available. We believe that it would be helpful in explicating the model further to give brief attention to illustrations of some of these expectations.[5]

Our model suggests that as sex role expectations become increasingly less differentiated and sex-linked structural barriers become less rigid, with a corresponding convergence of the adaptations and lifestyles of males and females, rates of victimization for males and females will tend to converge. This is true primarily for two reasons. First, females generally will increase their exposure to nonfamily members, and hence their victimization rate should increase relative to the male rate. Second, if the *offending* rate among females increases, as some have suggested it will (Adler, 1975: 251–2), then the lifestyle/exposure model predicts that females will have higher rates of victimization than would otherwise be expected. This is so because an offender characteristic (sex) would be shifting toward a characteristic of these individuals (female); according to Proposition 4, the more similar an individual's characteristics to those of offenders, the greater the chance of victimization.

To the extent that cohabitation outside of marriage continues to increase, we would expect that marital status will become less predictive of victimization. That is, persons who are not married (e.g., 'single') but who are cohabitating will have adopted to some extent lifestyles that are normally associated with marriage. This would be especially true to the extent that cohabitating and married couples are equally likely to incur childrearing responsibilities.

The lifestyle/exposure model also suggests that to the extent that trends toward age segregation in housing patterns increase, rates of personal victimization among age groups will diverge; conversely, to the extent that housing arrangements become age-heterogeneous, rates of victimization among age groups will tend toward convergence. We are not suggesting, of course, that in an age-heterogeneous setting, variations in rates of personal victimization across age groups would not exist; there are too many other factors that affect differential likelihoods of victimization by age.

A society that is fully integrated – in terms of housing patterns, lifestyles, and patterns of personal interactions with regard to such dimensions as race, socioeconomic status, age, sex, etc. – would likely be relatively homogeneous with respect to many important social consequences, including criminal victimization. Conversely, to the extent that patterns of interaction occur more within race-age-sex clusters, rates of victimization for demographic subgroups can, on the basis of our model, be expected to diverge, provided that there are demographic correlates of offending behavior.

Concluding remarks

The theoretical model that has been proposed grows primarily out of our research during the past four years on victimization survey results. Although the data and the theoretical model presented in this book deal with personal victimization, in prior research we have closely examined the correlates of household victimization – burglary, household larceny, and vehicle theft. We believe that with modifications the lifestyle/exposure model has some applicability to household victimization, primarily because lifestyles that disproportionately result in individuals being in public places also tend disproportionately to leave the households of those persons unoccupied and hence more vulnerable to household victimization. For example, age of head of household is inversely related to rates of household victimization; the lifestyles of younger persons which bring them into public places simultaneously tend disproportionately to expose their homes to household victimization. We are, however, pessimistic about the applicability of this model to victimization by corporate crime, white collar crime, and consumer fraud.

This lifestyle/exposure model of personal victimization has evolved as a result of a grounded theoretical approach. Although there are major advantages to a grounded approach to theory construction, there are some substantial shortcomings as well. Among the advantages are an intimate familiarity with the empirical patterns in the data, an empirical stance toward the concepts and indicators that are developed, and an appreciation for some of the measurement limitations inherent in the data. On the other hand, the greatest dangers are that grounded theory may be limited to ex post facto interpretation of the data and may not achieve a sufficiently high level of abstraction and generality. On balance, the advantages of a grounded theoretical approach seem to outweigh the disadvantages and such an approach has the greatest potential for advancing knowledge and explanations of social phenomena such as criminal victimization.

The lifestyle/exposure model is but a preliminary step toward an adequate explanation of personal victimization. Our own research will focus on testing, reformulating, and refining this theoretical model. To the extent that the model stimulates additional empirical and theoretical work on the part of others, it will have served an important function.

Notes

1   Throughout this chapter, our intent is to construct a theoretical model of the personal victimizations discussed in this book – rape, assault, robbery, and personal larceny. Although the model has some implications for household, business, and other forms of victimization, our discussion is not specifically designed to address these types of victimizations.

2   We are not arguing that behavior is completely determined by role

expectations and social structure. The constraints imposed by these factors delimit a range of behaviors from which even conforming members of society can choose. In addition, the individual can, with varying degrees of risk and success, resist or rebel against the constraints. Our argument is that the constraints do act to produce typical ways of behaving.

3 This differentiation is similar to the one used by Becker (1963: 31–35) in his designation of 'master statuses.'

4 In our usage here, 'family' refers to the extended family.

5 Unless otherwise noted, in these illustrations we will be assuming that patterns of offender characteristics remain constant.

Part 2

Vulnerable victims and critical responses

By Hannah Goodman Chong

This section will outline the development of victimological theory as it moved on from its positivist beginnings in the 1940s. The treatment of female victims of crime, both within the criminal justice system and wider society, prompted feminist writers to challenge the status quo. These developments, alongside similar moves within the field of hate crime and offending towards vulnerable victims, has challenged victimology to become more anti-oppressive in nature and to highlight the needs of specific groups of victims. This chapter moves beyond theoretical victimology by including readings about vulnerable victims which outline real experiences of victimization and subsequent contact with the criminal justice system. It has a broad context and furthers our understanding of victimology by examining victimization where the characteristics of the victim, such as age, gender, ethnicity or disability, are triggers rather than the individual themselves.

Our understanding of vulnerable victims is important because these victims were often those most in need of adequate services and also often the most overlooked or ill-protected groups. Victims who have been identified as vulnerable or intimidated within the Criminal Justice System are now eligible for enhanced services under the Code of Practice for Victims of Crime and are to be informed of key developments in their cases, on much tighter timescales (available to download from the Home Office website http://www.home office.gov.uk/documents/victims-code-of-practice?view=Binary).

The first reading in this chapter is a piece by Gwyneth Boswell looking at the needs of child victims of crime. This is a field often neglected by both academics and practitioners. Until recently many support services for victims of crime would not work with child victims. This was often because of issues around confidentiality and needing permission from parents to provide a service.

Boswell's article highlights the needs and responses to child victims of crime. The article outlines forms of child victimization including child abuse, abduction, homicide and smacking. Until recently many cases where the victims were children did not progress through the criminal justice system. Our greater understanding of the effects of victimization on children and methods introduced to help them give them their evidence has begun to remedy this in recent years.

Boswell has also written previously about the group who overlap categorization and are both victims and offenders (for example see Boswell, 1999). This challenges writers to see past the traditional stereotype of a victim as identified by earlier victimologists and to understand that experiences of being a victim of crime are more complex.

The insights of hate crime activists and the practitioner movement on anti-oppressive practice influenced thinking about victims and the study of victimology. Against a backdrop of social activism, researchers also began to write about the treatment of victims of racism and hate crime.

Bowling writes about experiences of racial harassment in an area of East London. The selected reading outlines findings from a survey which found that crime was considered to be a huge problem in the area but that the issue was surprisingly complex. People's experiences and opinions about crime were affected by their gender, and their ethnicity, with Asian women reporting far higher levels of fear of crime than African men, for example. The reading also contains descriptions of harassment experienced which offer a thought – provoking insight into the day-to-day lives of people from ethnic minorities living in this area.

The article by Jon Garland and Neil Chakraborti highlights the needs of victims who live in rural areas, and those who experience racist offending. The authors discuss the forms of racism experienced by people living in rural areas, and the impact that global events such as 9/11 had on people's experiences of victimization and the wave of racism that followed this. Garland and Chakraborti go on to make suggestions to services who work with these victims. This highlights an important aspect of the study of victimology. Victimology is not simply about understanding systems that already exist but is also forward-thinking in nature. Findings from research can have direct impact on improving services to victims of crime in the future. Perhaps this owes something to the background of feminist activist researchers who challenged the earlier positivist nature of victimology and used their research to try to improve the experiences of female victims.

Research such as this has helped further our understanding of the effects of victimization and demonstrated the need to tackle racism and also to provide appropriate support to those who have experienced it. Garland and Chakraborti call for more resources to meet the needs of victims of rural racism, and point out that these need to be allocated on a long-term basis in order to make services sustainable. This is a common criticism of funding for services to victims of crime, which on the whole tend to be located within the voluntary sector and exist on a succession of short-term funding streams.

The next theme in this section explores violence against women. There were two key areas of the criminal justice system that were in dire need of reform and became the centre of much attention from the 1970s onwards. These were awareness of and acceptance of domestic violence and sexual violence against women. Feminist writers began to research and write about these topics and also to set up practical support systems such as refuges and rape crisis services. An increasing pool of data about domestic violence began to highlight that violence against women within their own homes was endemic. Research studies showed that women experienced a wide range of forms of violence from partners, ex-partners and other family members including physical, emotional and financial abuse. Women experienced violence over long periods of time, sometimes even decades of abuse, and often suffered through 30 incidents before they reported this to anyone.

Once women had reported the violence, this was not the end of the story. More recently, there has been more awareness of what it is that women in violent relationships want. In some cases, this may be to remain within the relationship but for the abuse to stop. The problem remains however, and on average, two women a week are still being killed by their current or ex- partner.

Writers such as the late Sue Lees were instrumental in raising awareness of the degrading treatment of rape victims in the criminal justice system (for an example see Gregory and Lees, 1996). This reader contains an article written by Jan Jordan which discusses the issue of how female victims of rape were treated by the police. Difficulties included the need for female doctors to carry out medical examinations of victims, and the attitudes that victims were faced with when reporting their experiences to police officers. Research such as this has challenged commonly held stereotypes about sexual violence by finding that in the vast majority of cases the violence was perpetrated by someone known to the victim.

Improvements were slow in being introduced, although some were eventually made, such the special measures introduced by the Youth Justice and Criminal Evidence Act (1999) entitling vulnerable and intimidated witnesses to give evidence from behind screens or by video link. The creation of additional Sexual Assault Referral Centres (SARCs) is also aimed at improving services for victims, however, problems around short-term funding for services remain (for further information about SARCs, see Lovett et al., 2004). The rates of reporting or sexual assaults have gone up in recent years, though the conviction rate has steadily declined over the same period of time. Currently, only around 5.6 per cent of reported rapes result in a conviction (Travis, 2005) so there remains much work to do to improve this.

Methods brought in to try to increase victim's satisfaction with the criminal justice system sometimes have unexpected consequences. For example, mandatory arrest policies brought in to try to protect female victims of domestic violence actually led to an increase in the rates of females arrested. Women were often distressed and reacting to their situation when police arrived, even where they were the victims of the violence in the first instance, leading to them being removed from the home, rather than their partner. Stephens and Sinden (2000) found that victims appreciated being treated positively by officers, being believed and not dismissed.

There are also certain groups of people who are more vulnerable to suffer abuse, such as people with disabilities who may be dependent on their abusers to meet their day-to-day care needs. Christopher Williams outlines the problems faced by people with learning disabilities, including the higher levels of vulnerability to crime and subsequent difficulties in reporting these and having cases progress through the criminal justice system. Recent introductions to try to improve the experiences of people with disabilities in the criminal justice system include the special measures available to all vulnerable witnesses, but also the use of trained intermediaries to aid communication between the victim and the court.

Overall, the work of writers such as those included in this reader have increased our understanding of the scale and effects of a number of forms of victimization. They have also increased our understanding of the needs of vulnerable victims of crime and developments of services to meet their needs.

Recommended further reading

British Medical Association (2007) *Domestic Abuse: A Report from the BMA Board of Science*. London: British Medical Association.

Gregory, J. and Lees, S. (1996) 'Attrition in rape and sexual assault cases', *The British Journal of Criminology*, 36(1): 1–17.

Hester, M. (2006) 'Making it through the criminal justice system: attrition and domestic violence', *Social Policy and Society* (5): 79–90.

Stephens, B.J. and Sinden, P.G. (2000) 'Victims' voices: domestic assault victims' perceptions of police demeanor', *Journal of Interpersonal Violence* 15(5), 435–47.

2.1

Child victims
by Gwyneth Boswell

[. . .]

Introduction

The law in England and Wales classifies a child as anyone under the age of 18 years. This means that any consideration of child victims necessarily spans the range of those who might be victimised as babies, as toddlers, as primary schoolchildren, and as early or late adolescents.

Child victims have tended to be somewhat overlooked as a category within the literature on victimisation. This is in spite of the fact that there is much in the published domain about the types of crime which have frequently been perpetrated upon them. In all likelihood this is an omission which reflects both their structural location within family/state care, education and community systems and the priorities of the adult world upon which they are dependent.

This article will examine the ways in which crimes against children may be categorised, how society and the law respond to children as victims and why some children may be victimised on the grounds of their personal characteristics alone. It will chronicle some of the outcomes of victimisation as a child, and consider appropriate methods of working more proactively to support those who are, have been, or may become child victims.

Categorisation of and data about child victims

There is currently no single national source on the nature and prevalence of childhood victimisation. Discrete sets of statistics on specific crimes to children can, however, be found in annual publications such as *Criminal Statistics in England and Wales*; the *British Crime Survey* sections on the self-reports of 12–15 year old victims; *Mortality Statistics* sections on children up to 15 years; *Children and Young People on Child Protection Registers*; and in one-off pieces of published research about, for example, the prevalence of school bullying and particular types of child abuse, both of which, in common with around 58% of all offences (Ashworth, 2000) are liable not to be reported to the police. This in itself constitutes a major omission in the fund of data available about children.

As the Gulbenkian Report of the Commission on Children and Violence notes, '. . . children suffer far more violent victimisation than do adults' (Calouste Gulbenkian Foundation, 1995: 256). The report argues that this level of victimisation is because of their largely dependent status, which renders them more vulnerable to 'conventional' crimes such as homicide and assault, to family violence including violent punishments, sexual abuse by parents and others, and assaults by siblings, and to institutional violence such as bullying in schools. To this list might be added abuse and bullying in children's homes, secure units and juvenile Young Offender Institutions (YOIs), in all of which children and adolescents have variously sustained racist attacks, other serious assaults including rape, and have in some cases died or committed suicide as a result.

Two reports by Sir William Utting (1997, 2004) set out graphically the way in which social care systems are still failing to safeguard children living away from home. Reference is made, for example, to the Staffordshire 'Pin Down' Inquiry (Levy and Kahan, 1991) and to the case of Frank Beck, a social work training manager who was found to have carried out systematic rape and buggery in Leicestershire Children's Homes from 1973 to 1986; and to the Clwyd Inquiry (Waterhouse, 2000) which revealed abuse of children in residential care in the possible context of a paedophile ring.

Between 1990 and 2002, 152 juveniles died in custody as a result of self-inflicted injuries (Amnesty International, 2002). Amnesty's report chronicles prominent cases of children who have died in custody in recent years including: 17-year old Kevin Henson who hanged himself in Feltham YOI in 2000, not having been placed on suicide watch despite known emotional and anxiety disorders; and 16-year old Kevin Jacobs, who also hanged himself in Feltham, having been placed on suicide watch but with lack of clarity as to whether hourly checks had been carried out during the night he died.

As Goldson (2002: 9) notes, secure accommodation which is for the express purpose of restricting a child's liberty, 'straddles the conceptual space that awkwardly separates the child welfare and youth justice systems'. Deaths in secure care during 2004 included 15 year old Gareth Myatt who died while being restrained in the privately-run Hassockfield Secure Training Centre, and 14 year old Adam Rickwood, the youngest person ever to die in custody, who took his own life also in Hassockfield. In this connection, it is material to note that children in England and Wales are criminalised from the age of 10, and have been more likely to be so since Jack Straw, as Home Secretary, rescinded the rebuttable presumption of *doli incapax* (incapability of understanding the difference between right and wrong) for 10–13-year olds, in 1997, following its unsuccessful application to the two 11-year old children convicted of the murder of James Bulger in 1993. In the majority of European countries, children's offending would be a matter for the welfare agencies up to at least the age of 14, and in some cases up to 18 years.

Finkelhor (1997) suggests a framework of four categories for child victimisation:

1. Conventional specialised crimes – homicide, assault (on young children mostly by parents; on adolescents mostly by peers and other acquaintances); sexual assault; theft and robbery.
2. Child abuse (emotional, physical, sexual) and neglect.
3. Specialised crimes – abduction of children by (a) strangers or (b) family members
4. Non-criminalised violent acts – e.g. assault by other children including siblings; corporal punishment (including smacking); child prostitution. Child labour, female circumcision and witnessing domestic violence (where a child may be an indirect victim) constitute other examples.

Although exact numbers cannot be ascertained through current data systems, some of the victimisation types referred to in each of Finkelhor's four categories will be discussed here.

Homicide

Homicide is the rarest, but clearly the most serious crime to be committed on children. Criminal statistics show an average of 79 child deaths per annum for the last 28 years (babies being the most at risk); in 78% of these cases, parents are the principal suspect (Creighton and Tissier, 2003). Those killed by friends, acquaintances, other associates and strangers are, thus, very much in the minority.

It is important, however, to underline that there is general dissatisfaction with the reporting, recording and analysis of deaths of children and young people. Current statistics are thought to afford a significant underestimate of prevalence. As one example, in the case of suspicious deaths of babies and younger children, where parents deny guilt and there is insufficient evidence for a prosecution, open verdicts are usually recorded. As shown earlier, annual mortality statistics published by the Office for National Statistics do not include rates for 16 and 17 years olds who are at much higher risk of death than younger children.

Child abuse

In the UK, child abuse is generally recognised as belonging to one or more of the categories of physical, emotional, sexual abuse or neglect. There is debate about the definitions of these terms, but those seeking more information may refer to the Government guide to inter-agency working to safeguard and protect the welfare of children (Dept. of Health et al, 1999). As with child deaths, the prevalence of child abuse is generally believed to be seriously under-reported and recorded and also frequently to go unrecognised. Recent figures suggest the following in relation to the year 1st April 2002 to 31st March 2003.

- There were 4109 reported offences of 'cruelty or neglect of children' and 1880 of 'gross indecency with a child under the age of 14' in England and Wales
- There were 30,200 children's names added to child protection registers in England
- There were 570,000 referrals concerning child maltreatment to social services departments in England.

A breakdown of all these cases shows the following proportions: Neglect, 39%; Physical abuse, 19%; Emotional Abuse, 18%; Sexual Abuse, 10%; Mixed categories, 15%. (Creighton, 2004). As in the case of child deaths, much of the abuse is parental.

Child abduction

Abduction constitutes a very small proportion of all offences against children. In 2002/3, just over half of abductions were attempted only; 56% involved a stranger and 47% of these were unsuccessful. Of the remaining 9% of abductions which were successful (68 in number) at least 6% were sexually motivated. These figures represented an increase on previous years, but this is generally put down to greater public awareness and higher levels of reporting and recording (Newiss and Fairbrother, 2004).

Smacking

In their national study of parents, children and discipline in the UK, Ghate et al (2003) included in the category of severe violence, 'smacking/slapping of the head or face', and found a rate of 90 per 1000 children in this category. Eight European countries have now imposed a complete ban on the physical punishment of children. In England and Wales, smacking remains legal but, since the Human Rights Act 1998 (incorporating the United Nations

Convention on the Rights of the Child, 1989) came into force in October 2001, courts have been obliged to consider whether punishment amounts to 'reasonable chastisement'. The factors to be weighed are the nature and context of the treatment and its duration; its physical and mental effects and, in some circumstances, the sex, age and state of health of the victim.

At the same time, protection from harm is as much of a human rights issue for children as it is for adults – arguably more so as they are both smaller and more fragile. The Convention on the Rights of the Child may now have acquired the status of international law, but children cannot on their own seek justice through the courts when they are victimised (frequently behind the closed doors of their own family) and their Convention rights are breached. On the day this article was finalised (2 November 2004), a majority of MPs voted against an outright ban on smacking within the new Children Bill, and in favour of an amendment allowing light chastisement, with the caveat that no grazes, scratches, minor swellings, cuts or bruises should ensue. In the event that they do, the maximum sentence will be 5 years' imprisonment. It was notable, however, that the Government allowed a free ('conscience') vote on fox-hunting but retained its three-line whip on the question of physical punishment to children.

Victimisation on the basis of personal characteristics

As is the case for adults, some children are more likely to fall prey to victimisation by reason of identity-based characteristics such as gender, race, religion, disability and so on:

> Certain groups of children are particularly at risk of violence, including disabled children and children from some minority ethnic groups. Victimisation statistics in crime surveys and other interview research provide *prima facie* evidence of discrimination. Racial harassment, always a form of violence and often involving physical violence, threatens many children in the community and in schools. (Calouste Gulbenkian Foundation, 1995: 115)

Children may be singled out for school bullying and find themselves victimised as members of families of black and ethnic minority origin and/or of minority religions. Added to this is the risk of such victimisation going unrecognised by schools and criminal justice agencies because of institutional racism (Macpherson, 1999) and despite the requirement of the Race Relations (Amendment) Act, 2000 for public bodies to have due regard to the need to eliminate unlawful racial discrimination. More recently, the misperception of Muslims as terrorists, linking them with al Qaida and the attacks on the World Trade Center on 11th September 2001, has triggered well-documented victimisation and 'hate crime' towards Muslim families and communities. The Nottinghamshire Common Monitoring Scheme found that 11.4% of the victims of racially motivated crime were under the age of 10 years (Midlands Probation Training Consortium, 1998). Other studies have shown the pervasiveness of racial bullying, harassment and attack across the lifespan, beginning in childhood. (Bowling, 1998; Clancy et al, 2001; Garland and Chakraborti, 2004).

In terms of gender characteristics, a review of the research shows that boys are more vulnerable than girls to physical abuse and non-family assaults, whilst girls are more vulnerable than boys to sexual abuse (Calouste Gulbenkian Foundation, 1995). Female children are particularly (though of course not exclusively) likely to become the subjects of child pornography, and increasingly so on the internet, where it is fast becoming a major social problem. The debate surrounding the issue of what actually constitutes child pornography, and at what point viewing it actually becomes a crime, serves only to reduce the significance of the child victim concerned. Two researchers in this field make the point that the process of trying to understand an unpalatable phenomenon brings with it the accompanying danger of appearing to condone it; they refer to a 6 year old female child victim whom no-one could actually remember, and this is reminiscent of the victim 'grid' which depicts a victim submerged and faceless under a density of psychosocial projections and legislative paraphernalia (Boswell et al, 2002). They also note the pervading tension of official reluctance to censor on the internet versus obvious child protection issues, both set against the increasing sexualisation of childhood in the media. (Taylor and Quayle, 2003)

Research on children with disabilities has been sparse, but recent work has shown that they are a distinct high-risk group for victimisation and maltreatment, being on average two to three times more likely to be abused than non-disabled children. (Little, 2004). Further, while they often come to the attention of the health services, their condition may mask the fact that they have been abused or otherwise victimised, thus undermining the quality of the assessment and treatment they receive.

Legal responses to child victims

As Walklate (1989) noted, many professionals have been concerned at the potential for the formal court processes to intimidate victims, particularly existing vulnerable groups, such as children, and to victimise them further in the process. This is likely to be especially true in cases where children have been abused and have to face both their abusers and an adversarial system in a judicial climate not known for its sensitivity to children or indeed its understanding of abuse and its effect on the victim. Thus, until relatively recently, the Police and Crown Prosecution Services have tended to take the view that it is not in the public interest to proceed with a prosecution.

This is one example of the way in which children have historically been denied their right to due process. It may be argued that everyone, whatever their age, should be entitled to a full public hearing, when judge, jury and society at large can weigh up the evidence and draw conclusions appropriate to their role. Adolescents, in particular, may also wish to be credited with the capacity for independent thought, judgement and decision-making. In recent years, however, courts have begun to adapt their procedures where child victims are involved, so as to make those procedures both meaningful and non-intimidating. For example, there have been moves by court personnel to remove wigs and other formal trappings. Courts have used video recordings and live link facilities in an attempt to make children more relaxed when giving evidence. These developments culminated in the guidance issued to Crown Prosecutors under the Youth Justice and Criminal Evidence Act 1999, to the effect that children should now automatically be entitled to these special measures.

Prior to this enactment, however, an evaluation of the use of videotaped evidence in England and Wales, had found that this facility had not been used as widely as expected. Only a low proportion of cases led to a recommendation of prosecution, though the number of cases to reach court was rising. Most applications to show videotaped evidence during a trial, however, were granted. The majority of cases using videotaped evidence at trial were cases of child sexual abuse (Bull and Davies, 1996). Follow-up research found that children using tape seemed significantly less anxious than those using the live link facility (now installed in over half of all Youth Courts) and that there appeared to be no impact on the apparent credibility of the child as a witness. The researchers also observed that one of the most critical factors in the extent of distress levels was the approach and questioning tactics of the defence barrister, again highlighting the dependence of children on the adult world for sympathetic and just treatment (Wilson and Davies, 1999). It is also important to note that not all courts by any means yet have special facilities in place for child victims to give evidence by video tape or live link.

Prior to 1990, in England and Wales, the Rules of Evidence determined that it was unsafe to convict on the uncorroborated evidence of a child (in practice under the age of 6) again reducing the ability of child victims to make their voices heard. However, the Court of Appeal subsequently ruled that evidence could be given by children of any age if they could understand the need to tell the truth. More recently, the Youth Justice and Criminal Evidence Act 1999 introduced a presumption of 'competency' for all witnesses, children included, except where there were queries over their ability either to understand the questions or give comprehensible answers. However, there is a long way to go before courts can be persuaded to take fully into account the developmental stages of childhood (Erikson, 1968), how these can affect child perceptions, levels of understanding and articulacy, and how they may be profoundly damaged by prolonged victimisation (Cameron, 2000).

The Criminal Injuries Compensation Authority is a non-departmental public body, which administers the Criminal Injuries Compensation Scheme for England, Scotland and Wales. Under this scheme, children of parents or carers who have died as a result of their criminal injuries can claim an award for 'loss of parental services', for 'fatal injury' and 'dependency'. The numbers of claims made by adult former victims of child abuse are also steadily climbing. These measures are reinforced by Article 39 of the UN Convention on the Rights of the Child, 1989 which requires that all appropriate measures be taken to promote the physical and psychological recovery and social integration of child victims. However, where children make a claim, the claims officer will make an award only where he (*sic*) is satisfied that it would not be against his (*sic*) interest for an award to be made. While this is intended as a protective measure, in the wrong hands it could be misapplied.

Power relations between societies and their children

Beyond the formal, legalised responses which society makes to its child victims are other powerful responses, to be found for example in the media, which offer very mixed messages about crime, particularly violent crime. In the UK, this has impacted upon the populace as a consequence of public inquiry either because of abusive practices in children's homes, as discussed earlier; or because of the mismanagement of suspected child abuse; or because of child death within or outside the family. High profile examples in respect of the latter three arenas have included: Cleveland, where large numbers of children suspected of having been abused were taken into care, and the social work and health professionals vilified for unwarranted interference (Butler-Sloss, 1988); the long-term abuse and eventual murders in their families of Jasmine Beckford (Blom-Cooper, 1985) and Victoria Climbié (Laming, 2003), where professionals were accused of neglecting their duty of intervention; and the murders in Soham of Holly Wells and Jessica Chapman, where the failure of professionals to communicate and liaise effectively about a known sex offender was highlighted (Bichard, 2004).

According to the particular circumstances, then, those with professional responsibility have been criticised either for intervening too much or intervening too little. Public feeling seemingly runs as high about the increase of state interference in domestic and family life as it does about that same state's failure to prevent the death or abuse of a child. Cleveland or Climbié – which is worse? Either way, the child is the victim.

Power relations within and beyond UK societies have similarly institutionalised the victimisation of children. For example, Governmental regimes predicated upon political oppressions have both portrayed violence as a behavioural norm for children and engaged them in it. In other parts of the world, child soldiers are the epitome of state-sanctioned violence for the young. The apartheid regime in South Africa prompted strikes and demonstrations by school children against 'Bantu Education' in 1976; the response of the authorities was to shoot them. In the Western world, children in Northern Ireland lived through the longest period of sustained conflict in recent times. In all these situations, children died, witnessed death, were maimed, lost parents through imprisonment, were themselves imprisoned and saw or used guns in their daily lives.

Further, violence is enshrined in the response of a range of justice systems to criminalised anti-social behaviour – that is to say torture and other forms of physical retribution, and capital punishment – all of which, in some countries, may be applied to children and young people, despite wide ratification of the UN Convention on the Rights of the Child, 1989. Similarly, reports from the Bureau of International Labor Affairs (1996, 1998) emphasise that mental and physical violence to victims of child prostitution and child labour is to be seen not only in Asia, the Far East, Central and South America, as popularly imagined, but also in parts of the 'developed' world – Europe, North America and Australia. Physical violence between family members is frequently seen as normal for many societies (Gelles and Straus, 1988).

At national and international levels, then, these issues raise fundamental questions about how children experience power and its applications. As John (2003) notes, democracies are created both in the public sphere and within the emotional intimacies of the family. In these settings, without either fully developed cognitive skills or legal standing, it is highly problematic for children to engage in the process of recognising and realising their rightful autonomy and agency.

Some outcomes of victimisation as a child

The foregoing sections have described the structural settings in which children are most likely to become victims. The aetiology of their victimisation may produce a range of outcomes either within these settings as they become older, or beyond them when they reach adulthood. As one writer observes. 'Children are both victims and survivors of many violent acts . . . whether within the family or outside it' (Yule 1993: 153).

In terms of bullying which frequently takes place in school settings, there is evidence to suggest that those most likely to become bullies tend to live with (male) models of dominance and aggression who abused their power over their children (Bowers et al, 1992). Similarly it has been suggested that children who have been sexually abused and subjected to the abuse of authority coupled with the perversion of physical intimacy are conditioned to respond along a domination/submission continuum (Sanderson, 1992). Bagley and King in their search for the meaning that attaches to sexual abuse in childhood provide a wide range of published personal accounts of such abuse, most of which have in common feelings of anger, rage and hate which, set against positions of utter powerlessness, have to be internalised but nevertheless endure over time and surface in a variety of ways during adolescence or adulthood (Bagley and King, 1991). Earlier, Miller had studied the child-hoods of some authoritarian personalities and in the case of Hitler, for example, who was responsible for mass oppression and murder, had traced his actions back to a physically, emotionally (and possibly sexually) abusive father who persistently humiliated the young Adolf (Miller, 1987). Such well-organised and unrelenting compulsive destruction has been described as narcissistic rage, an extreme form of self-defensive revenge against early childhood helplessness and humiliation (Kohut, 1985; Wolf, 1988).

If young people have been denied their victim status by having no-one to confide in about what has happened to them then it is possible that they will seek redress by finding their own form of domination, sometimes within the family but, where this is unfeasible, sometimes also as a 'displacement' activity beyond it. In attempting to illustrate the latter form of redress Miller, for example, offers the speculation that millions of Jews might have escaped persecution if Hitler had had children of his own upon whom he could have taken revenge for his father's abuse of him (Miller, 1987). Although speculative, this is nevertheless a sobering thought which, again, leads back to a realisation of the crucial nature of preventive, protective action for victims of child abuse. It is also a further reminder that many societal structures render it more difficult than it should be for an abusive act against a child to merit a formal response. As two authors writing about child victims aver, 'Routine acts of minor violence such as bullying, chastisement or assault appear resist-ant to being defined as criminal when committed against children' (Morgan and Zedner, 1992: 22).

In more extreme cases of abuse, children have been likened to hostages or to concentration camp inmates whose 'captors' are also their significant attachment figures and whose means of survival will often be a direct func-tion of the only relationship dynamic they know – that of the captor/hostage relationship (Goddard and Stanley, 1994). In such circumstances it seems not implausible that without any intervention to tell them otherwise, children may come to believe that to take 'captives' for the purpose of physical, sexual and emotional abuse is the norm for adult behaviour. At the extreme of this spectrum (i.e. with no mediating factor to intervene) the victim may seek to become the survivor by finding her or his own victim to dominate in turn.

Studies of violent young people in a range of countries have shown how the oppressed may evolve into the oppressor and the victim and the offender become located in one single, damaged young person (e.g. Boswell 1995, 1996, 2000 in the UK: Widom and White, 1997, in the United States; Wedge, Boswell and Dissel, 2000 in South Africa). Although there are clearly differ-ences which relate to cultural and political variables, these studies show remarkably similar retrospective patterns in terms of earlier traumatic experi-ences. The UK study, for example, found that 72% of children sentenced between the ages of 10 and 17 years inclusive for murder and other grave crimes had experienced abuse of some kind-physical, sexual, emotional or combinations thereof; 57% had experienced traumatic loss of a close family member or friend (Boswell, 1995, 1996).

Indeed there seems little doubt that childhood abuse and loss, when no effective opportunity is provided for the child to make sense of these experiences, constitutes unresolved trauma which is likely to manifest itself in some way at a later date. Many children become depressed, disturbed, violent or all three, girls tending to internalise and boys to externalise their responses (American Psychiatric Association, 2000).

Working with those who are, or have been, child victims

Henry Kempe, who first identified the 'battered child' syndrome over four decades ago, pointed out in 1978 that the first stage of addressing the problem is to recognise the denial that it exists other than in 'people not like us' (Kempe, 1978). Society holds dear its warm images of childhood play, happiness and innocence. As another author observes:

> Our culture's view of childhood is built upon images of sweet-smelling babies, chubby hands dragging teddies, pony rides, science projects, piano lessons, prom dresses and graduation ceremonies. Sadly, for many children, the list would be more accurate if it included broken bones, chipped teeth, black eyes, burns, unexplained vaginal or anal infections, night terrors, empty stomachs and lonely hearts. (Everett and Gallop, 2001: 3)

In a critique of issues and findings relating to childhood abuse, one author has pointed out that 'one reason why professionals did not believe that children were subject to physical or sexual abuse, or suffered from PTSD (post-traumatic stress disorder) was simply that they never asked them!' (Yule, 1993: 165). Yule's view confirmed an earlier study of 105 hospitalised psychiatric patients, which found that 51% of them had been sexually abused in childhood or adolescence, but that in the majority of these cases hospital staff were unaware of the sexual abuse (Craine et al, 1988). Further, only 20% of the abused patients believed that they had received adequate treatment for their abusive experiences. Everett and Gallop, who make the important point that 'the denial of abuse can also mean the denial of recovery' (2001: 4), point to a series of systemic barriers which cause society to suppress or ignore the existence of child abuse. Broadly, these may be represented as follows:

- The family as sacred
- Authority should not be questioned
- Violence is normal

- The victim is at fault
- We are not our brother's (or our sister's) keepers
- Gender stereotypes
- Taboo subjects
- Nature versus nurture
- Finding the words (to name the unpalatable)

These issues have all been touched upon in previous sections and are more or less self-explanatory. What is important, here, is for professionals and policy-makers to consider how these barriers may impinge upon both society's and their own attitudes and behaviour towards children who have been victimised in any way and to seek ways of raising the visibility and voices of those children.

Conclusion

This paper has critically reflected on the topic of child victims with the intention of highlighting gaps and anomalies in the framework of statistical, legislative and societal responses which surround them. Noting, in particular, the need for improved interprofessional working and for sound preventive measures, three main suggestions are now offered for improving the quality of professional and policy responses in the process of working effectively with child victims.

Firstly, those likely to be in formal contact with children, such as health and social care professionals and teachers must be furnished with a firm knowledge base about the nature of the trauma which can follow childhood victimisation, and also acquire the relevant skills to make accurate assessments which lead to appropriate treatment and measures which will prevent adverse responses.

An important example of such a knowledge base is the growing body of work on post-traumatic stress disorder (Wilson & Raphael, 1993) which confirms that children suffer the after-effects of traumatic stress in the same way as adults. The set of criteria commonly used to establish whether an individual is suffering from post-traumatic stress disorder (PTSD) is set out by the American Psychiatric Association (2000). Professionals need to be equipped with the knowledge which will help them recognise these signs and to be provided with the training and resources which will enable them to intervene appropriately before behaviour manifestations along the risk continuum become entrenched within young adulthood.

Secondly, children and young people who have been victimised, abused and otherwise traumatised need communities which support them by validating rather than ignoring their experiences, making it more acceptable for them to report, describe and discuss these traumatic events, and placing emphasis on prevention, also offering support to parents in difficulty, and providing parenting classes in schools. As Morgan and Zedner observe:

> Child victims and their families have a diversity of needs. Many of them could best be met by the development of child-centred assistance. It is important that children be given a voice to express their feelings, needs and wishes. Listening to child victims themselves will allow criminal justice and support agencies to take greater account of their needs and, in doing so, to respond more effectively. . . . There should be far greater public awareness of the needs of child victims, better publicity about possible sources of support, improved interagency co-operation, and easier accessibility for victims seeking help for themselves. (Morgan and Zedner, 1992: 183)

Such awareness would require a genuine commitment to interprofessional working, possibly even beginning with interprofessional training so that commonalities rather than differences are emphasised, and the risk of children falling through professional safety nets, because vital information has not been shared, is eradicated. It would also require a much more developmental perspective on child victims. 'Understanding and appreciating the emotional and developmental levels of children and the developmental issues they are experiencing are extremely important first steps when assessing the impact of stress and crises' (Zubenko, 2002). It would further be enhanced by the introduction of a national database integrating annual figures on all officially reported crimes and forms of abuse committed against children, supplemented with regular national studies to assess the undoubtedly high levels of unreported direct and indirect victimisation of this age group. Though the role of the Children's Commissioner for England, due to take up post in April 2005, is widely seen as insufficiently independent of Government, this is a development which could very usefully be instigated by the post-holder. The new independent Commissioner for Victims, to be appointed under the Domestic Violence, Crime and Victims Act 2004, might also take this work forward.

Finally, there is a need for full integration of research programmes into the process of policy formulation and effective application in the justice system for young people. Such a process should take into account the views of professionals, the public, and the young victims themselves, moving society towards a greater sense of collective responsibility in the process. It is necessary to ensure that what Saunders (2003) refers to as the 'Balkanisation' of the professionals and the academics is diffused by a framework of interdisciplinary working and sharing of information about the complex and under-studied phenomenon that is childhood victimisation.

2.2

Violent racism: victimization, policing and social context
by B. Bowling

[. . .]

The views of survey respondents

Views about the locality

By almost any 'objective' criterion, North Plaistow is not the best place to live. In terms of its economy, the physical condition and cleanliness of its environment, the quality of its housing stock, its facilities for young and old people, and its rate of recorded crime and racial harassment, it is among the very worst-off localities in the whole of England and Wales. Despite this, many more respondents thought their area to be a good (60 per cent) rather than a bad one (28 per cent) to live in, and ethnic minority respondents rated the area considerably more highly than white ones. 55 per cent of white respondents said that the area was a good one, compared with 65 per cent of Asians and 70 per cent of Africans and Afro-Caribbeans.

Respondents were then read a list of things 'that are a problem in some areas', and were asked to what extent they themselves felt each were a problem. The things most likely to be seen as a big problem in the area were rubbish and litter (51 per cent), crime (44 per cent), and unemployment (32 per cent). 29 per cent of the sample thought that racial harassment was a problem—12 per cent thought it a big problem and a further 17 per cent a bit of a problem. As expected, ethnic minorities were more likely than white people to think that racial harassment was a problem.

Views about racial harassment in relation to other problems

Respondents were also asked what they thought to be the three greatest problems in the project area (see Table 2.2.1). Crime was considered the

Table 2.2.1 Respondents' opinion of the greatest 3 problems in the area (%)

	All	WM	WF	ACM	ACF	AM	AF	V	MV
Crime	48	48	51	41	30	60	52	57	61
Rubbish/litter	43	44	52	30	40	31	28	31	30
Unemployment	24	26	22	25	28	20	20	14	11
Housing conditions	19	19	21	24	19	14	15	11	6
Youth facilities	18	18	25	11	19	9	6	12	11
Leisure facilities	15	19	15	11	12	10	6	12	12
Rowdy youths	14	16	10	14	15	31	14	14	11
Council services	13	11	14	17	18	13	9	18	21
Schools	12	11	11	14	15	13	14	14	11
Graffiti	12	16	13	8	9	4	6	11	13
Racial harassment	10	8	5	3	16	22	28	27	36
Police service	9	9	5	16	10	14	12	18	14
Race discrimination	8	7	3	6	15	17	23	16	15
Noisy neighbours	8	10	5	11	9	10	5	2	2
Public transport	6	7	6	6	10	4	3	2	2
Rank order of racial harassment	11th	13th	12th	15th	8th	3rd	2nd	3rd	2nd

[. . .]
WM = white male
WF = white female
ACM = African/Caribbean Male
ACF = African/Caribbean Female
AM = Asian Male
AF = Asian Female
V = racial harassment victim
MV = multiply victimized

greatest problem, followed by rubbish and litter, unemployment, and housing conditions.

Ten per cent of the sample said that racial harassment was one of the three greatest problems in the area, ranking eleventh out of a list of fifteen problems. Racial harassment was for the sample *as a whole* more important only than police service provision, racial discrimination, noisy neighbours, and public transport. As expected, this picture changed substantially when desegregated by ethnic and gender group. Now, racial harassment emerged as a problem second only to crime and on a par with rubbish and litter for Asian women and as the third greatest problem for Asian men. Other ethnic and gender groups ranked racial harassment much lower—seventh for African and Afro-Caribbean women, thirteenth and twelfth for white men and women, respectively and fifteenth (bottom of the list) for African and Afro-Caribbean men.

Views about problems relating to law and order

Narrowing the focus somewhat, the survey next asked respondents to say whether or not they found specific forms of crime and disorder to be a problem in their area (see Table 2.2.2).

As might be expected, a large proportion of African and Afro-Caribbean and Asian respondents considered 'racial attacks on Afro-Caribbean and Asian people' to be a problem. Nearly two thirds of Asian women and men, about half of African and Afro-Caribbean women and men thought it was either a big, or a bit of a, problem in the area. However, there was also a considerable degree of concern among the white majority community about attacks on ethnic minorities; one quarter of white women and one third of white men said they thought that racial attacks *on Afro-Caribbeans and Asians* were a problem in the locality.

Views about police priorities

Views about policing priorities reflected, to some extent, beliefs about the greatest crime problems, although some forms of crime and harassment (e.g. sexual assault and pestering) were rated higher as police priorities than as crime problems (see Table 2.2.3).

Racial attacks were the third highest police priority for Asian men and women (after burglary and street robbery), fourth for African and Afro-Caribbean women, sixth for African and Afro-Caribbean men, and

Table 2.2.2 Respondents' opinion of the greatest 3 'crime' problems in the area (%)

	All	WM	WF	ACM	ACF	AM	AF	V	MV
Burglary	55	49	57	57	61	57	61	63	68
Street robbery	39	40	39	30	39	50	39	37	37
Vandalism	35	37	34	43	36	31	21	35	32
Car theft	35	36	33	33	39	42	29	39	37
Sexual assault	21	19	29	25	7	13	14	21	22
Youth misbehaviour	17	18	15	19	9	18	20	21	25
Women pestered	16	14	24	13	15	6	7	18	20
Racial attacks[1]	15	7	11	11	25	28	33	27	28
Fights in street	9	11	9	6	6	8	9	5	3

[1] The question referred to 'racial attacks on Afro-Caribbean and Asian people'.

Table 2.2.3 Which crime should the police concentrate on most? (%)

	All	WM	WF	ACM	ACF	AM	AF	V	MV
Burglary	50	45	49	54	55	57	58	52	49
Street robbery	36	38	34	25	42	42	40	34	32
Sexual assault	32	30	39	32	31	20	20	24	22
Car theft	27	27	26	27	28	32	25	32	24
Vandalism	26	26	24	32	28	23	24	26	26
Women pestered	21	20	30	21	15	10	7	16	18
Racial attacks[1]	19	16	13	21	28	33	39	30	30
Youth misbehaviour	10	11	8	16	1	12	14	15	21
Fights in street	8	9	7	10	6	7	10	7	8

[1] The question referred to 'racial attacks on Afro-Caribbean and Asian people'.

seventh for white men and women. Despite the differences in views among ethnic groups, some white people thought that racial attacks on African and Afro-Caribbean and Asian people were one of the three most important police priorities. The proportions of white people believing that racial attacks on ethnic minorities are a problem (32 per cent) and should be a policing priority (14 per cent) suggests that there is considerable concern about such attacks among the white majority community.

Fear of racial harassment

Fifty-eight per cent of Asian women worried either a great deal or a fair amount about being victimized, compared with 51 per cent of Asian men, 37 per cent of African and Afro-Caribbean women, 26 per cent of African and Afro-Caribbean men, 20 per cent of white women and 13 per cent of white men. Most white men (64 per cent), African and Afro-Caribbean men (57 per cent) and white women (54 per cent) did not worry at all about being victimized, compared with only 12 per cent of Asian women, 20 per cent of Asian men, and 29 per cent of African and Afro-Caribbean women. When asked whether they worried about the possibility of their families being victimized, the number of those fearful rose for each ethnic-gender group. Most worried of all were Asian women, only 10 per cent of whom claimed to live free from this anxiety (see Table 2.2.4)

Experiences of racial harassment

Respondents were next asked about experience, if any, of racial harassment. Interviewers explained that the term racial harassment referred to 'any form

Table 2.2.4 Respondents' worry about themselves becoming victims of racial harassment (%)

	All	WM	WF	ACM	ACF	AM	AF	V	MV
A great deal	10	5	6	10	18	19	29	35	39
A fair amount	15	8	14	16	19	22	29	25	27
Not very much	23	20	24	16	22	33	24	22	13
Not at all	50	64	54	57	39	20	12	18	19
Don't know/not stated	3	2	3	2	1	5	6	*	*

of insult, threat, violence, damage to or theft of property, or any attempt to do any of these things which was racially motivated. By racially motivated I mean an act directed at you because of your race.'

Respondents were then read a list of some types of offences and were asked to say whether any of them had happened to them personally within the previous eighteen months (January 1988–June 1989). 163 of the 1,174 survey respondents said they had experienced some form of racial harassment, about one in five ethnic minority respondents—21 per cent of African and Afro-Caribbean women (14 respondents), 19 per cent of Asian men (57 respondents), 18 per cent of Asian women (43 respondents) and 17 per cent of African and Afro-Caribbean men (n = 11). A small proportion of white people also said that they had experienced a racial incident—8 per cent of white men (n = 14) and 7 per cent of white women (n = 21).

Between them, these 163 victims mentioned approximately 831 actual incidents over the eighteen-month period.[1] This figure assumes that respondents' descriptions of the number of times they were victimized was accurate. They may not be able to recall the number and nature of incidents accurately over a period of eighteen months—some may be forgotten; others may have occurred longer ago and 'telescoped' forward into the reporting period; others may have occurred during the reporting period, but 'telescoped' backward and thus not been mentioned by the respondent. Because of the problem of defining racial harassment, discussed at some length in Chapter 2, some respondents may have defined incidents as *racial* when the motivation was arguable, or when they could not even be certain that a person from another racial group was responsible for the incident. Others may have ignored incidents they regarded as minor or unimportant.[2]

Despite this, it must be concluded that in the eighteen-month period in question, there were many thousands of incidents defined by the victim as racial harassment in North Plaistow. Given that roughly 10 per cent of the adult population of the area was interviewed, as many as 7,000 instances of insulting behaviour, threats of or actual violence, theft, damage to property (or attempts to do any of these things) where the victim believed that the incident was directed at him or her because of their race may have occurred in the eighteen-month period in question.

Detailed description of incidents

The preceding results are based on information supplied by the whole sample of 1,174 people. Of the 163 respondents who said that they had experienced one or more incidents, 114 agreed to provide details of 158 incidents.[3] These were between two thirds and three quarters of all those who stated that they had experienced a racial incident in the previous eighteen months. The information in the following section is based on their accounts of what happened. The victims detailing an incident were slightly more likely to be male than female, were much more likely to be under 45 than over, and were little different from the occupational class structure of the sample as a whole. Of the 158 incidents described in detail, the race—gender breakdown is as follows: fifty-eight Asian males, forty-five Asian females, thirteen African and Afro-Caribbean males, thirteen African and Afro-Caribbean females, fourteen white males, twelve white females, and three others.

By far the most common form of harassment consisted of insulting behaviour or verbal abuse (42 per cent), which the majority of victims suffered (see Table 2.2.5). Next were actual damage to property (16 per cent), actual physical assault (10 per cent), and actual theft (7 per cent). There were a very large number of 'less serious' incidents and many 'very serious' ones. Some appeared to be one-off events, while others were said to be part of a pattern of repeated attacks and harassment. This is consistent with the views of officers from local agencies who said that persistent door-knocking, egg throwing, damage to property, verbal abuse, threats, and intimidation had a cumulative effect on victims, even though the events may not look serious as individual 'incidents'.

Nearly six out of ten incidents occurred in the immediate vicinity of

Table 2.2.5 Types of harassment and number of incidents suffered by respondents over an 18-month period (weighted figures)

Form of harassment	Incidents
Insulting behaviour/verbal abuse	303
Threatened damage or violence	98
Attempted assault	81
Actual assault	72
Actual and attempted damage to property	114
Actual and attempted theft	53
Actual and attempted arson	3

Unweighted n = 163

victims' homes (see Table 2.2.6). This including incidents which occurred at the home address[4] (23 per cent), those that occurred in the street outside the victim's home (16 per cent), outside or inside the building in which their home was located (12 per cent and 4 per cent respectively), and near their garage (4 per cent).

Incidents happened at all times of the day and night, 29 per cent sometime during the daytime, and a further 13 per cent occurred in the morning, 30 per cent between 6 pm and midnight, 11 per cent between midnight and 6 am, and 4 per cent sometime during the hours of darkness.

Patterns of victimization for each ethnic-gender group

It is evident that a wide range of different experiences have been defined by respondents as racial incidents. The data suggest that there are very different experiences among the various ethnic and gender groups. Thus, it becomes impossible to speak of the *typical* case of racial harassment or attack. The experiences are so varied that one hesitates to include every instance in the same class of events, behaviours, or experiences.

In addition to differences between groups, there are differences *within* groups. Thus, the incidents mentioned in the survey by a single ethnic-gender group appear to cover a wide range of activities, with regard to the characteristics of the victim and perpetrator, or the context of the incident. In the following analysis, the quantitative data from the survey, *selected* quotations from the survey's openended questions are used to illustrate specific points as they emerge.[5]

Table 2.2.6 Where the incident took place (%)

Location	All	WM	WF	ACM	ACF	AM	AF	R[1]
In/around the home[2]	23	21	25	31	15	21	31	37
Street outside home	16	14	17	8	8	31	18	10
Inside own building	4	–	–	–	15	2	9	2
Outside own building	12	14	17	15	–	17	11	20
In garages for houses	4	21	–	–	8	4	–	8
All in vicinity of home	59	70	59	54	46	66	69	77
At work	7	–	–	–	31	7	–	3
All others[3]	33	29	42	39	23	28	17	17

[1] Incidents reported to an official agency (e.g. the police or the Housing Department).
[2] Includes attempted break-ins, incidents on the doorstep, material through the letter box.
[3] Includes school/college, in street near work, in/near a pub, at place of work out of doors and place of worship, and 'don't know'/not stated, all of which were very small numbers. The bulk (33% of the whole sample) were 'other' responses.

Asian people

Of the 103 incidents mentioned by Asian respondents, no fewer that thirty-nine of them (38 per cent) were directed at Asian council tenants. Only 14 per cent of the Asians sampled were council tenants, suggesting that those living in council accommodation were almost three times as likely to have provided detail about an incident as Asians as a whole. The majority of council estates in North Plaistow are away from the eastern portion of the study site, which has a high proportion of Asian residents (more than 50 per cent). Council housing lies mainly in the centre of the area (e.g. the Chadd Green estate) or on the western edge of the area where there is a low proportion of Asian residents. These facts support the view that the geographical spread of racial incidents reflects the targeting of ethnic minorities living outside the areas of high ethnic minority concentration.

The survey showed that seven out of ten incidents mentioned by Asian women happened close to home, with three out of ten occurring directly on or immediately adjacent to their homes and a further four out of ten in the street, walkway, or passageway outside their home. The remainder occurred elsewhere. The pattern was similar for Asian men, though more were incidents which occurred in the street outside their homes.

Most recent incident
> I was watching TV at home, and a gang of kids come, shouted abuse, and started throwing stones, hitting and breaking windows in my house, and of my car. *What was it about the incident which makes you believe that the attack was racially motivated?* They call me a black fucking Paki, and they said I shouldn't be here, to go home.

Second most recent incident
> It was some kids I chased off earlier in the day, they come and threw stone at my windows breaking them, shouting 'Go away Paki'. *What was it about the incident which makes you believe that the attack was racially motivated.* The fact that they hate anyone who is a 'Paki' as they call us. They tell me to go away.

Third most recent incident
> We were at the back of our garden, and we heard a noise. We come out to find the windows of our car broken. *What was it about the incident which makes you believe that the attack was racially motivated?* Because I'd had trouble with racial harassment before [Indian man].

The survey found that many incidents consisted of racist abuse, graffiti, window smashing, and egg throwing. There are three reasons for considering what are sometimes referred to as 'low level' or merely 'nuisance' incidents, very serious in their impact and their effect on the security of the victim.[6] First, any type of incident becomes serious when it is repeated frequently enough. Repeated or persistent incidents undermine the security of the victim and induce fear and anxiety. The sense of the cumulative effects of repeated instances of stone throwing, name-calling, and harassment are evident from this example:

Most recent incident
Came in and called me Paki and started throwing bricks at me. They didn't hurt me because I had thick coat on. They called me Paki before they started throwing the bricks at me.

Second most recent incident
A gang of teenagers started shouting at me 'Paki' go home and abuse. Nothing else.

Third most recent incident
It's happened so many times—they come up in groups and call me names—they call me rude names and call me Paki. I want to move away from here because I'm frightened to live here now because it happens so often.

A second reason for taking seriously the effect of repeated harassment directed specifically against ethnic minorities is the apparent exclusionary intent and impact of this form of victimization. The two examples cited above illustrate the exclusionary language and practice of the perpetrator. The phrases such as 'go home', 'go back to your own country' challenge the human rights of the people who are victimized (made into a victim) with the obvious effect of undermining their sense of security and sense of belonging (Hesse et al., 1992). The eventual impact is to create fear about living in a particular locality and to inspire a wish to move away. This aspect of racism is what Hesse et al. refer to as the 'logic of white territorialism':

What then is the context and objective of 'white territorialism'? . . . Consider the discursive resonances wrought by expressions like 'Pakis go home', 'go back to your own country', 'alien cultures swamping British identity', 'immigrants colonizing Britain', 'blacks ghettoizing the inner-city' or more recently 'Islamic fundamentalism sweeping the nation'. At least two things should be apparent from these spatial obsessions. First there is heightened anxiety about these 'subordinate', 'other' populations resisting regulation and getting out of 'our' control; and secondly, there is a sense in which 'our' British identity (for 'our' read 'white') is under threat because 'our right' to dominate is being questioned; this is the expressive logic of the desire for racial exclusion [Hesse et al., 1992: 172].

Even the most mundane instances of racial abuse may be seen as an exclusionary practice, one which acts to 'defend . . . space against change and transformation' (Hesse *et al.*, 1992). In this way spaces are created within which black people are made to feel unwelcome and vulnerable to attack, and from which they may eventually be excluded.

Finally, mundane but persistent attacks *on property* are also attacks on *those inside* the dwelling (whether or not they are present at the time of the incident). Graffiti, window breakages, and other forms of criminal damage on the fabric of the building and physical attacks nearby the building violate the security of the place where an individual is often considered safest. Although an Englishman's home is (metaphorically) his castle, in actual fact the physical fabric of a house (particularly those in localities such as Newham) provides only an illusion of defence against attack from without.[7] Being a static object makes a dwelling an easy target—one which is open to repeated and persistent attack, and one where the potential for escalation is tied specifically to a fixed location (Hesse *et al.*, 1992). Several respondents mentioned instances of attack which resulted in damage to property where their personal security was at great risk. Such instances include shooting a window with an air gun and attempted arson attacks using inflammable fluid squirted through the letterbox:

> A bullet came through the bedroom window and broke it bringing the bullet into the room. An air gun was used. *What was it about the incident which makes you believe that the attack was racially motivated?* It's happened several times [involving] the same person. I have got NF written outside my wall and I don't know what to do about it this time. I have been attacked right in my bedroom [Other Asian].

> Someone put container of liquid through letter box. Failed to make a fire. Could have been serious. *What was it about the incident which makes you believe that the attack was racially motivated?* Because of the sort of attack putting fire through letter box. Neighbours had one similar incident [Pakistani].

In several cases documented during the study period attacks have occurred in which groups of assailants have smashed their way through the front door and assaulted the victim with weapons (including knives, a hammer, and a pool cue) inside their homes. In other instances, attacks which started in public space led to attacks on the victim's home:

> My children went to the park, under the supervision of my sister, and they were set upon, by these white kids, when they finished beating my kids up they followed them to my address, and threw stones at my window, breaking it. *What was it about the incident which makes you believe*

that the attack was racially motivated? Because they shouted, abusive names like Pakis and many other insulting words.

Many of the incidents described by Asians in the survey are of a type identified in the Home Office (1981) study and noted by Walmsley (1986 drawing on Brown, 1984):

> Many attacks on Asians and West Indians are attacks in the street when there is clearly no background of a prior argument or misunderstanding. In such incidents strangers may simply approach others and hit them, kick them, throw stones at them or even use knives and bottles to assault them [Walmsley 1986: 26].

In North Plaistow, respondents described walking along the street near to their homes or while shopping, going to work or worship, and being unexpectedly verbally abused or being physically attacked or menaced:

> Me and my husband were taking our children to mosque in the afternoon. some young white man just said verbal abuse—'Paki' and things like that [Indian woman].

> As I was coming home there were some kids playing on the road—16 or 17 years old. They said 'You Paki. Why don't you go away from here'. Sometimes when I move my car they are there and won't move to let me get out [Indian].

> Guy was drunk, he hit me with a piece of [wire]. Line on my face straight through where he hit me then he ran away—I didn't have time to do anything to defend myself. It happened very quickly, he didn't say anything but he wouldn't have done it if I was white. *What was it about the incident which makes you believe that the attack was racially motivated?* We had no conversation—didn't know the guy—first thing that happened was that he hit me. He just wouldn't have done it if I was white. No [Iranian].

> I was shopping once [when a] white young girl came and stood in front of me. I told her I am in the queue and you should wait for your turn. But instead she started saying racially names and slapped on my face as well. *What was it about the incident which makes you believe that the attack was racially motivated?* That is quite obvious. If there was another white woman, first thing she would not jump the queue and secondly in the case of white women, if she had protested, this white girl would never slap her or abuse her [Pakistani].

Some incidents mentioned by Asian men (7 per cent) occurred while at work.

> Argument over prices. Bloody Indian, bloody immigrant. Fucking bastard! *What was it about the incident which makes you believe that the attack was racially motivated?* Wording racial. Bloody Paki. Bloody immigrant [Indian shopkeeper].

The only Chinese victim in the sample who gave details of their experience also suffered harassment at work:

Most recent incident

> [I work in a] Chinese fish and chip shop. I come to work the next morning to find our shop window smashed. *What was it about the incident which makes you believe that the attack was racially motivated?* Because they smashed my window without stealing anything. [I] must be someone they don't like.

Second most recent incident

> Two kids came in. Got a drink and tried to steal it. I went out of the counter and said 'You've got to pay for the drink'. They started arguing. Finally he paid for it and on his way out, he was very angry and said 'I'm gonna put a brick through that door'. *What was it about the incident which makes you believe that the attack was racially motivated?* I just felt it could have been because of us [Chinese] living here.

The majority of the incidents experienced by both Asian men and women involved groups of young white males who were unknown to the victim. Very few incidents targeted at Asian women were one-to-one confrontations, with 85 per cent involving more than one perpetrator. More than one third of the incidents involved a group of four or more perpetrators. Four out of ten incidents directed against Asian men were carried out by a group of four or more. Asian men and women were harassed by a group of males in two thirds of the incidents. Also in two thirds of the incidents the perpetrators were aged 16–25, and in one quarter were school age.

In just over one incident in ten the victim knew all or some of the people involved and, where they were known, they were not known well, most often by sight only. Two thirds of the Asian victims said that their assailants were white, one fifth that they were African or Afro-Caribbean, and one tenth a 'mixed' group.

The question of whether African and Afro-Caribbean people can exhibit racist attitudes or behaviour toward Asian people has been a recurrent one since the emergence of the problem of racial violence as a policy issue in the early 1980s, though many reports simply duck the issue altogether.[8] In North

Plaistow there is no doubt that some of the Asians interviewed believed themselves to have been the victims of anti-Asian racism perpetrated by groups composed solely of young men of African or Afro-Caribbean origin, or groups of blacks and white acting together. In some instances, the belief that attacks by African/Caribbeans were racially motivated was simply because the assailant was black. In other instances, African/Caribbean young people were perceived by the victim to engage in anti-Asian racist behaviour that was not readily distinguishable from that perpetrated by their white counterparts:

Most recent incident

Graffiti. Very abusive and dirty words were written on both the . . . front door and refuse box. All over the front walls. Some words are still visible. It happen[s] . . . frequently. *What was it about the incident which makes you believe that the attack was racially motivated?* It must be done by white or black kids. We are only two [Asian] families in this block. Everybody know[s]. That is why making our life very hard.

Second most recent incident

My husband was coming back. A group of young kids push my husband and started kicking him. *What was it about the incident which makes you believe that the attack was racially motivated?* Because the gang was mix[ed] group. Two white and one black youth. They were awaiting for him [Indian woman].

There are also instances of African/Caribbeans echoing the racist epithets more commonly associated with white racism:

A couple of whites and a couple of blacks called me racist names. They pushed me around . . . *What was it about the incident which makes you believe that the attack was racially motivated?* The verbal abuse. That's all [Pakistani].

Just came and asked me for money. They punched me—black and white gang—there were lots of them. They threatened me but I didn't give them anything. They were carrying knives and a screwdriver. *What was it about the incident which makes you believe that the attack was racially motivated?* Paki—they called me a Paki—if I'd been white I don't think they'd have stopped and asked me for money. Nothing else. No [Bangladeshi].

One Indian person said that he had been assaulted by 'eight black people' who held him to the ground and kicked and hit him. When asked what was it about the incident which made him believe that the attack was racially motivated, he said, 'because they told me it was. There you bloody Paki that will show ya'.

For both Asian men and women, the most common reason for believing that the incident was racially motivated—in 54 per cent of those directed against men and 40 per cent against women—was that the perpetrator had referred to their actual or supposed race. This racial ascription was very often wrong, with people of Indian origin frequently called 'Paki'. The second most common reason, in about one fifth of cases, was the victim's belief that such attacks would not happen to them if they were white. In one in ten incidents directed against Asian men, the victim was told to 'go back to where you came from', or 'to your own country'. Often these racist epithets were combined, such as '[t]hey call me a black fucking Paki, and they said I shouldn't be here, to go home'. In other instances, the victim ascribed a racial motive to the perpetrator because of the circumstances of the incident. This was sometimes because the incident had occurred without prior history, warning, or provocation: '[w]e had no conversation—didn't know the guy— first thing that happened was that he hit me. He just wouldn't have done it if I was white.' On other occasions, this perception stemmed from the fact the victim was one of a few or the only Asian family living in the block; that similar incidents had occurred to minority families living nearby; or that other expressions of racist antipathy had occurred in the past.

Africans and Afro-Caribbeans

About half of the incidents mentioned by African and Afro-Caribbean men (54 per cent) and women (46 per cent) took place at, around, or near their home addresses. All the incidents mentioned by African and Afro-Caribbean respondents involved white perpetrators. In common with the experience of the Asian respondents, most of these incidents consisted of insults and verbal abuse (54 per cent for women and 69 per cent for men) involved unprovoked abuse or harassment:

Most recent incident

A white guy came out of a pub and started abusing me. He called me a 'wog' and a 'nigger'. He first called me a wog and when I challenged him he called me nigger. It nearly turned [in]to a fight but a police car drove by and we broke it up. It ended in just words between us. *What was it about the incident which makes you believe that the attack was racially motivated?* Well his words. Wog and nigger. If that isn't racial, what is?

Second most recent incident

I was walking down this road. I had a suit on as I was going for an interview when a blue van drove past and a white guy threw an egg at me. It was a fresh egg. Well the egg broke and stained my suit. I . . . had to go back home to change. I was late for the interview and didn't get the job [African].

Two white boys in a car slowed down as they passed me and shouted 'get out of the way stupid nigger'. *What was it about the incident which makes you believe that the attack was racially motivated?* Well, they shouted nigger didn't they and they were white. So it's obvious isn't it [Afro-Caribbean].

A number of other incidents arose out of a conflict with neighbours:

We had a party. Neighbours were informed before hand. My neighbours threw a bag of rubbish at my guests. *What was it about the incident which makes you believe that the attack was racially motivated?* The person involved was white. The type of language used by the man [African].

The woman's [neighbour] dog kept on barking and barking that it was so loud my baby couldn't sleep so I went to the woman and complained. She told me to get lost, called me a black bastard and slammed the door in my face. The dog was so disturbing that I reported it to the council. *What was it about the incident which makes you believe that the attack was racially motivated?* She said I was a black bastard and that I shouldn't bother her. Yes, she's white so it was a racial thing wasn't it? [African].

African and Afro-Caribbean men were the most likely of all ethnic-gender groups to mention threatened or actual property damage (in 46 per cent of cases).

Petrol was poured through the letter box and set alight. That's all [Afro-Caribbean].

Came home from college and found damage on my door and it has been set on fire, with graffiti on the wall calling me names.

First incident
Someone smashed my car windscreen. Nothing was taken. It happened in the evening or night. *What was it about the incident which makes you believe that the attack was racially motivated?* All over the car was written 'Out, out Paki' [*sic*].

Second incident
I came back in my car with children from shopping. I parked my car. Then the youngest son from next door (about ten) went to my doorstep, took down his trousers and urinated in front of me and my children. *What was it about the incident which makes you believe that the attack was racially motivated?* In relation to all the other things that they had done

like cutting my telephone wires at least twenty times, stealing my son's glasses and me and my children were racially abused every single day [African].

African and Afro-Caribbean men mentioned incidents perpetrated by other males either in a group (60 per cent) or alone (40 per cent) In just under half of the incidents (45 per cent) the perpetrators were aged between 16 and 25, one fifth were school age, and one in three older people.

When explaining the basis for their perception that the incident was racially motivated, African and Afro-Caribbean men most often said that the perpetrators had referred to their race (54 per cent). They also mentioned that damage had been done to their property with no apparent motive other than racism, that they were told to 'go back to your own country', and that they were the only black people in the neighbourhood and were being singled out as victims of crime. Three out of ten respondents said that they felt that the incident was racially motivated, but had no proof.

About one in three of the incidents mentioned by African and Afro-Caribbean women occurred in their place of work. They were also more likely than any other group to know the perpetrator involved, suggesting that some of these incidents involved co-workers. In six out of ten incidents they were harassed by a sole male perpetrator and in more than half of them they knew the perpetrator involved. In more than half of the incidents described by African/Caribbean women, their race was mentioned and in one incident in ten they were told to 'go back to your own country'. 15 per cent of the incidents were said to have been part of a process of harassment over a longer period.

White people

In many ways the incidents mentioned by white women were similar to those mentioned by Asian and Afro-Caribbean women. A large proportion occurred in the vicinity of their home; many involved unprovoked abusive language and insulting behaviour. However, one very important difference between the incidents mentioned by white women and other groups was the likelihood of it involving theft. Those mentioned by white women were twice as likely to involve theft as those mentioned by Asian women and four times as likely as those mentioned by African and Afro-Caribbean women.

A striking feature of the incidents described by white women is the large proportion of cases in which white perpetrators were involved. White people were said to have been involved as aggressors in more than four out of the ten incidents directed at white women when the race of the perpetrator was known. In three incidents the perpetrators were *all* white and one other involved a mainly white group. Of the remaining six cases, four involved

African/Caribbeans, one Asians, and one involved a mixed but mainly black group.

[. . .]

Effects of victimization

Taking aggregated figures for all groups, racial harassment appears to be thought of as a relatively unimportant problem. It is not considered by many to be a priority for the police, nor does it comprise a particularly salient fear for the majority of residents. When these figures are disaggregated, however, the picture changes dramatically. Particularly striking is that one quarter of the Asian women thought racial harassment a big problem; they ranked it second only to crime and a police priority after only burglary and street robbery.

Some of the victims said that the experience had made little impact on them, while for others the experience, threat, and fear of racial harassment had a considerable effect. The most common emotional reaction to the incident among the sample as a whole was anger (70 per cent), followed by shock (44 per cent), and fear (27 per cent) about 10 per cent mentioned no emotional reactions. The pattern is similar for different ethnic groups, with the exception of Asian women, 60 per cent of whom said that they became fearful as a result of their experience. When asked how long the worst effects took to wear off, one quarter of the whole sample said they had worn of within a few hours and a further quarter within a few days. For more than one fifth, however, the effects were still continuing. Again, Asian women were more likely than any other ethnic-gender group to feel the effects for longer, nearly one third of whom stated *that the worst effects of the incident were still continuing* at the time of the interview.

The gender differences in fear of racial harassment and in the extent to which it is thought to be a problem observed in this survey broadly confirms existing research on fear of crime. However, such differences are not explained easily with survey data, as is evident in academic debate on this subject. In this survey, the small differences in victimization rates between sexes might account for a small proportion of the difference in concern between African-Caribbean men and women, the latter being somewhat more likely to be victimized and were more fearful. Among Asians, however, men were more likely to be victimized and yet they were less fearful.

Stanko, reviewing explanations of gender differences in fear of crime, notes that many focus on issues related to gender experience and gender role expectations (Stanko, 1987: 126). From this perspective, researchers speculate whether men are simply reluctant to report fear and feel less vulnerable to interpersonal violence and more secure than women because of the social expectations upon them to be brave and fearless. This speculation is, as Stanko suggests, 'squarely located in one gender expectation: men's bravado'

(Stanko, 1987: 126), a display which is clearly linked to what men are supposed to live up to:

> A 'real' man is a strong, heterosexual male protector, capable of taking care of himself and, if necessary, guarding his and others' safety aggressively. He is the man who will stand up in a fight, but will not abuse his power by unnecessarily victimising others. And, according to the mythology of the 'real man', he will do so fearlessly [Stanko, 1990: 110].

Alternatively, gender differences in fear of crime may be explained because of differences in perception of social and physical vulnerability (Skogan and Maxfield, 1981). For Skogan and Maxfield, physical vulnerability concerns 'openness to attack, powerlessness to resist and exposure to physical and emotional consequences if attacked'; and social vulnerability involves 'daily exposure to the threat of victimization and limited means for coping with the medical and economic consequences of victimization'. Thus fear is a logical assessment of the ability of women and the elderly physically to withstand violence. (Skogan and Maxfield, 1981: 77–8; cited in Stanko, 1987: 128).

Turning attention to feminist theory and the subjective reality of lived experience, Stanko argues that women's fear of crime is related to a fear of and vulnerability to rape (Riger and Gordon, 1981). It is also from feminist literature that the extent of under-reporting of women's experience of male violence to both official agencies and surveys in apparent. Thus, 'daily, commonly taken-for-granted experiences of women contribute to the hostile and intimidating atmosphere wherein women are presumably supposed to feel safe' (Stanko, 1987: 130). Throughout this work, emphasis is placed on the importance of understanding how different people experience their lives and how this is affected by where or how they live and who they are (Stanko, 1990: 6). For men, an additional sense of security and perhaps actual avoidance of danger: 'comes from strength, backed up by physical ability and enhanced by the advantages of economic, racial or sexual status' (ibid.).

The data from this survey go some way to supporting a theory based on actual risk of attack. Although it seems very likely that this survey will have been as unsuccessful as others in capturing the full extent of the experience of victimization (in terms of its estimate of the number of victims and the frequency of their victimization), it is evident that some people are more likely to become victims than others, and that this has an effect on their perceptions of themselves as vulnerable and in need of protection. Specifically, white people are at less risk of experiencing a racial incident, and this appears to be related to the extent of fear, concern about the problem, and beliefs about policing priorities. However, the data also suggest that vulnerability must also play a part, particularly when explaining gender differences.

Notes

1 Because Asians were believed, *a priori*, to be those most likely to be victimized, they were deliberately oversampled in order to have enough 'victims' in the sample for meaningful analysis. As a result, the number of incidents in the sample reduced to 724 when weighted to correct for oversampling.

2 An attempt was made to offset this problem by explaining to respondents that: 'I don't just want to know about serious incidents, I want to know about small things too. It is often difficult to remember exactly when the small things happened so please try to think carefully.' Nonetheless, the well-documented under-reporting of incidents to the police may also apply to reporting incidents to survey interviewers. The authors of the ICS, for example, concluded from one interview that 'some segments of the population are so over-exposed to [racist assaults] that it becomes part of their everyday reality and escapes their memory in the interview situation' (Jones *et al.*, 1986).

3 118 when weighted to compensate for oversampling Asians.

4 This includes actual and attempted break-ins, damage to property (including window breakages), incidents on the doorstep, and offensive material through the letterbox.

5 Most of the survey items were precoded, leaving open-ended only questions such as what actually occurred in the incident, why the respondent believed the incident to have been racially motivated, why the incident was not reported to the police and other local agencies (in cases where it was not), and what happened as a result of a police detection (in cases where perpetrators were detected). The responses to these questions as recorded by the interviewer were transcribed in full. Because details were not recorded in every instance and because of the poor quality of some of what was recorded it must be stressed that the quotations selected for inclusion in the text are intended only to *illustrate* the quantitative survey findings.

6 See also FitzGerald and Ellis, 1990: 59; Hesse *et al.*, 1992; Sampson and Phillips, 1992.

7 Some of the quotations provided in this section illustrate the vulnerability of houses and flats to attack through windows, glass door fronts, letterboxes, etc. Local authority flats, in particular, have been shown to be quite penetrable. In several instances which came to the author's attention while working in Newham, flats have been entered by perpetrators jumping through the thin ceiling of top floor flats having gained access to the eaves.

8 FitzGerald and Ellis (1990), for example, state that: 'Initial perceptions of the problem (which was first brought to light in respect of Asian communities in the East End of London) have tended to frame the

assumptions on which discussion has taken place and to limited the categories covered by surveys. Political pressure (with a small 'p') has also
been brought to bear, with strong exception being taken in some quarters
to the notion that black people can exhibit racial hostility either towards
whites or towards each other. . . . With regard to the survey data, it will be
noted that even the Home Office (1981) report does not cover harassment
between Afro-Caribbeans and Asians, while most of the other surveys
implicitly deny that whites could be victims of racial harassment at all'
(*ibid.*: 58). Small notes that 'conflicts between subgroups, ethnically or
otherwise, within the black population' are 'a topic of tremendous taboo'
(1991: 525).

2.3

Recognising and responding to victims of rural racism

by Jon Garland and Neil Chakraborti

[. . .]

Introduction

The needs and concerns of victims of crime have featured increasingly prominently on the agendas of academics and policy-makers in recent times. Following various localised studies of victimisation in the United States in the 1960s, and then the United Kingdom in the 1970s, the establishment of the British Crime Survey (BCS) in 1982 was the first attempt in the UK to measure, at a national level, victims' experiences of crime (Kershaw *et al.*, 2001). Coupled with the emergence of the BCS as a tool to measure victims' perceptions and experiences has been the growth in the 'veritable industry of services' (Newburn, 2003: p. 224) aimed at improving the existing support that victims receive from statutory and voluntary agencies. After the establishment of the entitlement of victims to receive compensation from central government in the 1960s and the subsequent founding of Victim Support in the 1970s, there have been a range of other initiatives, including victims' charters, the use of victim personal statements in courts, the growth in the importance of the principles and deployment of restorative justice, and the establishment of the Victims' Advisory Panel, that have resulted in victims being placed, according to some, 'at the heart of criminal justice considerations' (Goodey, 2005: p. 4).

An important piece of legislation in this regard was the Criminal Justice Act 2003, which offered protection for victims of crime from civil proceedings instigated by convicted offenders attempting to obtain damages from the victim by claiming that they had suffered some form of financial, physical or emotional damage or loss. This section of the Act was partly inspired by the furore and fallout from the Tony Martin case which gained extensive tabloid publicity and symbolic importance in the early part of the twenty-first century (Jones, 2002). Martin, a farmer based in a remote part of the west Norfolk fens, was sentenced to five years imprisonment in 2000 for the manslaughter of teenager burglar Fred Barras, who had broken into Martin's isolated farmhouse one night in August 1999. Martin had been awoken by noises downstairs and, startled by having a light shone in his face, fired his unlicensed shotgun, killing Barras. The teenager's accomplice, 30 year-old Brendan Fearon, was then shot in the leg by Martin, wounding him but not preventing his escape. Following Martin's conviction, Fearon served a writ upon the farmer, claiming £15,000 in lost income caused by his inability to work due to the injuries that Martin had inflicted upon him. This prompted the *Sun* newspaper to launch a fundraising campaign on Martin's behalf, and to donate £5,000, in order to help Martin defend himself against Fearon's action (Tendler, 2003).

The *Sun*'s action revealed a number of pertinent facets of the Martin case. Not only had the farmer apparently touched a raw nerve with the public regarding the rights of householders to defend themselves against intruders, but also Martin himself had become something of a *cause célèbre* and had attracted the sympathy of the popular press. To newspapers like the *Sun*, Martin himself had been the victim of the whole episode, rather than those he had wounded or killed, as it was felt he had been unjustly jailed, and given a harsh sentence, for merely defending himself when frightened by intruders in his home (Ford, 2003). To others, Martin was a 'dangerous' and 'reclusive' man who 'had it in for burglars' (Asthana, 2003: p. 6). One significant outcome of the Tony Martin case, aside from precipitating the section of the Criminal Justice Act 2003 mentioned earlier, was to bring the issue of rural crime and victimisation, if only briefly, to the forefront of political debate. Whether Martin was the 'real victim' or not, the episode highlighted the absence of available police cover in many rural areas during the hours of darkness. Martin lived in a remote farmhouse that had been burgled twice in the 12 months prior to the shooting. Despite reporting these incidents to the police, he had been left feeling isolated and vulnerable due to the lack of assistance that the police could provide for him at night, something with which many rural residents could empathise (Dingwall and Moody, 1999). It had, however, taken such a drastic and tragic event to bring the issue of rural crime and victimisation to the attention of the wider public. As Zedner (2002: p. 424) suggests, there is a 'paucity of information about victimisation in rural areas' and even the annual BCS has had something of an urban focus.

Moreover, it has also been argued that historically the BCS has overlooked certain groups, including minority ethnic populations (Fitzgerald and Hale, 1996). Indeed, the needs and circumstances of such groups in the countryside are still largely neglected by criminologists who have continued to focus attention towards the urban, despite a number of recent high-profile incidents of racism in the rural[1], including a spate of assaults upon Chinese residents in Cumbria (*Whitehaven News*, 2005), the uncovering of a small white supremacist cell in Shropshire (Newey, 2005) and the daubing of swastikas upon the statue of an Indian prince in Thetford, Norfolk (*The Times*, 2005). These types of incidents, and the apparent lack of willingness on behalf of minority ethnic groups to spend leisure time in the countryside, caused the Chair of the Commission for Racial Equality, Trevor Phillips, to state rather emotively in 2004 that a form of 'passive apartheid' exists in the rural and that white rural dwellers and minority ethnic visitors greet each other with 'mutual incomprehension' (Smith, 2004).

Yet, despite the continuing nature of such incidents and the publicity surrounding Phillips's comments, there still appears to be little academic or practitioner understanding of the concerns and needs of rural minority ethnic populations, of their risks of victimisation, nor of their ways in which different forms of victimisation can impact upon their quality of life and take-up of services in the countryside. As Magne (2003: p. 6.23) says, there is often:

> . . . a focus on the source of the racism to the exclusion of its impact. The natural consequence of this is that support for the victim is relegated to bottom of the procedural list for appraisal of an incident – often by victims as well as agencies.

This article attempts to redress this situation by examining the nature and forms of racist victimisation suffered by minority ethnic populations in the rural. Drawing upon the small but growing body of work in the area of rural racism, including research undertaken by the authors in three rural counties of England – specifically Suffolk, east Northamptonshire, and north and south Warwickshire[2] – the article assesses the characteristics of rural village communities, and in particular the lack of familiarity with difference evident among many of its white inhabitants that only serves to marginalise incomers from mainstream village activities, and especially those from minority ethnic backgrounds who are subjected to a process of 'othering' from many white villagers. In some cases, this process can manifest itself as racist hostility and harassment that can take a number of forms, ranging from verbal abuse to physical attack that can have devastating emotional and financial effects upon recipients. However, it is argued that victims of racism are often 'invisible' to service providers who do not realise the significance of the problem of racism in the rural. These agencies therefore frequently provide an inadequate and ill-informed response to incidents of harassment that merely exacerbates an already traumatic situation for victims. It is suggested in the conclusion that not only do service providers and policy makers need to recognise the seriousness of the problem of rural racism, but that they need to adopt a range of long-term, sustainable initiatives that fully recognise the unique characteristics of rural environments, if the needs of victims are to be properly met.

[. . .]

Contextualising racist victimisation in the rural

The image of the countryside as a peaceful and idyllic environment, where communities are warm and welcoming and crime levels are low, has enjoyed a lasting popularity amongst rural populations. The romanticised notion of the village being a locale 'where everybody knows and cares for each other' (Francis and Henderson, 1992: p. 19) was, for many of the white residents interviewed by the authors, an important part of their own rural community identities. Indeed, the majority of interviewees maintained that their village communities were both welcoming to incomers and yet also 'close-knit'. The key components of that notion – familial ties, long-term residency (including the ability to trace one's ancestral roots back several generations) and a low turnover of population – are reflected in the views of the rural residents who took part in Abrams' (2002: p. 82) study based in Buckinghamshire, who saw their village 'as a timeless place of long-established families forming a stable core of "real community" '. Another oft-cited and much-cherished component of village identities – 'Britishness' – was invoked by the prospective Conservative candidate for the Surrey Heath constituency for the 2005 general election, Michael Gove, who commented (Gove, 2005: p. 19):

> Settled communities have different ways of reacting to new arrivals. On the whole, tolerance, generosity and a sense of fair play has characterised the British response.

Gove made these comments in response to the criticism that some rural communities and Conservative party politicians had received in the Spring of 2005 from sections of the media for their opposition to the establishment of gypsy and Traveller encampments that only retrospectively applied for planning permission to develop their sites (Hurst, 2005). For Gove, this opposition was not an example of what the Commission for Racial Equality called the 'vilification' of gypsies (Hinsliff, 2005: p. 8), but was merely an attempt to stop such minorities from 'jumping queues' and 'claiming special privileges on the basis of their membership of specified groups' (Gove, *op. cit*: p. 19). By invoking the quintessential 'British' qualities of tolerance and fair play in order to justify his opposition to the presence of 'illegal' Traveller and gypsy sites, Gove was unwittingly echoing the sentiments of many of those white research participants interviewed as part of this study:

> We're pretty tolerant here . . . Obviously when you get a group of Travellers coming in the village, then you have to be careful about locking the back door.
>
> White male, south Warwickshire

They [travellers] used to hang around work and stuff and come in at night and nick all the computers. They'd planned the whole thing. There was quite a big problem with that.

Member of white youth focus group, south Warwickshire

Whilst often relatively guarded, at least initially, with regards to their use of language when referring to more established minority ethnic groups, many of the white interviewees felt that it was acceptable to express hostility and to use inflammatory language towards Travellers and gypsies; indeed, it appeared that these groups were regarded as 'fair game' for vitriolic abuse, in much the same way that asylum seekers have also been scapegoated by sections of the public and the tabloid press in the last decade. Whilst only a handful of white research subjects had actually come across asylum seekers in the flesh, they nevertheless had formed strong, and mostly negative, opinions about this group, perhaps reflecting the influence of the xenophobic and somewhat histrionic coverage of asylum in certain sections of the tabloid press that have contributed to the perception of asylum seekers as modern-day 'folk devils' (Garland, 2004).

These sentiments are illustrative of the lack of familiarity with difference that characterises many rural and isolated areas (see, for instance, Chahal and Julienne, 1999; Cloke, 2004; Chakraborti and Garland, 2004b). This does not just apply to the presence in the countryside of those from a minority ethnic background, but also affects those who, for whatever reason, do not conform to the rural 'norm', including those who lead an alternative lifestyle, or who are gay (Kirkey and Forsyth, 2001) or who experience poverty or homelessness (Cloke, 1997). Indeed, a number of minority ethnic interviewees from the three counties studied mentioned the tacit pressure that exists in such close-knit communities to 'fit in', feeling what Giddens (1994: p. 126) calls a 'compelling pressure towards conformism' that is heightened for anyone perceived to be somehow different. Similarly, Abram (2002) reveals that those newcomers who did not join in with village social activities in her study were disliked and marginalized, whilst those who did participate were more readily accepted. As Magne (2003) points out, those from a minority ethnic background who do make an attempt to participate in village life may experience hostility and resentment when they try to do so. As one dual heritage female based in north Warwickshire explained to the authors:

I still think you have to go to the pub, as they think you are different if you don't do that. It's bad that you have to go to the pub and mingle with the locals but by the same token if you don't they are going to think you are strange and different and not want to talk to you anyway.

Female of dual heritage, north Warwickshire

[. . .]

Such 'low-level' forms of racist harassment were reported to be commonplace by many minority ethnic participants in the three research projects undertaken by the authors, and formed part of a continuum of incidents that are a constant feature of living in the rural. The types of 'low-level' incidents described include verbal abuse, unnecessary or persistent staring, the throwing of eggs or stones, 'knock-down ginger', the blocking of driveways with cars, being sprayed with air freshener and being the subject of racist 'humour', reflecting patterns of racist harassment noted in other contexts (see for example, Jay, 1992; Bowling, 1998; Rowe, 2004). Typical of these experiences were those detailed by an Indian male based in south Warwickshire:

> One girl of about 18 years old was just bullying her [interviewee's daughter] all the time, and at that time she was only seven . . . Saying things like 'You can't use the slides, you can't do this, you lot are dirty people, go and take a bath'. Calling her all sorts of swear words, 'Paki', 'Nig-nog' . . . She'd start crying and come back to the house, and they [the bullies] just followed her making all sorts of racial comments. That type of incident happened so many times.

Other less frequent, but equally disturbing, incidents of 'high-level' racism were also reported by minority ethnic participants, including criminal damage, physical assault and even attempted petrol bombing. One Indian male living in Northamptonshire reported to the authors that his attacker yelled:

> 'You black bastard, you fucking Paki!' and he started pounding me. Then he gave me a couple of blows and by this time I was already fazed by what's happened and he was a big guy. He literally put me in a head lock, and he was shaking me about and I was trying to get free. I nearly passed out.

This incident left the victim badly shaken, as well as needing hospital treatment. Others reported being spat at, kicked and having their hair or clothes set alight, and some had suffered regular damage to their property, including having windows smashed, cars damaged or even defecated upon, doors kicked-in and property daubed with racist graffiti. The recipients of this harassment were not just those from visible minority ethnic backgrounds, but also included those of white Irish or American descent, or asylum seekers and Travellers. The experience of dual heritage rural residents and their families is also worth noting here. Some of those from a dual heritage background who were interviewed by the authors spoke of receiving racist abuse and intimidation from white villagers whilst also being the subject of some hostility from African Caribbean or Asian populations. This often left the recipient feeling confused and hurt, compounding their sense of social isolation. It is acknowledged here, however, that the situation for those of dual heritage needs further exploration more generally to unpick the particular issues facing those whose ethnicity can pose problems for researchers in terms of confusing perceptions of belonging and challenging apparently established boundaries of 'race' and identity (Chakraborti *et al.*, 2004: p. 34). As Tizard and Phoenix suggest (2002: p. 15), 'it is increasingly being asserted that people of mixed parentage have a separate identity . . . whilst their fortunes have been intimately linked with those of other black people, their experiences have not always been the same'. In the present study, the white parents or even grandparents of dual heritage children related that they too had been the victims of verbal or even physical harassment, reflecting the situation that, for some rural people, 'mixed-race' relationships are still unacceptable and unpalatable.

A substantial number of research participants who defined themselves as being from a Muslim background felt that they had been subjected to a higher number of incidents of harassment following the terrorist attacks of September 11th 2001, and also that, more generally, there was a level of 'racial tension' that had not existed in the countryside previously. A concern expressed by non-Muslim south Asians was that they too had been the subject of Islamophobic hate since 9/11 from those who were not minded to distinguish between those from different Asian backgrounds. As two research participants stated:

> I've had . . . people calling me 'Paki' and other comments since all this stuff in New York. I went to the fish and chip shop and there was a guy behind me and the news was on and he was pointing at me, I could see him in the reflection, he was saying 'Kill 'em all, the bastards'.
>
> Muslim male, Suffolk

> The new problem seems to have come up with this 9/11 incident in America. People get confused about our identity, whether he is a Sikh or he is a Muslim, and there is something now in the air.
>
> Indian male, north Warwickshire

[. . .]

However, the authors' research also indicated that minority ethnic villagers were perhaps more likely to be accepted by white rural householders if they possessed a degree of 'social status', and if their values and norms were compliant with those of their local white middle-class community. In the more affluent villages within the three research areas it seemed in some cases that as long as minority ethnic households conformed to certain predominant codes of behaviour, then they were more likely to be welcomed by local white villagers. As a District Councillor in south Warwickshire stated to the authors:

The ethnic minorities we have got are well-educated professionals, there-fore they're not perceived as spongers off the state or anything like that. They're really part of the community.

Of course, such attitudes serve to exclude those from minority ethnic backgrounds who are unemployed or in 'low-status' occupations, and they also reveal the complexities of the othering process, and suggest that the rural 'other' can take many guises. It is therefore also acknowledged that it is unwise to make generalistic assumptions about the 'minority ethnic experi-ence' in the countryside as this can be multi-faceted and contingent upon social, spatial and temporal elements. Indeed, there were a handful of minor-ity ethnic interviewees who *did* speak favourably of their own villages and felt that such places had a greater sense of shared values and togetherness than larger conurbations that they had previously lived in. These interviewees also stated that they felt safer and more secure in the countryside and that other residents 'looked out' for them and their children in a way that would not occur in the city.

These findings have resonance with those of Robinson and Gardner (2004), whose study of the minority ethnic experience in South Wales revealed more positive aspects of living in the rural. Robinson and Gardner found that some of those they interviewed were happy living in the country-side and indeed had thrived in the kind of environment where their ethnicity had made them stand out from the 'white landscape'. Some of those they had spoken to had mentioned that they enjoyed being an 'exotic, mysterious other' and one even stated that they felt like a 'celebrity' for being the only local person of colour. Others felt proud of their dual minority ethnic/Welsh identity and had not suffered the kinds of sustained racist harassment that had blighted the lives of many of those who had been interviewed by the authors of this article.

For the most part though, the experience of those who participated in the authors' own research was typified not by feelings of 'celebrity' but instead by those of anxiety, worry and depression brought on by persistent racist victimisation. Some of those interviewed were receiving medication for mental distress, whilst others had become reclusive. One participant told the authors that fear of violent attack had caused him to alter his sleeping patterns and habits:

[The racist harassment] wasn't over one day, it was spread over nearly two months, going on every night. We were mostly worried about petrol bombing, you know. That's the bit we were worried about. Especially as I've been sleeping here since then, I now sleep down here.
Pakistani Muslim, Suffolk

Others spoke of a loss of confidence and self-esteem, and some mentioned that they felt 'embarrassed' by their victimisation and yet powerless to do anything about it. However, one important and common aspect of the rural victimisation experience was an overwhelming sense of isolation, with victims lacking the formal and informal minority ethnic community support networks more commonplace in urban areas, and tending instead to be one of few (if that) from a particular ethnic background living in their locality. As a result of being 'the only ethnic [sic] in the village', as one interviewee put it, victims would often feel that they had no-one to confide in who would understand what they were going through, and so instead internalised their anxiety and anger.

Whilst a small number of male interviewees had claimed that they had reacted violently to being racially abused, it was more often the case that victims would develop their own coping mechanisms, which included 'keeping their heads down' and leading unobtrusive and 'quiet' existences. Some felt that the key was to develop better lines of communication with their fellow villagers, although, for some elderly interviewees, this was also problematic:

> [My children] fight it, because they're born and bred here, they're educated with them. They know their mentality, they know them quite closely, you see. They answer them back in exactly the language they speak. We are not in that sort of category. We really are too polite, too shy, too hesitant to create any disturbance or anything.
>
> Pakistani male, Suffolk

The authors' research also highlighted that an overwhelming majority of victims had, at one point or another, reported incidents of racism to the police, and many of these victims had also sought help from other statutory and voluntary agencies. It is to an analysis of their experiences of interacting with such agencies that this paper now turns.

Responding to racist victimisation in the rural

[. . .]

Concern about the ways in which the criminal justice system has dealt with victims of crime has, however, been an issue for a number of years preceding the Macpherson report. As Maguire and Pointing (1988: p. 11) noted, crime victims sometimes suffer a form of 'secondary victimisation' due to the poor service that they receive from agencies such as the police and the Crown Prosecution Service who have, on occasion, been insensitive and 'heavy handed' with the victim and have not kept them informed about the progress of their case nor provided an adequate explanation for the dropping of charges.

A number of the victims of racist harassment interviewed for the authors' own research echoed many of these concerns. In the three areas studied, victims often spoke of their frustration at the way the police had handled their case, and some thought that officers had failed to take the incident seriously enough or appreciate the impact that racism can have. Although these types of complaints are made regarding the police in urban contexts too, there was a suggestion, even from the police themselves, that they may be more common in the rural, where police are not as used to dealing with racist incidents as those working in urban areas:

> Officers don't necessarily perceive they're going to come up against it [racial harassment] that often. So that causes some problems in terms of trying to make officers aware and bringing them up to speed with issues about dealing with racial harassment.
>
> Inspector, Suffolk Constabulary

The inability of some officers to recognise incidents as having a racist element was also echoed by victims:

> The police asked me 'Do you feel it's racial?' I couldn't believe it. Somebody's just shouted at me 'You fucking Irish bastard!' and then the officer said, 'Do you class that as racist?'
>
> White Irish male, Suffolk

Other victims suggested that the police had been slow to respond to the reporting of an incident, or had treated them brusquely or contemptuously. A small number even felt that the police had behaved aggressively towards them. More often, victims had the perception that officers did not appreciate the trauma that even so-called 'low-level' harassment can cause the recipient and were instead prioritising other forms of crime that they could more readily recognise as being significant or important. As was mentioned above, Magne (2003) found that victims' feelings are often neglected during the process of investigating an incident, as the police and other agencies channel their energies towards gathering evidence with a view to prosecuting the offender.

However, as Rowe (2004) notes, generally there is a low rate of detection for 'minor' racist incidents, and this may be because officers seek to take a more 'practical', 'order maintenance' strategy towards dealing with the incident, rather than adopting a 'law enforcement' route which is much more complicated and time-consuming. Burney (2002: p. 108), whilst acknowledging the symbolic importance of prosecuting low-level offences, nevertheless advocates the use of informal cautions or warnings by the police in such incidents where 'the racial hostility displayed is a very minor element, or in which words referring to ethnicity may not even be genuinely "hostile" '. Whilst taking such an informal approach may have its benefits (including those of saving cost and time), a lack of formal punishment of the perpetrator may leave the victim still feeling vulnerable and intimidated, especially if threats of violence have been made (Bowling, 1998).

[. . .]

Some of those victims living in local authority accommodation spoke of their frustration at the apparent reluctance of local authority housing departments to impose injunctions or eviction orders against tenants who were perpetrating racist harassment.[3] Others mentioned that the deployment of some target hardening measures on their properties by local authorities, such as stronger locks or closed circuit television, offered some reassurance for the victim but did not, of course, actually address the root cause of the problem. In addition, as Goodey (2005) points out, some victims may simply be unaware of the full range of available services or may not possess the necessary skills to take advantage of them. Zedner (2002) argues that it is often those victims who are the most assertive or articulate, or who are the best informed, who can make the most of support services, whilst those less fortunate, or who have lower expectations of what is on offer, may miss out. A common suggestion made by interviewees for improving the situation was that agencies should publicise their services more widely, as those who most needed them were simply not aware of their existence. However, as Pugh (2004: p. 181) observes in the following quotation, it may well be the case that the range of comparable services that are available in urban environments simply are not present, or do not operate as extensively, in the rural:

> While the costs of service delivery in rural communities are often 20 to 30 per cent dearer than in urban areas, there has been no comparable uplift in funding for most public services. Thus delivering services to small and scattered populations, combined with fewer opportunities for economies of scale, result in reduced levels of provision for many rural dwellers.

A number of agency representatives interviewed by the authors also lamented the lack of financial and human resources available to them. Interestingly, others also felt that agencies did not pool the resources that actually are available, a worrying admission in the light of the impetus given to the principle of multi-agency working practices by the Crime and Disorder Act 1998 and other government reports and initiatives. The authors' research uncovered the existence, at least on paper, of extensive multi-agency networks that operate outside of the statutory crime and disorder reduction partnerships and whose principal aim was to help victims of racism. These partnerships, however, appeared to suffer from a number of common problems that affected their ability to provide the types of support that victims were seeking. These included a lack of information sharing within and between organisations; the existence of personal and political rivalries that damaged inter-agency relations; the poor or inconsistent recording of racist incidents; perceptions that some agencies were not fully committed to tack-ling racist harassment or that the bulk of the work was being done by just a handful of agencies involved; or that other forms of crime that show up more clearly in official statistics should be prioritised over those, such as racist harassment, that do not. Others spoke of unnecessary delays in dealing with cases due to the time it takes to convene multi-agency meetings, a concern that was echoed by a number of victim interviewees. Some agency repre-sentatives also complained that there were organisations involved in their networks whose participation was merely tokenistic:

> I was fairly horrified when talking to more than one senior area education officer when I was told to take a book along to [multi-agency meetings] because they're really boring meetings . . . there's no point in people attending meetings concerning racism because someone's told them they've got to be there. They've got to be committed.
>
> Agency representative, Northamptonshire

A lack of genuine commitment to challenging racism and helping those who suffer harassment was one of the most common reasons that inter-viewees gave for not reporting incidents to the police and relevant bodies, echoing the findings of researchers in other rural areas (Derbyshire, 1994; de Lima, 2001; Magne, 2003). A further oft-cited factor behind victims' reluctance to report incidents was a fear of repercussion. Victims were wor-ried that they would draw attention to themselves in their village, and stand out even more than they already did, if they were to get the police involved. Many felt it was better to develop their own 'coping strategies' and to just put up with the harassment, than risk the disfavour of their local community. Significantly, some were afraid that the harassment they had experienced would escalate if they informed the police, as one interviewee stated:

> When they [the police] ask him [the interviewee's grandson] if he wants to take it further, I think he does, because he's had enough of it, but he won't because he's scared of what the outcome might be. Because they have threatened 'If you tell the police we'll cut your fucking throat', and stuff like that. He gets really scared, I mean he does get really frightened.
>
> White grandmother of dual heritage grandson, Northamptonshire

[. . .]

Conclusions: developing effective responses to incidents of racism in the rural

This article has charted the nature and context of racist harassment in the countryside. It has shown that racism is a significant problem in the rural arena, where there is an inherent lack of familiarity with difference that causes those from minority ethnic backgrounds to be 'othered' and marginalized from mainstream white rural communities. This process of 'othering' can often be coupled by feelings of hostility which can manifest themselves through both 'high-' and 'low-level' forms of harassment that cause distress and anxiety for victims. Such incidents are rarely 'one-off' events, however, and instead occur as part of a pattern of victimisation that can continue over a sustained period of time, leaving the victim feeling isolated and vulnerable as they cannot access the kinds of 'in-built' support networks that characterise more numerically substantial minority ethnic communities in urban locations.

Also, as was noted above, victims of racism in rural areas tend not to receive the kind of help from statutory or voluntary agencies that their needs require. Reasons for this include agencies not taking the problem of rural racism seriously; a lack of sympathy and understanding on behalf of the police, and a lack of effective multi-agency partnership working. These flawed responses can cause recipients of racism to suffer a kind of 'secondary victimisation' that compounds the stress that they are already experiencing. These factors, coupled with a common reticence to report incidents, combine to paint a picture of rural service provision for victims of racist harassment that is particularly bleak.

However, it is argued there that the problem of rural racism cannot continue to be given such a low priority by agencies, not least because the rural minority ethnic population is growing rapidly and this increased numerical strength will make victims' demands harder to ignore[4]. Other sources also appear to confirm the notion that predominantly white areas can experience worse 'race relations' than other, more ethnically diverse areas. For example, data contained in the Home Office's *Citizenship Survey* for 2003 indicate that those living in areas with the lowest density of minority ethnic households felt that there was currently 'more racial prejudice' than existed previously (Home Office, 2004; p. 64). Similarly, statistics for the years 2000–2004 suggest that the most significant increases in the numbers of racist incidents occurred in the 'most sparsely populated areas, home to the smallest, most isolated minority communities' (Rayner, 2005: p. 1).

Yet there still appears to be a widespread reluctance to admit that racism is a problem in the rural. Indeed, acknowledging the existence of such harassment is something that some white rural residents can find unpalatable, due to the fact that, as was suggested earlier, their self-identities are formulated around notions that their communities are warm and welcoming to outsiders. To suggest that perpetrators of racist harassment are 'ordinary' members of village populations is an assertion that is commonly met with expressions of incredulity and resentment from rural communities and stakeholders, as the authors found first-hand during their own research studies (see, for example, Garland and Chakraborti, 2004). However, as Ray *et al.*

(2004: p. 364) found, the racist sentiments held by the offenders that they studied 'are widely shared in their local communities' and are not solely the province of small sections of the population that can be conveniently dismissed as 'extremist'. These findings are similar to those from Iganski and Kosmin's examination of the motivations of the perpetrators of racist hate crime, which found that (2003: p. 278):

> A deep-seated bigotry arguably plays little role in the motivations of many of the perpetrators of such incidents. Where it does come into play, rather than acting out extremist ideas, offenders draw on 'everyday' bigotry to decide who, and who is not, an appropriate victim.

It is this 'everyday' nature of much racist harassment that can cause difficulties for the police, who, it was agued above, are more used to dealing with distinct, stand-alone incidents of crime. They therefore might not afford such 'low-level' but commonplace harassment the gravity it deserves[5], and may choose to use informal methods, such as verbal warnings, or employ mediation, in an effort to resolve the situation without having to undertake a formal prosecution. Pursuing such a course of action may, however, merely exacerbate an already difficult situation for the victim and leave them feeling more vulnerable that they did prior to the intervention (Goodey, 2005).

Other measures are also needed to help rural victims. For instance, Magne (2003: p. 6.34) calls for the police to ensure that those 'low-level' incidents that are recorded as racist but that cannot be prosecuted as crimes are nevertheless reported to specialist support agencies, and that sufficient resources should be allocated to make sure that these specialist case workers are easily accessible to victims. Pugh (2004) suggests that these interventions, however well supported in terms of resources, will be flawed unless they acknowledge the *rural* nature of the environment they are operating in and therefore do not attempt to impose urban models in unsuitable environments.

As Jalota (2004) persuasively argues, responses to incidents of rural racism must acknowledge as a starting point that the issue itself is significant and is worthy of the application of substantial financial and human resources. These resources must be allocated on a long-term basis as a series of short-term responses are unsustainable and therefore impractical. Such resources could be integrated within the work of local crime and disorder reduction partnerships in an effort to get the issue of rural racism consistently on the agendas of those who are supposedly co-ordinating efforts to challenge it. If this happens, then those who urgently need the help and assistance from these agencies may stand a chance of receiving the levels of support that they deserve.

Notes

1   The term 'in the rural' has been used generically in this article to capture
    the different types of rural environments that exist in the UK, in prefer-
    ence to more recognisable terms such as 'in the country' or 'in the
    countryside', which tend to convey a more narrow conception of rural
    landscapes.
2   For more specific and detailed findings from these studies, see Garland
    and Chakraborti (2002); Chakraborti, Garland and Keetley (2003); and
    Chakraborti and Garland (2004a).
3   This is despite the fact that the Housing Act 1996 strengthened the
    power of these local authority housing departments to act against a range
    of different types of 'anti-social' behaviour.
4   Magne (2003: p. 11.11) notes that, overall, the rural minority ethnic
    population has increased by over 100 per cent over the ten year period
    from 1991 to 2001.
5   In light of the serious emotional, physical and financial implications that
    can often arise as a consequence of this 'low-level' harassment, the
    authors would advocate that such a description be used with caution.
    Referring to incidents as 'low-level' can in itself trivialise their potential
    impact upon the victim, and may lead agencies, academics and policy-
    makers to underplay their significance.

2.4

Worlds apart? Women, rape and the police reporting process

by Jan Jordan

[. . .]

In the 1970s women's rights activists around the world criticized the ways in which rape victims were treated by the police (Brownmiller 1975; Donat and D'Emilio 1992; London Rape Crisis Centre 1977; Rose 1977; Russell 1990). The experience of reporting rape was so arduous, they argued, that for many women it replicated the violation felt in the rape itself. Academic research in the 1980s endorsed these sentiments (Adler 1987; Temkin 1987), likening the reporting process to a second victimization. In response to mounting criticism, substantial legal and procedural changes were introduced in many countries aimed at improving victims' experiences of police and judicial processes (Adler 1997; Berger, Searles and Neuman 1988; Donat and D'Emilio 1992; Lees 1996; Lees 1997; Los 1990). However, as Temkin has pointed out in the British context (Temkin 1997), until recently there had been virtually no research conducted since these reforms to assess whether they had in fact improved women's experiences and increased their satisfaction levels. This article is based on recent New Zealand rape research conducted with women concerning their experiences of the police reporting process in the 1990s (Jordan 1998a, 1998b). It summarizes the women's experiences of reporting, police interviewing, and statement-taking, and identifies the factors associated with the extent to which they expressed satisfaction or dissatisfaction with the police response. The women's experiences of the medical examination are also documented and assessed. The results of this study are compared both with the findings of an earlier New Zealand study (Young 1983), and with Temkin's more recent British research (Temkin 1997, 1999). Jennifer Temkin concluded, on the basis of her study of women rape victims in Sussex:

> It seems that old police attitudes and practices, widely assumed to have vanished, are still in evidence and continue to cause victims pain and

suffering. Research of the type that has been undertaken here does not lend itself to sweeping statements and conclusions but it does suggest, at the very least, that more research is now urgently needed to discover whether the treatment of adult rape victims by police in other areas of the country is quite as benevolent as is commonly supposed. (Temkin 1997: 527)

The findings of this study, conducted in a country geographically located on the other side of the world, albeit based on the British policing tradition, echo closely those found by Temkin (1997). The thesis proposed here suggests that the similarity in findings is not surprising but instead reflects organizational responsibilities, police cultural realities and the legacy of patriarchy. Accordingly, the replication of Temkin's study in other parts of Britain would be expected to yield similar findings.

[. . .]

New Zealand rape study 1983

The first comprehensive examination of rape law and procedure in New Zealand was a research project conducted by the Institute of Criminology and the Department of Justice in 1983 (Young 1983). Included in this project was an interview-based study documenting the concerns and experiences of women who had been victims of rape. The findings reinforced what many women working in this area had long observed: namely, that the existing system was experienced by many complainants as a repeat violation, similar in its effects to the original rape incident (for example: Adler 1987; Allen 1990; Gilmore and Pittman 1993; Holmstrom and Burgess 1978; Medea and Thompson 1974).

Mounting criticism of the criminal justice system's response to rape victims prompted the introduction in 1985 of substantial reforms, including a broadening of the definition of rape to incorporate other sexual violation offences, the abolition of spousal immunity, and changes to courtroom practice and procedures. Significant changes were also made in relation to police training, the conducting of post-rape medical examinations, and the provision of crisis support counselling.

Ten years after these reforms were introduced, the Institute of Criminology and the Faculty of Law at Victoria University of Wellington began a research project to assess, from the woman's perspective, how she experienced now both the reporting of the offence to the police and any subsequent trial processes (Jordan 1998a). The data-gathering phase of the study was funded by the Foundation for Research, Science and Technology.

Methodology

The overall aim of this research project was to evaluate how rape and sexual assault victims' complaints to the police were responded to and dealt with by the various agencies involved. In-depth, qualitative interviews were conducted with 48 women who had approached the police between 1990 and 1994 with a complaint of rape/sexual violation or the attempt thereof. The study aimed to obtain accounts of the women's dealings with the police, doctors, and support agencies (Jordan 1998a) as well as their experiences in court and during the trial (McDonald 1997).

[. . .]

Limitations

As with any piece of research, there are limitations in this study's methodology and generalizability which need to be acknowledged.

First, only women were included in the study. This decision was made both to ensure comparability with the earlier women-only study, and because the overwhelming majority of reported sexual assaults involve female victims. Male rape victims may encounter additional credibility issues when reporting sexual offences to the police, and this is clearly an area requiring further sensitive research.

The women were questioned only about incidents which had happened to them over the age of 16 (i.e. once they had reached the legal age of consent), thereby excluding cases of historic child abuse. The information was obtained retrospectively and, for some women, the events they described had occurred several years before the interview was conducted. Their accounts may have been affected by subsequent events and experiences. No attempt was made to verify the women's accounts from other sources, since the explicit focus of this research was on how the women perceived their treatment and recounted their experiences.

Recruitment of the sample was dependent primarily on referrals from counselling agencies and, to a lesser extent, the police and self-selection. The agencies we contacted were primarily those whom the police routinely refer women to following a rape complaint, and efforts were made by these agencies to inform every woman who was eligible for inclusion in the study about the research.

Participants for the study were drawn principally from the cities of Auckland, Wellington and Christchurch, although in some cases the incident had occurred and been reported in smaller provincial areas. Primarily, however, the research is likely to be more indicative of women's experiences of reporting sexual assaults in larger, metropolitan areas—the experiences of women in rural areas may be different.

It is also the case that, despite employing Maori and Pacific Island interviewers in Auckland (the largest city), very few non-New Zealand European/European women were interviewed, and so the research primarily reflects the experiences of New Zealand European/European women. Anecdotal evidence suggests Maori women who have been raped find it even more difficult to approach the police, and are less confident of the response they will receive from them, than New Zealand European/European women.

One further point of clarification needs to be made concerning language—the word 'victim' is used here in contexts where it seems appropriate to acknowledge the impact of the incident, and the resultant needs it gives rise to, rather than the woman's capacity to survive what has happened.

Characteristics of the women in the sample

A total of 48 women participated in the study. They had reported a total of 50 incidents of rape or sexual assault to the police since 1990—two women had been raped on two separate occasions by the same perpetrator.

Age
The ages of the women interviewed at the time of the rape/assault ranged from 16 to the mid-70s. The single biggest category of women were young women in the 16–20 age group, who accounted for nearly one-third of those interviewed (31 per cent).

Relationship status
In terms of their relationship status, the women were divided approximately equally between those who were currently partnered (i.e. either married or in a de facto relationship) (N = 18); those who had been partnered (i.e. divorced or widowed) (N = 15); and those who were single (N = 15).

Ethnicity
Despite considerable effort to obtain Maori and Pacific Island participants for the study, the vast majority (92 per cent) of the sample identified as New Zealand European/European. Only three women described themselves as Maori, and one woman described herself as belonging to a specific national identity (which is not disclosed here for reasons of confidentiality).

Occupation
The women came from a diverse range of occupational backgrounds. The two largest groups represented were students (19 per cent, N = 9) and professionals (17 per cent, N = 8); the next most frequent categories were those who described themselves as homemakers (13 per cent, N = 6) and those on benefits (13 per cent, N = 6); the remainder included secretarial/office

workers (4 per cent; N = 2), kitchen/domestic workers (4 per cent; N = 2), and individual women who worked as a waitress, dancer, baker, fitness instructor, sex worker, or shop assistant.

Relationship to perpetrator

Of the 50 incidents reported to the police, fewer than one third involved an offender who was a stranger. In 35 of the incidents (70 per cent), the rape/ sexual assault was perpetrated by someone previously known to the victim. This figure included spouses and ex-spouses, boyfriends, family members (including brother-in-law, future father-in-law), neighbours, acquaintances (including friends of friends or of partners, co-residents, fellow party guests), and those with whom the woman may have had a professional relationship (such as a doctor, teacher, counsellor, or masseuse). In one case, two perpet-rators were involved in the assault, one known and one a stranger, and another case involved two known perpetrators.

Complainants' previous contact with the police

For more than one-third of the women in the sample (37 per cent; N = 18), the reporting of this incident marked their first significant contact ever with the police. The majority, however (63 per cent; N = 30) stated that this was not the first time they had been in contact with the police. Typically, their previous contact had been in the context of earlier victimization experiences, such as burglary, theft or assault (80 per cent; N = 24).

Summary of research findings

The women were asked to provide details of their interactions with the police at different stages of the reporting and investigation process. Although individual variations occur, there are recognizable stages through which most rape victims proceed when contacting the police following a rape/sexual assault. These are set out below:

(1) Initial contact and reporting;
(2) Medical examination;
(3) Statement-taking and interviewing;
(4) Case progress.

The women were asked to comment on their experiences at each stage of the process, where applicable.

(1) Initial contact and reporting

Whom she first told about rape/assault

In only six of the cases in the research sample were the police the first people the woman told about the incident. The women were, in fact, three times more likely to tell a friend about what had happened to them (36 per cent; N = 18) rather than call the police in the first instance. Others disclosed what had happened initially to family members or their partner, colleague, neighbour, or counsellor, before deciding to approach the police.

Who informed the police

Although it may not have been the police whom the woman told first about the incident, nevertheless in over half the situations (54 per cent; N = 27), she was the person who informed them of the incident. On seven occasions it was a friend who told the police, and less frequently it was either other people she knew (such as her partner or other family members), or those she approached for assistance directly after the rape/assault.

How the police were contacted

The most common way of informing the police was by telephone. Of the 27 women who reported the incident themselves, 21 (78 per cent) did so by telephone. The remainder did so in person: one went to a police caravan based at a music festival and the rest went to the police station. In two situations, it was the police who first contacted the woman as part of their investigation of the offender; in another, the woman's ex-husband went in person to the station; the remainder (N = 20) all involved friends or family phoning the police on the woman's behalf. Some women referred to the embarrassment they felt at having to disclose sensitive information over the phone, especially when their call was passed around the station.

> When you finally make the decision to report it, you just want to talk to one person—you don't want to go through three or four different people. It's a very hard and very personal thing.

Factors influencing decision to report

In those instances where the complainant herself reported the rape/sexual assault to the police, she was asked what factors influenced her decision to do so. One-third of the women simply said: 'I felt I should'; almost a further third (30 per cent) said 'to protect others'; more than a quarter (26 per cent) said they 'didn't want him getting away with it'; and almost a quarter (22 per cent) said they reported the rape because they were scared of a repeat attack. Other factors present in their decision included being persuaded to report by others or feeling pressured to report the rape.

For some women the decision to report appeared straightforward, as if it was an automatic reaction to the incident:

> When you're attacked you go to the police. I didn't even think about it—just dialled 111.

> It was the first thing I thought of.

Several women spoke of the reporting decision being related to a sense of personal empowerment:

> He attempted to rape me, threatened to kill me and he assaulted me. He's always had a bad temper and been highly strung, but this time I thought, 'No, he's not going to get away with it.'

> It's part of the healing process, part of saying it's not right, part of getting my control back.

How soon was the incident reported
Of the 50 incidents, well over half (62 per cent) were reported to the police either immediately after the rape/sexual assault or on the same day. There were delays in reporting the rape/sexual assault in just under two-fifths of cases (38 per cent). While half of these were reported within a fortnight of the incident's occurrence, the remainder took considerably longer to be brought to police attention, and in three cases, it took more than ten years.

It is clear from the above that not all women will choose, or be able, to report a sexual assault at the time of its occurrence:

> I think I was really numb for the first two days and really mulling the whole thing over in my mind and trying to come to terms with it and thinking, 'OK, I know I'm a person of quite strong character, I think I can deal with this myself', and it wasn't until I got to work on Monday and started to deteriorate there that I realized I wasn't coping with it and I had to do something about it.

At least two of the women said they held back because they felt confused about the incident and whether it constituted rape:

> It wasn't physically violent and I wasn't sure if what he'd done was illegal or not.

Sometimes the reason given for delayed reporting seems to have been fear-based, arising from the woman's concern over how the offender, the police, or family and friends would respond. In one case, the offender's death threats against the woman and her relatives kept her *silent* for ten years.

Women's satisfaction with police treatment at the reporting stage
Nearly two-thirds (64 per cent) of the women felt either satisfied (40 per cent; N = 20) or very satisfied (24 per cent; N = 12) with the treatment they received from the police during the initial reporting phase. Thirty-two per cent, however, were either dissatisfied (20 per cent; N = 10) or very dissatisfied (12 per cent; N = 6). The remainder (4 per cent; N = 2) felt neutral in their response.

The women who rated the police highly cited the importance of being believed, being taken seriously, and feeling cared for and supported. Even small gestures of friendliness counted for a lot when the women were feeling so vulnerable—for instance, the police officer getting the woman a cup of coffee, allowing her a smoke, or letting her stop and have a break when she got upset. Some women felt they needed clear information at this stage about the procedures to be followed and appreciated being provided with this and given some choice over whether and how to proceed.

The women who were dissatisfied with the initial police response identified particular behaviours and attitudes which they found distressing. Several commented on the lack of empathy they felt they encountered at a time when they really needed some caring.

> They were doing the interview like it was just a burglary, or a petty theft—it was just mundane to them.

> They were just throwing questions at me. They had me in a corner . . . It was disgusting—no wonder they are working with dogs—something to yell at and boss around. It felt like, 'Look, she's pissed so she asked for it.' I felt like they came up with their own decision on the spot.

Feeling as if the police did not believe them and that they were judging them was mentioned by several of the women.

> I went seeking help but then it turned and I was accused of false allegations.

> He talked to me like I was dirt . . . He said he wanted to get the truth out of me.

> They asked me so many questions *I* felt like the bad person. They really made me feel so stink. I just wanted to cry. They should be more sensitive. He was like a pig to me (you know how they call police pigs?—he even looked like a pig, he reminded me of a pig.) They should be more direct and up front, and say they have to sort out the truth for court. It made me very angry.

A further source of dissatisfaction for some women arose from their feeling that their complaint was unimportant to the police. This could be conveyed in various ways, including a cold and dismissive attitude or indicating other jobs had greater priority.

> He looked like—huh? Like he didn't know what the hell to do and he didn't really care.

Summary of initial contact and reporting
It is clear that the initial reporting experience is a critical determinant of whether complainants will be able to develop sufficient trust in the police to feel able to proceed with an investigation. It occurs at a time when the woman is feeling highly vulnerable, with heightened needs for safety and reassurance. For the police, then, it is critical in the first instance that the person who answers the telephone is adequately trained and suitable to respond to calls from rape complainants. Even though the majority of these will be referred immediately to the appropriate officer, a distressed victim may be required at this time to disclose the nature and details of the incident. It is also imperative that the number of referrals on to other officers needs to be kept to an absolute minimum.

It follows also that any police officer likely to attend situations involving rape/sexual assault victims needs to be selected and trained to respond sensitively and appropriately to their needs and concerns. A good understanding of the nature and effects of rape trauma is essential in this regard. Overall, the comments made by the women reflected their desire for the entire reporting process to become more victim-centred and cognisant of their needs rather than being oriented exclusively around police operational requirements.

(2) Medical examination

The medical examination is extremely important both for obtaining forensic evidence and assessing the woman's health and emotional state following a rape/sexual assault. In terms of providing reliable forensic evidence, doctors in New Zealand are advised that ideally the examination should be conducted within 72 hours of the rape/sexual assault, although in some cases this can be extended to seven days (Fancourt et al. 1994: 55). The examination itself is a lengthy and acutely sensitive procedure, involving rigorous tests, measurements and specimen collection. These include examination of external genitalia, speculum examination of the vagina and anal examination, as well as requiring the woman to provide samples by chewing gum, having her pubic hair combed, and her fingernails scraped (ibid: 60–8).

The way in which this examination is conducted is of critical significance, given the invasiveness of the procedures and the vulnerability of the victim. In New Zealand, it was common practice for police surgeons to perform such examinations, sometimes in police cells, until, in the late 1980s, concerned doctors formed a nationwide organization called Doctors for Sexual Abuse Care (DSAC). This is a voluntary organization which any doctor involved in the care of sexually abused patients is encouraged to join. One of DSAC's aims is to improve the knowledge base concerning the most appropriate ways to respond to and treat sexual assault victims, and the organization now operates a call-out system throughout most of the country to ensure that specially trained DSAC doctors are available to undertake forensic examinations on contract to the police. Thus, at the time of this study, the preferred practice was for the police to contact a local crisis support agency as soon as a rape was reported, who in turn would notify the doctor on call, arrange for the medical examination to be conducted in a clinic or other suitable venue, and provide a support worker for the victim as she underwent the examination.

The majority of the women interviewed in this study (68 per cent; N = 34) had undergone a medical examination as part of the overall reporting process. In cases of delayed or historical reporting, which accounted for 18 per cent of the cases in the sample (N = 9), the passage of time usually renders a forensic examination unnecessary, although it may often be advisable for sexual assault victims to have a general medical examination and be tested for possible infections and/or pregnancy. One woman, for example, said she did not report the rape to the police and left town instead, hoping to forget the incident. She began to feel terrible and, on returning to her home town, visited the family doctor, only to be told she was pregnant, at which point she was referred for an abortion.

Gender of the doctor

One significant change which has occurred since the 1983 Rape Study concerned the gender of the doctor conducting the medical examination. In 1983, all but two of the doctors who conducted the medical examination were male (Stone et al. 1983: 45), while in this study this had reversed, with the women being examined by a female doctor in by far the majority of cases (88 per cent; N = 30).

Virtually all of the women (97 per cent; N = 29) remarked that they were pleased and relieved that the doctor was a woman. In describing the comprehensive nature of the examination, one woman remarked:

> I had to chew chewing gum . . . she took finger-nail scrapings, she took everything, it was really gung-ho. It was degrading, but it was no more degrading than a cancer smear, I suppose. But there is no way I could have done it with a male doctor, there is no way.

What the women repeatedly stressed was the necessity of having a woman doctor, given both the intentionally invasive nature of rape and the unavoidably invasive nature of post-rape forensic examinations.

> Because the examination is so intimate—after having had a man do that to me I didn't want another staring at me.

> I wouldn't let a male touch me. That would be the worst thing you could do to a female, I think.

> I didn't think much of males at that point in time.

Issues concerning safety and empathy with the victim were also stressed by the women:

> I would have felt dominated if it had been a male—with a woman I felt safe.

> I thought she'd be able to be more in tune with how I was feeling.

Overall, it appears that while gender was not a consistently critical factor in relation to police interviewing, it emerged as a much more critical consideration for women undergoing the medical examination. Since the procedure itself is, by its very nature, invasive and distressing, virtually all of the woman said they were pleased and relieved to be examined by a woman doctor.

Women's satisfaction with the way the doctor dealt with them
Very high satisfaction levels were recorded overall by the women regarding how they felt the doctor treated them during the medical examination. Over 80 per cent said they felt either very satisfied (N = 18) or satisfied (N = 10). Only one woman expressed strong dissatisfaction, saying she found the attitude of the police surgeon who examined her aggressive and distressing.

> He treated me like I was just some bit of rubbish off the streets. He didn't talk to me or explain anything. He just said, 'Take off your clothes, hop into this,' then started measuring.

A number of particular themes and issues emerged from the women's accounts of the medical examination. These included the need to be guaranteed safety and privacy during the conducting of the examination and the need to feel they were treated with respect and sensitivity, especially given the invasive nature of the procedure.

The women said the behaviours they appreciated from the doctors involved being called by name, being talked to, being given explanations, having their feelings checked, being asked if it hurt or if they were comfortable—in other words, being treated with both caring and professionalism.

> She made me feel as comfortable as I could given the circumstances. She kept making sure I was OK, that I was comfortable, she explained everything—she was excellent.

> She was definitely professional but she offered more than that. She was giving me credit for being intelligent, she treated me with dignity, she wasn't at all patronizing—she was lovely.

It was clear from some women's comments that a professional stance alone was not always enough for what they felt they needed at this time.

> There was a sound of compassion in her voice but I felt it was robotic. Like she was just going through the procedures.

> She was professional but not very warm. When you've been through that you do need a bit of warmth.

The issue of control also featured repeatedly in the women's accounts. During the examination itself, control arose as an issue for some women in relation to who was present, with it clearly being important that the women be offered a choice in this matter. Not every woman wanted a support person in the room with her during this intimate procedure. Some preferred more anonymous professional support and did not want close family members to be present during the examination, while others thought they would have found it extremely difficult to manage such a procedure *without* close support. Such opposing views reinforce the need for the woman to be consulted as to her wishes so that her choice in these matters is able to prevail.

Summary of experiences of the medical examination
The high overall level of satisfaction with the doctors noted by the women suggests most are conducting these difficult examinations with care and sensitivity. This contrasts sharply with a London study in which only one of 24 rape complainants felt the medical examination had been conducted sympathetically; the rest experienced it very negatively (Lees and Gregory 1993: 29–30). The obvious improvement in how these examinations are being conducted in New Zealand is testimony to the work of a small team of dedicated medical practitioners (DSAC). This group has worked hard in recent years to provide appropriate training and supervision for, mostly, the women doctors prepared to undertake such examinations and the results presented here indicate the importance of their being able to extend and consolidate this service.

(3) Police statement-taking and interviewing

Following the reporting of a rape/sexual assault, the complainant will usually be referred for the forensic medical examination and put in contact with a support agency before returning to the police to provide a full statement. Subsequent police interviews may also eventuate as details are checked and the court case prepared.

Location and atmosphere during statement-taking

In the main, the woman's statement was taken in a police station. This occurred in nearly three-quarters (73 per cent; N = 35) of cases. Less commonly, it took place in the victim's home (19 per cent; N = 9) or in support agency rooms (4 per cent; N = 2). In one case, the interview was conducted in the woman's workplace, and in the remaining situation, the level of injuries sustained in the rape attack necessitated the statement being taken while the woman was in hospital.

Nearly half (49 per cent; N = 21) of the 43 women who commented on the atmosphere during interviewing and statement-taking considered it to be warm and supportive.

> It was nice, they were watching cricket on TV, it was the middle of the night. They made me a cup of coffee, they let me smoke . . . it was all quite relaxed.

> It was just a normal office, but they offered me drinks, they tried to make me feel comfortable.

Other women experienced the interviewing atmosphere in less positive ways. Nearly a quarter (23 per cent; N = 10) described it as a cold, clinical environment, and the remainder (28 per cent; N = 12) used a range of other descriptions, such as 'unreal', 'grotty', or 'overwhelming'.

> The atmosphere was terrible—just a room with very bright lights, a desk and a chair. And when you're tired those lights are hideous!

> They interviewed me in the same room where they interview the criminals. I felt like I was guilty and being charged.

> I think the room needs to be more comfortable. The room I was in had riot gear in it. I think they should have counsellors there when you give your statement.

Overall, what the women said they valued the most was being in a comfortable and relaxed environment where they were treated in a friendly, caring manner and could be guaranteed privacy.

Number of people present during the interview

The most common interviewing scenario involved the woman complainant with one police officer, which occurred in 41 per cent (N = 20) of cases. The next most common arrangement was when the woman had one support person present (22 per cent; N = 11). Sometimes, two officers would be present with the woman on her own (8 per cent; N = 4), or with her and a support person (14 per cent; N = 7). On other occasions (14 per cent; N = 7), there could be five or more people present during the interview, and there were up to eight in one case.

Whether or not it was possible to have a support person present during statement-taking became problematic for some women. Not all the women who wanted support during the interview felt strong enough to request this, and occasionally a request for support was refused.

Gender of the interviewing officer

Half of the women (51 per cent; N = 25) were interviewed by male officers; most of the remainder were interviewed by female officers (41 per cent; N = 20), although a small number of women (8 per cent; N = 4) were interviewed by officers of both genders. In general, a preference for women officers being involved was apparent (Jordan 1998b).

Given the sensitive nature of the incident, and the intimate questions which needed to be asked, some of the women found it very difficult to be questioned by a male. Several said categorically it *had* to be a woman, especially if the interview was conducted in their own home. Disclosing details of the incident to male officers could compound the woman's sense of vulnerability:

> It's like you're sitting there with your legs open, you might as well be.

Some women also commented about the lack of sensitivity and awareness displayed by male detectives towards them as rape victims. In relation to Lisa's case, she feels the police forced her to watch pornography tapes because they were trying to work out which ones her abuser had made her watch. She said:

> I got back to work and I just threw up—it made me that sick.

Lisa thinks a woman officer may have been more sensitive about this aspect, saying:

> She'd have been more understanding of what I had to go through to watch it again, because it brought back heaps of feelings, whereas the male cop just put the tape straight on.

Maleness per se did not appear to determine the quality of an officer's response to sexual assault victims. Several of the women interviewed, in fact, said they had requested a woman officer only to end up feeling disappointed with the outcome. Ruth, for example, observed of the police:

> The fact that they'd given me a female to interview me was seen to be enough, and that she could slack off on the other issues. *She* [the detective] thought the fact that she was a woman should be enough, but in actual fact it wasn't.

Some of the women expressed surprise when the women officers they saw displayed hostile, disbelieving attitudes. Since policewomen operate within the same organizational culture as policemen, and may struggle even harder for acceptance within it, such outcomes should probably not be totally unexpected.

In terms of gender, then, it was clear that while some women found it traumatic being interviewed by a man, others felt this was not nearly as important as the officer's attitude. This could be conveyed non-verbally at times and, for some women, it was reflected in the tone of the general interviewing environment. For instance, one woman felt uncomfortable being asked intimate details about her rape in a room in which pictures of semi-naked women were displayed on the wall calendar. Likewise, another felt the detective interviewing her was being reasonable until she overheard his male colleagues telling a sexist, anti-woman joke in the next room, which went unacknowledged by him.

Overall, the characteristics the women said they appreciated in the police can be summarized as those reflecting a caring professionalism underpinned by respect for and belief in the victim/survivor. Gender alone is no guarantee of such attitudes being present (see also Lees and Gregory 1993:6). It would, therefore, seem imperative to ensure that *all* officers, both male and female, who are likely to have contact with rape and sexual assault victims should demonstrate the appropriate aptitude and undergo the necessary training for this task. Once this is established, it may also be appropriate to offer rape complainants a choice, wherever possible, in terms of the interviewing officer's gender.

Number of interviews

Approximately three-quarters of the women (N = 35) were interviewed by the police more than once. These ranged from one additional interview just to clear up a few details, to at least five of the women having six or seven follow-up sessions with the police. Multiple interviewing appears to have arisen for a variety of reasons. In some cases, additional details needed to be obtained from the woman, her assistance was required in assembling an identikit, or the police wanted her to return to the crime scene for a reconstruction of the incident. In two cases, further details were necessary to enable the police to arrange appropriate witness protection measures.

Continuity of interviewing officers

Approximately half of the women (N = 18) who had more than one police interview had the same interviewing officer throughout; the remainder were interviewed by different officers. The women who were re-interviewed by the same officer often felt pleased at the continuity:

> I don't feel like I'm being put off from one person to another. I've just got this one person who seems to be wholly involved even though she's got all these other cases and who is genuinely interested. It's not like she's just doing her job. It's like she cares. I was lucky—I got a good one from the word go.

Of those who experienced a change of officer, their feelings varied depending on whether or not they felt the change was for the better. Some did not mind:

> I was not in the least worried—the first one (detective) was awful!

Other women, however, found it difficult to manage the lack of continuity:

> I don't know whether they're talking to each other or not. I mean, none of them knows what the other's doing, and one of them was so off-putting—he kept saying, 'Is that all?' Then when I couldn't stand it any longer I rang the police and found out the case officer I had had gone on holiday! I mean, I saw him a week before, so why didn't he say he was going on holiday and let me know who was taking over?

Advice to women in a similar situation about contacting the police

Three-quarters of the 40 women who answered this question (N = 30) said they would advise someone who was a victim of rape/sexual assault to report it to the police. Some added qualifiers to their answer, such as:

> Only if it was to a policewoman.

> Definitely—but I would say give so and so a ring, not phone up the watch tower and get Starsky and Hutch out.

Nine of the women said they would advise women to go to the police only if they had a support person to accompany them, with even women who expressed very negative views concerning how their case was treated saying they would still advise others to go to the police.

Six women (15 per cent) were emphatic, however, that after their experience, they would not encourage others in a similar situation to report:

> Going through that—it's not worth it.

A further four women (10 per cent) indicated that they were unsure what they would advise, and articulated mixed views on this question:

> If the rapist was unknown to them, I would; if the offender was known to them, I'd advise them to do it themselves! (laughs) I think the odds are stacked so heavily against getting a conviction. I know that more women need to go to court, but the system operates for the defendant. I think it's just too hard on people. Everyone wants a victim to come forward and give evidence and let's get this guy off the street, ra, ra, ra . . . but you lose your life. Then it's gone, there's no-one there, and because of the way the system operates, that's what you're left with—nothing. You feel as if you've been abused by the offender, you go to court, you're abused well and truly by the court system, and then afterwards it's like, 'It was all your fault so this is your punishment—now piss off!'

Extent to which the complainant was satisfied/dissatisfied with the police response overall

With each woman interviewed, we explored the extent to which she felt satisfied with the police response at different stages of the reporting process. The final time this question was asked the women were invited to provide an overall rating as to how they felt their complaint was responded to and dealt with by the police. Table 2.4.1 sets out this information.

It is striking that there was virtually a 50:50 split between those who expressed overall satisfaction or dissatisfaction with the police. A total of 20

Table 2.4.1 Women's overall satisfaction with police: numbers and percentages

	N	%
Very satisfied	11	22
Satisfied	9	18
Neither/nor	0	0
Dissatisfied	6	12
Very dissatisfied	13	26
Both/mixed	6	12
Not sure/can't say	3	6
Didn't proceed with complaint	2	4
Total	50	

women (40 per cent) said they were either satisfied/very satisfied compared with 19 (38 per cent) who said they were dissatisfied/very dissatisfied. At the two extremes within these categories, 11 women were very satisfied and 13 were very dissatisfied. Generally, therefore, the women's responses were quite polarized. In addition, a small number (6) felt unable to summarize their overall satisfaction level because, while they were pleased with some aspects of the police response, this was compromised by their dissatisfaction with other aspects. A further two women could not provide an overall satisfaction rating, stating that the negative police attitude expressed when they made their initial complaint deterred them from proceeding any further with it.

Comments made by the women further illustrate the intensity with which they described their experiences of the rape reporting process. Some women who felt satisfied referred to having their impressions of the police changed for the better as a result of reporting this incident.

> I'm glad they're there. I've changed my opinions of them. I was very pleased with how they treated me and think better of them since the incident. I don't think of the police as 'the enemy' any more, which is a bit of a juvenile thing anyway.

> The police were just wonderful to me . . . It gave me a lot of confidence in my belief of myself as a person of worth.

Those who felt dissatisfied complained of not feeling believed by the police and of not having their experience understood by them.

> I feel it was wrong to tell the police because they haven't helped me in any way. Now I'll never tell them ever again because I always believed they were there to help.

> The police are a big waste of time, and they really haven't got the complainant's interest and priority right. If only they knew how victims felt . . .

In Beth's case, she was 16 when she was raped at a party. She went to a neighbour's house for help at 3am and they called the police. Beth reports finding it difficult to convince the police that she had been raped.

> Right from the very beginning I think they thought I was a little slut—I even told them 'I'm not a little slut', because I was a virgin . . . But I always thought they thought I was a young stupid girl who had got drunk and had sex.

Another woman said she resented their assumption:

'that I was telling lies, like I was the bad person. What had I done wrong?'

Sometimes, the women felt the police's focus on information gathering prevented them from recognizing the needs of the victim.

They don't think about you needing support. They just think about the 'finding the person' side—they don't think about rekindling the person who's hurt.

When Stevie, aged 16, was raped by a young man she met at a music festival, she felt her obvious distress during the interview was unacknowledged by the police, leading her to say:

They need to stop just getting information and be a bit more personal, like see what I really need. They should have tissues in the rooms—I had to smear it all over my jersey, all the tears and snot, it wasn't very nice. They didn't even show me where the toilet was.

One woman said she now feels so disgusted with the police that she can't watch their family violence campaign advertisements on television any more:

I feel so disgusted with them. 'You're not alone, just contact the police.' Well, I did that and I didn't get anywhere. They did nothing. I was in the very same situation as those women and I did act, I did seek help, and I felt very threatened that they didn't act as they made out—or as you'd expect them to, as well. I just turn them off now, or walk out of the room.

It is, therefore, clear that while a significant number of the women felt very positive about the response they received from the police, an equally significant number were highly dissatisfied. Precisely why such a polarization exists is difficult to determine. It may be related in part to the nature of rape itself, and the fact that it is such an overwhelmingly traumatic experience for the woman to experience, combined with the undoubtedly strong views held by many police officers on its occurrence. Because rape is such an intense and sensitive area, when the police act with professional caring and demonstrate their respect for the victim, this is noticeable and greatly appreciated. When such qualities are lacking, however, their absence is also very noticeable. Either way, this results in heightened emotional responses and polarized views.

The women's satisfaction ratings were correlated with several key variables, in order to determine the possible impact of these. No significant differences emerged in women's overall satisfaction with the police depending on the age of the complainant—of those aged 25 and under (N = 24), 10 expressed overall satisfaction and 10 dissatisfaction. Similarly, of those aged over 25, 9 expressed overall satisfaction and 10 dissatisfaction. In both age groups, the remainder gave a mixed response in their replies to this question.

Similarly, no significant differences emerged which were related to whether or not the perpetrator was a stranger. Of those attacked by strangers (N = 15), half expressed satisfaction (N = 7) and half dissatisfaction (N = 7), while one gave a mixed response. Of those attacked by someone known to them (N = 35), 13 women expressed satisfaction and 14 dissatisfaction, with the remainder giving mixed (N = 5) or unsure (N = 3) responses.

The only variable analysed that did seem to be associated with the women's satisfaction ratings of the police was that relating to case outcome. Of the 20 cases where the offender was either not detected (N = 8) or detected but not prosecuted (N = 13), three-quarters of the complainants (75 per cent; N = 15) stated their dissatisfaction with the police. A further two said they decided not to proceed with the case because of encountering a negative police response. One said she felt she had received a mixed response, leaving only two women expressing any level of satisfaction with the police. Conversely, of the total number of cases resulting in prosecution (N = 31), 18 women recorded satisfaction with the police; four dissatisfaction; seven had a mixed response and two felt unsure. In ten cases the offender pleaded guilty while the remaining 21 went to a defended hearing. The eventual case outcome did not appear to be as influential on women's views of the police as the fact of prosecution—the four women who expressed dissatisfaction with the police all had cases resulting in conviction (including one offender who pleaded guilty), while none of the seven women whose cases resulted in acquittals expressed clear dissatisfaction with the police (although two women had a mixed response).

(4) Case progress

Being kept informed by the police about progress on one's case has emerged as a factor of vital importance to rape complainants (Adler 1991: 1115; Chambers and Millar 1986: 51; Temkin 1997: 517; Temkin 1999: 28–30) and this finding was further reinforced in the New Zealand study.

Informing the women about what would be involved in a prosecution
Over half the women (59 per cent; N = 26) said the police gave them information concerning what would be involved in a prosecution, and some commented that they appreciated in particular being fully informed as to what the trial would involve.

> She (detective) told us (complainant and support person) it's not like you see on TV—they're (defence lawyers) not allowed to bang the table

and swear and yell at you. She told me how I'd get looked after in court, that I could have all the support people I want, that it would be a closed court—just what to expect.

The police were very straight, they were blunt, saying it was more or less my word against his word and they couldn't promise anything. That was really good, because it meant I went in there with open eyes.

They made it very clear how arduous it was going to be for me and they made it clear there'd be support for me and that everyone, from the Crown Prosecutor to the police and stuff, they all *hated* these guys and were going to get them for me. A couple of times they said they'd like to do them over and what not for me—it was like having a pack of big brothers around that wanted to protect me. Maybe they were saying some of it to make me feel better, but I really think they genuinely dislike people like him.

Eighteen women (41 per cent) said they were not told what would be involved in a prosecution. In five cases this was related to the offender not having been identified or apprehended, and in at least two others it was related to the police deciding not to press charges. In the remainder, the women said that although their case appeared to be proceeding, they felt ill-prepared by the police and uninformed as to how the process should operate and what to expect. Some of the women remarked that they were given no explanations by the police concerning reasons for case delays or postponements, and felt frustrated that they were unable to meet the Crown Prosecutor until the day of the trial. Concern was also expressed by some that the police asked them to proceed to trial without explaining exactly what would be involved, leaving them to ask support agencies for information they believed the police should have provided. One woman, for instance, said she specifically asked the detective what kinds of questions she might face only to be told dismissively that he did not know, leaving her to seek preparation for court from elsewhere.

One aspect that she and other women felt strongly about concerned their perception that at times the police deliberately withheld information from them regarding the most potentially harrowing aspects of a courtroom trial in order to try to protect or insulate them. The women criticized this practice for its potential to misinform and mislead them about the realities of the trial process. As one woman said about the police:

They didn't want to frighten or upset me, but I think that's wrong. It leaves you impotent, not knowing what to expect. I think you really need to know what you'll be up against when you go in there. I've spoken to several lawyers since and they've told me the tactics they use to break rape victims down on the stand and so I think rape victims should be taught what's going to be thrown at them.

On the other hand, over a quarter of those who were given information about the prosecution process believed that this was for negative reasons and that the police wanted to deter them from continuing with the case. Some related this to a perception that the police did not believe them:

> They said to me that if there's anything in my statement that I'm lying about then to fix it up now before it went to court, otherwise if it went to court and they found out I was lying I'd get imprisonment for lying in my statement.

Undoubtedly the issue of courtroom preparation is a complex one for the police to negotiate with complainants. If officers detail how aggressive defence lawyers can be towards the complainant then the police can be criticized for scaring her from proceeding; if they fail to warn her of the possible rigours of the trial, however, then they may stand accused of insensitivity to her vulnerability on the witness stand. This need not be an intractable catch-22 situation for the police. Comments from the women suggest that what is valued most is realistic information from the police concerning how they expect a trial to proceed, with the most important factor being that this is communicated in a way which validates the woman's experience, irrespective of the eventual case outcome. Knowing that the police believed them and that the justice system was often flawed helped some women to accept the possibilities of a 'not guilty' verdict without feeling completely invalidated by the process.

Often, therefore, it seemed to be the process that mattered more to many of the women, rather than necessarily the final case outcome. This factor possibly underlies the apparent tension which exists at times between the police and rape victims, and which is explored more fully later in this article. Some women complained, for example, that once their case entered the criminal justice system, the police overlooked their need to be kept informed of progress and developments. In Susan's case, for instance, she was very pleased with how the police responded to her stranger rape and appreciated being informed when the accused pleaded guilty before the trial. She was upset, however, that they had said they would let her know what sentence he received but she read it first in the paper. She felt, she said, as if the police were too busy with their own agenda:

> It was all tied up for them but I felt they forgot to let me know . . . They need to keep the victim informed—I thought that was rude. If you're going that far, it's very important to know they're locked up, they've got them, and they've dealt to them.

[. . .]

Comparison with the 1983 rape study

The results of this study, compared with that conducted in 1983, suggest that, despite changes in the law and police training, little has changed in terms of women's experiences of the reporting process. Analysis of the content of the women's concerns, as revealed in their stories and comments, confirms that, as Temkin also found recently in the Sussex study (Temkin 1997), little of substance has changed. Despite apparent improvements in police processes, women reporting rape/sexual assaults to the police now are likely to encounter similar police attitudes and behaviours to those experienced by women in the early 1980s. While it is clear that some individual police officers may respond supportively to rape complainants, it is equally apparent that such a response cannot be guaranteed. This lack of consistency runs counter to increasing expectations of acceptable professional conduct in the 1990s. As one of the women in this study commented:

> Individual cops are really, really good and deal with these situations really, really well, and probably now there are more individual cops who are good than there were, but it shouldn't be an individual thing. They're paid by us and they need to be able to respond to things appropriately and it's not good enough when it's just left up to individuals. It shouldn't be a case of just who you happen to get.

Being lucky in 'the police rape lottery' is incompatible with the current police focus on increased professional service delivery and quality customer service. Yet rape victims and police officers often present in ways suggesting they are worlds apart in their needs and perspectives, leading us to consider more closely the tensions between them.

Tensions between victim needs and police responsibilities

A common source of concern is the perceived failure of the police to strike a consistent and compassionate balance between the victim/survivors' needs and the demands of investigative and administrative priorities (LRCV 1991, in Gilmore and Pittman 1993: 12).

The attitudes expressed, both verbally and non-verbally, by those with whom a rape victim has contact dramatically contribute to the process of restoring her sense of self and safety in the world. Of critical importance is the extent to which she feels believed by those she entrusts with her confidence, and the degree to which they are able to validate that what happened to her was both traumatic *and* not her fault. Since rape by its very nature involves a loss of control and autonomy, the victim needs to begin rebuilding her own sense of autonomy as soon as she is able. This may mean enabling complainants to exercise some choice, for example, over who they are interviewed by, medically examined by, and supported by, although it is also important to appreciate that some women may still be too traumatized to want or be able to make such decisions at this time.

The women's efforts to regain power and autonomy can be either enhanced or undermined by the police response. Police practice following a rape complaint is primarily oriented around the need to establish the nature of the offence, the identity of the offender, and the obtaining of evidence. Since rape historically has been perceived as a charge easy to be laid and hard to be proven, the police are intent on establishing the extent to which sufficient evidence of any kind exists on which to identify and/or charge the alleged offender and take him to court. Their role at this time must necessarily reflect a detached and evaluative assessment of the incident characterized by professional distance and impartiality. An individual officer cannot afford to empathize too closely with the victim, since over-identification carries with it the risk of loss of perspective and emotionally based decision-making. An additional factor in the officer's mind is the arrest imperative, the pressure to be the one who 'nails' the offender and can then add a new notch to his/her police arrests' belt. A sense of urgency therefore prevails, and influences the pace of the proceedings. Furthermore, the police, although undoubtedly seen by many victims as there to support them and their interests, must also be cognisant of the alleged offender and his rights.

From the above, it is evident that at the very time that a raped woman is seeking to be believed and validated, the police will be intent on obtaining proof and verification that she is telling the truth. Her need for validation may clash with the police search for verification, and the techniques used by the police in their quest for evidence may threaten and undermine her sense of confidence and safety in them. While she struggles to regain a sense of autonomy following the rape, the police feel they as professionals must retain control of the proceedings.

Police professionalism requires control and decisiveness on their part, and a determination to ascertain the legitimacy of any complaint and establish its suitability to proceed to court. Yet the complainant may not be able initially to provide a coherent account of the events, nor to recall details with sufficient clarity and consistency. The impact of trauma is such that the very information the police require may be that which she is the least likely to be able to provide. Moreover, police efforts to obtain this information may, depending on how they are conducted, convey to the woman a sense of suspicion and hostility that will trigger her into being even less trusting and available.

From comments made by the women interviewed, it appears that, as indicated earlier, some of the tension may result from the police focus on *outcome* at a time when complainants are more concerned about *process*. This is not to deny that many victims may also want to see their attacker caught and prosecuted, although this is by no means a universal desire on the part of victims (e.g. Jordan 1998a: 43). *All* victims, however, expressed a wish to be treated with respect, sensitivity and professionalism. At times, however, the police's focus on their own procedures appeared to obscure their appreciation of how these might impact on the victim. A clear example of this clash can be seen in Kylie's case.

Kylie felt misunderstandings arose from her being interviewed by the police and expected to provide details when she was too exhausted to think straight. Of the police interview she says:

> I did feel they were calling the shots. I was too tired and distressed to think that I had a right to say, 'This is enough . . .' It didn't really occur to me that I could say I was too tired and wanted to go home.

Kylie felt it was the police's insistence on continuing to obtain details from her when she was '*past it . . . that began the slippery slope*'. When the police subsequently re-questioned her, they became upset at apparent inconsistencies and gaps in her memory. The requestioning culminated in the police cautioning Kylie three times and threatening to charge her with making a false allegation.

In recognition of this particular tension, police in some jurisdictions have begun recommending the practice of delayed statement-taking when the complainant is exhausted and in need of rest (Epstein and Langenbahn 1994:19; Temkin 1997: 514). For some officers, however, it is clear that such a departure from traditional police practice may threaten their sense of control over procedures (personal communication, New Zealand Police 1999), making it likely that other rape complainants in future may have experiences similar to that described by Kylie.

Overlooking the women's needs led to other women saying they experienced the interview process in ways similar to the original abuse. Sarah expressed strong views on this:

> The police are hopeless! They don't care at all. It's like you're an instrument for their cause, a means to an end, in the sense of how they use you, and they don't care about all the effects these things have on you psychologically.

These comments suggest that there are undoubtedly tensions between the needs of rape victims and the responsibilities of the police, to the extent that we might wonder if it is inevitable that rape complainants will feel dissatisfied with the police response.

> I was definitely a case; I was not a rape victim . . . She [the policewoman] didn't even recognize me as a victim—I was a client, a case study. It's really important at that stage that people do see you as rape victims, or there's just no understanding—it's just a case, facts and figures, and whether there's enough evidence to convict.

When we consider the respective focus and needs of women rape complainants and the police, it is clear that, at times, a vast gulf separates the two. Although there may be some overlap between what victims want and what the police seek, the issues are complex and suggest that at times the police may appear to victims to be overly ends-oriented and insensitive to the impact of both sexual assault and their own procedures on complainants. It is also apparent that despite this clash in roles, it *is* possible for the police to achieve high levels of client satisfaction in some cases. Analysis of those situations resulting in favourable police ratings reveals that these are most likely to arise when complainants feel they are believed, treated with respect and caring, and enabled to retain some degree of control over proceedings (Jordan 1998a; Temkin 1997, 1999).

Of concern, however, in this study was the lack of consistency evident in relation to the quality of response complainants received. Such inconsistencies did not appear, in any systematic way, to be related to identifiable factors such as whether or not the victim knew the alleged perpetrator, or whether or not she had been drinking. In some situations the victim had approached the police in trepidation, fearing that the context within which the rape occurred would result in their blaming her, only to be relieved by the sensitivity of their response (e.g. Jordan 1998a: 44–5). At other times victims who felt their case was clear-cut, for example, involving obvious physical injuries, were stunned to encounter disbelief and threats from the police (e.g. Jordan 1998a: 34–5).

Elsewhere it has been suggested that the increasing attrition rate in rape cases may be related to the increasing number of reported sexual assaults involving perpetrators already known to the victim (Harris and Grace 1999). The findings from this New Zealand study suggest that case progression through the system is not solely related to the stranger rape scenario, and also that case outcome is not the central determinant of victim satisfaction. Police decision making continues to occur within an occupational culture profoundly influenced by traditional patriarchal thinking and within such an environment it is inevitable that rape myths will still be apparent in some officers' responses to rape complainants. The fact that individual variation exists suggests both that this occupational culture is no longer hegemonic, if indeed it ever was, and that the possibility of further reform exists even within the currently flawed system.

[. . .]

2.5

Vulnerable victims? A current awareness of the victimisation of people with learning disabilities
by Christopher Williams

[. . .]

Introduction

Care in the community presents the likelihood of new perspectives on the victimisation of adults with learning disabilities. Police and court procedures are not conducive to obtaining convictions on their behalf. There is, consequently, a low expectation of redress and a low rate of reporting. Whilst much has been written concerning people with learning disabilities as defendants or offenders it appears that little significant attention has been given to general victimisation *against* this group, in the UK or abroad.

This position paper outlines relevant literature, and a current awareness of the nature of victimisation, police and reporting, and court procedures. Informal research at the Norah Fry Research Centre (University of Bristol) suggests some of the issues for more thorough investigation. The paper aims to provide a basis for research or other actions, which can contribute to minimising victimisation and maximising the means of support and redress for victims.

Relevant Literature

A formal awareness of the vulnerability of people with learning disabilities seems to stem from the 1970s:

> . . . the scandals surrounding the treatment of . . . mentally retarded . . . persons . . . require that an enlarged list of victims receive the attention of criminologist and other scholars. (Drapkin & Viano, 1974, p. 121)

The theme was taken up in the United States by Balkin (1981) in a paper called 'Toward victimisation research on the mentally retarded'. In the UK, *Disability, Handicap & Society* provided some preliminary thoughts from Hewitt (1987) concerning 'The abuse of deinstitutionalised persons with mental handicaps'. The author was a former police officer.

More recently Margaret Flynn (1989) included an excellent overview of general victimisation as part of her study, *Independent Living for Adults with Mental Handicap: a place of my own*. This covers descriptions and types of victimisation, consequences, associated factors, and prevention. From the United States *The Criminal Justice System and Mental Retardation* (Conley *et al.*, 1992), although largely concerned with people with learning disabilities as defendants, also includes a short chapter on victimisation, dealing with prevalence, limitations of data, crime patterns, fear of crime and its consequences, possible strategies for the justice system, and victim assistance.

A number of recent papers deal with a specific aspect of victimisation: sexual abuse. Dunne & Power (1990) have documented a small, community-based study of sexual abuse in Dublin, and a broader study is in progress in England, funded by the Joseph Rowntree Foundation (Brown, 1991). The Roeher Institute has published *Vulnerable: sexual abuse and people with an intellectual handicap* (Senn, 1988) which deals with Canada; Marchetti & McCartney (1990) investigated the characteristics of the abused, the abusers and the informers in residential settings in America; Tharinger *et al.* (1990) dealt more generally with sexual abuse. Valerie Sinason (1992) deals with the topic from the perspective of a psychologist in *Mental Handicap and the Human Condition: new approaches*. A meeting at the House of Commons in June 1992, chaired by Edwina Currie, promoted the work of the organisation VOICE. The organisation was founded by parents who successfully pursued a case of sexual abuse, at a MENCAP home, through the courts (Cervi, 1992a).

There has been discussion of coping with the effects of sexual abuse. In 1982 Anderson produced a paper, 'Teaching people with mental retardation about sexual abuse prevention'. More recently *Community Care* (1991b) published an account of counselling for women who have experienced rape, and Haseltine & Miltenberger (1990) have considered 'Teaching self-protection skills to persons with mental retardation'. The Family Planning Association publish a comprehensive booklet, *Working with the 'unthinkable': a trainers manual on the sexual abuse of adults with learning difficulties* (Brown & Craft, 1992).

On a more general level, the London Borough of Hammersmith (LBH) embraced the victimisation of disabled people in a survey of needs, finding that people with disabilities are three times as likely to be conned into letting someone into their home and twice as likely to be attacked in the street (LBH, 1992). Unfortunately surveys such as the British Crime Survey (BCS) and the General Household Survey (GHS) omit the experiences of many people with learning disabilities. The definition of 'household' is limited; so-called 'institutions' are not embraced by the surveys. Health Authority or Social Service staffed 'group homes' are excluded, and the status of a house with day-time staff or weekly visits is unclear. Research officers from the BCS are aware that 'better educated respondents seem more adept at recalling relevant events at interview', but no formal attempt has been made to include the views of less intellectually able people. As these surveys influence government policy, the lack of representation of people with learning disabilities raises important democratic questions.

There seems to be no comprehensive study of the victimisation of people with learning disabilities, which would provide the type of information gained by the standard victim studies concerning others. The Home Office *Victims' Charter* (1990) sets out expectations concerning the general population, which provides a good starting point for arguing for equitable outcomes for people with learning disabilities.

The nature of victimisation

The nature of victimisation of adults with learning disabilities is likely to be different to the general picture. For example, current surveys suggest that about one third of crime concerns cars and 95 % of total recorded offences involve property (Home Office, 1991). People with learning disabilities rarely drive, and usually own little more than personal effects. The type of victimisation they are likely to suffer is suggested by recounts from the Bristol area. Incidents include harassment in public places, verbal abuse, simple assault, a murder, abduction by car, arson at a group home, and a taxi driver who exposed himself to a female passenger. Vandalism of group homes and day centres seems common (especially of greenhouses), and it is interesting to note that residents and users are not usually considered to be victims in these circumstances, although feelings of annoyance and trauma may be considerable.

Language is often used in a manner that disguises that particular incidents, if perpetrated on members of the general populace, would clearly be labelled as crimes. 'Abuse' of a person with learning disabilities might be considered an 'assault' of anyone else; 'sexual abuse' is often used when, more accurately, the crime is 'rape' or 'indecent assault'. The title of a recent journal article, 'Role inappropriate sexual behaviour between therapist and client', could be used to embrace anything from embarrassing comments to rape.

A further perspective is the strong likelihood of victimisation by others with learning disabilities. Reports of minor incidents are numerous, but there have also been serious outcomes. In January 1992 a man living in a Health Authority unit in Sheffield was charged with murdering his companion by setting fire to their house (Community Care, 1991a, p. 3). A recent study of sexual abuse indicates that most of the perpetrators were other people with learning disabilities and that 'nearly 60% of the victims were still accessible to the perpetrators' (Turk, 1991, p. 18).

Identifying victimisation

Accurate recognition of victimisation is a prerequisite of seeking redress. Events such as these are not usually pursued through criminal or civil actions:

— youths paying a young person with learning disabilities to swear and goading others into petty crime. This might constitute incitement.
— verbal abuse of people waiting at a bus stop outside their day centre. Verbal abuse may be covered by the offence of, 'Use of threatening, abusive or insulting words or behaviour likely to cause harassment, alarm, or distress to others'.
— a defamatory description in a newspaper. In May 1991 the *Sun* newspaper was successfully sued for describing a child with behaviour problems as the 'worst brat in Britain' (*Guardian*, 1991b, p. 3).
— locking someone in their bedroom or otherwise restricting their liberty, at a group home. This could be 'false imprisonment'.

Mike Gunn (1990) proposes that crime committed by 'omission', (such as neglect by a carer), rather than 'act' (such as assault) may be a significant aspect of the lives of people with learning difficulties. Crimes of 'omission' are more difficult to identify and prove. Instances of alleged neglect at a mentally handicapped unit in Colchester included the failure to respond to a man with a cut lip who 'was left to drip blood into his lunch', and leaving a female patient alone in a bathroom of males (Cooper, 1992, p. 11). The case resulted in the judge directing not guilty verdicts because of the unavailability of a witness.

A greater awareness of what might be pursued through the courts (both through criminal and civil proceedings), by professionals, carers and people with learning disabilities, is fundamental to encouraging reporting.

The effects of victimisation

Even the effects of a moderate victimisation can be serious. The *Independent*, under a headline stating that a man 'died alone in his flat, a victim of Care in the Community', reported,

> Shortly before he died, he was found with paint spattered in his dark hair. He said his 'friend' had done it. Kay believes these same 'friends' took his money and cigarettes, and saw him as a figure of fun. He was an easy and vulnerable target. (Sage, 1991, p. 21)

In 1984 *The Times* (p. 2) reported that a mentally handicapped man jumped to his death after being urged on by 'goulish yobs' shouting, 'We want some blood.'

Margaret Flynn (1989) indicates more general, but certainly not unimportant, outcomes.

(i)   Personal 'debts are significantly more likely to occur when people are victimised' (p. 113).

(ii) Concerning 'relationships'—'Arguably people who experience victim- isation are unable to trust others and, regarding themselves as prey, they do not or cannot take the necessary steps to form relationships. Some people are too frightened to leave their homes, and inevitably this reduces their opportunities to meet others' (p. 118).

(iii) Victimisation is a factor 'associated with satisfaction with the home and location'. 'Victimisation lowers the quality of people's lives and imposes restrictions on them.' (p. 121)

A students' evaluation of a Community Service Volunteers work experience project in Bristol disclosed circumstances when victimisation interfered with employment. They complained of people begging from them, the fear of harassment at bus stops and of problems if the last bus failed to arrive. These situations reduced the number of locations in which they would seek employment.

Despite a growing awareness, the likelihood of victimisation rarely seems to feature as an aspect of planning for people with learning disabilities.

Reporting and the police

Reporting seems low. One Canadian study found that almost 75% of sexual abuse cases were not reported (Sobsey & Varnhagen, 1989). There may be fear of further traumatising a victim through questioning. The case of exposure by a taxi driver in Bristol was not taken further for this reason, although the taxi firm dealt very responsibly with the matter.

Police procedures and attitudes, are also likely to have an influence. After difficulty reporting an incident against a group home in the West of England, a sympathetic police officer is said to have told social workers informally not to give the name of the group home if they contact the police station in the future. To do so would probably lead to the report being ignored. In contrast, a police investigation of a sexual abuse case in the North of England was handled with extreme sensitivity by officers who were experienced in working with children. The result was a successful prosecution.

Sir Frederick Lawton, a retired Lord Justice of Appeal, considers that there is a 'widespread belief among officers, and probably reality, that promotion depends upon having a record of successful prosecutions' (Dyer, 1991, p. 3). If the police generally view crime against people with learning disabilities as unlikely to lead to convictions, their interest and support is likely to be less than for other citizens.

Police procedures concerning offenders are laid down in Home Office Circular 66/90—Provision for Mentally Disordered Offenders. It recommends that 'particular care' is taken with interviewing, that a parent or other responsible person should be present, and that this person should also sign any document arising from an interview. Although similar approaches would be valid when people with learning disabilities are victims, these ideas have not been formally applied to mentally disordered victims.

Low reporting may also result from ignorance of procedures. The Scottish Society for the Mentally Handicapped provides brief guidelines in *Sex, Laws and Red Tape* (McKay, 1991). More comprehensively, *Abuse of Adults with a Mental Handicap/Learning Disability: procedural guidelines*, prepared by the Nottingham Health Authority and Nottinghamshire Social Services Department, describes formal procedures in detail for professionals (Notts. HA/SS, 1992). This also contains a valuable Outline of the Legal Position, by Mike Gunn.

Of equal import to a concern that crimes are not reported to the police is an almost total absence of civil proceedings on behalf of people with learning disabilities. A 'mentally disordered' individual may sue by the help of a 'next friend' under Order 80, Rules of the Supreme Court.

Victims who do not want to pursue an incident provide another aspect. The Law Commission concludes, 'It is not generally clear at what stage intervention against the person's apparent wishes is justified, or who should be responsible for taking this action,' (1991, p. 7). The wishes of victims must remain central, but can be difficult to reconcile if they appear based on minimal knowledge and experience of how police and justice systems work, or on fear of retaliation. People with learning disabilities will sometimes consider the maintenance of social harmony more important than retribution or punishment. An individual relating a story of sexual harassment in a Day Centre photographic dark room placed more importance on ensuring that the perpetrator's wife did not find out, than on reporting and official action.

Even when a report is made and taken seriously, general attitudes can hinder investigation. *The Independent* (Dunn, 1991, p. 5) pointed out the difference in media attention given to the disappearance of an attractive Oxford student and that given to Jo Ramsden a young woman with Down's Syndrome. The paper suggested that because 'She's not attractive in the classic way,' Ms Ramsden did not capture press imagination. Her abduction did not receive the immediate press publicity that may have helped trace her. Ms Ramsden's body was found 11 months later, 10 miles from home. In June a retired psychiatric nursing assistant was charged in connection with this incident.

Court procedures

Few cases reach the courts. In a Rowntree-funded study, of 77 cases of strongly suspected sexual abuse, only four came to court (Cuffe, 1991, p. 15). If cases reach the courts, conviction rates seem low. Sobsey & Varnhagen (1989) found that in Vancouver of 20 cases where charges were laid only nine resulted in convictions. A small-scale survey by the Zonta Club of Hong Kong found conviction rates concerning sexual abuse 'disturbingly low' (Lau, 1988, p. 3).

Court attitudes may underlie some of this failure. Following the case of an alleged attack on a 48-year-old man by a member of staff at a day centre, it was reported

> 'It was not a serious act of violence,' said Judge Williams, who likened the incident to a parent smacking a child and later regretting the action.
>
> (Western Telegraph, 1991)

Attitudes also seem to influence sentences. Recently, a man who had sexual intercourse, illegally, with a 'defective' was given two years in prison although the usual sentence for rape is from five years to life imprisonment (McCormack, 1991, p. 144). In a similar case, a judge stated that he was, 'taking an exceptionally lenient course' in sentencing a social worker to three years probation for having sexual intercourse with a 20-year-old woman in his care. The reason was that the man had been promoted from maintenance worker to social worker without training, and that this mitigated his actions (Guardian, 1991a, p. 5).

Evidence-giving

The Law Commission (1991, p. 40) concludes that, 'Evidential problems may make it particularly difficult to obtain convictions for offences against mentally disordered people.' In a recent court case concerning alleged rape of a 16-year-old woman, her evidence was deemed unacceptable because her 'mental age' was stated to be less than eight, and children younger than eight cannot give evidence under oath (McCormack, 1991, p. 143). The judge apparently considered that actual age referred to by law and a subjective view of mental age proposed by a professional were synonymous. There is no indication as to why the evidence was not heard without an oath, as is sometimes the practice with children under eight. The transcript of another case depicts the confusion of a 20-year old women which could have been avoided:

> Judge: Do you understand what an oath is?
> Mary: No.

Judge: When you swear to tell the truth, will you tell the truth?
Mary: (No answer)
Judge: If you are asked to tell the truth, will you tell the truth?
Mary: I don't know.
Judge: Does an oath on a Bible bind you?
Mary: (No answer)
Social Worker: Would it be all right if I help her out with the question?
Judge: No, it would not.
Prosecuting counsel: My Lord, I wonder if the term 'bind you' would be understood by this lady?
Judge: Do you believe in God?
Mary: Could be yes, could be no.
Judge: Let her be shown a bible, please, usher. If you are asked to tell the truth today, will you tell the truth?
Mary: Yes.
Judge: That book will make you tell the truth, will it?
Mary: Yes.

(Cuffe, 1991, p. 15)

A paper from the United States in 1988 (Kaufhold & VanderLaan) argued that mentally retarded victims could give evidence leading to successful convictions, if procedures are sensitive. Preparation seems a key to successful evidence-giving. Thomas & Mundy (1991) describe work with a woman, who had been sexually abused by her father, which included visits to a court, role plays, and familiarisation with court language. On a practical level, the Crown Office in Edinburgh has just produced a training booklet on the interviewing of witnesses with a learning disability by Ray Bull.

In a recent case of sexual abuse in the UK, the victim was permitted to give evidence from behind a screen, and barristers and judges removed their wigs and gowns to create a less intimidating atmosphere (see Downey, 1992). The prosecution was successful, and the parents of the victim have now formed an organisation, VOICE, to promote the lessons from the case. VOICE identifies points for consideration:

support and belief in the person,
allowances for their disability,
pre-trial methods of court familiarisation,
duration of time to bring to trial,
the laws of advocacy,
awareness of the witness's limited ability by the judiciary/jury,
the role of liaison with the police authorities and the Crown Prosecution Services,
the use of a video link at disclosure interviews,

the recognition (of the difference) between the chronological age and the age determined by psychometric testing procedures.

(VOICE, 1991)

Colin McKay (1991) makes similar recommendations in *Sex, Laws and Red Tape*:

> Special procedures must be adopted to make it more feasible for witnesses with learning difficulties to give evidence in court. These may include videotaped statements; making pre-trial statements admissible in court; expedited trials; screens; less formality in courtrooms. There is also need for improved interview techniques at pre-trial stages. (p. 42)

On an academic level, a recent conference organised by the Department of Psychology at Portsmouth Polytechnic addressed the question, in relation to sexual abuse, 'How may victim's evidence be relied upon to produce more prosecutions?' Papers dealt with collecting evidence via interview (Ray Bull), suggestibility and admissibility (Gisli Gudjonsson), and statement reliability analysis (Günter Köhnken).

In Nova Scotia a court protocol has recently been introduced to provide support and accommodation to all victims and witnesses who have communication problems, including those with mental disabilities (Nova Scotia, 1991). Viewing evidence-giving more as a matter of facilitating communication as less as one of competence, might provide a productive way forward. In Australia, formal Facilitated Communication (supporting an individual to communicate via a computer keyboard or letterboard) is reported to have been used successfully in a court setting. But the likelihood of courts generally accepting evidence in this manner seems minimal without convincing research and acceptance by senior judges.

There are two important arguments for the improved facilitation of evidence-giving. First, there is need to prevent the further traumatisation of victims through unnecessary court procedures. A guilty plea will usually spare a victim unpleasant questioning in court. An offender who suspects that a victim's evidence will not be accepted is very unlikely to plead guilty. An increased probability that evidence from people with learning disabilities will be successful would lead to more guilty pleas and less traumatisation through court procedures. Secondly, the decision whether or not to proceed with a case, by the Crown Prosecution Service, is based in part on the likelihood of a successful prosecution. If it is believed that prosecutions are difficult to achieve on behalf of people with learning disabilities, there is the possibility that cases will not be pursued as they would for other members of the public (see Cervi, 1992b).

Conclusions

Comprehensive research, building on work that has focused on specific aspects of abuse, but which examines *all* facets of victimization and subsequent processes, is a starting point for improving the achievement of justice and the minimisation of victimisation for people with learning disabilities. This paper provides an awareness of the current position, which prompts the following questions:

(i) The experience of victimisation

- What types of crimes occur?
- Do some adults seem more vulnerable, e.g. age, sex, gender?
- Are crimes recognised as such by victims, carers and professionals; if not, why?
- How are victims affected in the short- and long-term? Does victimisation create a fear of leaving the house, for example?
- How might surveys such as the British Crime Survey embrace the adults with learning difficulties who are victims?

(ii) The causes of victimisation

- What are the common settings of victimisation, e.g. in the street, on public transport, in shopping centres, or in rural locations?
- What seem to be the precipitating factors and what are the stated motives of offenders?
- Are there reasonable means of avoidance, that do not culminate in blaming the victim?
- How can public or police awareness minimise the incidence of victimisation?

(iii) Reporting

- Why are some incidents reported and some not?
- What is the police response?
- How can reporting be encouraged?

(iv) Court procedures

- How many cases reach the courts and why/why not?
- How many convictions are obtained?
- What are the perceived and stated reasons for success or failure in court?
- What are the attitudes of court officials?

(v) Other actions

- Is the Victim Support Scheme used? If so, how?
- Are there other channels of formal or informal victim support?
- Are people insured against theft and are claims made?

- What is the involvement of the Criminal Injuries Compensation Board?

The eventual achievement of justice for people with learning disabilities seems dependent on a familiar circle of interdependent factors. Reporting will be improved by better identification of victimisation and the likelihood of greater success in the courts. Success in the courts will be achieved by better investigation, preparation, and improved procedures which are likely to be prompted by more reporting. Success in the courts is likely to deter victimisation and increase access to support and redress through Victim Support and the Criminal Injuries Compensation Board. The need to encourage productive attitudes is common to all levels of involvement.

Note

Dr. Christopher Williams is a Joseph Rowntree Fellow.

Part 3

Religion, spirituality, work with, and research on, victims

by Basia Spalek

Before the emergence of victimology as a social scientific discipline, beginning with Von Hentig's *The Criminal and His Victim* (1948), understandings of crime and victimization included theological and philosophical frameworks, involving concepts such as fate, demons, original sin, the devil or human depravity (Garland, 2002). Originally, victimology constituted an attempt at developing a scientific approach to the study of victimization, involving the discovery of factors that influence a non-random pattern of victimization, and examining how victims contribute to their victimization (Miers, 1989), and so questions of religion and/or spirituality were largely marginalized, even though these continue to be present in contemporary society.

Interestingly, religious convictions have been a motivating factor for those individuals who have volunteered their services towards rehabilitating offenders and helping victims. For example, the historical roots of the probation service lie in the police court missionaries in England in the late 18th and early 19th centuries, many of whom had religious convictions (Whitfield, 1998). Religion continues to influence work with victims today. With respect to restorative justice, a process whereby all those with a stake in a particular crime, including victims, come together to try and deal with its aftermath, religious influences can clearly be seen. For instance, the idea of a 'good society' that underpins restorative justice might be linked to Christian teachings, in particular those of the Quakers in the UK and, in the USA, the Mennonites. More recently, academic work has been exploring restorative justice in relation to a wide variety of religions, including Buddhism (Loy, 2001), Christianity (Allard and Northey, 2001), Hinduism (Neufeldt, 2001), Jewish perspectives (Segal, 2001), and Sikhism (Singh, 2001). The first reading in this section features a chapter about restorative justice in Islam by Nawal Ammar. According to Ammar, advocating restorative justice in Islamic communities is not a difficult task because Islam allows for the encounter between victim and offender, imposes reparation of some form, and to a certain degree allows the participation of interested parties. Indeed, this author shows that many Muslim communities already practise forms of mediation, which include compensation and forgiveness. Importantly, Ammar concludes that 'restorative justice in Islam requires a feminization', which involves exploring the role that women play as witnesses, judges, as well as the role of community in compensation. The second suggested reading in this section is an article by Mark Umbreit, who presents a humanistic model of mediation, which can help practitioners to tap into the transformative and healing possibilities within mediation work. Umbreit argues that complex disputes are characterized by strong emotions, which require specific skills and perspectives on the part of practitioners, skills which non-western indigenous cultures are more comfortable with than those in the West. For Umbreit, 'the practice of mediation can intentionally and more consistently tap into its transformative and healing powers' when consisting of a dialogue-driven approach that seeks to promote the healing of relationships within communities rather than merely seeking to find a solution to a problem. According to Umbreit, important changes are required to dominant Western European styles of mediation, so as to embrace a humanistic model of mediation, including such things as recognizing and using the power of silence, conducting premediation sessions and connecting with parties by building rapport and trust.

Research on victims is increasingly focusing upon questions of religion and spirituality. Faith minorities can be the victims of religious hate crime. For example, the Community Security Trust (CST), which represents the Jewish community on matters of anti-Semitism in the UK, recorded 455 anti-Semitic incidents in 2005, this being the second-highest annual total since the CST started recording incidents in 1984 (CST, 2006: 4). In a post-9/11 context, Muslim men, women and children, as well as places of worship, have become the targets of hate crime. Following the bombings in London on 7 July 2005, the Metropolitan Police Service recorded a sharp increase in faith-related hate crimes, including verbal and physical assaults (European Monitoring Centre on Racism & Xenophobia, 2005). In some parts of Germany, violent attacks on fast-food outlets owned by Muslims are a regular occurrence, and mosques and other Muslim-owned establishments have been attacked. Attacks on Muslim-owned establishments in France, as well as in other countries of the European Union, have also been documented (for more details see EUMC, 2006). A suggested reading for those interested in this topic is a study by Spalek (2002) about Muslim women's experiences of victimization immediately after the 9/11 attacks in the USA. The women taking part in this study felt more vulnerable to harassment and to becoming the victims of crime in the immediate aftermath of 9/11. These women turned to their faith to help them deal with their increased sense of vulnerability, also to help them cope with any crimes that they had experienced. For example, one woman described her father going to the local Imam to ask for special prayers of protection after being burgled. This study also raises wider epistemological questions, asking whether frameworks of understanding that have developed from within social science disciplines are appropriate for analysing religious aspects of individuals' lives. Spalek argues that feminist frameworks of understanding that focus solely upon the role of societal and cultural traditions in religion may be inappropriate, since it might be argued that these ignore the centrality of faith, thereby giving insufficient space to a consideration of women's beliefs or values.

The ways in which religion and/or spirituality is used by victims as part of their coping strategies are evident in other research studies as well. For example, according to Shorter-Gooden (2004), participation in a congregation or spiritual community is, for some African-American women, part of their coping strategies against the debilitating consequences of racism and sexism. According to a study by Kennedy et al. (1998), looking at changes in spirituality for the female victims of sexual assault, the majority of the female victims (60%) revealed an increased sense of the spiritual in the aftermath of the crimes that had been committed against them. Furthermore, those victims with increased spirituality appeared to cope better than those victims without increased spirituality. Ganzevoort's (2005) paper, a suggested reading, looks at the theme of religious coping, this being an important area of study in the psychology of religion. Ganzevoort draws upon his experiences of pastoral counselling, specifically in relation to a woman whose parents had died and who had previously been in a coercive and exploitative sexual relationship with a man. This author distinguishes between the notions of tragedy and malice, illustrating that, depending upon whether a victim views their experiences as being the result of tragedy or of malice, this may influence their coping strategies in the aftermath of crime as well as other traumatic experiences.

Recommended further reading

Spalek, B. (ed.) (2002) *Islam, Crime and Criminal Justice*. Cullompton: Willan.
Ganzevoort, R. (2005) 'Coping with tragedy and malice'. Available at: www.ruardganzevoort.nl/a05malice.htm

3.1

Restorative Justice in Islam: theory and practice

by Nawal H. Ammar

The discussion of Restorative Justice and Islam is both new and old. For centuries scholars have been debating the meaning of justice in Islam as it relates to mercy, forgiveness, and equity. With an emerging sense of urgency about crime and punishment in many countries—including those with Muslim citizens—the question of how we should punish more effectively is being debated in all sectors of society. Although scholars of Islam, and Muslims *in praxis* (in action), have not debated the issue of Restorative Justice per se, the major elements of the discussion exist in diverse works. This chapter, which could readily be expanded to fill an entire volume, examines the old debates with the new language, and asks age-old questions about crime and punishment in Islam within a Restorative Justice framework.

Western criminologists are generally suspicious of any mix between religion and crime. Ideas and attitudes to the effect that Islam is 'only' a religion, or indeed that Islam is an outside 'foreign religion,' complicate the discussion of the relationship between Islam and Restorative Justice within the criminal justice system.

Islam, as will be discussed later, is a holistic system of paths—*Shari'a*—where any examination of it falls within the domain of some particular sphere of social, political, and theological legal knowledge and opinion. As a religion, it is a total way of life, one that includes how we punish crime. At the end of a millennium that has seen the resurgence and reinterpretation of Islam as a violent, blood-thirsty religion, this discussion of Islam and Restorative Justice ought to be seen as a theology of crime and punishment.

Moreover, the notion that Islam is a 'foreign religion' in North America makes a mockery of the reality that prison or jail wardens in the United States recognize daily. Today, it is estimated that Muslims constitute the largest 'minority religion' in the United States, comprising over six million adherents. In prisons and jails too, Muslims are also a growing population. In the

United States, where African Americans are disproportionately represented in prisons, between 10–12 percent of this population is Hanifa Muslims.[1] (Over 45 percent of prisoners at the state level are African American, while constituting only 12 percent of the general population). While in the 1960s and 1970s many African Americans were converted to Islam in prison, today most enter prison as Muslims. In addition, Muslim immigrants are increasingly involved in the various North American criminal justice systems. As a translator, observer, and expert witness I have personally encountered many immigrants in the U.S. system on various charges: domestic violence, illegal trading with food stamps, or even physicians overprescribing pills containing illegal substances. In short, Islam is a universal religion and is a growing religion in North America. Hence, the discussion of Restorative Justice in Islam is useful at both the North American and at the international/global level of criminal justice.

Two other issues complicate the discussion of Islam and Restorative Justice. The first relates to the debate about the applicability of so-called Western concepts such as Restorative Justice to communities and societies that have different socioeconomic and historic origins and cultural systems. There is no doubt that modern Restorative Justice has its beginnings in Canada, where in Kitchener, Ontario, a Mennonite probation officer established a victim-offender reconciliation program in 1974. But Restorative Justice is in fact not a Western concept at all, for one can trace it back to the Babylonian code of Hammurabi (circa 1700 B.C.E.). Ironically, the criminal justice systems that exist in many Muslim countries today are not so much molded by Islam, but rather by Western systems. They are the product of either the Norman invasion of Britain in the eleventh century or the Napoleonic codes of the eighteenth century which were imposed on many developing countries during nineteenth century colonialism. The second issue that complicates the discussion of Islam as it relates to Restorative Justice involves questions about whether a single Islamic criminal justice system actually exists. Are these systems restorative and healing? And if they are not, can we transform them to become restorative and healing?

Today, although most Muslim countries have codified laws, many countries use some form of Islamic law in the formal civil/criminal or administrative courts. Since Colonial times in the 18th and 19th century there have been demands in Muslim countries to reassert *Shari'a* law. In the wake of national independence in many Muslim countries, constitutions have proclaimed *Shari'a* the principal source of legislation. This means that 'gaps in the codes are to be filled by rules of Islamic law. It also means that interpretation of the provisions of the codes are to be carried out in light of the principles and the rules of Islamic law.'[2] The problem, however, is that Islamic law, as I will discuss later, is not a unified body of legislation; hence the various interpretations currently in existence render inaccurate any discussion of it as a monolithic, unified code. Hence, the dilemma of discussing

Restorative Justice in Islam: How can we accurately discuss a core approach of justice, such as Restorative Justice, in a legal system that is so diverse and eclectic? Certainly, a single chapter such as this does not permit comprehensive discussion. The essential thing to remember, however, is that Islamic law, like all other laws, is an intricate system of social control that evolved over time; it did not 'pop out of the head of the Prophet' in one day and stay that way for fourteen centuries unchanged. Though derived from the holy texts, the system is socially constructed to serve communities in certain historical situations. The Islamic legal system, like all other legal systems, is challenged with the tidal waves of social change in contemporary societies. Sometimes the change is swift and dynamic; at other times it is resisted by either those already in power, or with power to change the status quo.

In the light of these critical considerations, the chapter first provides a theoretical overview of the eclectic legal system in Islam. It addresses key issues such as what is crime and punishment in Islam? How does the legal system organize punishment? Where do the victim, offender, and community fit in this system? And finally, are the 'four corner posts of encounter, reparation, re-integration and direct participation'[3] articulated by Dan Van Ness relevant in the Islamic system of crime and punishment? The second section of the chapter examines actual cases of Restorative Justice from empirical data that I collected either from field research or literature reviews. In this section, I aim to show the importance of viewing the Muslims *in praxis*, or as Durkheim referred to it, the 'profane' aspects of Islamic religion in Restorative Justice. It is my intention to underscore that the most successful programs of Restorative Justice have emerged from the communities dealing with conflict. In Islamic communities, the profane aspects of religion and the universal needs to heal the injuries of crime are similar. Hence, an examination of living examples provides a sense of the dynamic communities actually thriving in Islam. The life of these communities negates the stereotypical notion beloved of Orientalists and fundamentalists alike that Muslims belong to a religion with neither society nor nation.

Restorative justice in Islam: theoretical perspective

Although the traditional crime rates in many countries with a Muslim majority are not as high as those in Western countries, yet the increased call for more punitive measures against 'the criminal' is similar to those in the West. Some even argue that the 'few true Islamic' punitive measures that some Muslim societies apply contribute to the lower crime rates. Ayatollah Khomeini of Iran has pushed this argument furthest by stating:

> If the punitive laws of Islam were applied for only one year, all the devastating injustices would be uprooted. Misdeeds must be punished by the law of retaliation: cut off the hands of the thief; kill the murderer; flog the

adulterous woman and man. Your concerns, your humanitarian scruples are more childish than reasonable.[4]

Islamic legal codes and their retaliative nature are much more complex, responsive, and dynamic than the above quote suggests. At the most dog-matic/theoretical level, law in Islam is God-given in the Qur'an, but 'between the original divine proposition and the eventual human disposition is inter-posed an extensive field of intellectual activity and decision.'[5] Qur'anic verses in many cases provided general rules. Sometimes these rules were 'absolute' and clear, while in others the meanings were complex and hidden, leading to variegated interpretations. During the years of the Qur'anic revelation, the Prophet provided the interpretation. After the completion of the revelation and the Prophet's death, however, the Caliphs (as the Prophet's successors) disagreed on the interpretation, and as such Muslim legal theory was required to explain and understand divine revelation. The human interpret-ers of divine revelation in Islam developed the science of jurisprudence, or *Ilm al-Fiqh*. The Arabic word *fiqh* is used to denote both the basis of law and the means of understanding the reason/cause of the speakers' words.

The content of *fiqh*, however, varies according to the various schools of thought. Some, like the Hanafi'i School include pure questions of faith; others, like the Shafi'i School, see it as relating exclusively to human action. The process by which knowledge is derived from the sources also varies according to the different schools of interpretation. Some see the strict inter-pretation from divine sources as the sole basis for interpretation (Shafi'i), others, for example Maliki'i, view the application of reason as essential.[6] In the tenth century C.E. (fourth century Hijri) the doors of interpretation (*ijtihad*) closed for Sunni Muslims. The disagreement among jurists led them to agree that 'all principles had been completely settled.'[7] Today, in Sunni Islam the Islamic legal codes are based on four schools of jurisprudence (*Mathahib*). These are Hanafi'i, Shafi'i, Maliki'i, and Hanbali.

Shia' Islam differentiates between the issue of interpretation of the divine revelation, and the sources of the law itself. While Sunnis view the literary and explicit meaning of the text, Shia's and Sufis look at its internal and hidden symbolism. This difference for Shia' Muslims lies in the concept of 'Imam's judgement.' According to the Shia' Muslims in general, 'the Imam is not there by the sufferage of people, but by divine right. And He is the final interpreter of the Qur'an.'[8] For the Shia', the Prophet's sayings, called hadiths, are a source of law. However, whereas the Shia' accept only hadiths related by the Imams descended from the Prophet, the Sunni's have developed a science (*Ilm al-hadith*) to ascertain genuine from fabricated hadiths.[9]

Turning now to examine Restorative Justice in Islam, we see at the theor-etical level three parameters. The first is the Sunni parameter of interpret-ation. The second is the parameter of legal codes in Sunni Islam. These latter are derived from a sacred source, though the codes themselves are not.

Instead, these codes are the product of fallible humans striving to understand God's sacred words. (They were mostly men, although early in Islamic history there were a few women jurists). Hence, while based on holy sources, most of the codes are socially constructed. The third parameter explores Restorative Justice from the perspective of crime and punishment.

Crime and punishment in Islam

In Islam the concept of unity (*Tawhid*) places the individual in direct obligation towards serving the one God, and in an integrated relationship of solidarity with the community (*Ummah*). The individual is 'part and parcel of society . . . society is not a system, but the highest form of integral and integrated collectivity.'[10] Each individual within this integral collectivity is God's vice-regent (*Kahilfa*), and hence is obligated to preserve His creation.[11] This by no means suggests, however, that the individual thereby becomes unthinking or unreasoning. Within this view of the intimate interrelationship between community and individual, crime is seen as an abrogation of the individual's responsibility towards God, as well as of the harmony and solidarity of the community in both the public and private spheres. This concept of crime leads to the classification of crime and punishment into three categories: *Hudud, Quisas*, and *Ta'zir*. These categories indicate different bases of infringed rights, God's right (public), or individual rights (private). These categories have a number of implications as well: various levels of judicial discretion in implementing punishments; the harshness of penalties imposed; and different evidentiary or fact-finding standards. Whatever the category or the implication, however, all jurists agree that the final objective in this classification of crime and punishment is to achieve a just society.

In the past quarter century, Islamic criminal law has turned to its most punitive methods. The media have reported Islamic law as a savage system. We have witnessed, for example, the murder of a 'princess' for adultery in the late 1970s; the hunting of Salman Rushdie and Abu Zeid because of their alleged blasphemy and apostasy; the cold-blooded murder of the famous Egyptian thinker Farg Fouda; and the attempted killing of the Nobel Prize Winner for Literature, Naguib Mahfouz for apostasy. All these so-called executions are deemed examples of Islamic justice. Importantly, however, these extreme measures of justice and the call for their implementation in the formal system are inherent neither in the Islamic message nor the Muslim people. Such extreme miscarriages of justice must be understood within the socioeconomic and political contexts of particular societies and have a number of causes: maldevelopment, inequity, increase in poverty and marginality, lack of genuine democratic dialogue, deteriorating educational systems, shrinking employment opportunities, and the disparity between the oil-rich countries and other Muslim nations. According to Houidi 'the Qur'an in general is not "obsessed" with crime and punishment. This is evidenced by the fact that only 30 Ayah (units of revelation) out of 6236 address crime and punishment.'[12] In actual fact, the Qur'an is a message of mercy and forgiveness. Thus one reads verses such as: 'Allah forgives not that worshiping others with him, but He forgives anything else' (al-Nisa: 48); 'If anyone does evil or wrongs his own soul but afterwards seeks Allah's forgiveness, he will find Allah oft-Forgiving, most Merciful' (al-Nisa: 110); 'Say: O my adherents who have transgressed against their souls! Despair not the Mercy of Allah. For Allah forgives all sins for He is oft-forgiving most merciful' (al-Zumar: 53); 'When they are angry, even then forgive' (al-Shura: 37); 'The recompense for an injury is an injury equal thereto (in degree); but if a person forgives and makes reconciliation, his reward is due from Allah.' (al-Shura: 40)

Islamic classifications of crime and elements of restorative justice

This section provides a brief account of Islamic classification of crimes and punishment namely *Hudud, Quisas*, and *Ta'zir. Hudud* crimes include: 1) theft, 2) adultery, 3) slander, 4) drinking alcohol, 5) highway robbery, 6) rebellion, 7) apostasy.[13] *Had*, the singular, refers to both the crime and the penalty.[14] According to jurists, the penalties for *Hudud* crimes are mandated in the Qur'an and not by a judge. *Hudud* crimes are the most serious of crimes, and their punishments are the harshest. This is because the individual has violated God's right (*Haq Allah*) by injuring the harmony of the community that is His creation, a public right. Offenders of God's Right/public right are perceived as people who have strayed from the straight path and require a hand in leading them back to it. The Prophet recommended respect towards the person being punished. In a hadith, the Prophet brought a drunk in front of the community and said: 'beat him, 40 slaps for a drunk is the penalty. Some slapped him, some beat him with their garments and others with their sandals. When he was leaving some of the people present said: "may God shame you." The Prophet in response said: "don't say this, never demonize him for his crime" ' (Bukari Sahih).[15]

In the case of *Hudud* crimes, an offender can only be found guilty under specific condition: the offender must have committed the act under no coercion, have been adult, have been in full possession of his/her mental faculties, must not have been ignorant of the law; and evidence must prove guilt beyond any doubt.[16] In all cases, the judge has to follow very precise procedures to ensure the accuracy of the evidence against the offender without any doubt or uncertainty. Historically, this rule has often made the *Had* crime and punishment difficult to prove and execute; for that reason, the crime was reclassified to the lower categories of *Quisas* and *Ta'zir*, the nullification of *Had*. In numerous cases where adultery was a consequence of rape, or where apostasy was extracted for certain benefits, the charges against the accused were nullified. In cases of adultery where four witnesses to the actual act don't testify, or where there is no repeated self-incrimination, the *Had* (crime) charges are dropped. Significantly, *Hudud* crimes apply only in a just society. For example, during the reign of the second Caliph after the death of the Prophet Umar, the punishment of cutting off hands for stealing was universally dropped because there was a famine, and a society that is starving is not just.

The victim in *Hudud* crimes is a more silent participant than in the other categories of crime. The state commences the criminal procedure, and the victim has no right to intervene at any stage of the process, except as a witness, and then only according to certain schools of jurisprudence.[17] In all testimonies the witness and offender encounter each other. But if the witness is also the victim, different rules obtain: only the Hanafi'i school permits their encounter with the offender for *Hudud* crimes. The Maliki'i school allows their encounter only in highway robbery *Had* crimes. The Shafi'i and Hanbali schools disallow the victim's testimony altogether because it is viewed as the testimony of 'enemies against each other.' Neither the arbitrator nor the victim have much freedom in their participation in the *Hudud* criminal process. The punishment is predetermined, and hence the arbitrator's function is to determine the accuracy of the testimonies and evidence.

Regarding the integration process in *Hudud* crimes and punishment, jurists have argued that there is a built-in component of integration or restoration. The offender is viewed as someone who has strayed and needs to be returned to the straight path. The offender is integrated back into society because he/she has never been isolated in a prison and has stayed in the community and within his/her context (i.e., family). Jurists have also made the argument that in the larger theological question, the offender in the *Hudud* crime is punished only on earth and hence, is forgiven by God; this in turn allows him/her to be reintegrated into the community of believers both on earth and the hereafter. All this, however, is valid only on the ideal, orthodox level. Yet at the practical level, the physical stigma of some of the *Hudud* punishments (cutting off the hand of the thief) and the fatal nature of others (such as stoning the married adulteress to death) precludes reintegration of the offender.

The ultimate Restorative Justice notion in this *Hudud* crime classification is that of the public or community right. The very basis of the crime falls into the category of injuring a public right and requiring the individual to amend it. At the same time, the harshness of the penalties requires the public as represented by the arbitrator to be careful in deciding guilt or innocence. This often results in the nullifying of *Hudud* crimes and transforming potentially punitive/retributive justice to the more transformative categories of *Quisas* and *Ta'zir*.

Quisas is the second category of crime in Islamic criminal *fiqh*. These crimes include all types of murder—voluntary and involuntary—and crimes against persons including assault, battery, mayhem, and other bodily harm that results in injury or death.[18] The kind of rights that are violated in *Quisas* is subject to debate. Modern Islamic jurists, however, agree that this category combines both public and private rights in the case of intentional homicide. It is public because humans are God's creation, and private because the victim's family has lost a loved one. The penalties for *Quisas* are not strictly mandated in the Qur'an, but a range of retaliation, compensation, and reconciliation is prescribed. It was within the pre-Islamic context of retaliating against the murder of even one person by annihilating entire clans that the Qur'an stated the range of possible punitive measures:

> O ye who believe the law of equality is prescribed to you in cases of murder: the free for the free, the slave for the slave, the woman for the woman. But if any forgiveness is made by the brother of the slain, then grant any reasonable demand, and compensate him with handsome gratitude. This is a concession and a mercy from God. (al-Baqarah: 178)

The Qur'an cautions against vengeful retaliation:

> We ordained therein for them life for life, eye for eye, nose for nose, ear for ear, tooth for tooth and wounds for equal. Anyone remits the retaliation by way of charity, it is an act of atonement. (al-Maidah: 45)

To guarantee the equitable application of punishment in *Quisas* crimes, the administration of justice should be in the hands of an 'appointed guardian' (*wali amr*, a mediator who can be a judge or local administrator) and not left to the community or the victim or his/her family. The procedural rules for dealing with a *Quisas* crime have been a subject of disagreement among the various schools of Sunni jurisprudence. Some argue that retaliation by death is prescribed; others note equitable methods of retaliation, and yet others argue that while retaliation is the maximum penalty, it is not the recommended one. Judicial opinion notes that the legislative rule of dismissing any crime that has inadequate evidence and the strict evidentiary procedures required, encourage remorse and forgiveness. More specifically, retaliation is quite categorically *not* recommended in the Qur'an, particularly in crimes of murder: 'If you stretch your hand against me, to slay me, it is not for me to stretch my hand against thee: for I do fear Allah, God of the universe.' (al-Maidah: 28)

Forgiveness, notes Houidi, 'is desirable in *Quisas* crimes particularly the verse 178 of surat al-Baqarah that follows the mention of *Quisas* which states: "but if any forgiveness is made by the brother of the slain, then grant any reasonable demand and compensate him with handsome gratitude".'[19] Also all the Prophet's sayings related to *Quisas* include indications that forgiveness is desirable in order to strengthen solidarity and mercifulness. Bahnasi notes that forgiveness from the victim's family in intentional homicide does not abrogate the state's right to punish less punitively by either imprisonment or compensation.[20]

An offender in cases of *Quisas* crimes is granted the same respect and rights as in those of *Hudud*. Here, however, alternatives to retributive punishment can be given including a *Diyya* (victim's compensation) or reconciliation. The appointed guardian (*wali amr*), victim, or victim's family can order the forgiveness and consider the alternatives. Complete forgiveness in *Quisas* crimes can only be granted by a victim who forgives and then dies. In all other cases, forgiveness is conditioned by compensation and reconciliation. Such cases have been documented by many sociologists and anthropologists of the Middle East and will be explored later in this chapter.[21]

Compensation (*Diyya*) in *Quisas* crimes is procedurally complex. Generally, it is due in cases where there is doubt in evidence, in cases of involuntary manslaughter, in cases where a juvenile is the perpetrator, or the offender is insane. *Diyya* should be accepted as an option by the offender, otherwise the *Quisas* punishment applies. The amount of compensation is paid by the offender according to a predetermined amount and over a prescribed period of time. In cases where the offender has neither the funds nor resources to pay, the immediate blood relatives are responsible. If, however, the offender is a female or a juvenile offender, then their immediate relatives are exempt from repayment.[22] If the offender has no immediate blood relatives living, then the state is responsible to pay the compensation amount. *Diyya* can be revoked in cases where the guilty is subsequently found innocent, or else, according to the Maliki school, if the victim requires the cessation of payment and then dies; some argue that after a period of fifteen years without legal inheritors, the *Diyya* payment should stop.[23]

The amount of *Diyya* (compensation) payment is nowhere mentioned in the Qur'an, but jurists have agreed that an amount equivalent to 100 camels be the minimum. Some (for instance communities in Syria, Egypt, and the Maghreb) have added gold to the camels; others (for example communities in Iraq and Iran) have added legal tender. There is also a system of compensation called *Errish*, which is calculated in terms of the value of loss. This applies to cases where there is injury, including the loss of a pregnancy due to beatings and broken bones. This form of compensation does not apply to loss of life. The *Diyya* system is not equivalent to victim's compensation in the same manner as civil damages in the Western criminal justice system; rather, it carries an element of punitive damage. The money, however, goes to the victim or his/her inheritors and not to the state.[24]

Reconciliation (*Solh*) is not an alternative to compensation (*Diyya*), but rather an additional step in the process. It is highly recommended in cases where injuries have not led to death. *Solh* takes the place of forgiveness and requires negotiations in the presence of an appointed guardian (*wali amr*). *Solh* does not have to occur between all injured parties and offenders, but can be partial, i.e. between the offender and one of the injured.

In the case of *Quisas* crimes, action is mostly initiated by the victim or the victim's family. As mentioned earlier, the victim or his/her family has a very active role in the procedures of this crime. Their role is instrumental in transforming the punishment from retributive to restorative. This is because forgiveness that leads to compensation (*Diyya*) and reconciliation (*Solh*) can only be initiated with the agreement of the victim. The offender also has an important role in transforming *Quisas* punishment into Restorative Justice by accepting to pay the *Diyya* and be forgiven. Once again, in *Quisas* crimes the community's role of appointing a guardian (*wali amr*), through the authority of the democratically elected ruler, is essential since this person guarantees equitable punishment of the crime; but more important, however, is the role this person plays in transforming the process of justice. The judge/arbitrator in *Quisas* crimes is the one who sets the stage for moving the punishment from retributive to restorative by advising the victim of his/her 'forgiveness obligation' and hence of the right to *Diyya*; he sets the reparation amounts and conditions, and finally attempts to bring about reconciliation among the parties. The encounter between the offender and the victim or his/her family is arranged by the guardian or judge/arbitrator (*wali amr*) whose task it is to mediate the conflict to a peaceful or punitive resolution.

The participation of the victim, the offender, and the community is very clear in this process. The victim plays a full role in either granting forgiveness or not. The offender also participates by accepting the ruling on compensation, or rejecting it. Finally, the community plays the role of the arbitrator in choosing the judge/arbitrator (*wali amr*) through the ruler, as well as by providing compensation to the victim or his/her family in cases where either the offender or his/her family is indigent. One can argue in the case of *Quisas* crimes that reintegration is not a necessary corner post, since offenders almost always remain in the community anyway, and hence the need to return them to the community is unnecessary. Again, the combination of public and private rights in this category of crime (especially in intentional homicide) brings forth issues of obligation, injury, and reparation. The harshness of punishment obligates the public (represented by the judge/arbitrator) to take care in deciding guilt or innocence. This often results in suspending judgment of this particular crime and considering less punitive options that in effect transform retributive justice, including compensation, reconciliation, or the reduction of the crime to the lesser *Ta'zir* crimes.

Ta'zir (chastisement) is the third category of crime in Islam. This category includes all crimes for which the Qur'an or Sunna do not prescribe a penalty, or where there was doubt on the evidence for the more serious *Hudud* or *Quisas* crimes. The punishment for these crimes is left to the discretionary power of the ruler and his/her delegates. *Ta'zir* literally means chastisement for bad behavior. The aim of this chastisement is the public good. This public good is not fixed, but evolves with society and in history, hence the flexibility of the legal system. *Ta'zir* crimes and punishment have been defined by the Hanafi school of jurisprudence as the 'politics of punishment' rather than the 'science of punishment'; its aim is the rehabilitation of the criminal. It is the discretionary power of the judge, the contextual setting of the society, and the status and personality of the offender that contribute to the definition of a crime and the implementation of a penalty. *Ta'zir* crimes have not been codified by all countries where Islamic law is practiced. Yet even in those where the laws have been codified, they are not divine revelations, but formulated by human beings. Precisely because they are man-made, they can be changed. It is, hence, in this category of crime that the practice of Restorative Justice in all its programs—mediation, victim-offender conferences, victim's compensation programs, and so forth—can be implemented with little resistance.

In *Ta'zir* crimes and punishment, forgiveness and minimum punitive measures are central features of punishment. Penal sanctions can be abolished in four cases: the death of the convict; the granting of grace (*afw*)—initially by the victim and then by the judge/arbitrator; if the victim and the offender had forgiven each other prior to the matter appearing before the judge or sovereign; and if the offender had repented.[25] This category of crime is the most amenable to transforming justice in the Islamic criminal justice system from retributive to restorative.[26]

Yet, the politics of the larger contemporary state have been problematic. Muslims are governed by undemocratic institutions, by values of consumerism, by a New World Order where the law of military might reigns over justice, and by patriarchal norms that bend Qur'anic prescriptions. In this contemporary reality of Muslims, any potential for Restorative Justice within the criminal justice system has been blocked by external, conflicting norms of injustice. Prisons provide a good case-example of how *Ta'zir* punishments that are potentially restorative, have become retributive in the context of contemporary warring societies.

The Qur'an contains nine references to prison as an institution, and all are in Surat Yusuf (Joseph) relating to pre-Islamic times. Also, the Prophet and his first Caliph had no specific space to imprison people, but placed them in custody in homes, mosques, or kept someone guardian on them while they were at home. This was virtually house arrest without its military symbols. It was not until Islam had expanded beyond the bounds of Arabia, that the second Caliph, Umar, bought a home in Mecca and transformed it into a prison. As such there is great disagreement about whether Islam views prisons as legal. Regardless, however, the prison became an institution of punishment at later times in Islamic civilization. Jurists agree that in Islamic prisons inmates should not be chained as this would prevent their praying. Murderers should be chained, but only at night. Prisoners should be given ample food and drink. They should also be given clothing suitable to the winter and summer seasons. Prisoners who die in prison are buried at the expense of the state. Prison sentences vary according to crime and are divided into determinate and indeterminate duration. Generally, however, jurists agree on a month for investigation, and six months for rehabilitation and punishment.[27]

The modern use of prisons in many Muslim countries generally follows the example of many Western countries such as the United States, and their conditions violate any humane standards of punishment. Just how a justice system with the potential for restoration and healing could have been transformed into a punitive, retributive system requires further examination in the context of the relationship between Islam and Restorative Justice.

At the theoretical level, then, we have seen that Islamic criminal law (*fiqh*) has some basic elements of Restorative Justice. These elements vary according to the classification of crime. In crimes where public rights have been infringed upon, Restorative Justice elements relate more to the offender and the community than to the victim. The victim as an individual is silenced, and some schools regard his/her participation as a hindrance to the justice process. In these crimes the harshness of punishment is mediated by the burden of strict and comprehensive evidentiary rules, which often lead to reducing the crime to a lesser degree. Reduction of the crime to a lower level of classification is not a way of absolute forgiveness, but an attempt to punish justly without vengeance. In nullifying the higher-order crime, the offender is not exposed to the most punitive system of justice, but continues to be shamed by a responsible and merciful community. Shaming offenders by punishing them for a *Hudud* crime by invoking the lesser *Quisas* punishments, or for *Quisas* crime by invoking the lesser *Ta'zir* punishments makes the punitive measures particularly restorative. The aim of shaming in this case is to uphold the norms of the superiority of the community through forgiving, rather than punishing unjustly out of vengeance. Such communal behavior accords with God's description of Muslims in the Qur'an: 'Let there arise out of you a band of people inviting to all that is good, enjoining what is right and forbidding what is evil' (al-Imran: 104).

In *Quisas* crimes, where the crime is an infringement on both public and private rights, Restorative Justice elements are seen in the central role of the victim in the process. The active voice of the victim as a participant and as one who actually confronts the offender is seen through initiating the complaint and either accepting or rejecting the compensation or reconciliation. *Quisas* crimes and punishment also have an already built-in program of Restorative Justice, namely, mediation. It can be argued that the role of the judge/arbitrator (*wali amr*) is also to mediate the conflict in order to lead to the most merciful, and least burdensome, resolution for victim, offender, and the public good alike.

Ta'zir crimes and punishment are the classification that is most amenable to contemporary programs of victim-offender reconciliation, conflict resolution, anger management, and compensation. This category of crime and punishment is seen as an infringement on private rights and hence the judge/arbitrator has a wide range of options within the historical, socio-economic setting. Imprisonment, as a *Ta'zir* punishment, also contains many elements of Restorative Justice including respect and dignity for the offender. Hence, Islamic criminal *fiqh* regulates the operation of prisons along the lines of mercy, rather than retaliation. Again, the contemporary conditions of many prisons operating in oppressive socioeconomic and political conditions require special attention in future discussions of Restorative Justice in Islam. There is a need to explore the conditions of particular societies and communities where Muslims live and to elaborate on the forces that lead people to reinforce punitive justice, when they in fact have a theoretical basis of mercy for instituting restoration. Suffice it to say nonetheless, that one can indeed implement elements of Restorative Justice in Islamic criminal law.

The only element of Restorative Justice lacking in Islamic law is the notion of reintegration. This does not mean that the concept is incompatible with most of the principles in the system. Rather, it is a generally under-developed concept and in certain categories of crime, such as *Hudud*, it may be impossible. In cases where reintegration is impossible, however, the term cannot be developed and may need to be replaced. The Islamic *ummah*, rejecting individuals on the basis of apostasy, is a case in point: it means no return; there is room neither to negotiate, to mediate, nor even to reach a middle ground. The encounter between the community and the offender(s) in such crimes (*Hudud* especially) is one either of reconciliation or elimination, but not one of reintegration. There are, however, other categories of crime in Islamic criminal law where reintegration is very relevant, especially those of *Ta'zir*. Hence, the need to operationalize such a term within Islamic *fiqh* more clearly in order to create programs that would facilitate the reintegration process.

[. . .]

In conclusion, this chapter provides one of the first written treatments of Restorative Justice and Islam. It both summarizes basic ideas and raises questions for future work. Islam contains many elements required for Restorative Justice. The essential component of mercy and forgiveness in Islam facilitates both the ideals and programs of Restorative Justice. Moreover, the various classifications of crime and punishment in Islam do incorporate the community, the victim, and the offender. The community is represented in terms of rights and obligations, as well as having a role in mediation through the appointed guardian or judge/arbitrator. The offender's human rights are respected and his/her obligations to the victim and the community are clearly defined in the style of punishment and/or forgiveness. Also, the strict rules of proof in the Islamic justice system often lead to a lessening of the charges, thus dictating that less punitive measures be applied. This transformation of justice—from certain and swift to hesitant and less punitive—is restorative and healing. Most of all, however, the reduction of punishment to the lowest classification (i.e. due to lack of proof) leaves a large space for human discretion, and hence a place for advocating Restorative Justice programs. Such negotiations require a serious attempt by Restorative Justice advocates at 'selling' the idea to legal practitioners, administrators, and politicians in Islamic countries and communities.

Advocating Restorative Justice in Islamic communities is not a difficult task. According to most interpretations, Islam allows for the encounter between victim and offender; it imposes reparation of one kind or another, and to some degree permits participation of all parties. Hence, at the theoretical level Restorative Justice programs are not alien to the process of conflict resolution in Islam. Additionally, as illustrated earlier, many Muslim communities already practice forms of mediation, arbitration, compensation, and forgiveness. Restorative Justice, therefore, is not alien to Islam and Muslims, neither at the theoretical nor at the practical level.

By concentrating on crime and punishment, this chapter has necessarily omitted discussion of other arenas of conflict such as civil, administrative, and family disputes which require a systematic inquiry within the Islamic framework.

A final word of caution regarding the above treatment of Restorative Justice and Islam is in order: namely the place of women in such a view of justice. Clearly, Restorative Justice in Islam requires a feminization. Such a process requires among other things an examination of women as witnesses, the role of the community in paying their compensation, and women as judges/arbitrators.

Though more work is needed to provide a clearer picture of Islam and Restorative Justice, of which this chapter constitutes a first building block, nothing detracts from the fact that the basic elements of a restorative approach already exist in Islam at both the theoretical and practical level.

Notes

1 Personal communication with head chaplains in the Ohio state prison system.
2 G. M. Badr, 'Islamic Law,' 1987, 29.
3 Dan Van Ness, 'Perspectives on Achieving Satisfying Justice Values and Principles of Restorative Justice,' a paper presented at the Achieving Satisfying Justice Symposium, Vancouver, B.C., 21 March 1997, 1.
4 Cited in Virginia Mackey, *Punishment*, 1981, 36.
5 N. J. Coulson, *Conflicts and Tensions*, 1969, 2.
6 A. M. Khoja, *Elements*, 1978, 37–8.
7 Ibid., 52.
8 Ibid., 54–8.
9 Ibid., 59.
10 M. C. Bassiouni, 'Sources of Islamic Law,' 1982, 14.
11 Ibid., 204–205.

12 Houidi, 1994, 73.
13 A. F. Bahnassi, *Tatbiq al-hudad*, 1988, 99–268.
14 *Had* punishments are the cutting of hands for theft and highway robbery;
     100 lashes for adultery for the unmarried, and stoning to death for those
     married; 80 lashes (40 beatings) for drinking (jurists disagree on this);
     100 lashes for slander; for rebellion, a range from forgiveness to killing;
     for apostasy, a range from imprisonment for three days until return to
     Islam or immediate return to Islam or immediate killing (jurists disagree
     on this).
15 Bahnassi, *al-uqubah fi al-fiqh al-Islami*, 1983, 233.
16 There are seven types of evidentiary processes in Islamic criminal *Fiqh*:
     1) evidence of lay witnesses, 2) self-incrimination, 3) presumption,
     4) expert witnesses, 5) personal knowledge of the judge, 7) written evi-
     dence left by a deceased, or written evidence accepted by the offender as
     belonging to him/her.
17 M. M. Salama, 'General Principles,' 1982, 141. The state is represented
     in the governor, the chief of police, since the jurisdiction of the judge was
     not usually over criminal cases. Some jurists expressed this distinction by
     saying that the purpose of the governor is to prevent public corruption in
     the community and to eradicate crime, while the purpose of the judge is
     to redress injuries to private rights.
18 Bahnasi, 1988; M. C. Bassiouni, 'Sources of Islamic Law,' 1982, 24.
19 Houidi, 1982, 75.
20 Houidi, 1982, 75–79.
21 H. Ammar, *Growing Up in An Egyptian Village*, 1954; Antoun, 1972;
     N. Ammar, 'An Egyptian Village,' 1988.
22 It is difficult in the limited space available to provide a comprehensive
     discussion of how Restorative Justice in Islam requires an attempt at
     'feminizing justice.' In many cases relating to witnessing (evidence), par-
     ticipation as a victim or an offender, justice as written by the jurists is
     'gendered.' This 'gendered' justice in crime and punishment and Islam
     requires an independent study.
23 Bahnassi, *Tatbiq al-hudad*, 1988, 160.
24 Bassiouni, 'Quesas Crimes,' 1982, 206.
25 G. Benmelha, 'Ta'zir Crimes,' 1982, 224.
26 The politics of Islam encourages the reduction of burden in numerous
     sources: In the Qur'an verses such as: 'Allah doth wish to lighten your
     burdens for humans were created weak (al-Nisa: 28); in the Prophet's
     hadiths 'this is a religion of ease' (Bukahri and Muslim Sahih). Also,
     the juristic rule of gradual application of punishment beginning with
     'soft' and ending with 'harsh.' One very good example of how Islamic
     criminal *fiqh* has within it a framework for Restorative Justice is the prac-
     tice of capital punishment. Islamic criminal *fiqh* has determined that
     crimes punishable by death can be handled with great restraint. Only in

acts of *Hudud* and *Quisas* where there is no doubt in the evidence, can the death penalty be applied. As stated earlier, these cases often have insufficient evidence and are reduced to *Ta'zir* crime and punishment. Additionally, the Qur'an is very clear that punishment should not be excessive, and hence the verse: 'Slay not the life that Allah hath forbidden save with right. Whoso is slain wrongfully, We have given an authority unto his heir, but let him not commit excess in slaying. Lo! He will be helped' (al-Isra': 33). Due to such prescriptions, therefore, many judges are reticent about inflicting the death penalty in *Ta'zir* crimes.

27 Bahnassi, *al-uqubah fi al-fiqh al-Islami*, 1983, 208–211.

3.2

Humanistic mediation: a transformative journey of peacemaking
by Mark S. Umbreit

[. . .]

The impact of mediation in resolving a wide range of interpersonal conflicts is well documented. The application of mediation consistently results in high levels of client satisfaction and perceptions of fairness within families (Emery and Jackson, 1989; Depner, Cannata, and Simon, 1992; Duryee, 1992; Kelly, 1989, 1990; Slater, Shaw, and Duquesnel, 1992; Umbreit and Kruk, 1997); among coworkers (Umbreit, 1995c); and in neighborhoods (Clark, Valente, and Mace, 1992; Cook, Roehl, and Sheppard, 1980; Davis, Tichane, and Grayson, 1980; Kolb and Rubin 1989); schools (Araki, 1990; Moore and Whipple, 1988; Stern, Van Slyck, and Valvo, 1986); and the criminal justice system (Coates and Gehm, 1989; Umbreit, 1991, 1993, 1994, 1995a, 1995b; Umbreit and Roberts, 1996). The achievement in mediation of a written, mutually agreed upon settlement between the involved parties is often an important outcome. However, if the field of mediation becomes driven by the desire to reach settlements in the quickest way possible at the expense of understanding and addressing the emotional and relational context of the conflict, it may evolve into little more than another impersonal, mechanical, and routine social service. This article presents a model of mediation that intentionally taps into the full potential of mediation to offer a genuine transformative journey of peacemaking that is grounded in compassion, strength, and our common humanity.

Although some conflicts, such as complex commercial disputes, clearly require a primary focus on reaching an acceptable settlement, most conflicts develop within a larger emotional and relational context characterized by powerful feelings of disrespect, betrayal, and abuse. When these feelings about the past and current state of the relationship are not allowed to be expressed and heard in a healthy manner, an agreement might be reached but the underlying emotional conflict remains. Little healing of the emotional wound is likely to occur without an opening of the heart through genuine dialogue, empowerment, and a recognition of each party's humanity despite the conflict. This requires moving far beyond the well-known techniques of active listening or reflective listening and their emphasis on paraphrasing, summarizing, and related skills. Clearly, these techniques, when used by disputants or mediators, can often be very helpful in resolving conflict. The "techniques" of listening skills, however, can also get in the way of genuine dialogue, particularly when their use leads to the inability to honor and feel comfortable with silence, to deeply reflect upon what is being said, and to reflect upon what you (the mediator) are feeling and experiencing in the present moment. The clearest example of technically accurate reflective listening skills inhibiting genuine communication is when a mediator paraphrases every bite-size chunk of verbal conversation in such a way that the disputant experiences it as intrusive and insensitive, if not obnoxious.

Genuine dialogue, in which people feel safe enough to speak and listen in a nondefensive manner, requires skills and a life perspective that many non-Western indigenous cultures are far more comfortable with than we in the West are; that is, speaking and listening from the heart, as well as feeling comfortable with and honoring silence. The basic elements of dialogue as promoted in Western culture (Teurfs and Gerard, 1993) consist of suspension of judgment; listening as the key to perception; identification of assumptions; maintaining an attitude of learning and a spirit of inquiry; looking within one's self; keeping the focus on context and meaning; and releasing the need for outcomes.

After many years of application in diverse setting, the field of mediation now faces a wonderful opportunity to build on the many anecdotal stories of how mediation periodically has often been far more than simply working out a settlement. By moving from a settlement-driven to a dialogue-driven approach to mediation, the practice of mediation can intentionally and more consistently tap into its transformative and healing powers. These healing powers are intrinsic to the process of mediating conflict between individuals but need to be consciously drawn out and utilized.

The potential of effective conflict resolution to promote healing of relationships within communities rather than just immediate resolution of problems between individuals is particularly well grounded in the traditions of many indigenous people throughout the world. The practice of ho'oponopono by native Hawaiians (Shook, 1989), family group conferencing by Maori people in Australia (Alder and Wundersitz, 1994), and healing circles and other practices among aboriginal and First Nation people in Canada (Griffiths and Belleau, 1993) and Native Americans (LeResche, 1993) all provide beautiful examples of spiritually grounded forms of resolving conflicts through a journey of healing and peacemaking. As Diane LeResche (1993) points out, "at its core, Native American peacemaking is inherently spiritual; it speaks to the connectedness of all things; it focuses on unity, on harmony, on balancing the spiritual, intellectual, emotional and physical dimensions of a community of people" (p. 321). These principles of balance have also been adapted by tribal leadership in Canada (Huber, 1993) for use in urban tribal settings, using the traditional symbol of the medicine wheel.

Within Western culture, the transformative dimensions of mediation have been eloquently described by Bush and Folger (1994) in their widely acclaimed book *The Promise of Mediation*. They emphasize the importance of genuine empowerment and mutual recognition of each party's humanity in addition to the value of compassionate strength among parties in conflict. Bush and Folger emphasize that through empowerment parties grow calmer, clearer, more confident, more organized, and more decisive. They regain a sense of strength, of being able to act and handle life's problems. Through recognition, the parties in conflict voluntarily choose to become more open, attentive, and responsive to the situation of another, thereby expanding their perspective (if expanded) to include an appreciation for the circumstances that the other person is faced with. Whether an actual settlement occurs is quite secondary to the process of transformation and healing that occurs in their relationship. One of the most powerful, yet controversial to some, expressions of the transformative qualities of empowerment and recognition has been consistently observed in the small but growing application of mediation and dialogue between parents of murdered children and the offender (Molhan, 1996; Umbreit, 1995c). After lengthy preparation by the mediator, involving multiple individual meetings, the parties frequently experience each other's humanity (despite the evil and traumatic event that has occurred, as well as the inconsistency of some facts) and gain a greater sense of closure through a genuine dialogue about what actually happened and its impact on all involved.

A specific application of transformative mediation practice that is particularly suited to family, community, workplace, and victim-offender mediation is the humanistic model of mediation (Umbreit, 1995c). In fact, the elements of a humanistic model are grounded in the experience of many mediators over the years and have been applied in areas ranging from family conflict to criminal conflict involving such offenses as burglary, theft, and minor assaults. Instead of the highly directive settlement-driven model practiced widely in civil court settings, a humanistic mediation model is very nondirective and dialogue driven. It prepares the parties, through separate premediation sessions with the mediator, so that they feel safe enough to have an opportunity to engage in a genuine conversation about the conflict, to experience their own sense of empowerment, and to express what Bush and Folger call "compassionate strength," including empathy for the other party in the conflict. The emphasis is on the mediator facilitating a dialogue that allows the parties to discuss the full impact of the conflict, to assist each other in determining the most suitable resolution (which may or may not include a written agreement), and to recognize each other's common humanity, despite the conflict.

A humanistic model of mediation, in some respects, parallels a humanistic style of psychotherapy or teaching, which emphasizes the importance of the relationship between the therapist and client or teacher and student and embraces a strong belief in each person's capacity for growth, change, and transformation. Carl Rogers (1961), a pioneer in humanistic psychology, emphasized the importance of empathetic understanding, unconditional positive regard, and genuineness. Although his theories were developed in the context of psychotherapy, they have enormous implications for mediation practice and life in general.

Parties in conflict may be more likely to experience emotional benefits from the practice of humanistic mediation because of the healing that often occurs in the relationship encounter in the present. It is important to note, however, that such a process is not psychotherapy, nor does it require a mediator to have training in psychotherapy. Acknowledgment of brokeness or hurt is intrinsic to humanistic mediation. Working on that brokenness and dealing with the past emotional issues that have contributed to these feelings, however, is the domain of therapists, not mediators (Bradshaw, 1995; Kelly, 1983).

Underlying values

A humanistic mediation model is grounded in underlying values and beliefs about the nature of human existence, conflict, and the search for healing, as follows:

- Belief in the connectedness of all things and our common humanity
- Belief in the importance of the mediator's presence and connectedness with the involved parties in facilitating effective conflict resolution
- Belief in the healing power of mediation through a process of the involved parties helping each other through the sharing of their feelings (dialogue and mutual aid)
- Belief in the desire of most people to live peacefully
- Belief in the desire of most people to grow through life experiences
- Belief in the capacity of all people to draw upon inner reservoirs of strength to overcome adversity, to grow, and to help others in similar circumstances
- Belief in the inherent dignity and self-determination that arise from embracing conflict directly.

Practice implications

In order to consistently embrace a more humanistic model of mediation, a number of significant changes in the dominant Western European model of mediation are required. Although clearly not capturing the full spiritual richness of many traditional practices of indigenous people, these changes in the dominant Western European model of mediation will lead to a more transformative and healing experience of mediation. Each change in the practice of mediation that is necessary to more closely follow the humanistic model will be discussed in greater detail but is outlined here:

- Centering. Clearing the mind of clutter and focusing on the important peacemaking task at hand.
- Reframing the Mediator's Role. Facilitating a process of dialogue and mutual aid instead of directing a settlement-driven process.
- Conducting Premediation Sessions. Listening to each party's story, providing information, obtaining voluntary participation, assessing the case, clarifying expectations, preparing for the mediation.
- Connecting with the Parties. Building rapport and trust beginning in premediation phase.
- Identifying and Tapping into Parties' Strengths. Beginning in premediation phase.
- Coaching on Communication. If required, during premediation sessions.
- Using a Nondirective Style of Mediation.
- Face-to-Face Seating of Victim and Offender. Unless inappropriate because of culture of parties or individual request.
- Recognizing and Using the Power of Silence.
- Conducting Follow-up Sessions.

Centering

A humanistic mediation model emphasizes the importance of the mediator clearing away the clutter in his or her own life so that he or she can focus intensely on the needs of the involved parties. Prior to initiating contact between people in conflict, the mediator(s) is encouraged to take a few moments of silence, through reflection, meditation, or prayer, to reflect on the deeper meaning of his or her peacemaking work and the needs of the people in conflict. The centering of the mediator throughout the entire process of preparation and mediation also helps the parties in conflict to experience it as a safe, if not sacred, journey toward genuine dialogue and healing. Through the practice of centering, the humanistic mediator is more likely to stay grounded in a deeper sense of spirituality that recognizes the interconnectedness of all people (regardless of our many differences) as well as the sacred gift of human existence.

Reframing the Mediator's Role. Tapping into the full power of mediation in resolving important interpersonal conflict reframes the mediator's role. Instead of actively and efficiently guiding the parties toward a settlement, the mediator assists the parties to enter a dialogue with each other, to experience each other as fellow human beings, despite their conflict, and to seek ways to help them come to understand and respect their differences and to arrive at a mutually acceptable way to deal with those differences. This may or may not involve a formal written settlement agreement. Once the parties are engaged in a face-to-face conversation, the mediator intentionally gets out of the way. For example, the mediator might pull his or her chair back further away from the table and adopt a more informal posture. It should be noted that rarely does the mediator totally get out of the way, never saying anything or intervening to redirect communication. This is especially true during the later stages of mediation when the parties in conflict may need assistance to construct a formal settlement agreement if one is needed. In all cases, it is important for the mediator to provide a brief closing statement that thanks the parties for their work and schedules a follow-up meeting if necessary.

Conducting Premediation Sessions. Routine use of premediation separate sessions with the involved parties should become a standard practice. These individual sessions should occur at least a week or more before the mediation session. Collection of information, assessment of the conflict, description of the mediation program, and clarification of expectations are important tasks to complete. The first and most important task, however, is that of establishing trust and rapport with the involved parties. The development of trust and rapport enhances any dialogue process, but is particularly beneficial in intense interpersonal conflicts. For this reason, the mediator needs to get into a listening mode as quickly as possible during the initial meeting, inviting the involved parties to tell their stories of the conflict and how it affects them. Clearly explaining how the mediation process works and what they might expect to experience will likely put the involved parties at ease.

Connecting with the Parties. A far greater emphasis needs to be placed on the mediator establishing a connection with the parties in the conflict. Instead of viewing mediators as technicians who are emotionally distant and uninvolved with no prior contact with the involved parties, emphasis would be placed on mediators establishing trust and rapport with the involved parties before bringing them to a joint session. A mediator does not need to lose his or her impartiality in order to effectively connect with the involved parties before bringing them together. The art of mediation, as well as teaching, nursing, therapy, and social work, is found in connecting with people at a human level through the expression of empathy, warmth, and authenticity. The late Virginia Satir, a world-renowned family therapist, teacher, and trainer, recognized the supreme importance of the "presence" of the therapist. Authentic human connection was regarded by Satir as being fundamental to change processes (Gold, 1993). Making contact with people on a basic human level requires "congruence," a condition of being emotionally honest with yourself in which there is consistency in your words, feelings, body and facial expressions, and your actions. Authentic connection with others, through therapy or mediation, first requires looking inward. According to Satir (1976), there are four key questions.

1. How do I feel about myself? (self-esteem)
2. How do I get my meaning across to others? (communication)
3   How do I treat my feelings? (rules)
    *   Do I own them or put them on someone else?
    *   Do I act as though I have feelings that I do not or as though I don't have feelings that I really do?
4. How do I react to doing things that are new and different? (taking risks)

The process of connecting with those involved in mediation takes energy. As Satir points out, "making real contact means that we make ourselves responsible for what comes out of us." Although Satir developed her concepts of making contact and congruence within the context of family therapy, her material is highly relevant to a humanistic model of mediation. Humanistic mediators can have a powerful presence with their clients, as Virginia Satir did, through a more spiritual understanding of life that embraces the connectedness of all people along with the connectedness of the mediator's actions and belief system with the core of his or her being.

Building on the earlier work of Virginia Satir, Lois Gold (former chair of the Academy of Family Mediators) identifies four specific elements of presence that can increase the effectiveness of mediators: (1) being centered, (2) being connected to one's governing values and beliefs and highest purpose, (3) making contact with the humanity of the clients, and (4) being congruent (Gold, 1993).

Identifying and Tapping into Parties' Strengths. When people become engaged in conflict, it is common for them to communicate and interact in highly dysfunctional ways. The careless expression of intense anger and bitterness along with the inability to listen to the other party or effectively communicate their own needs can mask many strengths that they may have. It is the mediator's task, during separate premediation sessions, to learn the communication style of each party and identify specific strengths that may directly assist in the mediation-dialogue process and to encourage the expression of those strengths in mediation. An example would be a mediator discovering that an individual has a difficult time responding to questions of a global, if not abstract, nature, such as "How are you feeling about all of this?" When asked more concrete questions related to the individuals specific experience, however, he or she may feel quite comfortable responding. Tapping into the strengths of individuals and coaching them in how to effectively communicate their feelings can contribute greatly to the mediator's ability to use a nondirective style of mediation as noted in the following section.

Coaching on Communication. The open expression of feelings related to the conflict is central to a humanistic mediation model. Because of the extreme intensity of those feelings, it may become necessary during the separate premediation session for the mediator to coach the disputant on helpful ways of communicating those feelings so that they can be heard by the other party. Coaching one or both parties on the communication of intense and potentially hurtful feelings may be required. This coaching focuses on how to own one's feelings rather than projecting them onto the other party. Projecting intense feelings through aggressive communications often will trigger defensiveness in one or both parties and shut down honest dialogue. To avoid this, the speaker needs to own his or her feelings and communicate them as an "I" statement rather than attacking the other party. Furthermore, through coaching the mediator works to help identify and tap into the strengths of each of the parties in conflict, despite any emotional baggage that is present. In the process of coaching, however, the mediator is careful not to suggest what specifically should be said.

Nondirective Style of Mediation. The practice of humanistic mediation requires a nondirective style of mediation in which the mediator assists the involved parties in a process of dialogue and mutual aid, of helping each other through the direct sharing of feelings and information about the conflict with little interruption by the mediator. The mediator opens the session and sets a tone that will encourage the parties in conflict to feel safe, understand the process, and talk directly to each other. The mediator's ability to fade into the background is directly related to having connected with the parties before the joint session and having secured their trust. Without routine use of one or more separate pre-mediation meetings with the parties in conflict, it is unlikely that a truly nondirective style of mediation can be employed. It is also unlikely that the parties will be able to participate in a process of dialogue and mutual aid unless they trust the mediator, are prepared for the process with clear expectations, and feel safe and reasonably comfortable.

A nondirective style of mediation is not meant to be confused with a passive style in which the mediator provides little direction, leadership, or assistance. Instead, the mediator remains in control of the process and, although saying little, is actively involved nonverbally in the encounter and is able to respond or intervene at any point required, particularly when people get stuck and indicate a need for assistance. By setting a clear and comfortable tone, the parties are put at ease so that they can talk directly to each other and a far more empowering and mutually expressive form of mediation can then be experienced by the involved parties. This style of mediation, which can only be used effectively if the mediator conducts separate premediation sessions, will frequently result in the mediator saying very little after the opening statement.

Face-to-Face Seating of Involved Parties. Seating arrangements during a mediation session are important. Routine use of a seating arrangement in which the involved parties are sitting across from each other, allowing for natural eye contact, is central to the process of direct communications and dialogue. If a table is required, the mediator(s) would be at the end and the parties in conflict would sit across from each other. A major blockage to mediator-assisted dialogue and mutual aid occurs when the involved parties are seated next to each other behind a table facing the mediator, who is on the other side of the table. A clear exception to this arrangement is when, because of the culture of one or both parties or personal preference, such seating would create discomfort, if not offensiveness, and therefore would be inappropriate.

Recognizing and Using the Power of Silence. Moments of silence in the process of dialogue and conflict resolution are inherent to a nondirective style of mediation. Recognizing, using, and feeling comfortable with the power of silence (qualities that are more commonly found in non-Western cultures, as noted previously) is important to the humanistic mediation process. By honoring silence and patiently resisting the urge to interrupt silence with guidance or questions (by, for example, slowly counting to ten before speaking), the mediator is more consistently able to assist the involved parties in experiencing mediation as a process of dialogue and mutual aid—a journey of the heart in harmony with the head.

Conducting Follow-up Sessions. Follow-up joint sessions between the parties in conflict are central to a humanistic mediation model. Because of the nature of conflict and human behavior, problems are often far too complex to resolve in only one session, particularly when the conflict involves an important relationship. Oftentimes, the full range of issues and concerns cannot be addressed in only one session. Even in those cases when the conflict is largely resolved in one session, conducting a follow-up session several months later to assess how the agreement is holding or to resolve any issues that may have emerged can be important in the overall process of healing and closure.

The paradigm of healing

A humanistic, dialogue-driven model of mediation is grounded in what Lois Gold (1993) describes as a paradigm of healing. She identifies twelve characteristics that differentiate the paradigm of healing from the more well-entrenched paradigm of problem solving with its settlement-driven emphasis (see Table 3.2.1).

Table 3.2.1. Comparison of Problem-Solving and Humanistic Mediation

	Classic Problem-Solving Mediation	Humanistic-Transformative Mediation
Primary focus	Settlement driven and problem focused.	Dialogue driven and relationship focused.
Preparation of parties in conflict	Mediator has no separate contact with involved parties prior to mediation. Intake staff person collects information.	Mediator conducts at least one face-to-face meeting with each party prior to joint mediation session. Focus is on listening to their stories, building rapport, explaining the process, and clarifying expectations.
Role of mediator	Directs and guides the communication of the involved parties toward a mutually acceptable settlement of the conflict.	Prepares the involved parties prior to bringing them together so that they have realistic expectations and feel safe enough to engage in a direct conversation with each other facilitated by the mediator.
Style of mediation	Active and often very directive; mediator speaks frequently during the mediation session and asks many questions.	Mediator is very nondirective during the mediation session. After opening statement mediator fades into the background and is reluctant to interrupt direct conversation between parties. Mediator is not, however, passive, and will intervene if parties indicate a need.
Orientation to emotional context of conflict	Low tolerance for expressions of feelings and the parties' story-telling related to the history and context of the conflict.	Mediator encourages open expression of feelings and discussion of the context and history of the conflict. Recognizes the intrinsic healing quality of storytelling when speaking and listening from the heart.

Moments of silence	Few moments of silence. Mediator is uncomfortable with silence and feels the need to speak or ask questions of the parties.	Many prolonged moments of silence. Mediator is reluctant to interrupt silence and honors silence as integral to genuine empowerment and healing.
Written agreements	Primary goal and most likely outcome of mediation. Agreements focus on clear, tangible elements.	Secondary to the primary goal of dialogue and mutual aid (the parties helping each other through the sharing of information and expression of feelings). Agreements may often focus on symbolic gestures, personal growth tasks, or affirmations of the new relationship between the parties.

1. Demonstrating caring, nonjudgmental acceptance of the person's humanity
2. Building rapport and emotional connection . . . "being there"
3. Helping people listen to their innate wisdom, their preference for peace
4. Generating hope . . . "with support, you can do it"
5. Tapping into the universal desire for wellness
6. Speaking from the heart
7. Thinking of clients in their woundedness, not their defensive posture
8. Being real and congruent
9. Creating safe space for dialogue
10. Creating a sacred space
11. Recognizing that a healing presence does not "fix it"
12. Understanding that a healing presence acknowledges brokenness and shares the journey.

Although this conceptual framework has grown out of her extensive experience as a family therapist and mediator, the paradigm of healing presented by Gold (1993) has enormous implications for humanistic mediation practice in any context in which the nature of the conflict relates to broken relationships. This is particularly so in those cases in which one or both parties are grieving the loss of a relationship that once existed, whether this was among colleagues at work, friends, spouses, partners, parents and children, or neighbors. It is also highly relevant in response to the needs of many crime victims and offenders who, although most often unknown to each other, are suddenly in a type of situationally induced relationship (certainly not by the victim's choice) because of the nature of the criminal act and its effect on their lives. Crime victims, particularly in more serious offenses, often are grieving the loss of a sense of safety, if not invulnerability, that has been shattered because of what has occurred. Understanding and practicing humanistic mediation in the context of the paradigm of healing offered by Gold (1993) is ultimately grounded in a profound recognition of the precious gift of human existence, relationships, community, and the deeper spiritual connectedness among all of us in our collective journey through this life, regardless of our many religious, cultural, political, and lifestyle differences. Lois Gold describes the language of healing as the language of the soul, not the language of problem solving.

Conclusion

The dominant model of settlement-driven mediation in Western culture is clearly beneficial to many people in conflict and superior to the adversarial legal process and court system in most cases. Using a different model, one that embraces the importance of spirituality, compassionate strength, and our common humanity, holds even greater potential. As an expression of the transformative power of conflict resolution, a humanistic mediation model can lay the foundation for a greater sense of community and social harmony. With its focus on the intrinsic healing power of mediation and dialogue, this model can bring a more complete resolution to the conflict. Through a process of dialogue and mutual aid between the involved parties, humanistic mediation practice facilitates the achievement of outer peace. It addresses and often resolves the presenting conflict while also facilitating a journey of the heart so that participants may find inner peace. Real peace is the true goal of humanistic mediation.

Part 4

Corporate crime and state crime victims

by Sandra Walklate

Interest in this kind of victimization largely stems from the work of Quinney (1972) who asked the provocative question: who is the victim of crime? Quinney was primarily interested in extending the criminological agenda to include the kinds of crimes for the most part not recognized as criminal, like for example, crimes committed by the state, by agents of the state, or 'crimes' that were simply the product of what were considered to be a normal and routine result of what happens in the work place (like infringements of health and safety legislations). His question, who is the victim of crime, was embraced by two influential criminologists: Reiman in the United States whose book *The Rich Get Rich and the Poor Get Prison* (1979) (now in its 8th edition) set out a hard-hitting agenda that, for example, compared the chances of being murdered with the chances of dying at the hand of the surgeon's knife in which the surgeon might be deemed culpable. It made salutary reading. In the UK, Box's *Power, Crime and Mystification* (1983), an extract from which constitutes the first reading in this section of the book, outlined similar concerns.

Much of the work within this kind of victimology embraces this wider understanding of what counts as crime, who might be labelled the criminal, and as a consequence, who the victim of crime is, and is largely associated with what has been called 'radical victimology'. This version of victimology has struggled to maintain a presence within victimological studies since the work of Quinney (1972), however, its concern with state crime and corporate crime is clearly a legitimate one. Elias (1986, 1993) has linked this concern with the human rights agenda. As Elias (1985: 17) has stated, 'a victimology which encompassed human rights would not divert attention from crime victims and their rights, but would rather explore their inextricable relationship to more human rights concerns'. Indeed such a victimology has clear links with not only what might be understood as criminal but also has clear links with the policy agenda, like for example the move to introduce legislation to address 'corporate manslaughter, but also victims', organizations, like for example

Amnesty International. So this version of victimology shares in all the characteristics of mainstream victimology (discussed in Part 6) in relation to its policy and campaign links but has a much broader focus on who the victim of crime might be.

The extract from Box focuses our attention not only on what might be considered to be a radical criminological agenda but is also suggestive of a radical victimological agenda that is presumed in the question asked by Quinney (1972) and suggested in the previous paragraph. The headings used by Box send a clear message: corporate crime kills, corporate crime injures, corporate crime robs, the social and economic costs of corporate crime. These messages, while still not at the forefront of criminological or victimological concerns, are now no longer as hidden from the victimological gaze as they once were. Whyte (2007), for example, in exploring the relevance of corporate killing, estimates that over 24,000 people in England and Wales are 'murdered' as a result of the activities of business corporations: a concern that increasingly preoccupies both the theoretical, policy and activist agendas that are illustrated in the three readings that follow.

Kauzlarich et al. (2001) reopened the theoretical argument for a radical victimology, begun by Quinney (1972) in proposing a 'victimology of state crime'. This framework defines crime victims as

> Individuals or groups of individuals who have experienced economic, cultural, or physical harm, pain, exclusion, or exploitation, because of tacit or explicit state actions or policies which violate law or generally defined human rights.
>
> (Kauzlarich et al., 2001: 176)

They go on to suggest that ratified international law, domestic law, and human rights standards can be used to look to the criminal activities of the state and produce a fourfold typology that might be used to iterate the nature of victimization by the state. From this they generate six propositions that are designed to capture not only the extent of state crime, but also its hidden nature and who are most likely to be victimized as a result. So victims of state crime tend to be among the least socially powerful actors, victimizers generally fail to recognize and understand the nature, extent, and harmfulness of institutional policies, victims of state crime are often blamed for their suffering, victims of state crime must generally rely on the victimizer, an associated institution or civil social movements for redress, victims of state crime are easy targets for repeated victimization, illegal state policies and practices, while committed by individuals and groups of individuals, are manifestations of the attempt to achieve organizational, bureaucratic or institutional goals (Kauzlarich et al., 2001: 183–9) As the authors acknowledge, taking this kind of victimization into account is not without its problems. As Box (1983: 17) observed, 'the majority of those suffering from corporate crime remain unaware of their victimisation – either not knowing it has happened to them or viewing their "misfortune" as an accident or "no ones fault" '. A phenomenon Geis (1973) referred to as 'victim responsiveness'.

The extract from Braithwaite's *Restorative Justice and Responsive Regulation* (2002) asks the question: what can be done about corporate crime? Braithwaite starts from the position that it is first important to understand how well citizens or corporations are regulating themselves before stepping in with legislation to strengthen such regulation. Quoting his own earlier position he states that 'the hard question is how to decide when to punish and when to persuade' (p. 29). It is his view that this is the question that needs to be addressed whether we are thinking about a hardened burglar or a multi-national corporation. He argues that the regulatory pyramid offers a solution to the problem of when to punish and when to persuade and suggests that business regulatory processes contemporarily employ aspects of this pyramid in their practices since they recognize that sometimes punishment works and sometimes persuasion does. What this pyramid does is put restorative justice at its base thus giving it the privileged position of being the first response available. This reflects Braithwaite's view that restorative justice works better with the threat of punishment in the background rather than such a threat being in the foreground. Structured in this way the interests of the victim are best served since remorse, apology and forgiveness can be put to the fore: these are values that, in Braithwaite's view, can transform people's lives. It is interesting to note that these were the values embraced by the Truth and Reconciliation Commission commented on by Hamber (2002) that clearly worked for some people but not for all and the reader might like to reflect upon whether or not part of that failure was as a result of the rather stark relationship between persuasion and punishment that was embedded with the Commission's work. It is Braithwaite's view, however, that 'what the restorative and responsive position argues is not just that restorative justice is more effective that punitive justice. It is that restorative justice at the base of a regulatory pyramid increases the efficacy of punitive justice as well' (p. 42). In his view this is the case in the context of corporate criminal activity as with any other kind of more conventionally recognized criminal activity.

A knotty problem stalks those committed to restorative justice, however. That problem raises a similar question to that posed by Hamber when he asks: what do we mean by reconciliation? Here the question posed is: what do we mean by restorative? How do we know when an apology is genuinely and authentically given and genuinely and authentically received? This is especially the case when such giving and receiving is conducted in front of a third party? As Tavuchis's (1991: 122) analysis of different modes of apology highlights, 'If [as I have argued] sorrow is the energizing forces of apology, then what moves the offended party to forgive? In historical and cross-cultural terms, what is deemed forgivable and unforgivable?' Given the global presences of restorative justice these are good questions.

So these readings provide a flavour of the kinds of work that has endeavoured to embrace the victim of corporate and state crime. Not all the writers whose work is presented here would by any means claim the label 'radical victimologist' but the focus of their work clearly gels with the need for a 'victimology of state crime' as suggested by Kauzlarich et al. (2001). Since the pioneering work of Box (1983) it is fair to say that there is greater recognition of this kind of criminal victimization both within the academy and within the sphere of policy. However, the relative invisibility of both the nature and extent of victimization of this kind remains a problem (see for example the discussion by Whyte, 2007), that means that the possibilities of responsive regulation notwithstanding, much of corporate and state crime remains beyond regulation of any kind, and the victims of such neglected. These processes serve to remind us of how successful the assumptions that underpin who counts as a legitimate victim and thus who has a claim on victim status are. Little has served to undermine Christie's (1986) conceptualization of the 'ideal victim', the rise and rise of what Furedi (2002) has called the 'cult of victimhood' notwithstanding. In order to become a victim, claim victim status, and engage in any regulatory processes, people have to know of their victimization. For those who may be victims of corporate or state crime this is still a huge barrier to them moving on with their lives.

Recommended further reading

Quinney, R. (1972) 'Who is the victim?', *Criminology*, 10: 309–29.
Reiman, J. (1979) *The Rich Get Rich and the Poor Get Prison*. New York: Allyn and Bacon.
Whyte, D. (2007) 'Victims of corporate crime', in S. Walklate (ed.), *Handbook of Victims and Victimology*. Cullompton: Willan.

4.1

Corporate crime kills
by S. Box

Whereas a person involved in the American *Mafia* could say, quite reasonably, 'what's all the fuss about, we only kill each other', the same could not be said in defence of some corporate crimes. When these result in avoidable death, and they do, then it could be anyone who just happens to be there – employees, consumers, ordinary citizens. Thus, in September, 1976, a fire aboard HMS Glasgow, which was at the time undergoing repairs in the Swan Hunter shipyard, resulted in the death of eight workers. The fire was the result of the company failing to provide a proper safe environment for such work (Health and Safety Executive 1980: 15). Following a hoist accident at the power station Littlebrook Dee, Kent, on 1 September, 1978, four people died and five were seriously injured. The cause of this was identified as the company's neglect of safety equipment (Health and Safety Commission 1980: 16). In 1972 at Buffalo Creek, West Virginia, 125 people were killed when a carelessly maintained dam burst (Stern 1976: 3) and at Willow Island, West Virginia, fifty-one people died when a cooling tower collapsed as a result of safety violations (Kennedy 1978). Early in 1979, fifty people lost their lives as a result of an explosion aboard the tanker Betelgeuse whilst it was anchored at Bantry Bay in County Cork. An Inquiry headed by an Irish High Court Judge, Mr Justice Declan Costello firmly placed the responsibility for this on two corporations, Total and Gulf, 'who deliberately decided not to carry out necessary repair work costing a mere £130,000 because they intended to sell the tanker' (*The Observer* 27.7.80: 2). Similar considerations appear to have preyed on the minds of Ford executives during the early 1970s. According to Dowie (1977), this auto-company sold the Pinto model for a period of six years even though they knew from their own test researchers that the product, which had been rushed from design to production in the short period of twenty-five months instead of the planned forty-three, was dangerous. The trouble was the improperly designed fuel tank; this tended to fracture, particularly after rear-end collisions. Dowie claims that between 500 and 900 burn deaths resulted from ensuing explosions. During the period 1969–79 there were, according to the Department of Energy, 106 fatalities on or around installations in the British sector of the North Sea. According to Carson (1981) many of these were avoidable and only occurred because safety standards which applied to onshore industries did not apply to offshore installations. In 1976 twenty-six men died in the Scotia mine, which was unsafe and had been the subject of 652 citing-for-violations of safety regulations (Caudill 1977). And so on . . .

Corporate crime injures

In the early 1960s over 300 consumers suffered adverse side effects from taking the chemical MER/29 which was advertised as medically beneficial to heart sufferers. These 300 suffered from a series of various iatrogenic complaints, including occasional disruption of the reproductive system, loss of hair or a change in its colour and texture, and a variety of eye disorders including the development of cataracts. Ungar (1973) alleges that the test results on which Merrell secured permission from the Federal Drug Administration to market the chemical substance were proven to be 'doctored', thus concealing the extent to which the company knew of the drug's adverse side-effects. But this example of corporate induced injury pales beside one which followed closely afterwards. As a consequence of taking the prescribed drug thalidomide, something like 8,000 pregnant mothers in the United States, Germany, Japan, Britain, Ireland, Sweden, Australia, Canada, Brazil, Italy, and Spain gave birth to monstrously deformed babies. The company which had discovered and later granted licences for the drug, Chemie Grunenthal of Germany, had criminal charges brought against them for deliberately falsifying the test data and concealing the truth about the drug's serious side effects (Sunday Times Insight Team 1979).

Not only are many consumers injured by corporate crime; thousands of employees too suffer from 'accidents' at work (which are in fact not pure accidents but events which spring directly from the conditions of production and are in that sense avoidable) or work-induced diseases, such as asbestosis, lung cancer, and mesothelioma.

Corporate crime robs

For seven years prior to 1961, twenty-nine electrical corporations, including some of the best known names in the country, such as General Electric and Westinghouse, conspired illegally to fix prices on large, mainly government contracts, so as to avoid competition and hence reap enormous illegal profit (Geis 1967; Smith 1961). In July 1977, Revco Drug Stores, one of America's largest discount drug chains, was found guilty of computer-generated double-billing schemes that resulted in the loss of over a half-million dollars in Medicaid funds to the Ohio Department of Public Welfare (Vaughan 1980). A well known Swiss-based pharmaceutical company was suspected by the British government of overcharging the National Health Service for the drug Valium; their agreement to repay £4.5 millions tacitly admitted guilt but not what proportion of their 'extra-legal' profits this sum represented. But these and other financial swindles pale into insignificance when compared to the Equity Funding Scandal (Blundell 1978; Dirks and Gross 1974; Soble and Dallos 1974). The directors and executives of Equity Funding simply made up insurance policies to inflate the company's business and hence improve its share prices. When the whistle was finally blown on the crime by a disgruntled ex-employee, thousands of policy-holders and share-holders simply lost all or a substantial part of their savings or expected pensions, amounting to somewhere between two and three billion dollars.

All the above *examples* of deaths, injuries, and economic losses caused by corporate acts are not the antics of one or two evil, or mentally disturbed, or relatively deprived senior employees. Rather they represent the rational choices of high-ranking employees, acting in the corporation's interests, to *intend* directly to violate the criminal law or governmental regulations, or to be *indifferent* to the outcome of their action or inaction, even though it might result in human lives obliterated, bodies mangled, or life-savings lost.

The physical, economic, and social costs of corporate crime

The physical effects of corporate misbehaviour are difficult to quantify precisely. But if what is sought is merely a gross comparison between the damage of corporate and 'conventional' crimes, then the current level of official information available provides sufficient facts to get the ratio in perspective. Thus workers die of *avoidable* industrial diseases and accidents, and it is sobering to compare these with the conventional crime of homicide. Reiman (1979: 75) estimates that in 1972 the number of persons in the USA dying from occupational hazards (diseases and accidents) was 114,000, whereas only 20,600 died from being shot, cut, beaten, or poisoned, and being recorded as a homicide case. If there were a time clock for murder, it would show one every twenty-six minutes. But as Reiman so graphically points out:

> 'If a similar crime clock for industrial deaths were constructed . . . and recalling that this clock ticks only for that half of the population that is in the labour force – this clock would show an industrial death about every four and a half minutes! In other words, in the time it takes for one murder on the crime clock, six workers have died "just trying to make a living"!'

> (Reiman 1979: 68)

A similarly disturbing picture emerges if we consider the relevant data for Britain. In the table below (*Table 4.1.1*), which shows data for the years 1973–79, the combined number of employees dying from fatal accidents or occupational diseases (most of which are avoidable if employing corporations obeyed government regulations and designed safe production schedules or paid for hazard-free work environments) far exceed the number of homicide cases recorded by the police. Furthermore, this comparison becomes even more shocking when it is remembered that the population at risk of being killed at work is *less than half* those who could be 'murdered'. In other words, to obtain an initial fair comparison we would have to multiply the industrial related deaths by at least a factor of two and compare that figure with the number of recorded homicide cases. The result is approximately seven to one!

But even this ratio puts the *best possible* light on the contribution made by employment to the avoidable death toll. For although we can be fairly sure that the recorded homicide figure is reasonably valid, we cannot have the same confidence in the data on occupationally related deaths. The cause of death is frequently ambiguous and pinning it down to occupational environments, which may have been experienced years or even decades ago, is clearly no easy matter. Furthermore, in the processes of socially constructing

Table 4.1.1 Homicides finally recorded by the police compared with fatal occupational accidents and deaths from occupational diseases, England and Wales, 1973–79

	1 fatal occupational accidents[1]	2 deaths from occupational diseases[2]	3 col. 1 plus col. 2	4 deaths finally recorded as homicides by the police[3]
1973	873	910	1,783	391
1974	786	911	1,697	526
1975	729	957	1,686	444
1976	682	976	1,658	489
1977	614	916	1,530	418
1978	751	866	1,617	472
1979	711	752	1,463	551
total	5,146	6,290	11,436	3,291
adjusted for population at risk (approx)			22,872 7	: 1

[1] Health and Safety Executive (1980) *Health and Safety Statistics, 1977*. London: HMSO, p. 4 and (1981) *Health and Safety Statistics, 1978/9*. London: HMSO, p. 12
[2] Health and Safety Executive (1980) p. 58 and Health and Safety Executive (1981) p. 63
[3] *Criminal Statistics England and Wales, 1980*, London: HMSO, p. 61 (Murder, Manslaughter, etc.)

the cause(s) of death, there are considerable social forces directed towards minimizing the number of deaths certified as occupationally induced.

Since such fatalities are frequently *avoidable*, each one is an indictment of corporate practices, and consequently wherever pressure can be brought to bear, either in the process of recognizing a fatal disease-causing work condition or in the enforcement practices, corporate officials will lean towards favouring those definitions and arrangements which minimize the recording of deaths as arising from occupational hazards. Thus executives have successfully prevented most forms of cancer from being included in the list of occupationally-induced illness, even though the documentation on carcinogenic work environments is substantial (Epstein 1979).

In the endeavour to minimize the contributions work environments make to avoidable fatalities, state officials also play a significant part. They will probably err on the side of caution whenever attempting to unravel the cause of death because recording it as occupationally induced requires the subsequent payment of industrial death benefits. Evidence consistent with this view came to light recently whilst Yorkshire TV was making a documentary on asbestos. It discovered 'that death certificates often do not mention asbestos diseases even when the coroner has conclusive and documented evidence that they were the cause of death. As a consequence, spouses and relatives have been prevented from claiming compensation' (Cutler 1982).

These two forces tend to depress the level of recorded occupationally induced death below a level it would be otherwise. Therefore, to re-echo Reiman: you stand more chance of being killed *avoidably* at work than in any other sphere of your life, including being at home!

But don't feel safe staying at home! The long arm of the corporation's grim reaper is not deterred by such agoraphobic precautions. Consumers may be poisoned in their beds by improperly tested medical drugs, they may be killed over their dinner tables by unhygienically prepared food, they may be blown up to God knows where by the neighbourhood chemical complex exploding, and they may become fatally diseased in their living rooms by industrial pollution. For example, a recent chilling national survey of pollution and its chronic effects on the lives and deaths of American citizens concluded that approximately 9 per cent of all deaths, that is, 140,000 a year, may be attributable to air pollution.

It was because of this shocking rate of avoidable death that the British Society for the Social Responsibility of Science published *Asbestos – Killer Dust* in 1979. In this report, it accused the asbestos industry of deliberately pursuing profit in the face of known dangers, and 'in the light of the damage done to people working in the industry and likely to occur in the future, . . . it is simply incredible' that nothing much is done about it. It concluded that those responsible should be treated like criminals who allow dangerous cars on the road. But it is clear from the Asbestos Advisory Council's latest Report (1980) that this will not happen, so they remain, in Swartz's (1975) chilling words, 'silent killers at work', far more deadly than the phantom killer of the opera. But unfortunately this is not how most people see it. When they think of mass murderers, they normally think of one person killing unlawfully a handful of other people. But when many people die from known carcinogenic work-conditions or their employer's refusal to put right unsafe equipment, machinery, or buildings, this is normally seen as a 'disaster', even though their deaths were easily avoidable. In the case of asbestos for example, there has been a voluminous medical literature on its direct link with asbestosis, lung cancer, and mesothelioma. Of course employers can claim unawareness of obscure medical journals. But during a series of lawsuits against Johns-Manville, Pittsburgh Corning, and other asbestos manufacturers, it was revealed that they did know directly from their own scientific researchers whose implicatory findings were suppressed (Ermann and Lundmann 1982: 68–9).

Maybe the only, but significant difference between the two is that corporate crimes 'kill more people than are murdered by acts that come to be listed as criminal homicide in the (American) Uniform Crime Rates' (Geis 1975: 93).

On the occasions when corporate negligence, indifference, or apathy does not result in employees, consumers, or the public being killed, it often leaves them seriously injured or ill. Thus in Britain from 1973 to 1979 there was an annual average of 330,000 non-fatal accidents at work. The vast bulk of these were not caused by employees' carelessness or stupidity but by the conditions under which they are obliged to work. These put pressure on employees to take risks – even violating the corporation's own safety standards. But in this contradiction between productivity and safety, between speed and conformity to regulations, which does the corporation prioritize? A clear answer is given in Carson's (1981) analysis of the other price paid for North Sea oil. He claims that when oil companies were faced with the contradictory demand for speedy exploration and extraction and the requirements of safety they, with successive British governments' blessing, chose speed. Consequently most accidents, and there were nearly 500 of them during the 1970s, were not the result of employee thoughtlessness but emerged directly out of the contradictory demands made upon the workforce. Also during the period 1973–79, there was an annual average of nearly 14,000 persons diagnosed as suffering from an occupationally induced disease. The number of persons injured or made ill at work far exceeds the number against whom indictable crimes of violence, including rape and indecent assault, were committed. Thus in 1977 over 340,000 persons at work in the UK suffered through accidents and occupationally-induced ill health compared with 93,500 persons victimized by indictable crimes of violence. If we multiply the former figure by a factor of two to obtain a roughly comparable population at risk size, we arrive at a ratio of seven to one in favour (*sic*) of work-induced avoidable suffering. The magnitude of this ratio, rather than the exact validity of the aggregate figures on which it is based, ought to be stressed, for it reveals just how much more objective damage is caused to persons at work than members of the public experience through 'conventional' criminal violence.

But even these comparisons understate the excessive amount of corporate-induced death and suffering because they omit any reference to consumers *physically* harmed by the sale of improperly researched substances, dangerous or poisonous products, and so on, or citizens physically harmed through industrial air pollution. According to the American National Commission on Product Safety (1971: 1) approximately 20 millions out of a total population of over 250 million are seriously injured annually by consumer products, with 110,000 resulting in permanent disability and 30,000 resulting in death. And according to the American National Cancer Institute, one of the major causes of lung cancer is 'neighbourhood air pollution from industrial sources of inorganic arsenic' (Reiman 1979: 78). Other types of cancer were also found to be higher in geographical areas where chemical plants were situated.

So if consumer and citizen avoidable death and injury were added to workers avoidably killed and injured, then the ratio between corporate criminal violence and 'conventional' criminal violence would clearly put the former in an extremely unfavourable light. Indeed, it would be seen as a major source of avoidable and illegal human suffering. This conclusion should not be seen to reflect callous indifference to individuals who have suffered miserably or fatally at the hands of persons committing 'conventional' crimes; their agony is real and should never be ignored. But neither should we enable this sympathy to blind us to the greater truth that more persons suffer, many fatally, from corporate crime than 'conventional' crime. If we are to prioritize the study and publicization of one, surely it should be that which, in objective terms, causes more human suffering rather than the other which is *perceived* by the public to be the more serious even though they are clearly wrong.

In *Pretty Boy Floyd*, Woody Guthrie caught poetically the awesome and terrifying instrument through which corporate officials economically harm others. He wrote:

> 'Now as through this world I ramble,
>   I see lots of funny men,
> Some rob you with a six gun,
>   And some with a fountain pen.'

This irony was not lost on a US judge. 'In our complex society', he said, 'the accountant's certificate and the lawyer's opinion can be instruments for inflicting pecuniary loss more potent than the chisel or crowbar' (Morgenthau 1969: 17).

Robbing others, directly or indirectly, is a major form of corporate criminal activity. Price fixing (Geis 1967; Smith 1961) and illegal monopoly
pricing (Klass 1975) both mean that customers pay more than they would
under competitive conditions; bribing corrupt officials (Braithwaite 1979b;
Jacoby, Nehemlis, and Ells 1977) may mean reducing competitors' profit
margins or even driving them into bankruptcy; illegal mergers and take-overs
and other shady financial manoeuvres may result in many shareholders being
defrauded (Hopkins 1980b); misleading advertising as well as trimming production costs may result in customers buying goods whose quality fails totally
to match manufacturers' glossy claims, thus leaving a swindled consumer
population (Moffit 1976); corporate tax evasion and avoidance may mean
more average taxes paid by individual members of the public (Vanick 1977).

Given the relative invisibility of these crimes, even to those victimized,
the fact that they are infrequently reported to or detected by relevant authorities, the absence of any centralized data-collecting agency, and the inconsistent publication of those that are collected, it is impossible to quantify
with any accuracy just how serious corporate crime is in economic terms.
Furthermore, the figures involved are so astronomic as to be literally
incomprehensible. The public understands more easily what it means for an
old lady to have five pounds snatched from her purse than to grasp the
financial significance of 25 million customers paying one penny more for
orange juice diluted beyond the level permitted by law. The public tend to
focus more on the one penny than on the quarter of a million illegal profit
and conclude that the incident is insignificant. But it is not.

There have been attempts to estimate the economic cost of corporate
crimes and render these in a meaningful fashion (Bequai 1978: 1; Clinard
1978: 83–102; Conklin 1977: 2–8; Geis 1975: 95–7; Hills 1971: 167–68;
McCaghy 1976: 205; President's Task Force Report 1967: 47–51; Stotland
1977: 180–82). Although authors have arrived at different figures, thus
reflecting the inherent difficulty and speculative nature of the task involved,
they have been unanimous in one conclusion: persons are deprived of far
more money by corporate crimes than they are by ordinary economic crimes,
such as robbery, theft, larceny, and auto-theft. Conklin (1977: 4) estimates
that in 1977 these four offences in the USA accounted for between $3–4
billions compared with the annual loss of around $40 billions resulting from
various white-collar crime, of which consumer fraud, illegal competition, and
deceptive practices account for at least half. Johnson and Douglas (1978:
151) point out that the Equity Funding scandal, 'perhaps one of the largest
securities and investment frauds ever perpetuated on the American public,
. . . involved more losses than the total losses of *all* street crime in the US for
one year'. In a similar vein, Geis (1978: 281) writes that 'the heavy electrical
equipment price-fixing conspiracy alone involved theft from the American
people of more money than was stolen in all of the country's robberies,
burglaries, and larcenies during the years in which the price fixing occurred'.

Whether we are consumers or citizens, we stand more chance of being robbed by persons who roam corporate suites than we do by those who roam public streets. Furthermore, *in the aggregate* we stand to be robbed of far more by these fine gentlemen acting in the good name of their corporation than by the common rogues apparently acting from some morally worthless motive.

Finally, there are the social consequences of corporate crime compared with 'conventional' crime. A number of writers have recently argued very strongly that the *latter* is more corrosive to social life. Thus Wilson writes:

> 'Predatory crime does not merely victimize individuals, it impedes and, in the extreme case, even prevents the formation and maintenance of community. By disrupting the delicate nexus of ties, formal and informal, by which we are linked with our neighbours, crime atomizes society and makes of its members mere individual calculators estimating their own advantage, especially their own chances for survival amidst their fellows. Common undertakings become difficult except for those motivated by a shared desire for protection.'
>
> (Wilson 1975: 21)

And echoing this sentiment, a British criminologist claims:

> 'If the cities are to be saved as centres of a civilized urban life, and not plunged into gutted and fearful waste-lands . . . delinquency will have to be tackled as a problem with high priority – perhaps as *the* urban problem. City life cannot exist without security in its open spaces, some unarmed trust and reciprocity. In Britain . . . there is a mass exodus of skilled workers and middle class groups from the metropolis and other inner cities . . . these areas are left with heavily welfare-dependent populations; the old, the sick, the handicapped, the uneducated, the dull, the retarded, and the unskilled. What is not realized . . . is that although the movement from the cities has many other long-term causes, delinquency has now ceased to be merely a symptom of urban breakdown (if it ever was) . . . and has become a major contributor to it.'
>
> (Morgan 1978: 21)

Furthermore, she argues that unless some inroad is made now into reducing or containing the problem of street crime, the loss of community will spread outwards, like a cancerous growth, to desirable middle-class areas in the city.

At an abstract level, these arguments are probably true. Beyond historically determined levels of societal tolerance, crime is dysfunctional to social life. But the issue is, on which type of crime ought we to be concentrating? Surely the deleterious consequences street crime has on our sense of community pale beside the way in which corporate crime fractures the economic and political system. Thus Conklin, reiterating the President's Commission on Law Enforcement and Administration of Justice, writes that:

> 'such offences "are the most threatening of all – not just because they are so expensive, but because of their corrosive effect on the moral standards by which American business is conducted". Business crimes undermine public faith in the business system because such crime is integrated with "the structure of legitimate business". Such crime reduces willingness to engage in commercial transactions. Stock manipulations and frauds undermine the capitalist system, which requires public investment for capital. The discovery of fraud through adulteration and mislabelling of grain which is shipped abroad has created distrust among foreign businessmen who purchase grain from American companies.'
>
> (Conklin 1977: 7)

Writing on another type of corporate crime, Braithwaite argues that:

> 'Bribery and corruption by large corporations are most serious forms of crime because of their inegalitarian consequences. When a governmental official in a Third World country recommends (under the influence of a bribe) that his country purchase the more expensive but less adequate of two types of aircraft, then the extra millions of dollars will be found from the taxes sweated out of the country's impoverished citizens. For a mass consumer product, the million dollar bribe to the civil servant will be passed on in higher places to the consuming public. While it is conceivable that bribes can be used to secure the sale of a better and cheaper product, the more general effect is to shift the balance of business away from the most efficient producer and in favour of the most corrupt producer. The whole purpose of business-government bribes is after all, the inegalitarian purpose of enticing governments to act against the public interest and in the interests of the transnational. Every act of political corruption rewards corruptibility in politics and exacerbates the social selection into public office of those who are most adeptly corrupt. To the extent that politics and government administration become more corrupt, then to that extent will men and women of high principle find entry into politics repugnant. *Transnational corporate corruption is therefore perhaps the most pernicious form of crime in the world today because it involves robbing the poor to feed the rich, and brings into political power rulers and administrators who in general will put self-interest ahead of the public interest, and transnational corporation interest ahead of national interest.*'
>
> (Braithwaite 1979b: 126)

Whether one agrees with the sentiments expressed by Wilson and Morgan on the one hand or the President's Commission and Braithwaite on the other is not a matter of blind prejudice, but of weighing carefully the relevant evidence. From the evidence presented above – and this is merely illustrative of the evidence available – it should be clear that corporate crime ought to be a prioritized concern because it is the more serious. This concern should focus first on understanding 'how it is possible' for corporate crime to be endemic in our 'law and order' society, and second, and hopefully flowing from this understanding, 'how can it be contained or regulated?'

But before proceeding, a caveat needs to be made. Prioritizing corporate crime has to be set in context. It has been neglected relative to the study of conventional/street crime. To argue now for its prioritization means no more than demanding as much attention be given to it as there is to street crimes. There is no concealed value judgement here that street crimes are less of a social problem, particularly if the degree of fear and apprehension experienced by the majority of citizens is considered. Citizens in inner-city areas are desperately worried and rightly so, about street crime. That terrain, so proudly occupied by the radical Right's law and order campaigners, has to be won back, and Ian Taylor's (1982) recent attempt, following earlier sorties of Platt (1978) represents the appropriate move from the Left. But whilst the law and order debate ebbs and flows over the political terrain, there is a strategic need to establish a second front where radical criminology takes on corporate crimes and crimes of other powerful institutions and privileged people.

4.2

Responsive regulation
by J. Braithwaite

The basic idea of responsive regulation is that governments should be responsive to the conduct of those they seek to regulate in deciding whether a more or less interventionist response is needed (Ayres and Braithwaite 1992). In particular, law enforcers should be responsive to how effectively citizens or corporations are regulating themselves before deciding whether to escalate intervention. Responsive regulation is not only something governments can do; private actors in civil society can also regulate responsively, indeed, even regulate governments responsively (Gunningham and Grabosky 1998).

Regulatory formalism is the important contrast to responsive regulation. The formalist says to define in advance which problems require which response and write rules to mandate those responses. The formalist might say, for example, that armed robbery is a very serious evil. Therefore it should always be dealt with by taking it to court, and if guilt is proven, the offender must go to jail. Responsive regulation requires us to challenge such a presumption; if the offender is responding to the detection of her wrong-doing by turning around her life, kicking a heroin habit, helping victims, and voluntarily working for a community group "to make up for the harm she has done to the community," then the responsive regulator of armed robbery will say no to the jail option.

The problem many have with responsive regulation is that it is not designed to maximize consistency in law enforcement. Indeed, the idea of responsive regulation grew from dissatisfaction with the business regulation debate—some arguing that business people are rational actors who only understand the bottom line and therefore must be consistently punished for their lawbreaking, others that business people are responsible citizens and can be persuaded to come into compliance. In different contexts there is a lot of truth in both positions. This means that both consistent punishment and consistent persuasion are foolish strategies. The hard question is how to decide when to punish and when to persuade (Braithwaite 1985). What makes the question such a difficult one is that attempts to regulate conduct do not simply succeed or fail. As we will see in chapter 4, often they backfire, making compliance with the law much worse. So the tragedy of consistent punishment of wrongdoers of a certain type is that our consistency will regularly cause us to make things worse for future victims of the wrongdoing. In business regulation circles these days, there is not much contesting of the conclusion that consistent punishment of business noncompliance would be a bad policy, that persuasion is normally the better way to go when there is reason to suspect that cooperation with attempting to secure compliance will be forthcoming. But with individual criminal offending, there are still many who defend a consistent punishment policy, even though the meta-analyses of the effects of punishment suggest that increasing our investment in expanding criminal punishment increases somewhat the reoffending of those punished (Gendreau, Goggin, and Cullen 1999).

The regulatory pyramid

The most distinctive part of responsive regulation is the regulatory pyramid. It is an attempt to solve the puzzle of when to punish and when to persuade. At the base of the pyramid is the most restorative dialogue-based approach we can craft for securing compliance with a just law. Of course if it is a law of doubtful justice, we can expect the dialogue to be mainly about the justice of the law (and this is a good thing from a civic republican perspective). As we move up the pyramid, more and more demanding and punitive interventions in peoples' lives are involved. The idea of the pyramid is that our presumption should always be to start at the base of the pyramid, then escalate to somewhat punitive approaches only reluctantly and only when dialogue fails, and then escalate to even more punitive approaches only when the more modest forms of punishment fail. Figure 4.2.1 is an example of a responsive business regulatory pyramid from Ayres and Braithwaite (1992, p. 35). The regulator here escalates with the recalcitrant company from persuasion to a warning to civil penalties to criminal penalties and ultimately to corporate capital punishment—permanently revoking the company's license to operate.

The crucial point is that this is a dynamic model. It is not about specifying in advance which are the types of matters that should be dealt with at the base of the pyramid, which are the more serious ones that should be in the middle, and which are the most egregious ones for the peak of the pyramid. Even with the most serious matters—flouting legal obligations to operate a nuclear power plant safely that risks thousands of lives—we stick with the presumption that it is better to start with dialogue at the base of the pyramid. A presumption means that however serious the crime, our normal response is to try dialogue first for dealing with it, to override the presumption only if there are compelling reasons for doing do. Of course there will be such reasons at times—the man who has killed one hostage and threatens to kill

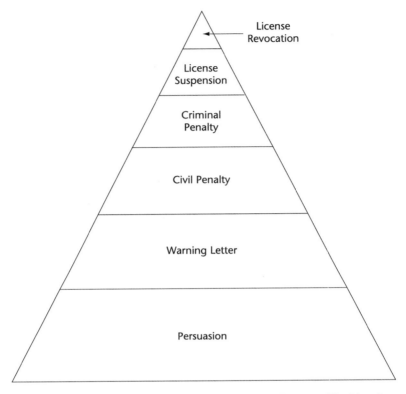

Figure 4.2.1 An example of a Regulatory Pyramid (from Ayres and Braithwaite 1992)

another may have to be shot without a trial, the assault offender who during the criminal process vows to go after the victim again and kill her should be locked up.

As we move up the pyramid in response to a failure to elicit reform and repair, we often reach the point where finally reform and repair are forthcoming. At that point responsive regulation means that we must put escalation up the pyramid into reverse and de-escalate down the pyramid. The pyramid is firm yet forgiving in its demands for compliance. Reform must be rewarded just as recalcitrant refusal to reform following wrongdoing will ultimately result in punishment.

Why the pyramid works with business regulation

Business regulatory agencies all over the world are today deploying the idea of the responsive regulatory pyramid. It is an influential policy idea because it comes up with a way of reconciling the clear empirical evidence that sometimes punishment works and sometimes it backfires, and likewise with persuasion (Braithwaite 1985; Ayres and Braithwaite 1992). The pyramidal presumption of persuasion first gives the cheaper and more respectful option a chance to work first, and there is empirical experience in some areas of business regulation that it does work in the majority of cases. The more costly punitive attempts at control are thus held in reserve for the minority of cases where persuasion fails. Yet it is also common for persuasion to fail. When it does, the most common reason is that a business actor is being a rational calculator about the likely costs of law enforcement compared with the gains from breaking the law. Escalation through progressively more deterrent penalties will often take the rational calculator up to the point where it will become rational to comply. Quite often, however, the business regulator finds that they try restorative justice, and it fails; they try escalating up through more and more punitive options, and they all fail to deter. This happens for a number of reasons. One is the so-called deterrence trap, where no level of financial deterrent can make compliance economically rational. Perhaps the most common reason in business regulation for successive failure of restorative justice and deterrence is that noncompliance is neither about a lack of goodwill to comply nor about rational calculation to cheat. It is about management not having the competence to comply. The manager of the nuclear power plant simply does not have the engineering know-how to take on such a demanding level of responsibility. He must be moved from the job. Indeed, if the entire management system of a company is not up to the task, the company must lose its license to operate a nuclear power plant. So when deterrence fails, the idea of the pyramid is that incapacitation is the next port of call (see Figure 4.2.2).

This design responds to the fact that restorative justice, deterrence, and incapacitation are all limited and flawed theories of compliance. What the pyramid does is cover the weaknesses of one theory with the strengths of another. The ordering of strategies in the pyramid is not just about putting the less costly, less coercive, more respectful options lower down in order to save money and preserve freedom as non-domination. It is also that by resorting to more dominating, less respectful forms of social control only when more dialogic forms have been tried first, coercive control comes to be seen as more legitimate. When regulation is seen as more legitimate, more procedurally fair, compliance with the law is more likely. Astute business regulators often set up this legitimacy explicitly. During a restorative justice dialogue over an offense, the inspector will say there will be no penalty this time, but that she hopes the manager understands that if she returns and finds the company has slipped back out of compliance again, under the rules she will have no choice but to refer it to the prosecutions unit. When the manager responds that this is understood, a future prosecution will likely be viewed as fair. Under this theory, therefore, privileging restorative justice at the base of the pyramid builds legitimacy and therefore compliance.

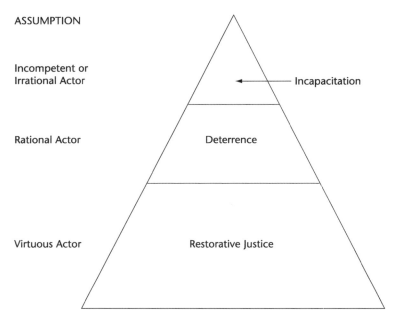

ASSUMPTION

Incompetent or
Irrational Actor — Incapacitation

Rational Actor — Deterrence

Virtuous Actor — Restorative Justice

Figure 4.2.2 Toward an Integration of Restorative, Deterrent and Incapacitative Justice

There is also a rational choice account of why the pyramid works. System capacity overload (Pontell 1978) results in a pretense of consistent law enforcement where in practice enforcement is spread around thinly and weakly. Unfortunately, this problem will be at its worst where crime is worst. Hardened offenders learn that the odds of serious punishment are low for any particular infraction. Tools like tax audits that are supposed to be about deterrence are frequently exercises that backfire by teaching hardened tax cheats just how much they are capable of getting away with (Kinsey 1986, p. 416). The reluctance to escalate under the responsive pyramid model means that enforcement has the virtue of being highly selective in a principled way. Moreover, the display of the pyramid itself channels the rational actor down to the base of the pyramid. Noncompliance comes to be seen (accurately) as a slippery slope that will inexorably lead to a sticky end. In effect what the pyramid does is solve the system capacity problem with punishment by making punishment cheap. The pyramid says that unless you punish yourself for lawbreaking through an agreed action plan near the base of the pyramid, we will punish you much more severely higher up the pyramid (and we stand ready to go as high as we have to). So it is cheaper for the rational company to punish themselves (as by agreeing to payouts to victims, community service, paying for new corporate compliance systems). Once the pyramid accomplishes a world where most punishment is self-punishment, there is no longer a crisis of the state's capacity to deliver punishment where it is needed. One of the messages the pyramid gives is that "if you keep breaking the law it is going to be cheap for us to hurt you because you are going to help us hurt you" (Ayres and Braithwaite 1992, chap. 2).

Paternoster and Simpson's (1996) research on intentions to commit four types of corporate crime by MBA students reveals the inefficiency of going straight to a deterrence strategy. Paternoster and Simpson found that where the MBAs held personal moral codes, these were more important than rational calculations of sanction threats in predicting compliance (though the latter were important, too). It follows that for the majority of these future business leaders, appeals to business ethics (as by confronting them with the consequences for the victims of a corporate crime) will work better than sanction threats. So it is best to try such ethical appeals first and then escalate to deterrence for that minority for whom deterrence works better than ethical appeals.

According to responsive regulatory theory, what we want is a legal system where citizens learn that responsiveness is the way our legal institutions work. Once they see the legal system as a responsive regulatory system, they know there will be a chance to argue about unjust laws (as opposed to being forced into a lower court production line or a plea bargain). But they will also see that game playing to avoid legal obligations, failure to listen to persuasive arguments about the harm their actions are doing and what must be done to repair it, will inexorably lead to regulatory escalation. The forces of law are listening, fair and therefore legitimate, but also are seen as somewhat invincible. The deterrence superiority of the active deterrence of the pyramid, as opposed to the passive deterrence of a fixed scale of penalties that are consistently imposed for different offenses, will be further developed elsewhere.

Corrupting restorative justice with coercion?

In the punishment-versus-persuasion debates among business regulatory scholars, while advocates of consistent punishment argued that cynical businesses abuse offers of cooperation (which they do if cooperation is not backed up by enforcement capability), advocates of consistent persuasion argued that punishment and persuasion involve incompatible imperatives. Theorists of this second sort believe that threat and coercion undermine goodwill and therefore the trust that makes cooperative compliance work. This, indeed, can also be pointedly true. Restorative justice advocates will be reading this chapter with very much the latter concern. How can we but corrupt the restorative justice values if we seek to coerce them?

The first point to make is a factual one. Very few criminal offenders who participate in restorative justice processes would be sitting in the room absent a certain amount of coercion. Without their detection and/or arrest, without the specter of the alternative of a criminal trial, they simply would not cooperate with a process that puts their behavior under public scrutiny. No coercion, no restorative justice (in most cases).

The question seems not one of how to avoid coercion, but how to avoid the escalation of coercion and how to avoid threats. A paradox of the pyramid is that to the extent that we can absolutely guarantee a commitment to escalate if steps are not taken to prevent the recurrence of lawbreaking, then escalation beyond the lower levels of the pyramid will rarely occur. This is the image of invincibility making self-regulation inevitable. In contrast, when it is seen as common that there are no escalatory consequences when young offenders flout their obligations under a restorative justice process, young offenders will often flout them. When the consequences of this become sufficiently serious, criminal enforcement will be belatedly mobilized in many of these cases. Without locked-in commitment to escalation where lives are not turned around, the system capacity crisis will rebound. The fundamental resource of responsive regulation is the belief of citizens in inexorability.

This does not mean that an offender should go to court as soon as he reoffends after a conference or fails to honor his undertakings at the conference. These are normally grounds for reconvening the conference. Until we get into the area of really serious sanctions—incarceration, confiscation of assets like houses and cars—conferences have a superior capacity to escalate remedies in any case. So at least the first few rungs of most enforcement pyramids will normally be restorative justice rungs. Arguments for attendance in a drug rehabilitation program or an anger management program will become more insistent, victims will insist on greater efforts at compensation, community service hours will be increased, curfews might be imposed until behavior improves. Again the message the restorative justice conference should give is that it is better to put your best self forward at the bottom rung of the pyramid because if you don't, you will end up going through this again, and next time it will be a bigger production, and the conference will be more demanding. And, ultimately, if again and again I fail to satisfy the conference agreement, I will end up in court, which will be more demanding again.

This inexorability is the reverse of the reality of current Western justice systems. In these systems, as a result of overload, it is the offenders who wear the system down rather than the reverse. The enforcement response is to hang back on confronting lawbreaking in a credible way early on, wait until really serious cases land in your lap, and then impose through the courts the harsh punishments that the media and a frustrated public demand in egregious cases. When the young offender finally ends up in jail, she is often genuinely shocked—after years of getting away with all manner of infractions with ten-minute appearances in court and good-behavior bonds, all of a sudden prison strikes like a bolt from the blue. The whole deal seems arbitrary and illegitimate, a perception reinforced by the prison culture offenders enter.

Many wrongly see inexorability as a responsive regulatory objective that requires participants in restorative justice processes to issue threats: the police officer who says, "Next time I'll be taking you to court and you'll probably go to jail." What is required is quite the reverse. It is for conference participants to identify with the offender as someone they are working with to prevent inexorable outside forces from taking over the case and putting it on a more punitive track. Inexorability is a societal accomplishment of the legal system—under a responsive regulatory regime everyone can see that it works inexorably. It is not an accomplishment of the issuance of threats in individual cases, which will only amount to bluff if there is in fact no inexorability in the system.

Threat is counterproductive because it increases a psychological process called *reactance* (Brehm and Brehm 1981), which undermines compliance. It is argued there that what is needed to achieve deterrence without reactance is societal inexorability of escalation (supporting deterrence) combined with offers of help without threat to avert that escalation—offered by others with whom one identifies (knocking out reactance). This is the way to improve compliance in a world where the impact of sanctions on compliance is the sum of a deterrence effect and a reactance effect.

Put another way, my hypothesis is that restorative justice works best with a specter of punishment in the background, threatening in the background but never threatened in the foreground. Where punishment is thrust into the foreground even by implied threats, other-regarding deliberation is made difficult because the offender is invited to deliberate in a self-regarding way—out of concern to protect the self from punishment. This is not the way to engender empathy with the victim, internalization of the values of the law and the values of restorative justice, the sequences of remorse, apology, and forgiveness that I will argue can transform lives in permanent ways. In contrast, contingent threats at best could only change lives in immediately contingent ways. The job of citizens in restorative justice is to treat offenders as worthy of trust. That is why the primary selection criterion for invitees to restorative justice conferences should be that these are the people offenders and victims nominate as those they most trust. Even though it might be trust in the shadow of the axe, there is nothing baffling about offenders actually feeling trusted in these circumstances. The fact is that it is in the nature of human beings to want to be trusted and to want to trust those they are close to. When lawbreakers believe they are treated as trustworthy by those who regulate them, they are more likely to comply with the law in future. [. . .]

Restorative and responsive regulation of the hardest criminal cases

These ideas seem plausible to many with respect to business regulation or juvenile justice but not so with "hardened" adult street criminals. I happen to think the approach has a lot of potential with the most serious repeat criminal offenders, and so I will outline in some detail how it might work there. The analysis starts with three propositions:

1. Most serious common crime (e.g., burglary) is perpetrated by a small proportion of the criminal population who commit very large numbers of offenses (Kelling and Coles 1996, pp. 244–45; Kennedy 1997).
2. Competent police services have the intelligence capability to know who most of those serious repeat offenders are (Kleiman 1997, p. 4).
3. But most police services do not have the resources to act on this widespread intelligence in any serious way.

The third of these points is the system capacity problem again. If the police really want to catch someone who is known to be a serious repeat burglar, they can. They can have him followed twenty-four hours a day, and when he ultimately goes a-burgling they can catch him in the act. But twenty-four-hour surveillance is terribly expensive—four shifts of police doing nothing but pursue one property criminal until he is caught. Police would never have the resources to touch many of the known repeat offenders this way, so instead they opt for reactive policing. Every now and then one of these people gets caught in the act for more fortuitous reasons, and the police settle for grabbing these opportunities when they come to them. Intensive surveillance and serious detective work are reserved for categories of serious offending that are more limited in numbers, particularly murders, though murderers are generally not offenders who will offend again.[1]

So here is the restorative and responsive option. Assuming proposition 2 is right, the police approach each of the known serious repeat offenders of a certain type—for example, those believed to commit a lot of burglaries. The offender is approached by a police officer who, in an unthreatening but authoritative manner, says something like the following:

> My name is Constable Bloggs, and I regret to inform you that you have been targeted for the Serious Repeat Offender Program. There are only two ways you can get off this program, John. One is that as a result of the police Serious Repeat Offender group having you under intensive surveillance (taking effect now), serious offenses will be proven against you, and you will be put behind bars. The other is that you desist from crime.
>
> That is where I come in, John. My job is to be available to help you

if you choose to get yourself dropped as a Serious Repeat Offender Program target. I work for the Restorative Justice Group. If you choose to work with me, I will set up a restorative justice circle of your loved ones, the people you most trust, those who care about your future. The objective of that circle will be to try to keep you out of jail, to give your life a new direction, and help you to open up new opportunities for yourself. If you genuinely convince everyone in the circle that you are going straight and will stay straight, then the circle has the power to recommend to the judge who approved putting you under surveillance that he should order that you be dropped as a Serious Repeat Offender Program target. To be convinced, the circle and the judge will normally want you to make concrete commitments. In your case, John, one of the things that would involve is your heroin habit. You see, the judge found that there was reasonable suspicion of a pattern of offending that justi-fied your being a suitable target for special surveillance. So, between us, we have to convince the judge that this is not true. To accomplish that we would need to work together as a team with your family and closest friends.

The deepest worry about this strategy is arbitrariness or prejudice in the selection of targets. The most promising approach to limiting such abuse would be the development of criteria for independent judicial approval of targeting.

My assumption is that these police visits themselves would have a small short-term effect on crime. That is, many of the targeted citizens who were intending to commit a crime in the next twenty-four hours would pause, considering their position before doing so. Perhaps in a day or two many of them would reject the offer of working with the Restorative Justice Group. Then they would have to be targeted for intensive surveillance, though not necessarily immediately. The important thing would be for the police to mobilize resources to secure arrests of some of these people and publicize the convictions. All targeted offenders should be advised by mail of convic-tions of other targeted offenders when they occur, have explained to them that the arrest of this high-priority target means that there will now be more resources for surveillance on remaining targets, and be reminded of the telephone number of the Restorative Justice Group should they want to get off the target list. For this group, there should be a reduction in crime both among those arrested and among those who are not arrested but who decide to reduce their risks by reducing their offending. These reductions in offend-ing will have been achieved at considerable cost in policing resources, however.

There can be a further escalatory element within the targeting option. Most known serious offenders are vulnerable. They commit a lot of minor offenses (like buying drugs) for which they can easily be charged, as well as a steady flow of major ones. They often breach probation or parole conditions; they often have outstanding warrants for things like failure to file a tax return or other infractions. They are accustomed to being allowed to get away with breaching parole or buying drugs because so much of that goes on that credible enforcement again confronts the system capacity problem. So the police understandably do not even try to make enforcement credible in these minor areas. However, the first arrest of targeted offenders has a new meaning as a step up the enforcement pyramid. They now realize that they are in a different category from others who buy drugs or breach parole. So targeted offenders are given another opportunity to respond to the inexorable fact that they will prove to be in a different category from other major burglars. They ponder the next rung of an enforcement pyramid that leads to prison.

Another kind of step up the enforcement pyramid can be to put temptation into the path of the target:

> [A] decoy-car program was established . . . The decoy car was a sports model chosen because of its popularity with thieves. Youths were enticed into it by leaving it running. When youths seated themselves in the car, the ignition system shut down and a remote control was used to automatically lock the door. Arrests and charges followed. (Ericson and Haggerty 1997, p. 273)

I assume that most offenders would opt for the restorative justice process. For many perhaps most, of these, this might be a purely strategic decision. That is, it would be a decision to try to get themselves dropped as a target without desisting from crime. While it is difficult to be optimistic about these hard cases, as a result of the program some of them may listen to the emotional pleas of family members that they opt for a different life, some of them may go to a new drug rehabilitation program and kick their habit for a period, others will take up an offer of a new job found for them as a result of the engagement of a specialized job placement agency with the process. Most will not do any of these things. Many of this group will con the conference into believing that they have changed their ways when actually they have not. The process will have no impact on this group. In summary, it is hypothesized that such a restorative and responsive regulatory program would have the following effects:

All targeted offenders	Initial twenty-four-hour fall in crime while they consider their position
Those who refuse restorative justice and are not convicted	Modest reduction in crime as a result of increased caution while targeted
Those who refuse restorative justice and are convicted	Significant reduction in crime

Those who accept restorative justice and con the conference	No impact on crime
Those who accept restorative justice and are reformed	Major impact on crime
Those who accept restorative justice, try to reform, but fail	Only short-term reduction in crime

Clearly, if most offenders opted to reject the restorative justice option, the program would fail totally because it would not solve the system overload problem—too many serious offenders committing too many crimes to be able to target a credible proportion. However, because it would be irrational even for the offender who has an iron determination to continue with a life of crime to opt for targeting in preference to restorative justice, we assume the greater problem would be insincere cooperation with the conference. This would cause only partial failure of the program. But it would enable a strategic solution to the system capacity problem. An interesting strategy for lending credibility to the targeting would be for it to be announced that a neighboring police service had a hundred police on call to supplement local police in targeting the serious repeat offenders. This offer could be reciprocated when the other police service launched its targeting program. Hopefully the announcement effect would lend sufficient credibility to drive offenders into the restorative justice option, making it unnecessary to import the extra police. A visible complementary change would be to shift normal enforcement to the targeting of geographical hot spots where a lot of crime occurs and which are frequented by the targeted offenders (see Sherman 1998).

In a jurisdiction with too many serious repeat offenders to be able to resource either the surveillance targeting or the intensive restorative justice conferences required, the solution is to apply the strategy first to an A-list of serious repeat offenders, and much later move on to B- and C-lists. The enforcement pyramid, both by rationing the targeting of punishment and by making it rational for offenders to punish themselves, can solve what Mark Kleiman (1993) has called the "enforcement swamping" problem. Here is how David Kennedy describes this enforcement swamping problem.

Imagine a neighbourhood in which the capacity of authorities to punish offenders is fixed. If the crime rate in that neighbourhood goes up, the punishment per offence must necessarily fall. If the new, lower level of punishment attracts new offenders, induces old offenders to offend more frequently, or both, there will be more offending, an even lower rate of punishment, and thus still more offending. When authorities' capacity to punish falls too low to prevent this kind of positive feedback cycle, we have enforcement swamping. A common contemporary example is street drug markets. As a stylized example of this process, when the volume of drug transactions in a particular location gets high enough, the author-ities lose their capacity to control the location. Their lack of control attracts more drug dealers, which further weakens control capacities. The market attracts more buyers, cementing the commitment of dealers to do business there. The result is the common phenomenon of flagrant street markets that appear utterly impervious to normal enforcement approaches: they have "tipped to the wrong side of the enforcement swamping divide." (1997, p. 476)

The phenomenon of crossing a tipping point into enforcement swamp-ing is a further reason that the attempt to create the appearance of equal opportunity enforcement is bad policy. It is better to start with an A-list and push those individuals back past the tipping point: "If you can't get past the crossover point for everybody, get past it for somebody and work outward" (Kleiman 1999, p. 21).[2] When we are swamped with enforcement opportun-ities, zero tolerance amounts to zero credibility. At the same time, equal opportunity enforcement is equal neglect.

Then, of course, the critical question is whether restorative justice pro-grams can be effective with hard-core repeat offenders. Bonta, Rooney, and Wallace-Capretta's (1998) study of serious offenders, 90 percent of whom were subject to a prosecution recommendation of prison sentences over six months and who went through a restorative justice program, found that their reoffending rate was about half that of a sample matched on risk who were sentenced to probation by the court. Burford and Pennell's (1998) study of serious cases of family violence found that abuse/neglect incidents halved in families that went through a restorative family conferencing process com-pared with a matched control group of families. [. . .]

Programs with considerable similarities to the responsive targeting part of the program proposed here, but without the restorative justice part, were the Boston and Minneapolis youth homicide projects, which were associated with almost a halving of youth homicides in Minneapolis and a two-thirds reduction in Boston (Kleiman 1999). The context was a familiar one—youth gang killings where everyone knew which gang had perpetrated the latest murder, but where proving anything in court was impossible. In Boston the Inter-Agency Operation Ceasefire group gave gang members the following message:

We know who you are. We know what you're doing. Most of it is illegal. You sell drugs, you carry weapons, you drive unregistered cars, you are truant from school, you are in breach of your probation terms, you drink alcohol from open containers. We can't crack down on everyone at once, but we can crack down on any group we choose. If we crack down on your group, you can't live your (mostly illegal) life.

Here are the new rules: no deadly violence. Here are the

consequences of breaking the rules: concentrated attention until the whole group says "uncle" and turns in its guns. No deal: you break the law at your own risk. But if you or any member of your group shoots someone, the risks will become, and remain, intolerable.

The first Operation Ceasefire intervention involved the Vamp Hill Kings in 1996 after a quick succession of three homicides. Street drug markets were disrupted, warrants were served, probation conditions enforced, and some indictments launched. Compliance did not come readily. A further homicide occurred during the intervention, but eventually sit-down forums with gang members got the message through.

[. . .] Restorative justice is not a utopian option even for the most serious and organized of criminals, even for the most powerful corporate criminals, as we will also see in the next chapter. However, for restorative justice to be effective with such tough nuts, it must be backed by an enforcement pyramid that is seen as having credibility and inexorability. Even the toughest nuts are capable of being surprised by someone treating them with respect, a person who cares about the effects offenders have on others. As Ayres and Braithwaite (1992, pp. 30–35) report, regulatory ethnographies show regulated actors to have contradictory multiple selves. Even the worst of us have a caring, socially responsible self as well as an exploitative self. The idea of starting at the bottom of the pyramid with the most ruthless criminals is to surprise them with a show of trust and respect, to give them a chance to put their best self forward:

> INSPECTOR TO NURSING HOME ADMINISTRATOR: What you want and what we want more than anything else is to improve the quality of care your residents are getting . . .
>
> (later) INSPECTOR TO BRAITHWAITE: When you say to them that we all agree that the care of the resident is what we are all concerned about, you know that's not true, that they're concerned about making money. But what are they going to say? They can't turn around and say, "Hell no, I don't care about the residents; all I care about is profits."

Mafia bosses (some of whom own nursing homes), tobacco executives and other kinds of drug barons, serial wife beaters (Braithwaite and Daly 1994), professional hit men, perhaps even Saddam Hussein,[3] can be surprised by being given an opportunity to put their socially responsible self forward, to be touched by the love of those who care for them most, and in particular to be touched by the way those they love suffer for the evils they do. As Hollywood teaches us, it is with drug barons and Saddam Husseins that we are willing to tolerate good cops who do bad things to protect us from a greater evil or marines who commit war crimes. The philosophy of restorative justice does not allow us to do this. We must always remember that the

192 VICTIMS AND VICTIMIZATION

constraining values and fundamental human rights . . . are our first priority. If they are the only priority we can accomplish in confronting a great evil, then it is them we must honor. That said, restorativists must not duck the responsibility to work through how they can respond to intransigent evils to which we must respond, both with credible clout and determination and with even more credible commitment to imposing a new set of checks and balances on the kind of freewheeling cops so valorized by our folklore.[4]

Evaluating the elements of responsive regulation

I have conceived responsive regulation here as a presumption in favor of trying restorative justice first, then deterrence when that fails, then incapacitation when that fails. Elsewhere I will evaluate the prospects of efficacy at these three levels and will evaluate whether restorative justice works on the basis of the evidence we have at this time. Yet really the question to be answered here is more demanding from a responsive regulatory perspective. Does restorative justice work so much better and more decently than deterrence to justify a general presumption for trying it before resorting to deterrence? [. . .] It will be argued that the active deterrence of escalation from restorative to punitive justice is likely to be much more effective than traditional passive deterrence as conceived in criminological theory since Bentham. It will also be argued both that restorative justice is generally more effective than the punitive incapacitation of selective incapacitation theory in criminology and that a restorative and responsive account of incapacitation might make for a superior model of incapacitation.

Hence, what the restorative and responsive theoretical position argues is not just that restorative justice is more effective than punitive justice. It is that restorative justice at the base of a regulatory pyramid increases the efficacy of punitive justice as well. It accomplishes the latter by increasing the effectiveness of both deterrence and incapacitation. All this, according to the theory, is especially true with the most hardened, sophisticated, and powerful criminals. The radical implication of the theory is that for no type of offending is imprisonment the normal response that is needed; for all types of offending we are best to have a presumption in favor of restorative justice first, combined with an expectation that restorative justice will often fail. Most of our prisons can be closed and sold. The conservative implication of the theory is that we cannot be abolitionists; restorative justice must be backed up by deterrence and incapacitation options that sometimes must include imprisonment.

Notes

1   In some parts of the world, notably the United States, there are substantial numbers of repeat murderers who are hit men or gang leaders; these are suitable targets for the kind of program I describe.

2   Also relevant here is what we know about salience and conditional prob-
     abilities: "Tax-payers focus on the most salient link in the chain of con-
     ditional probabilities that influence the likelihood of getting caught, rather
     than on the overall probability. Thus a 10 percent chance of getting
     caught and punished is treated as a lower risk than a combined 50 percent
     chance of getting caught and a 20 percent chance of being punished
     if caught, even though the actual risk in both situations is the same
     $(.5 \times .2 = .10)$. The salience of the higher probabilities leads people to
     overcompensate in determining the joint effect on risk, a heuristic that
     has been called the 'conjunctive effect.' Given this effect, compliance
     levels increase when the salience of high-probability links is increased,
     even when the underlying risk is unchanged" (Scholz 1998, p. 143).
3   UN Secretary-General Kofi Annan to Saddam Hussein: "You're a
     builder, you built modern Iraq. It was destroyed once. You've rebuilt it.
     Do you want to destroy it again? Look how you talk about the suffering of
     your people. It's in your hands, we can do something about this. If we can
     work out an agreement that will prevent military action and you would
     undertake to comply, it will save the day" (Shawcross 2000, p. 241).
4   The beginnings of an attempt to work through my favored civic repub-
     lican way of accomplishing this can be found in Braithwaite and Pettit
     (1990) and in chapter 5 of Braithwaite (2002). In this chapter the
     important point I am emphasizing is judicial approval of targeting, so
     judges are guardians of rights and limits. Hence, controversial tactics like
     the use of decoy cars to catch car thieves are not precluded, but are
     subjected to a new form of judicial regulation that limits their application
     to cases of reasonable suspicion of serious repeat offenders who have
     been warned. Being warned, they can appeal any injustice of the target-
     ing to the judge.

4.3

Toward a victimology of state crime
by David Kauzlarich, Rick A. Matthews and William J. Miller

[. . .]

The criminological study of immoral, illegal, and harmful state actions has not developed as fully as would have been expected from the explosion of research in the late 1980's to mid 1990's, which lifted the optimism about criminology's interest in understanding state malfeasance. Attempts to develop a sophisticated theoretical and empirical criminology of the state are currently declining, although conceptual and typological efforts abound (Friedrichs 1996; Kauzlarich 1995). Critical criminologists have historically been concerned with understanding and correcting harms caused by powerful corporate and state agents and organizations, yet few have followed Friedrichs' (1983) and Quinney's (1972) calls for a radical or critical victimology of state organized harms and immoralities.

In the 1970's and 1980's, some radical criminologists and other social scientists examined state crime (Falk et al. 1971) and a few issues of the journals *Social Justice* and *Issues in Criminology* were devoted to matters related to governmental crime. Crimes by political elites and institutions caught the attention of criminologists such as Clinard and Quinney (1973), Michalowski (1985), Quinney (1980), and Simon and Eitzen (1982), whose works are the foundation of the modern criminological study of organizational-level unethical and illegal state practices. Perhaps the most influential contribution was Chambliss' 1989 presidential address to the American Society of Criminology calling for the study of state-organized crime. Like Sutherland's American Sociological Society presidential address on white collar crime fifty years before, Chambliss' message challenged the prevailing epistemology of criminology, and called for the study of more harmful and insidious forms of crime previously neglected by mainstream criminologists.

By the early 1990's, state crime research increased dramatically in both quality and quantity. Barak's (1991) *Crimes by the Capitalist State* was the first anthology from a criminological perspective that brought together several papers on state crime. Tunnell (1993) produced an edited anthology, which, like Barak's reader, provided case studies and the application of the label "political crime" to phenomena such as the state's role in the undermining of labor movements, the facilitation of patriarchy, and corporate crime. Ross (1995) assembled a collection of papers that provided an understanding of how international, regulatory, and other forms of law and social control may contain, control, deter, or decrease incidences of unethical and illegal state actions. Interspersed with these anthologies were a few journal articles by criminologists as well (e.g., Chambliss 1995; Cohen 1993; Friedrichs 1996a; Kauzlarich et al. 1992; Kauzlarich 1995).

More recent works include those of Friedrichs (1998) and Ross (2000). Friedrichs' two volume anthology supplied reprinted journal articles on state crime and, interestingly, contained more articles by non-criminologists than criminology scholars. Ross' anthology on controlling state crime included studies of several countries, including many western countries as well as Japan, Italy, and Israel. In spite of these works, there appears to be only one scholarly monograph published since 1995 that adopts a chiefly criminological approach to state crime (Kauzlarich and Kramer 1998). While there have been a handful of journal articles written on state crime since 1995 (e.g. Green and Ward 2000; Kramer and Kauzlarich 1999; Matthews and Kauzlarich 2000; Mullins and Kauzlarich 2000; Ross, 1998; Ross et al. 1999), less than five sessions at each of the last three American Society of Criminology meetings explicitly pertained to state crime.

In sum, while there have been some important developments in the study of state crime over the past few years, the subject has yet to develop into a major sub-field of criminology, and the rate of theoretical and empirical progress is slow even within the ranks of critical criminology. Nearly all of the works on state crime in the last thirty years have included calls (and sometimes a desperate plea) for more criminological attention to unethical and illegal actions of states and governments, but the answer has been inadequate.[1]

Even more deficient, however, is the study of the *victimology* of state crime. There are some discussions of victimology in the literature (see Fox and Szockyj 1996); but beyond brief descriptions, there has been no attempt to establish the nature, extent, and distribution of the victimology of state crime. Incredibly, this lack of attention continues in the wake of state atrocities in Rwanda, the former Yugoslavia, Kosovo, and East Timor. Hundreds of thousands of people have been killed, physically assaulted, rendered homeless and hungry, raped, or emotionally abused by the actions and policies of governments and state officials. State sponsored genocide, ethnic cleansing, and imperialism are clearly not actions of the past, but current, compelling, and deeply disturbing problems which require immediate and rigorous scholarly study.

A radical victimology has developed in the areas of street crime (Elias 1986; Mawby and Walklate 1994), corporate crimes against women (Fox and Szockyj 1996), wife rape, and intimate violence (Bergen, 1998). It is now crucial to develop a sophisticated criminology of state crime to begin examining its victimology. This article is a step in that direction. It starts with a working definition of state crime. It then attempts to enumerate the range of victims by way of a typology whose cells are illustrated by examples of conduct, both foreign and domestic, that violate international or domestic law. Drawing on the illustrations in the typology and previous studies, the article posits a series of propositions about the harms resulting from state crime and policies.

What is state crime and who are the victims?

An important task in developing a victimology of state crime is to enumerate the victims, a task hindered by the lack of a uniform definition of state crime. While the labels differ (e.g. political crime, government crime, state-organized crime), most scholars working in the area agree that governmental or state crimes are illegal, socially injurious, or unjust acts which are committed for the benefit of a state or its agencies, and not for the personal gain of some individual agent of the state. This way of viewing crimes committed by political actors and organizations is consistent with the classic distinction made by Clinard and Quinney (1973) between occupational and corporate crime, and points to the importance of viewing governmental and state crime as a form of organizational crime.

Scanning the criminological literature, scholars have identified victims of state crime as: Civilians and soldiers in war (Kauzlarich, 1995), peoples targeted for genocide (Friedrichs 1996, 1996a), individuals suffering from racism (Hazlehurst 1991; Simon 2002), sexism (Caulfield and Wonders 1993), classism (Bohm 1993), crack using mothers (Humphries 1999), research subjects (Kauzlarich and Kramer 1998), countries and nations oppressed by powerful states (Barak 1993, 1991; Kauzlarich and Kramer 1998), workers (Aulette and Michalowski 1993; Friedrichs 1996), union organizers (Tunnell 1993), immigrants (Hamm 1995), prisoners (Kauzlarich and Kramer 1998), the natural environment (Kauzlarich and Kramer 1993, 1998), astronauts (Kramer 1992), suspects in criminal cases (Hazlehurst 1991; Henderson and Simon 1994), those subjected to cultural imperialism (Ross 1995), and passengers on planes (Matthews and Kauzlarich 2000).

Likewise, there are numerous definitions of a victim, and hence what is victimology. Stitt and Giacopassi's (1995: 67) conceptualization of corporate crime/harm victimization includes individuals or groups who "(a) have not given informed consent, (b) are incapable of making a reasonable judgement, and (c) are forced or deceived into participation in a situation that results in adverse consequences to them." This way of thinking about victims of state crime is helpful but ignores the structural patterns and relationships often preceding or facilitating state crime victimization. For example, the poor, racial and ethnic minorities, and women are explicitly or tacitly victimized by the state partly because of its support of larger structural and cultural definitions of worth, status, power, authority, and prestige. Ultimately, stratification produces inequality in social relationships between the state, groups of citizens, and the interests of capital. To the extent that the state supports immoral and illegal inequalities and their harmful manifestations, a state can be in whole or in part considered responsible for victimization. This approach is consistent with literature identifying governmental complicity through unjust and immoral social structural arrangements (Bohm 1993; Kramer and Michalowski 1990; Aulette and Michalowski 1993). The working definition, drawing on Kauzlarich (1995: 39), thus includes as state crime victims:

> Individuals or groups of individuals who have experienced economic, cultural, or physical harm, pain, exclusion, or exploitation because of tacit or explicit state actions or policies which violate law or generally defined human rights.

This definition, while somewhat broad, encapsulates most of the substance and spirit of the criminological literature on the varieties of state crime, and sets the stage for an inclusive typology of victimization. Also, international and domestic laws and human rights standards can be used to define certain state activities as criminal. Thus, in defining the activities of a state as criminal, one may employ ratified international law and customary international law (i.e., which may or may not be codified) in addition to domestic law or human rights standards.

In a broad sense, victims of state crime generally fall into two categories: (1) victims of domestic state crime and (2) victims of international state crime. Domestic state crime occurs when a government acts to undermine the social, economic, or political rights of its own citizens. International state crime occurs when a government violates the economic, political, or social rights of citizens in other countries. Also, various international and domestic laws can be legitimately employed as an epistemological framework for criminology (Kauzlarich 1995: 41). Thus, in defining the activities of a state as criminal, one may employ international law, human rights standards, and domestic law. The resultant typology is captured in Table 4.3.1, based on whether the victims were domestic or international and whether the action was a crime under domestic or international law and humans rights standards.[2] The remainder of this section defines the contents of each cell in the typology illustrated in Table 4.3.1, and provides examples to demonstrate the utility of the typology. This enumeration of the victims, in turn, will be the basis for a series of inductive propositions intended to advance a victimology of state crime.

Table 4.3.1. Types of governmental crime

Crime type	Abbreviation	Definition	Examples
Domestic-International Governmental Crime	DIGC	Occurs within a state's geographic jurisdiction against international law or human rights.	Institutional Racism DOE Human Radiation Experiments
International-International Governmental Crime	IIGC	Occurs outside a state's geographic jurisdiction against international law or human rights.	Economic Terrorism
Domestic-Domestic Governmental Crime	DDGC	Occurs within a state's geographic jurisdiction against domestic criminal, regulatory, or procedural laws or codes	COINTELPRO DOE Environmental Degradation
International-Domestic Governmental Crime	IDGC	Occurs outside a state's geographic jurisdiction against domestic criminal, regulatory, or procedural laws or codes	Iran-Contra

Source: Kauzlarich (1995).

Domestic-International Governmental Crime (DIGC)

DIGCs are "acts which occur within a state's geographic jurisdiction which run contrary to the state's obligations under international law" (Kauzlarich 1995, 40), or human rights standards. Examples include violations of International Covenants (e.g., the Covenant on Civil and Political Rights, the International Convention on the Elimination of All forms of Racial Discrimination, and the Convention on the Political Rights of Women), and injury from the fallout of nuclear tests. The discussion below elaborates on two additional examples: (1) institutionalized racism, sexism, and classism in social and criminal justice policy; and (2) human radiation experiments.

Although there have been no appreciable changes in African American crime rates over decades, the percentage of African Americans incarcerated since 1980 has increased tremendously. This trend has continued throughout the 1990's with the advent of get tough on crime measures such as three strikes and truth in sentencing laws (Tonry 1995). Miller (1996) argues that the war on drugs has a racial bias that has increased the prejudice that already exists throughout the criminal justice system. This bias increases the likelihood that young black males will come into contact with the criminal justice system and will be disproportionately under some form of correctional control. For example, nearly one in three (32%) black males in the age group 20–29 is under some form of criminal justice supervision on any given day – either in prison or jail, or on probation or parole; and 49% of prison inmates nationally are African American, compared to their 13% representation in the overall population (Mauer 1999: 3). Racial disparities are also found in drug sentencing policies (e.g. higher sentences for crack than powder cocaine) and the imposition of the death penalty. The treatment of racial minorities by the criminal justice system through practices like detaining them for "Driving While Black" violates not only common decency and ethical standards, but also the International Convention on the Elimination of All forms of Racial Discrimination.

Finally, as Johnson and Leighton (1999; 126) have argued, the effects of incarceration are only a small part of the problem:

> On release, their records will follow them, making them harder to employ and in many cases rendering them unemployable. Young men with nothing more than an arrest record – no conviction, no confinement – may increasingly find themselves in the same predicament. Jobs, housing, insurance – the essentials of a secure life – may be placed beyond their reach (Johnson and Leighton 1999: 126).

Another example of Domestic-International Governmental Crime is the human radiation experiments funded and managed by the U.S. Department of Energy and a host of other federal agencies. Several of these experiments have been conducted in violation of the Nuremberg Code, which outlaws non-consensual, reckless, deceptive, and coercive experiments.

From 1945 to 1947, a series of Manhattan Project and Atomic Energy Commission (AEC) supported plutonium injection studies were conducted on people expressly deceived into participating in the study. They were told that they were being treated for a life-threatening disease when in fact the studies were designed to help the state understand the effects of plutonium on the human body in the case of nuclear war. The victims of these experiments were poor and uneducated. The second series of experiments in violation of the Nuremberg Code were prison radiation experiments conducted from 1963 to 1973. One hundred and thirty one prisoners at the Oregon State Prison in Salem and the Washington State Prison in Walla Walla were subjects in a study to determine the effects of irradiation on the function of testes. Prisoners received $25 per irradiation, and were informed of only some of the possible risks. Prisoners are not in a position to exercise the type of free will envisioned by the Nuremberg Code, which among other things requires that research subjects have the legal capacity to give their consent free from force, fraud, deceit, or duress (Kauzlarich and Kramer 1998).

Domestic-Domestic Governmental Crime (DDGC)

DDGCs include those "acts which occur within the state's geographical jurisdiction in violation of the criminal or regulatory code of that state" (Kauzlarich 1995: 41). Such crimes include police violations of procedural, constitutional, and civil law. Illustrations of such crimes include the Tuskegee syphilis experiments, the injury and disease of workers and communities as a result of nuclear and atomic production, the undermining of political rights (e.g., the FBIs COINTELPRO program), and environmental degradation through the U.S. nuclear weapons industry complex.

There is little question that the Federal Bureau of Investigation (FBI) has engaged in activities directed toward U.S. citizens that were unethical at best and illegal at worst. One of the most widely recognized forms of state suppression of political rights was the FBI's COINTELPRO program. Waged by the FBI against numerous dissenting groups, the political rights of dissident political groups like Communist Party of USA (CPUSA), Socialist Workers Party (SWP), the Southern Christian Leadership Conference (SCLC), the Black Panthers, the American Indian Movement (AIM), and the Committee in Solidarity with the People of El Salvador (CISPES) were violated (Caulfield 1991; Churchill et al. 1990; Davis 1992). The covert and illegal activities of the FBI to "neutralize" political dissent by members of targeted organizations has been well documented, and included such illegal tactics as wiretaps, bugging, mail-openings, and breaking and entering (Beirne and Messerchmidt 2000). Other activities included group infiltration and death threats (Churchill and Vander Wall 1990; Davis 1992).

The production of atomic and nuclear weapons by the U.S. Department of Energy has resulted in serious environmental contamination. In violation of U.S. EPA laws, the Clean Water Act, and the Resource Conservation and Recovery Act, at least 17 areas in the country have been substantially damaged and polluted. At one time in Hanford, Washington, there was 100 square miles of groundwater contaminated with extremely high levels of tritium, iodine, and other toxic chemicals. Near the Savannah River Plant in the Carolinas, there have been large releases of mercury into the air and tritium, strontium, and iodine into the soil (Kauzlarich and Kramer 1998).

There is evidence to show that there are higher rates of miscarriages, leukemia, and other health related problems in the areas where nuclear weapons have been produced, stored, or tested. The human effects of environmental degradation as a result of the hundreds of nuclear weapons tests in the Western part of the U.S. are also examples of state crime. A recent study by the National Cancer Institute estimates that tens of thousands of people have developed thyroid cancer as a result of nuclear tests (Neergaard

1997). The victims of these environmental crimes were not only the unknowing civilians who simply happened to be living near the test sites, but also military personnel who were forced to witness nuclear blasts and then tested for any negative side effects (Kauzlarich and Kramer 1998). In these cases, the victims were easily exploitable because they were either unknowing, powerless, or in subordinate organizational positions.

International-International Governmental Crime (IIGC)

IIGCs are "criminal acts by governments which occur outside the state's geographic jurisdiction in violation of international law" (Kauzlarich 1995: 41) or human rights standards. Examples include: violations of international agreements like the Genocide Convention, the Geneva Convention, and the Nuclear Non-Proliferation treaty; various forms of overt and covert aggression representing state-sponsored terrorism (Herman 1982, 1987); political assassination (Hamm 1993); and subverting state sovereignty and political processes (Chomsky 1985, 1992, 1993; Chomsky and Herman 1979). All of these activities have been defined by the international community as undesirable, and have been prohibited by international law. States have historically committed these crimes by facilitating the repression of economic, political, and social rights of citizens in other countries by either implicitly or explicitly supporting brutal dictatorships. Because many forms of IIGC are well documented, this section focuses on the less commonly considered practice of the economic sanctions placed on Cuba.

While the scope and nature of economic sanctions[3] may differ, they can be a form of coercion that is directed toward the civilian population of the target country to bring about a desired political or economic change, or to simply punish the target country (Hass 1998; Hufbauer et al. 1990). Historically, the use of economic sanctions has been viewed under both domestic law and international law as a humanitarian alternative to military force. There have been instances where economic sanctions have been very successful in bringing about a desired political change (e.g., Haiti and South Africa) or have been nearly universally supported by the international community (e.g., Iraq). As Weiss (1997) argued, however, even successful sanctions may collide with humanitarian concerns:

> *although in theory sanctions are motivated by an implicitly humane rationale, their implementation often wreaks great havoc and civilian suffering. Inherent in sanctions policy are uncomfortable and, for the moment, still imprecise calculations about inflicting civilian pain to achieve political gain.* Where tolerable civilian discomfort ends and full-fledged humanitarian crisis begins is an elusive boundary, particularly because pre-sanction conditions in many countries are often so marginal (Weiss 1997: 30; emphasis added).

The passage of the Cuban Democracy Act (CDA) in 1992, and the passage of the Helms-Burton Act in 1996, were major steps in tightening the economic sanctions on Cuba. As the 1997 American Association for World Health (AAWH) found, the tightening of economic sanctions in 1992 created health problems for many Cuban citizens in the areas of malnutrition, water quality, and medicines and medical equipment shortages. Further, the ban on sales of American foodstuffs has contributed to serious nutritional deficits, especially among pregnant women, leading to an increase in low birth-weight babies. Additionally, food shortages have led to outbreaks of neuropathy (diseases of the nervous system), and the embargo has severely restricted the access to water treatment chemicals and the parts needed for Cuba's water supply system (AAWH 1997). The decrease in safe drinking water for many Cuban citizens led to rising incidences of morbidity and mortality from water-borne diseases (AAWH 1997).

The right of individual nations to place economic sanctions on other countries is usually enshrined in domestic law. For example, the legal justification of the U.S. economic sanctions against Cuba has been found under the authority of the Trading with the Enemy Act of 1917, the Foreign Assistance Act of 1961, and the Export Administration Act of 1919. Internationally, the UN permits the use of economic sanctions under Article 41 of Chapter VII of the UN Charter, which also contains provisions for the use of military force. Each year since the passage of the CDA in 1992, however, the U.N. General Assembly has passed resolutions condemning the sanctions placed on Cuba. Cuba has maintained that the U.S. economic measures (particularly the CDA and Helms-Burton Act), which are intended to coerce changes in Cuba's political and economic institutions, violate the fundamental international law principles of non-intervention and the sovereign equality of states (Krinsky et al. 1993). The issue that has been raised with concern to the CDA and Helms-Burton Act has been their extraterritorial nature and not necessarily the sovereign right of the U.S. to apply its own economic sanctions on Cuba.

International-Domestic Governmental Crime (IDGC)

IDGCs are "criminal conduct by a government abroad in violation of its own criminal or regulatory code" (Kauzlarich 1995: 41). Examples include violating domestic law like the Boland Arms Amendment, in the case of Iran-Contra, and assorted constitutional directives. On a technical level, any breach of international law or custom would also be an IDGC under Article VI of the U.S. Constitution, often referred to as the supremacy clause, that situates international treaties and the like as the "supreme law of the land." Given the tenuous status of international law in the American popular culture and in political circles (especially when its application is directed against U.S.

interests), it is not surprising that this technicality rarely surfaces in popular discussions of crime and law. If taken seriously, however, the supremacy clause further widens the scope of criminological analyses of state crime, and could prove useful in helping legitimize the study of state crime in traditional academic quarters.

Iran-Contra is a form of IDGC because the Reagan administration, through the covert activities of Oliver North, John Poindexter, Richard Secord, and Albert Hakim, violated U.S. domestic law in supplying the Contras with arms in spite of the Boland Arms Amendments of 1982 and 1984 (the 1984 Amendment expressly forbade the U.S. from supporting the Contras with military aid or financing).[4] Between 1984 and 1986, the Reagan administration deliberately ignored these amendments in supporting the Contras with arms and financing. In addition to illegally channeling arms and military support to the Contras, the Reagan administration also participated in an extensive program of bribery, coercion, and quid pro quos aimed at the countries of Central America whose political, military, and logistical support was pivotal to sustaining the Contra war. Quid pro quos, which Vice President Bush, at a June 1984 NSPG meeting, declared "would be wrong," were used to "entice" cooperation from Honduras, Guatemala, Costa Rica and Panama.

It is difficult to assess the extent of the harm caused by these illegal activities. As a start, a fact finding mission to Nicaragua between 1984 and 1985 revealed that the U.S. funded Contras had engaged in many forms of terrorism and war crimes which included killing unarmed men, women and children; torture, kidnapping and rape; assaults on economic and social targets; and, the kidnapping, torture and murder of religious leaders (Beirne and Messerschmidt 2000).

Propositions of a victimology of state crime

Propositions about the victimology of state crime can be developed from this review to help shed light on the larger phenomenon of state crime victimization, although a caveat is in order because state crime takes a variety of forms. For instance, it is difficult to compare the victimology of international economic terrorism against the people of Cuba and Iraq to institutionalized racism, sexism, and classism, or the suffering of human radiation subjects to unjust criminal justice system practices. Nevertheless, several general propositions about the victims of state crime may be formulated based on current and prior research in the area.

(1) *Victims of State Crime Tend to be among the Least Socially Powerful Actors*
    [. . .]
(2) *Victimizers Generally Fail to Recognize and Understand the Nature, Extent, and Harmfulness of Institutional Policies. If Suffering and Harm are*

Acknowledged, It Is often Neutralized within the Context of a Sense of "Entitlement"
[...]
(3) *Victims of State Crime are often Blamed for Their Suffering*
[...]
(4) *Victims of State Crime Must Generally Rely on the Victimizer, an Associated Institution, or Civil Social Movements for Redress*
[...]
(5) *Victims of State Crime Are Easy Targets for Repeated Victimization*
[...]
(6) *Illegal State Policies and Practices, while Committed by Individuals and Groups of Individuals, Are Manifestations of the Attempt to Achieve Organizational, Bureaucratic, or Institutional Goals*
[...]

Conclusion

Even with a universally accepted definition of state crime, the development of a victimology of the phenomenon is unlikely to occur soon. It is, however, time for state crime scholars to spend less energy arguing for the inclusion of this phenomenon into the criminological enterprise, and more time and energy studying the harms that result from state actions and policies.

One point of departure is the extant literature on victims of white-collar crime, including both occupational and organizational varieties. For instance, unlike many forms of traditional street crime victimization, victims of elite crime can be unaware of the source of the injury, or in some cases, unaware that they have even been injured at all (e.g. lags in correlating corporate and state eco-crimes with regional health problems). Just as price-fixing and other types of economic and financial fraud can often go unnoticed by the public, the larger cultural and political normalization of economic, racial, and gender inequalities shields some forms of resultant state crime from the kind of scrutiny they deserve. This is much less likely to be the case in state crimes such as genocide, imperialism, and perhaps economic terrorism – the problem shifts from acknowledging the fact that some harm actually occurred (i.e. visibility of the victim) to whether the behavior or policy is actually criminal. Then other questions surface such as whether the policy or behavior is an appropriate criminological subject, whether it is a potential candidate for legal proceedings (and if so, whether international or domestic), and whether the victims are entitled to restitution. Criminologists interested in advancing the study of state crime are not without guidance in addressing these issues – they were raised decades ago about retail terrorism, occupational crime, and many forms of corporate crime. Our response to these issues should be similar to those made by Sutherland (1945) on the topic of white-collar crime, Clinard and Yeager (1980) on corporate crime, and Barak (1991) on state criminality: State crime is real, it is harmful, it produces victims, and there-fore should be subject to social control and criminological analysis. In the end, the real significance of the study of state crime is found in its potential to reduce or eliminate human exploitation, suffering, and exclusion. The cur-rent body of criminological literature of the etiology, control, and victimology of state crime is unhelpful in this endeavor, much like the thousands of books and articles published each year that seldom have any affect on the safety of families and communities victimized by street crime and violence. For a host of reasons – *inter alia*, scholarly, political, and humanistic – the victims of state crime should be studied criminologically. It only stands to reason that the development of a victimology of state crime might help promote the social change necessary for state crime to decline in frequency and severity.

Notes

1 Additionally, small inroads have been made into mainstream arenas. Most white collar crime and elite deviance textbooks (e.g., Ermann and Lundmann 1996; Friedrichs 1996; Hagan 1997; Rosoff et al. 2002; Simon 2002; Simon and Hagan 1998) have at least one section on unethical or illegal, organizationally rooted actions of governments and government officials. Even then, with the exception of Friedrichs (1996), the examples are often unrepresentative of recent criminological work on state crime. Several criminology textbooks include examples of state crime as a part of their "white collar crime" or "political" crime chapters (e.g., Barlow and Kauzlarich 2002; Beirne and Messerschmidt 2000; Siegel 1998).

2 Kauzlarich (1995) notes that this typology is intended to be an alternative or complimentary conceptualization as opposed to a substitution for sociological and other definitions of crime.

3 The term economic sanctions, as used here, is consistent with the Hufbauer et al. (1990: 2) definition: "economic sanction means the deliberate, government-inspired withdrawal, or threat of withdrawal, of customary trade or financial relations. 'Customary' does not mean 'contractual'; it simply means levels of trade and financial activity that would probably have occurred in the absence of sanctions."

4 Additionally, some have suggested that these activities also violated other domestic laws such as the Arms Export Control Act, which prohibits the sale or export of arms to states that sponsor terrorism (i.e., Iran), and the U.S. Neutrality Act.

Part 5

The conceptual and theoretical basis of victimology: an introduction

by Joanna Shapland

The early years of the formation of criminology as a discipline were marked by debate about its scope and remit: what should be counted as a crime? What levels of explanation were the most useful to pursue in order to look at explanations for crime and criminality? There has been similar controversy over the last few decades about victimology, its baby sister. What should be the subject matter for victimology: merely victims of offences which are against criminal law in that country? Or should it have a wider remit, to include offences which are criminal anywhere, or are against human rights? The debate has been sharpened by the perceived negative connotations, for some, of the word victim. Should being a victim be self-defined, as is ethnicity? Doesn't 'victim' imply passivity, a separate status of 'ill'? Those who have experienced domestic violence would prefer the use of the term 'survivor'.

Another factor underpinning these questionings has been the close relationship between research and practice. Research on victimization has often been done to influence or reform criminal justice, social services or medical services. The scope of the definition of victim then acquires new, key political dimensions. If 'victim' is to be determined by the scope of the criminal law, then the implication is that reform should be within criminal justice parameters. But these are seen as traditionally failing the victim, with the key participants and priorities for criminal justice being offenders and the state. Should not then action be taken to help and restore victims to as near their everyday lives prior to victimization *outside* criminal justice? Perhaps using civil justice or restorative justice parameters, resources and values? But then this would reflect back on the scope of the population of 'offences' and 'victims' to be included – and the very small likelihood of any country finding the funding to help those harmed in matters covered by the civil law as well as the criminal law.

The debate has swung backwards and forwards. An initial concentration on victim of crime gave way in the 1970s and 1980s to wider conceptualizations, linked to despair about the potential effectiveness of correctional policies and hence sympathy with abolitionist views on criminal justice.[1] The growth of victimization and crime surveys in the 1980s resulted in considerable impact of data as to the effects of victimization and the need for victim assistance. This became linked to the parallel growth of crime prevention which put the emphasis back firmly on victims of crime. By the 1990s, the slow pace of reform of criminal justice so that it might be more in tune with the needs and expectations of victims was beginning to quicken, showing that it might be possible to undertake limited reform – and victim needs were beginning to be seen as more legitimate. In the new millenium, criminal justice reform has still proceeded slowly but was being accompanied by parallel processes, particularly for youthful offenders, such as restorative justice and restorative practice.[2] The debate about the boundaries of victimology is opening up again.

The readings in this section all consider the ways in which we should see victims, how to draw boundaries as to who should be considered a 'victim', and the results in terms of how we should see victims in relation to criminal and civil justice.

Who should be considered a victim?

The dominant strand in victimology would define a victim as someone who has suffered harm as a result of an offence which is against the criminal law. Because almost all criminal law is national criminal law, however,[3] there are some variations in what is defined by criminal law as a crime between one country and another. National differences in reporting and recording crime (Kangaspunta et al. 1998; Barclay and Tavares, 2003) and these definitional differences make it very hard to know the extent of victimization between countries. One solution is to design a victimization survey which is applied consistently between countries. The International Crime Victim Survey (ICVS), described by Alvazzi del Frate in this section, has been running since 1989. It has covered a large number of countries, including developing countries, from Africa, Asia, North America and Europe. It asks not only about victimization *per se*, but also about whether and why victimization is reported to the authorities, about crime prevention precautions taken, and about views on criminal justice.

Its major advantages are its standardized measurements and its wide geographical coverage. This makes it one of the very few studies which have looked at countries which have high victimization rates – where it could be said almost to be 'normal' to be a victim of crime, as opposed to the 'shock' experienced when victimization is rare (del Frate et al., 1993). However, the ICVS is a study of individual victimization, not the victimization of businesses, organizations or community groups. To gain a complete picture of the amount of victimization by criminal offences, separate victimization surveys of organizations and businesses also need to be considered (Shapland, 1995). Another major advantage of the ICVS is that it has included white-collar crimes, such as corruption and consumer fraud, which are rarely reported to the police and which rarely figure in national official statistics. It shows that victimization rates for such fraud are often higher than those for theft. This links with the ICVS findings of the major effect of corruption on the rule of law and political legitimacy in some countries – and also returns victimology to the original mandate of the UN Declaration on Victims of Crime and Abuse of Power (1985).

The scope of justice remedies for victimization

This same kind of question resonates across the broad range of studies looking at justice responses to victimization. Christie's (1986) classic article was one of the first to demonstrate how traditional western criminal justice has a very impoverished view of who might be involved in providing a justice response. Its focus on the offender and the professional representatives of the state (judge, prosecutor, police) have 'stolen' the original dispute between offender and victim and made it into a dispute between offender and state. Hence the justice response has also been confined to one between offender and state, one which, in today's popular punitiveness, emphasizes punishment and suffering.

For Christie, criminal justice has left the victim aside and depersonalized the conflict. What happens, though, if criminal justice is forced to acknowledge the victim, at least in name? There has been significant pressure on countries towards having victim impact statements read out in court or a victim impact statement made by the victim as to the effects the offence has had. Both South Australia and several states in North America now routinely allow this, with other countries permitting it in certain circumstances.

The reforms, however, have had only minor effects on sentencing practice, as Erez and Rogers document. Why? Erez and Rogers argue that it is because practitioners will resist reform initiatives which are contrary to their established world views. If the effects are 'normal' – those expected – then there is no need to change sentencing practice – the sentence will do very nicely within the usual range. This is in fact statistically correct, but, as they argue, it obviates any pressure to individualize sentencing – to make it demonstratively appropriate to that victim. I would argue that it is in fact a tactic not to attend to victims, even if that is only expressive rather than in terms of changing the substantive sentence. However, the reform does seem to be educating legal professionals as to victim needs and effects, and this was reflected in sentencing in a few cases.

The very slow pace of reform in relation to the criminal justice response to victims is documented by Shapland, as well as by Elias and Erez and Rogers. Shapland argues that it is because recognizing victims would affect existing professional power bases which have been negotiated over many years. Pressure groups representing victims have few funds and are largely voluntary. Since victim needs span many professionals' work (police, prosecution, courts, release authorities) but are central to none, the effort to meet victim needs, even though they are now acknowledged, tends to collide with greater organizational imperatives based on the core business of that professional group, as expressed in performance indicators. Serving victims rarely leads to promotion; failing victims rarely leads to censure.

Since the article was written, the history of victims and criminal justice in England and Wales has tended to reinforce these views. There have been major innovations, with the provisions for vulnerable witnesses to give evidence using special measures (screens, video, etc.) being probably the most major. The extent of the definition of a vulnerable witness has been extended from a child witness to any who have difficulties in giving evidence or who are intimidated or scared. The measures have been successful – and implemented (Hamlyn et al., 2004). Similarly, a service of support for victims and witnesses has been started in every court: the Witness Service. It is interesting, however, that these measures have been introduced to benefit 'witnesses' – not victims per se. Witnesses are a central concern of court-based professionals. Witnesses who are too scared or too ill at ease to give evidence threaten the path of criminal justice. Though victims will benefit from these measures, it is clear that they have not been introduced primarily to meet victim needs, nor recognize the victim as a party to criminal justice.

Christie considers that criminal justice is probably beyond reform. Instead, one should use civil justice, or introduce restorative justice. It is beyond the scope of this introduction to provide an overview of restorative justice. However, its values are, as Ashworth says, those of empowerment, dialogue, negotiation and agreement. It recognizes and includes victims in the justice response, by definition. Is this not then a more adequate justice response? Ashworth might cautiously agree, but he would also argue that many of the elements of criminal justice would need to be introduced if restorative justice is to deal with criminal offences. The state, for example, should be recognized as a party, as well as the offender, the victim and possibly the community – to provide a public response, and to guarantee human rights. The ways in which the community might be involved in our fragmented western societies need to be worked through – and the potentially biasing tendencies of local justice considered. Above all, Ashworth would prize values of consistency, proportionality and impartiality, and place 'public interest' values above those espoused by participants in a restorative justice event. These are traditional criminal justice strengths. The question is then whether they are necessarily threatened by restorative justice,[4] whether safeguards can be introduced to limit the potential for harm, or whether processes can be staged in time to prevent abuse.[5] If conflicts between restorative justice and criminal justice values remain after these possibilities have been considered, perhaps the fundamental question, which justice theorists have so far failed to consider, is whether values of, say, inclusion and communication are more important, or less important than those of consistency and 'impartiality'.

Notes

1   Abolitionists, including Matthiessen and Christie, believe that the criminal just-
    ice system is an outmoded and ineffective method of reducing reoffending
    and supporting victims, useful only to display the power of the state. They
    hence advocate the abolition of the traditional criminal justice system and its
    replacement by civil or restorative justice.
2   Restorative practice includes various schemes in which the offender works
    to benefit the community, whereas restorative justice is normally taken as
    involving the victim of that offence.
3   The exceptions being major human rights violations which are the subject of
    international instruments, such as genocide and trafficking in human beings.
    The only international treaties which have set up separate means for prosecut-
    ing and trying offenders, however, are those dealing with war crimes (such as
    those relating to the former Yugoslavia and Ruanda). Hence most offences
    under international treaties have needed to be incorporated into national
    legislation and are investigated, prosecuted and tried in national courts.
4   We have argued, for example, that the offender's interests are not necessarily
    in opposition to those of the victim or state (Shapland et al., 2006).
5   The staged pre-sentence or pre-prosecution decision restorative youth con-
    ferencing in Northern Ireland, whereby the results of the conference go to the
    sentencer or prosecutor for final decisions, is one example of such staged
    safeguards for proportionality and taking into account the public interest
    (Campbell et al., 2006). Circle sentencing techniques in Canada are another.

Recommended further reading

Shapland, J., Atkinson, A., Atkinson, H., Chapman, B., Colledge, E., Dignan, J., Howes,
    M., Johnstone, J., Robinson, G. and Sorsby, A. (2006) 'Situating restorative
    justice within criminal justice', *Theoretical Criminology*, 10: 505–32.

5.1

The voice of victims of crime: estimating the true level of conventional crime
by Anna Alvazzi del Frate

[. . .]

Introduction

The main objectives of the International Crime Victim Survey include:

- Providing comparative indicators of crime and victimization risks, indicators of perception of crime and fear of crime, performance of law enforcement, victim assistance and crime prevention
- Promoting crime surveys as an important research and policy tool at the international, national and local levels
- Enhancing adequate research and policy analysis methodology
- Creating an opportunity for transparency in public debate about crime and reactions to crime
- Encouraging public and criminal justice concern about citizens' participation in the evaluation of criminal policy and particularly in partnership in crime prevention
- Promoting international cooperation by providing an opportunity for a large number of countries to share methodology and experience through their participation in a well coordinated international research project

The International Crime Victim Survey shares with national crime surveys the objective of measuring crime beyond the information provided by police statistics. Indeed, one of the most important aspects of the Survey is its ability to measure the quantity of crime that is not reported to the police. The reasons for the non-reporting of crimes have to do with the inaccessibility of the authorities, which makes reporting difficult, complicated reporting procedures and a lack of confidence that reporting victimization to the police will result in solving the crime or punishing the perpetrator. Such measurements of unreported crime demonstrate that reports of official crime levels as outlined by Shaw, van Dijk and Rhomberg (2003) provide only part of the picture and that citizens' elementary right of access to justice, and that of victims to be heard and protected are not met. This is particularly true in developing countries and countries with economies in transition and among vulnerable groups such as women and children.

The study of corruption, including "street-level corruption" and the perception of corruption among the general population, is an important and unique feature of the Survey. The perception of corruption can be monitored over time and compared with an objective measure.

Participation in the Survey has been facilitated by the international community and donors who have taken an interest in and supported the reform process towards a market economy and a democratic political system. It is, however, important to repeat the collection of data on a regular basis. The fifth "sweep" of the Survey is planned for 2004.

Overview of the international crime victim survey, 1989–2002

Initially called the International Crime Survey, the International Crime Victim Survey was carried out for the first time in 14 developed countries in 1989. Subsequently, in 1992, a face-to-face interview for the questionnaire was developed to enable the participation of countries in which telephone interviews would not have been feasible at the time. From that time, it became possible to conduct standardized surveys on crime in a number of countries for which very little information on crime was available. The third Survey was conducted in 1996 and the fourth in 2000; the project now includes more than 70 countries, all of which have participated in the survey at least once. The fourth Survey was carried out in 2000 and included 17 national surveys and 31 city surveys (16 capital cities in Central and Eastern Europe, 4 in Asia, 7 in Africa and 4 in Latin America). (For a detailed list of survey participants, see Table 5.1.1.)

The regional breakdown used in the Survey is intended to be an approximate grouping of countries that are geographically close to each other and that share some cultural values. However, countries within each region may differ significantly in terms of gross domestic product and their ranking on the United Nations Development Programme human development index (www.undp.org/currentHDR_E/).

Methodology

The Survey targets samples of households in which only one respondent, aged 16 or above, is selected. National samples include at least 2,000

Table 5.1.1 Countries and territories that participated in the International Crime Victim Survey at least once, 1989–2002
(N = national survey; C = city survey)

Country or area, by region	Type of survey	Country or area, by region	Type of survey
Africa		**Western Europe**	
Botswana	C	Austria	N
Egypt	C	Belgium	N
Lesotho	C	Denmark	N
Mozambique	C	Finland	N
Namibia	C	France	N
Nigeria	C	Germany	N
South Africa	C	Italy	N
Swaziland	C	Malta	N
Tunisia		Netherlands	N
Uganda	C	Norway	N
United Republic of Tanzania	C	Portugal	N
Zambia	C	Scotland	N
Zimbabwe	C	Spain	N and C
Asia		Sweden	N
Azerbaijan	C	Switzerland	N
Cambodia	C	United Kingdom	
China	C	England and Wales	N
India	C	Northern Ireland	N
Indonesia	C	**Central and Eastern Europe**	
Japan	N	Albania	C
Kyrgyzstan	C	Belarus	C
Mongolia	C	Bulgaria	C
Papua New Guinea	C	Croatia	C
Philippines	C	Czech Republic	C
Republic of Korea	C	Estonia	C
Latin America		Georgia	C
Argentina	C	Hungary	C
Bolivia	C	Latvia	C
Brazil	C	Lithuania	C
Colombia	C	Poland	N and C
Costa Rica	C	Romania	C
Panama	C	Russian Federation	C
Paraguay	C	Slovakia	C
North America		Slovenia	C
Canada	N	The former Yugoslav	
United States of America	N	Republic of Macedonia	C
Oceania		Ukraine	C
Australia	N	Yugoslavia	C
New Zealand	N		

respondents, who are generally interviewed using the computer-assisted telephone interview technique. In the countries where that method could not be used because of insufficient distribution of telephones, face-to-face interviews were conducted in the main cities, generally with samples of 1,000–1,500 respondents.

The questionnaire includes sections on 11 types of "conventional" crime, for which standard definitions are provided. Questions on consumer fraud and corruption are included; those are also accompanied by standard definitions. The questionnaire is also used to gather data on whether crimes were reported to the police, the reasons for not reporting crimes, attitudes towards the police, the fear of crime and crime prevention measures.

Of the eleven "conventional" crimes, some are "household crimes", that is, crimes that can be seen as affecting the household at large. Respondents report on all the incidents involving household crimes that are known to them. A first group of crimes deals with vehicles owned by the respondent or other members of his or her household: theft of car; theft from car; car vandalism; theft of bicycle; and theft of motorcycle. A second group refers to breaking and entering burglary; and attempted burglary. A third group of crimes refers to crimes experienced personally by the respondent: robbery; theft of personal property; assault or threat; and sexual incidents (women only). Finally, the questionnaire addresses two more types of crime that may have been experienced by the respondents: consumer fraud; and bribery or corruption.

Regular meetings of survey coordinators from participating countries have helped to facilitate the translation of concepts and definitions into the various languages.

Data analysis

Each sweep of the Survey provides an enormous amount of information. In-depth analysis of the database is one of the objectives of researchers across the world. The wealth of data produced can hardly be analysed between two consecutive sweeps of the Survey. Analysis of the Survey has been carried out mostly within comparable groups of countries, for example, national surveys in the "industrialized countries" city surveys in Central and Eastern Europe and the developing countries (van Dijk et al, 1990). Analysis of the main comparative results concerning industrialized countries was published upon completion of the first, second, third and fourth international crime victim surveys (van Dijk et al, 1990; del Frate et al, 1993; Mayhew and van Dijk, 1997; van Kesteren et al, 2000); results from developing countries and countries with economies in transition were made available in numerous publications (del Frate et al, 1993; Mayhew and van Dijk, 1997; van Kesteren et al, 2000; Zvekic and del Frate, 1995; del Frate, 1998; Hatalak et al, 2000; Zvekic, 1998); and results from the International Crime Victim Survey 2000 were also widely published (del Frate, 2002; del Frate and van Kesteren, 2002, 2003; Naudé and Prinsloo, 2002). The present article will deal with some of the main findings of the Survey conducted in 2000. For international comparisons across groups, only respondents located in urban areas with populations of more than 100,000 are considered from national surveys.[1]

The crime count

The Survey provides an overall measure of victimization in the previous year through any of the 11 conventional crimes included in the questionnaire (which do not include consumer fraud and corruption). On average, approximately 28 per cent of respondents suffered at least one form of victimization over the twelve months preceding the interview. Overall victimization of around 27 per cent was observed in four out of six regions of the world (Western Europe, Central and Eastern Europe, North America and Australasia), while in Africa and Latin America much higher levels of victimization were observed (35 and 46 per cent respectively).

Figure 5.1.1 shows prevalence rates for burglary and robbery in the six world regions and Australia. In the Survey, burglary is defined as housebreaking for purposes of theft. It is a crime against the household that may involve very secure or poorly protected residences. While, in the

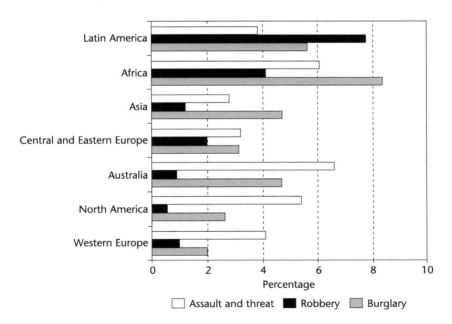

Figure 5.1.1 Victimization rates for burglary, robbery, assault and threat, one-year period.

industrialized world, burglars frequently steal objects of a very high value, such as jewellery or stereo equipment, burglary in developing countries is often aimed at stealing food, domestic appliances, linen or cutlery. In regions where households have installed various levels of protection against burglary, such incidents tend to involve damage to doors, locks or windows. The Survey shows that this occurs more frequently in Western Europe, North America and Australia. Interestingly, the Survey shows that high levels of damage also occur in Africa during incidents of burglary.

The consequences of burglary in terms of monetary value may be very different in different contexts, although it is generally considered very serious, since it is a violation of the domestic sphere. It is therefore a crime that is well remembered by survey respondents and provides a reliable indicator of property crime.

Robbery is defined as theft from the person by use of force, thus involving direct contact between victim and offender (called "contact" crime). The crime category of assault and threat is defined in the Survey as personal aggression, by a stranger, relative or friend, without the purpose of stealing and is another contact crime. Although physical consequences in most cases may be minor, the crime may well have significant emotional repercussions for victims.

Figure 5.1.1 shows the regional distribution of victimization rates for burglaries, robberies and assaults and threats, as observed in the Survey. The differences among the regions were larger for the two crimes involving property of which the highest number occurred in Africa and Latin America. Burglary was over four times more frequent in Africa than in Western Europe. Robbery was approximately eight times higher in Latin American than in either Western Europe, North America or Australia. The data on robbery confirm the regional distribution of this crime as observed in official statistics on reported crime.

Rates of assault and threat showed smaller variations among regions: they were lowest in Central and Eastern Europe and Asia, and highest in Africa, North America and Australia.

Previous analysis using the Survey data at the aggregate level showed a negative correlation between the human development index and property crime (del Frate, 1998) The 2000 Survey data confirmed that levels and effects of victimization are more pronounced in the developing countries than in the rest of the world. That contrasts sharply with the fact that official recorded crime levels in developed countries are far higher than in developing countries (Shaw et al, 2003).

Crimes reported to the police
Crimes are more frequently reported to the police in Western Europe, North America and Australia than in the other regions, thus showing an opposite trend with respect to the frequency of victimization. It is concluded that in the regions where more crime occurs, the police know less about it.

In general, car theft was the most frequently reported crime, followed by burglary (see Figure 5.1.2). However, the considerable differences that exist among countries and regions in respect of insurance coverage (since a valid report to the police is a requirement in order to submit a claim to an insurance company, it is expected that reporting is more frequent in the areas where house insurance is more common) and the ease of reporting (determined by factors such as access to the police, availability of telephones, and so forth) result in different reporting patterns. Burglary was more frequently reported in Western Europe, North America and Australia.

Robbery was also frequently reported in Western Europe, but much less in the other studied regions, in particular in Latin America, where only one victim of robbery out of five reported to the police. Again, this is consistent with the conclusions reached by Shaw, van Dijk and Rhomberg (2003). It appears that the greater the level of crime, the smaller the number of citizens willing to approach the police. More than 50 per cent of the Latin American victims of robbery who did not report the crime to the police said they did so because "the police would not do anything" and approximately 25 per cent of them said that they feared or disliked the police.

Assault and threat was the least frequently reported crime, with rates around or below 40 per cent in all regions. Significantly, levels of reporting did not show any variations since the previous analysis of the 1996 Survey results.

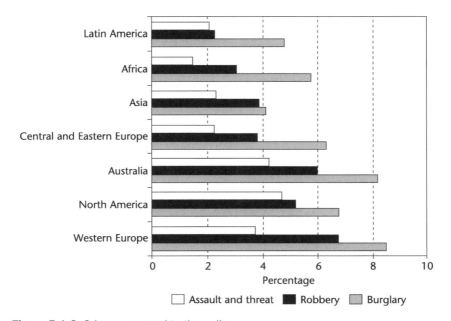

Figure 5.1.2 Crimes reported to the police.

Trends in victimization, 1996–2000

An analysis of regional trends can be made by comparing victimization rates in the countries that took part in both the 1996 and 2000 sweeps of the Survey.[2] The comparison reveals that victimization rates are consistent in most regions and modest variations have been registered, with an overall trend downwards for the three types of crime considered.[3]

The biggest changes, both upwards and downwards, were found in Latin America and Africa, where rates of robbery increased considerably (contrary to what was observed in the other regions) and burglary decreased more sharply than in the other regions (see Figure 5.1.3). This conclusion is again consistent with the analysis of Shaw, van Dijk and Rhomberg (2003).

As regards assault with force, aside from the relatively steady trend observed in Western Europe and North America and a slight decrease in Central and Eastern Europe, developing countries show large variations that do not allow for easy interpretation. While Asia and Latin America showed a downward trend, assaults increased in Africa.

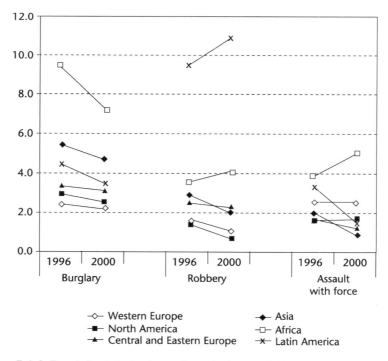

Figure 5.1.3 Trends in victimization, selected crimes, 1996–2000.

Corruption and consumer fraud

Questions on the direct experience of respondents with corruption or bribery of public officials are one of the unique features of the Survey.[4] Due to the scarcity of available information, corruption is often measured by surveys. The International Crime Victim Survey offers the advantage of addressing citizens with questions on corruption from the point of view of crime and victimization, thus highlighting that having to pay a bribe is a form of abuse of power that entails being victimized. Such an approach facilitates understanding of the question across cultures and partially lifts the burden from the respondent to admit that he or she also did something wrong by agreeing to pay. International Crime Victim Survey data have been extensively used for assessing corruption in several areas, if not as an absolute measure of the phenomenon, at least to compare with other available indicators (Hoddess et al, 2001; Zvekic and Camerer, 2002).

There is a high level of consistency between 1996 and 2000 results from the Survey, with a slight decrease in victimization rates for both corruption and consumer fraud. As regards regional comparisons, it should be noted that corruption in Western Europe, North America and Australia is almost non-existent, while it is a widespread phenomenon in the rest of the world.

The analysis of the type of public official who most frequently demanded bribes revealed the extensive involvement of police officers in corruption. This is a critical issue in the complicated relationship between the police and the community that is also reflected in the overall assessment of police performance.

Consumer fraud of some sort, especially when dealing with retail stores, was experienced by some 9 per cent of respondents in Western Europe and in North America and Australia. Victimization rates for such fraud were much higher in the other regions and especially in Central and Eastern European countries (see Figure 5.1.4).

Assessment of police performance

The section of the Survey dealing with the assessment of police performance (Figure 5.1.5) revealed that respondents in Latin America, Central and Eastern Europe and Africa had low levels of satisfaction with police efforts in preventing and controlling crime.[5] This suggests that in many countries there is still much to be done by police services in order to gain public confidence.

Because of a change in the 2000 questionnaire, it is not possible to analyse directly trends in public opinion of police performance. It appears, however, that respondents tended to express their opinion of the police more freely than in previous sweeps of the Survey. Indeed, the percentage of respondents falling in the "don't know" category was very small.

A correlation was observed between satisfaction with the police and

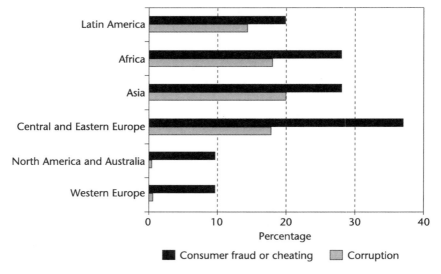

Figure 5.1.4 Victimization rates for corruption and consumer fraud, one-year period.

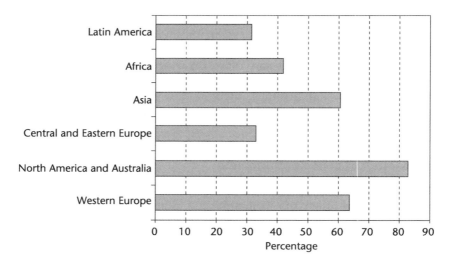

Figure 5.1.5 Satisfaction with the police in controlling crime.

reporting to the police for the various types of crime. The correlation is stronger for reporting assault and threat, which is the least reported type of crime (r 0.473, N = 47). It appears, therefore, that a good perception of the police may increase public cooperation with that service.

Conclusion

By disclosing previously unrevealed aspects of crime and victimization at the international level, the International Crime Victim Survey has become an indispensable source of information for researchers, policy makers and the international community. In particular, inclusion in indexes (such as the Transparency International Corruption Perceptions Index (www.transparency.org/cpi/index.html#cpi) and global reports (such as the *Human Development Report* (www.undp.org/currentHDR_E/), the *Global Report on Crime and Justice* (United Nations, 1999), the *World Report on Violence and Health* (World Health Organization, 2002), the *European Sourcebook of Crime and Criminal Justice Statistics* (Council of Europe, 1999), the *Global Corruption Report* (Hoddess et al, 2001) and *Crime and Criminal Justice in Europe and North America, 1990–1994*) (Kangaspunta et al, 1998). The International Crime Victim Survey has also been included in the United Nations *Manual for the Development of a System of Criminal Justice Statistics* (United Nations, Sales No. E. 03).

It is expected that, in the future, the International Crime Victim Survey will become an even more solid source of data, because a greater number of countries will be included and those which have already participated will continue to do so, thus reinforcing the longitudinal series. An effort in the direction of further standardization of data collection is currently being made by the group coordinating the project (del Frate, 2003). The involvement of institutional partners such as the Justice Department of Canada, the Ministry of Justice of the Netherlands and the Home Office of the United Kingdom of Great Britain and Northern Ireland, together with the United Nations Office on Drugs and Crime and the United Nations Interregional Crime and Justice Research Institute ensures the monitoring and coordination of activities at the central level. It is also expected that, in future, the International Crime against Business Survey and the International Violence against Women Survey, which are currently under development, will play important roles in complementing the International Crime Victim Survey in the areas of crime against business and violence against women.

Notes

1   More information is available at the International Crime Victim Survey web site (www.unicri.it/icvs). It should be noted that, due to the increased number of participating countries, the groupings by region described in the present article differ from those discussed in earlier publications, such that direct comparisons with data presented elsewhere are not possible.

2   The analysis of trends at the regional level only included the 31 countries that participated in the International Crime Victim Survey in 1996 and

2000. Fewer countries are therefore included in each region and they are not the same countries as those presented in the analysis of the 2000 Survey. Possible inconsistencies in sampling procedure suggest that some caution should be exercised in reading trends, especially as regards developing countries.

3   This section deals with data on burglary, robbery and assault with force, that is, only the portion of incidents in the assault and threat category that involved the use of force.

4   The question on corruption was as follows: "In some areas there is a problem of corruption among government or public officials. During 1999, has any government official, for instance a customs officer, police officer or inspector, in your own country asked you or expected you to pay a bribe for his service?"

5   The question on satisfaction with the police in controlling crime was as follows: "Taking everything into account, how good do you think the police in your area are at controlling crime? Do you think they do a very good job, a fairly good job, a fairly poor job, or a very poor job?" Figure V shows percentages for the answers "very good" and "fairly good".

5.2

Responsibilities, rights and restorative justice
by Andrew Ashworth

[. . .]

Restorative justice is practice-led in most of its manifestations (see Miers 2001). Although the writings of John Braithwaite (e.g. 1989, 1993, 1999), Howard Zehr (1990), Martin Wright (1996) and others may be a source of inspiration for some practitioners and policy makers, there is also a certain reflexivity at work. The theory of restorative justice has to a large extent developed through practice, and will probably continue to do so. One consequence of this is that there is no single notion of RJ, no single type of process, no single theory. Tony Marshall suggests that a commonly accepted definition of restorative justice would be: 'a process whereby parties with a stake in a specific offence collectively resolve how to deal with the aftermath of the offence and its implications for the future' (Marshall 1999: 5). This usefully identifies three central elements in restorative justice: the importance of process, the notion of stakeholders, and the fairly wide-ranging aspirations for outcomes.

In terms of restorative process, the keynotes are empowerment, dialogue, negotiation and agreement. Professionals should not be dominant: the voices of the stakeholders should be the loudest. The stakeholders are assumed to be the victim, the offender and the community. Turning to restorative outcomes, what is to be restored is broadly stated as 'whatever dimensions of restoration matter to the victims, offenders and communities affected by the crime' (Braithwaite 1999: 6). Restoration is often seen as a form of reintegration, of the community and of individuals. Outcomes are measured chiefly by the satisfaction of the stakeholders in each case, and not by comparison with the outcomes of like cases.

One of the aims of the restorative justice movement is to replace forms of state justice for a wide range of offences and offenders. This means changing the focus of the term 'criminal justice' itself, away from the assumption that it is a matter concerning only the state and the defendant/offender, and towards a conception that includes as stakeholders the victim and the community too. However, it will be argued here that such a process of change should not have the effect of depriving defendants/offenders of safeguards and rights that should be assured to them in any processes which impose obligations as the consequence of committing an offence. Important steps have been and are being taken to ensure that appropriate standards are respected in restorative processes and outcomes, notably in the United Nations draft 'Basic Principles on the Use of Restorative Justice Programmes in Criminal Justice Matters' (United Nations 2000; see further Braithwaite, this issue). However, there are further and deeper issues to be confronted.

The aim of this article is to generate discussion on four of those issues. First, what should be the role of the state and its organs in the administration of criminal justice and in the determination of criminal justice outcomes? Second, if it is argued that the community should have a more central role in criminal justice, what implications does this have? Third, what are the rights and responsibilities of victims in matters of criminal justice? And fourth, if it is accepted that there must be some kind of 'default system' to deal with cases that cannot be handled through restorative justice, what form should it take?

The responsibilities of the state

It is central to the philosophy of restorative justice that the stakeholders should be able to participate in dialogue about the offence. Undoubtedly the offender is one stakeholder, but who are the others? It may be claimed that the community and the victim also have a stake in the response to the offence, but what about the state? At a time when statist assumptions are crumbling, when 'neo-liberal' and 'advanced liberal' analyses (e.g. Rose 2000; Shearing 2000) point to the changing role of the state and governmentality, what should be the role of the state in matters of criminal justice?

It is common to refer to the 'public interest' in preventing or prosecuting crime: what does this mean? What is the significance of the phrase 'a crime against society'? The idea seems to be that, what it is decided to make certain conduct a crime rather than simply a civil wrong, this implies that it should not be merely a matter for the victim whether some action is taken against the malefactor; and even that there is a public interest in ensuring that people who commit such wrongs are liable to punishment, not merely to civil suit (Cretney et al. 1994). Thus Antony Duff argues for a category 'of "public" wrongs that are properly condemned and dealt with as wrongs by the community as a whole' (Duff 2000: 62), and he illustrates this with crimes of 'domestic' violence:

> But whatever else is unclear about the rights and wrongs of a domestic dispute . . . such violence should surely not be seen as a matter for nego-tiation or compromise. It should be condemned by the whole community

as an unqualified wrong; and this is done by defining and prosecuting it as a crime. (Duff 2000: 62)

These are not propositions with which a restorative justice advocate would necessarily disagree. But another element of the argument is more contentious: that it is the responsibility of the state to ensure that there is order and law-abidance in society, and to establish a system for the administration of criminal justice.

In crude terms, the political theory would be that citizens agree to obey laws in return for protection of their vital interests, though keeping their right of self-defence for occasions of emergency when state protection is unavailable. As David Garland puts it, 'over time, the effective control of crime and the routine protection of citizens from criminal depredations had come to form elements of the promise that the state holds out to its citizens' (Garland 2001: 109–10). This serves as the basis of the justification for maintaining a police force, a system of public prosecutions, the courts, and other aspects of the criminal justice system. Thus Duff regards it as obvious 'that the state owes it to its citizens to protect them from crime' through the criminal law and its administration (Duff 2000: 112).

> If a community is, through the legal organs of the state, to take seriously the public wrong done to a citizen, it must not only sympathize with the victim but also censure the offender. It owes it to the victim, whose wrong it shares, and to the offender as a member of the normative community, to try to get the offender to recognize the wrong and to make a suitable apology for it. (Duff 2000: 114)

These arguments in favour of the state's responsibility for criminal justice[1] are joined by other consequential justifications for the state taking over the administration of criminal justice from victims and other individuals— partly to avoid placing on victims the additional burden of having to bring offenders to justice (Reeves and Mulley 2000: 130), and partly to avoid the social instability that would result if people had to 'take the law into their own hands' in responding to offences, which might encourage vigilantism (MacCormick and Garland 1998: 22, 27).

None of this is to rule out some delegation of this function by the state (in whole or in part) to others, either by moving it down to the level of the local community (MacCormick and Garland 1998: 27) or by elements of privatization. Recent decades have seen increasing decentralization and 'responsibilization' in criminal justice (Garland 2001), for a variety of political reasons; one aspect of the restorative justice movement, too, is a relocation of authority over responses to crime (Bayley 2001: 212). It is important to question whether these changes are right in principle, but first we must acknowledge two major failures of the statist approach.

First, in many political systems the prevailing statist approach has neglected (some would say, reinforced) social inequalities. Thus Kent Roach writes of disadvantaged groups having to 'rely on the criminal sanction's false promise of security and equality' (1999: 117), and argues that the state's responsibility for protecting citizens should be viewed in the wider context of public health, and therefore tackled as one element in a social programme to improve the conditions of life of groups who are disproportionately victimized and are not in a position to buy private security or healthcare (*ibid.*: 261). This is a timely reminder of the limitations of focusing criminal policy initiatives on the criminal justice system, rather than locating them in the wider social structure.

Second, and more deeply, there are countries in which the legitimacy of the state and its apparatus, including the criminal justice system, has suffered a serious collapse-obvious examples were South Africa (van Zyl Smit 1999; Shearing 2001) and Northern Ireland (McEvoy and Mika 2001). Some of the restorative justice initiatives in the most difficult social conditions are as much about social control as about responses to crime (see McEvoy and Mika 2001 on Northern Ireland). In still other countries it is possible to say that there have been or are legitimacy deficits, particularly in respect of certain groups (Blagg 1997; Tauri 1999), which suggest that reality lies some distance from basic democratic theory. Conditions of this kind may provide fertile soil for initiatives based on restorative justice, with its emphasis on greater participation and community involvement, although even restorative justice initiatives intended to tap into the culture of indigenous communities court the risk of increasing the extent of official power over them (Cunneen 1997; Blagg 1997; cf. Braithwaite 1997).

These deficiencies in relation to social disadvantage and governmental legitimacy have led many restorative justice advocates to the view that the state should not have a prominent position in the administration of criminal justice, and should instead have a residual role in providing facilities and in enforcing post-offence agreements reached by conferences, etc. The facilitative state would leave restorative conferences with deliberative space in which to decide on the most appropriate response to an offender's crime, from which it seems to follow that they might select (within ill-defined outer limits) whatever approach the particular conference prefers. Would this confine the state's role too narrowly? Are there duties that the state should retain, no matter that there are elements of 'rolling back' or 'hollowing out' the state's functions which lead to a measure of privatization and responsibilization?

The focus of these questions must be on the process of responding to crime, a process that (even within restorative justice) involves a measure of public censure and the placing of obligations on offenders. Garland identifies:

> an emerging distinction between the *punishment of criminals* which remains the business of the state (and becomes once again a significant

symbol of state power) and the *control of crime*, which is increasingly deemed to be 'beyond the state' in significant respects. And as its control capacity comes to be viewed as limited and contingent, the state's power to punish takes on a renewed political salience and priority. (Garland 2001: 120)

What reasons can be given for state control over punishment and official responses to offences? Two arguments are that criminal justice must be administered 'in the public interest', and that it should ensure respect for human rights. Since, as argued above, a defining feature of criminal offences is that they are offences against the state or collectivity, it is right that the state should ensure that the response is based on general principles duly established and applicable throughout the jurisdiction. This connects closely with the second argument about respect for human rights. The state surely owes it to offenders to exercise its power according to settled principles that uphold citizens' rights to equal respect and equality of treatment. Decisions on sentence should be taken by independent and impartial tribunals (see below), operating on principle and transparently, within a legal framework. There is an important distinction between tribunals responding in a principled manner to relevant factual differences between cases, and responding on the basis of their own views or preferences. The latter is contrary to the rule of law, and at odds with the notion of a *Rechtsstaal*. As John Gardner has argued, one of the implications of acting according to the 'rule of law' is 'that questions of how people are to be treated relative to one another always come to the fore at the point of its application'. This is not to rule out mitigation or mercy in sentencing, but to assert that 'what falls to be mitigated is none other than the sentence which is, in the court's [judgment], required by justice' (Gardner 1998: 36–7). In other words, the power exercised by imposing obligations on offenders in response to their offending ought, in principle, to be exercised consistently as between citizens, according to settled standards.

Although the list of failures of state justice is a lengthy one, the state must, as the primary political authority, retain control over criminal justice and its administration. It must do so for pragmatic reasons concerned with security (Bayley 2001: 218), and it must do so in order to ensure respect for the rule of law and human rights standards. This is not to ignore the shortcomings of human rights declarations and their enforcement, or to overlook the malleability of the 'rule of law' principle. Rather it is to argue that these remain fundamental ideals, which should be taken more seriously rather than discarded. The state ought, out of fairness to the people in respect of whom its coercive powers are being exercised, to insist on 'rule of law' principles and so ensure consistency of response to offences. Insofar as restorative justice approaches are adopted, the state's responsibility should be to impose a framework that guarantees these safeguards to offenders—an aim no less worthy in those societies where state legitimacy is contested. The recent draft UN standards amount to a small but welcome step in this direction (United Nations 2000; Braithwaite, this issue). We should also recall that the state has responsibilities towards victims: in the context of restorative justice, this means that it is wrong in principle to place burdens on victims as part of any criminal justice initiative (Reeves and Mulley 2000).

The empowerment of communities

It is the hallmark of many restorative justice approaches that they draw into criminal justice both victims and the wider community (although there is no unanimity on this: some regard the involvement of community members as 'at odds with the principles underlying conferencing': Morris and Maxwell 2000: 215). Garland is among those who have argued for the delegation of sentencing powers to communities (to 'authorities intermediate between the state and the individual': MacCormick and Garland 1998: 27). He does this for reasons similar to those of many restorative justice theorists—that the closer the adjudicators and enforcers are to the offender, the more likely they are to be effective in bringing about the desired changes in behaviour (partly, perhaps, because their legitimacy is more likely to impress itself on the offender).

Much depends, of course, on the conception of community on which reliance is being placed. Every citizen may be seen as a member of several cross-cutting communities: each of us has 'a number of community attachments, articulated in terms of factors such as race, ethnicity, class, gender, age, sexuality, occupation' (Lacey 1998: 144). Some restorative justice advocates would probably claim to have an open and inclusive approach to 'community', but in practice most schemes seem to involve the families of victim and offender, and yet to regard the community (where there are 'community representatives') as a geographical entity. If this means that local communities can adopt separate standards, the result is likely to be a form of 'justice by geography' or 'postcode lottery'. Indeed, the empowerment of communities, howsoever defined, might involve a sacrifice of 'rule of law' values such as consistency, which, it was argued, ought to be standards for criminal justice. Is it right for the state, or for bodies exercising authority delegated by the state, to use its coercive powers differently against each of two people, one who commits an offence in one locality and another with exactly similar background who commits a similar offence in a different locality? Surely not; it happens in both 'conventional' and restorative justice systems, but the difference is that in the former it is regarded as a malfunction to be removed whereas in the latter it may be thought beneficial. The conflict can be represented as one between principle and pragmatism, since there are those who regard the use of local knowledge and local ordering as an essential element of successful social control in contemporary societies (e.g. Braithwaite 2000: 232, and Shearing 2001; cf. van Ness 1993). It is certainly true that policing policies are increasingly responsive to local concerns; and, as one looks across European countries or American states, there may be stark differences in criminal justice policy between neighbouring jurisdictions—federal systems differ, for example, in respect of the allocation of responsibility for the administration of criminal justice. The issue cannot be argued to a conclusion here, but the very least that is required by the principle of the consistent use of state power over offenders is that local decision making should be constrained by general standards of procedural and substantive justice.

Turning from restorative processes to restorative outcomes, what is meant by the goal of 'community restoration'? This is regarded by most advocates as one desirable outcome of restorative justice processes, but its practical meaning turns on two issues which remain unsettled. One is the conception of community that is being used. If the broad aim is to restore the 'communities affected by the crime' (Braithwaite 1999: 6), as well as the victim and victim's family, this will usually mean a geographical community; but where an offence targets a victim because of race, religion, sexual orientation etc., that will point to a different community that needs to be restored. This leads to the second issue: what exactly is community 'restoration', and on what criteria are the form and amount of community restoration to be calculated? Reintegration is a term often used in this context, but its practical implications remain unclear. Many restorative justice theorists and others (e.g. Zedner 1994; Walgrave 1995; Duff 2000: 99–106) regard as the paradigm of community restoration some form of community service (now termed 'community punishment orders' in England and Wales). This is largely a symbolic form of restoration, and therefore it must be necessary to devise a scale of 'wrongs to the community' and to match it with a register of degrees of community restoration (cf. Meier 1998). There seems to be little endeavour among restorative justice theorists to deal with this issue, and certainly nothing comparable to the efforts of desert theorists to work out parameters of proportionality (cf. van Ness 1993 with von Hirsch and Jareborg 1991, and von Hirsch 1993; chs 2 and 4).

A further issue of principle concerns impartiality. It is one thing for critics of 'conventional' criminal justice systems to argue that those systems fail to sentence 'objectively', despite their aspirations, because they fail to avoid discrimination on grounds of class, race or gender. It is quite another thing to devise a system that would avoid problems of bias, or of informal hierarchies growing up, or of local power structures tending to dominate (Lacey 1998: ch. 5). Advocates of community justice stress the importance of inclusion rather than exclusion, and the concept of community is often associated with self-regulation, consent and agreement (Pavlich 2001). There may be examples of sentencing circles and restorative justice conferences that appear to avoid these difficulties, but there is always the danger that, as

Adam Crawford has warned, 'the normative appeal of community [may be] confused with empirical reality':

> the ideal of community should be forced to confront the empirical reality, which reminds us that communities are often marked (and sustained) by social exclusion, forms of coercion, and the differential distribution of power relations. (Crawford 2000: 290–1; cf. McEvoy and Mika 2001)

Among the problems here might be that majorities in some communities might disagree with certain criminal laws, perhaps laws intended to protect the weak against the strong or to eradicate drunk driving (Johnstone 2001: 55–7). Allowing community-based tribunals to determine the response to such laws is fraught with difficulty. Impartiality is a key value in justice processes, and yet in restorative justice theory it stands in tension with other values such as participation, involvement and empowerment (see Johnstone 2001: 153–8). But the tension is not insoluble, since it would be possible to concede the case for greater participation by members of affected communities while insisting that the power of decision making remains in impartial hands.

Rights and responsibilities of the victim

It is common for those writing on restorative justice to insist that all parties 'with a stake in the offence' ought to be able to participate in the disposition of the case, through a circle, conference, etc. (e.g. Llewellyn and Howse 1998: 19). The victim certainly has 'a stake', and Christie's (1977) assertion that the 'conflict' in some sense 'belongs' to the victim has become a modern orthodoxy among restorative justice supporters (e.g. Morris and Maxwell 2000: 207, who write of 'returning the offence to those most affected by it and encouraging them to determine appropriate responses to it'). The approach has ancient roots (Braithwaite 1999: 1–2 for a summary and references), although the growing awareness of the existence of secondary victimization (e.g. Morgan and Zedner 1992 on child victims) demonstrates the complexity of the issues arising.

The politico-historical argument is that most modern legal systems exclude the victim so as to bolster their own power. Originally the state wanted to take over criminal proceedings from victims as an assertion of power, and what now passes for 'normal' is simply a usurpation that has no claim to be the natural order. My concern is not to dispute this rather romantic interpretation of criminal justice in early history (Daly 2000 does this splendidly; also Johnstone 2001: ch. 3) but rather to raise three points of principle which have a bearing on the nature and extent of victims' rights: the principle of compensation for wrongs, the principle of proportionality, and the principle of independence and impartiality.

The first point of principle is the most direct of all in its target. What I want to argue is that the victim's legitimate interest is in compensation and/or reparation from the offender, and not in the form or quantum of the offender's punishment. The distinction between punishment and compensation is not widely appreciated: when a court fines an offender £300 for careless driving in a case where death resulted (but where there was no conviction for the more serious offence of causing death by dangerous driving), newspapers will often report comments such as 'my son's life has been valued at just £300'. However, the size of the fine will usually be related to the offender's culpability (and financial resources), and will not be a 'valuation' of the loss. Compensation for loss, from whatever source, is a separate matter. It may not require a separate civil case: English criminal courts are required to consider ordering the offender to pay compensation to the victim or victim's family, so far as the offender's means allow. However, in many cases the offender will not have the funds to pay realistic compensation. It is now recognized as part of the state's responsibility for criminal justice that it should provide a compensation fund for victims of crimes of violence, at least (see Ashworth 1986 and, on the current scheme, Miers 1997). This is not to deny that victims primarily have a right to compensation from the offender: that is clear on legal and moral grounds, if not always practical.

The key question is whether the victim's legitimate interest goes beyond reparation or compensation (and the right to victim services and support, and to proper protection from further harm), and extends to the question of punishment. It would be wrong to suggest that the victim has no legitimate interest in the disposition of the offender in his or her case, but the victim's interest is surely no greater than yours or mine. The victim's interest is as a citizen, as one of many citizens who make up the community or state. In democratic theory all citizens have a right to vote at elections and sometimes on other occasions, and to petition their elected representatives about issues affecting them. If I am an ardent advocate of restorative justice or of indeterminate imprisonment for repeat offenders, I can petition my MP about it, or join a pressure group. Just because a person commits an offence against me, however, that does not privilege my voice above that of the court (acting 'in the general public interest') in the matter of the offender's punishment. A justification for this lies in social contract reasoning, along the lines that the state may be said to undertake the duty of administering justice and protecting citizens in return for citizens giving up their right to self-help (except in cases of urgency) in the cause of better social order. This returns to the earlier argument about the state's responsibility, and to the 'rule of law' values of impartiality, independence and consistency in the administration of criminal justice.

This principle is not opposed by all those who advocate a version of restorative justice. Thus Michael Cavadino and James Dignan (1997) draw a strong distinction between the victim's right to reparation and the public interest in responding to the offence. In their view it is right to empower victims to participate in the process which determines what reparation is to be made by the offender, and reparation to the victim should be the major element of the response. In serious cases some additional response (punishment) may be considered necessary, and they then insist on a form of limiting retributivism in which proportionality sets upper and lower boundaries for the burdens placed on offenders (and also serves as a default setting for cases where a conference or circle proves impossible or inappropriate). It is a matter for regret that few restorative justice theorists refer to Cavadino and Dignan's attempt to preserve as many of the values of restorative justice as possible whilst insisting upon principled limits. They rightly see the distinction between compensation and punishment as crucial, even though their proportionality constraints are looser than many desert theorists would require, and they regard victim involvement as a value to be enhanced where possible. 'Victim personal statements' must now be taken into account by English courts before sentencing: Edna Erez claims that 'providing victims with a voice has therapeutic advantages' (1999: 555; cf. Edwards 2001), but findings from the English pilot projects indicated no great psychological benefits to participant victims and some evidence of disillusionment (Sanders *et al.* 2001: 450).

The second point of principle concerns proportionality. Sentencing is *for* an offence, and respect for the offender as a citizen capable of choice suggests that the sentence should bear a relationship to the seriousness of the offence committed. To desert theorists this is axiomatic: punishment should always be proportionate to the offence, taking account of harm and culpability (von Hirsch 1993: ch. 2), unless a highly persuasive argument for creating a class of exceptional cases can be sustained. It is a strong criticism of deterrent sentencing and of risk theory that they accord priority to predictions and not to the seriousness of the offence committed: von Hirsch and Ashworth (1998: chs 2, 3). The proportionality principle is not the sole preserve of desert theorists: on the contrary, versions of it are widely accepted as limiting the quantum of punishment that may be imposed on offenders, whether as a major tenet of the Council of Europe's recommendation on sentencing (1993: para. A4) or as an element in Nicola Lacey's communitarian approach to punishment (Lacey 1988: 194). Other important functions of the proportionality principle are that it should ensure consistency of treatment among offenders, and that it should give protection against discrimination, by attempting to rule out certain factors from sentencing calculations. It is not being suggested that existing sentencing systems always pursue these principles successfully, but it is vital that they be recognized as goals and efforts made to fulfil them.

The principle of proportionality goes against victim involvement in sentencing decisions because the views of victims may vary. Some victims will be forgiving, other will be vindictive; some will be interested in new forms of sentence, others will not; some shops will have one policy in relation to thieves, others may have a different policy. If victim satisfaction is one of the aims of circles and conferences, then proportionate sentencing cannot be assured and may be overtaken in some cases by deterrent or risk-based sentencing. Two replies may be anticipated. First, it may be argued that in fact the involvement of victims assures *greater* proportionality (Erez and Rogers 1999; Erez 1999; cf. Sanders *et al.* 2001: 451): the actual harm to the victim becomes clear, and in general victims do not desire disproportionate sentences. But these are aggregative findings, whereas the point of the principle is to ensure that in no individual case is an offender liable to a disproportionate penalty. A second reply would be to concede that victim involvement should be subject to proportionality limits, so that no agreement reached in a circle or conference should be out of proportion to the seriousness of the offence. The significance of this concession depends on the nature of the proportionality constraint. There is a range of possible proportionality theories: desert theory requires the sentence to be proportionate to the seriousness of the offence, within fairly narrow bands (von Hirsch 1993: chs 2 and 4), whereas various forms of limiting retributivism recognize looser boundaries. Michael Tonry, for example, argues against the 'strong proportionality' of desert theorists and in favour of 'upper limits' set in accordance with a less precise notion of proportionality (Tonry 1994). Among restorative justice theorists, Braithwaite refers to 'guaranteeing offenders against punishment beyond a maximum' (1999: 105), but it is unclear whether his 'guarantee' adopts as much of proportionality theory as Tonry seems prepared to accept, and whether it imposes similar constraints or even less demanding ones. Most restorative justice theorists would insist that one of their objectives is to reduce levels of punitiveness, not to increase them; but some questions will be raised below about the contours of the 'background' penal system which is envisaged for cases where restorative justice processes fail or are rejected.

The third point is that everyone should have the right to a fair hearing 'by an independent and impartial tribunal', as Article 6.1 of the European Convention on Human Rights declares. This right expresses a fundamental principle of justice. Under the European Convention it applies to the sentencing stage as much as to trials. Do conferences and other restorative justice processes respect the right? Insofar as a victim plays a part in determining the disposition of a criminal case, is a conference 'independent and impartial'? The victim cannot be expected to be impartial, nor can the victim be expected to know about the available range of orders and other principles for the disposition of criminal cases. All of this suggests that conferences may fail to meet the basic standards of a fair hearing, insofar as the victim or victim's family plays a part in determining the outcome.

Most restorative justice supporters will be unimpressed with this, because the argument simply assumes that what has become conventional in modern criminal justice systems is absolutely right. But the issue of principle must be confronted, since it is supported by the European Convention, the International Covenant on Civil and Political Rights and many other human rights documents. One reply from restorative justice supporters might be that the required 'impartiality' and 'objectivity' produce such an impersonal and detached tribunal as to demonstrate exactly what is wrong with conventional systems, and why they fail. But that reply neglects, or certainly undervalues, the link between independence, impartiality and procedural justice. Might it be possible to sidestep the objection by characterizing conferences and other restorative justice processes as alternatives to sentencing rather than as sentencing processes, and therefore not bound by the same principles? This might be thought apposite where any agreement reached in the conference or circle has to be submitted for approval by a court, and where the offender may withdraw from the conference and go to the court at any time.

This is an appropriate point at which to question the reality of the consent that is said to underlie restorative justice processes and outcomes. The general principle is that 'restorative processes should be used only with the free and voluntary consent of the parties. The parties should be able to withdraw that consent at any time during the process' (UN 2000: para. 7). This suggests that the offender may simply walk out and take his or her chances in the 'conventional' system. However, the result of doing so would usually be to propel the case into a formal criminal justice system that is perceived to be harsher in general, or that the offender may expect to be harsher on someone who has walked away from a restorative justice process. On some occasions, then, as in plea-bargaining (Sanders and Young 2000: ch. 7; Ashworth 1998: ch. 9), the 'consent' may proceed from a small amount of free will and a large slice of (perceived) coercion. Where the 'consent' is that of young people, and it is the police who explain matters to them, the danger of perceived coercion may be acute (Daly 2001). The United Nations draft principles attempt to deal with some of these issues, by providing that failure to reach agreement or failure to implement an agreement 'may not be used as a justification for a more severe sentence in subsequent criminal justice proceedings' (UN 2000: paras. 15, 16). But it is right to remain sceptical of the reality of consent, from the offender's point of view.

Returning to the right to an independent and impartial tribunal, is it breached if the victim makes a statement about sentencing, written or oral, to the court or other body that is to take the sentencing decision? This refers to statements that go beyond a victim impact statement, and are not limited to the issue of compensation. The ruling of the European Commission on Human Rights in *McCourt* v. *United Kingdom* (1993) 15 EHRR CD110 may be taken to suggest that such a statement on sentence could prejudice the impartiality of the tribunal, but this might be thought to go too far, not least because defendants have the right to make a 'plea in mitigation', in which their lawyers usually argue against certain outcomes and (sometimes) for a certain sentence. A stronger argument here is to return to the principles of compensation and of proportionality, discussed above, and to assert that the victim's view as to sentence should not be received because it is not relevant. Consider the case of *Nunn*, where the defendant had been sentenced to four years' imprisonment for causing the death of a close friend by dangerous driving. When Nunn's appeal against the sentence came before the Court of Appeal, the court had before it some lengthy written statements by the victim's mother and sister, recognizing that some punishment had to follow such a terrible offence, but stating that their own grief was being increased by the thought of the victim's close friend being in prison for so long. They added that the victim's father and other sister took a different view. In the Court of Appeal, Lord Justice Judge said this:

> We mean no disrespect to the mother and sister of the deceased, but the opinions of the victim, or the surviving members of the family, about the appropriate level of sentence do not provide any sound basis for reassessing a sentence. If the victim feels utterly merciful towards the criminal, and some do, the crime has still been committed and must be punished as it deserves. If the victim is obsessed with vengeance, which can in reality only be assuaged by a very long sentence, as also happens, the punishment cannot be made longer by the court than would otherwise be appropriate. Otherwise cases with identical features would be dealt with in widely differing ways, leading to improper and unfair disparity, and even in this particular case . . . the views of the members of the family of the deceased are not absolutely identical. (*Nunn* [1996] 2 Cr. App. R. (S) 136, at p. 140; see also *Roche* [1999] 2 Cr. App. R. (S) 105)

This statement captures the principles well.[2] Neither one victim's forgiveness of an offender, nor another's desire for vengeance against an offender, should be relevant when the community's response to an offence (as distinct from compensation) is being considered. The plea in *Nunn* was for leniency in the outcome, as also in the New Zealand case of *Clotworthy* (see Braithwaite 1999: 87–8). There are other cases where victims and their families campaign for severity, some with a very high profile (e.g. the case of Thompson and Venables, convicted at the age of 11 of the murder of James Bulger, whose family campaigned, with considerable support from the mass media, in favour of prolonging the imprisonment of the offenders). In dismissing an application by James Bulger's father for judicial review of the tariff set by the Lord Chief Justice, the Queen's Bench Divisional Court noted with approval that Lord Woolf had invited the Bulger family to make representations about the impact of their son's death on them, 'but had not invited

them to give their views on what they thought was an appropriate tariff'
(*R* v. *Secretary of State for the Home Department, ex parte Bulger, The Times,*
16 February 2001).

The above discussion of the three principles of compensation for
wrongs, of independent and impartial tribunals, and of proportionality of
sentence, suggests that the substantive and procedural rights of victims at the
stage of disposal (sentence) ought to be limited. This should apply whether
the rights of victims are being considered in the context of restorative justice
or of a 'conventional' sentencing system. The rights of victims should chiefly
be to receive support, proper services, and (where the offender is unable to
pay) state compensation for violent crimes. There are arguments for going
further, so as to achieve some measure of victim participation: this would
require the provision of better and fuller information to victims, and the
objective would be to enable some genuine participation in the process of
disposal 'without giving [victims] the power to influence decisions that are
not appropriately theirs' (Sanders *et al.* 2001: 458). This would be a fine line
to tread, as the debate following the decision of the US Supreme Court
to allow victim impact statements in capital cases demonstrates: *Payne* v.
Tennessee (1991) 111 S Ct 2597, discussed by Sarat 1997.

Exploring the 'default setting': when restorative justice runs out

Although some restorative justice practitioners and writers express themselves
as if there are no aspects of criminal justice with which restorative justice
could not deal, most are realistic enough to recognize that provision must be
made for some cases to be handled outside restorative justice processes. We
have noted that Cavadino and Dignan provide for a 'default system' to deal
with cases in which a circle or conference does not prove possible, perhaps
because the necessary consents are not forthcoming. Certain writers make
much stronger claims for the ability of restorative justice to handle a wide
range of disputes in criminal justice, schools, industry, and business regulation (e.g. Wachtel and McCold 2001). But even some of those recognize that
there must be some form of 'background system' in place (Braithwaite
1999). If one adds together the groups of offenders for whom such a system
may be needed—those who refuse to participate in restorative justice, or
whose victims refuse to participate,[3] or who have failed to comply with previous restorative justice outcomes—the numbers might be considerable. It
has been argued above that some restorative justice processes themselves
are incompatible with principles of justice on independence, impartiality,
proportionality, and so on. How does the 'default' or 'background' system
measure up to these principles?

Braithwaite explains his background system by reference to this
enforcement pyramid, developed in relation to regulatory enforcement
(1999: 61):

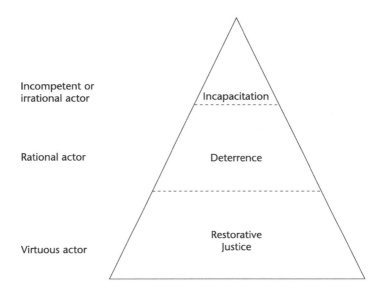

Incompetent or irrational actor — Incapacitation

Rational actor — Deterrence

Virtuous actor — Restorative Justice

The idea is that one starts with restorative justice at the base of the pyramid. It may be tried more than once. If it clearly fails, then one would move to an 'active deterrence' strategy, which Braithwaite distinguishes carefully from the 'passive deterrence' described in most of the punishment literature (see Ayres and Braithwaite 1992: ch. 2). To have this kind of deterrence in the background helps restorative justice to work, in Braithwaite's view. Nonetheless, he warns that:

> The problem is that if deterrent threats cause defiance and reactance, restorative justice may be compromised by what sits above it in a dynamic pyramidal strategy of deterrence and incapacitation ... The challenge is to have the Sword of Damocles always threatening in the background but never threatened in the foreground. (Braithwaite 1999: 63–4)

From the point of view of principle, this approach is troubling. It seems that, once we leave the softly, softly world of restorative justice, offenders may be delivered into raging deterrent and in capacitative strategies, with rogue elements like Uncle Harry calling the shots (see the remarkable paragraphs in Braithwaite 1999: 66–7, on Uncle Harry), and with only the vaguest of gestures towards 'guaranteeing offenders against punishment beyond a maximum' (*ibid.*: 105). When Philip Pettit and John Braithwaite state that, in pursuit of the goal of 'community reassurance', sentencers should take account of 'how common that offence has become in the community' and 'how far the offender is capable of re-offending again' (1993, excerpted in von Hirsch and Ashworth 1998: 326), the glass becomes very dark, and the excesses of the 'risk society' seem to beckon.

Braithwaite and Pettit (1990: ch. 7) would answer that current maximum penalties should provide the guarantee in the first instance, and that there should then be a 'decremental strategy' of lowering those maxima progressively so as to reduce levels of punitiveness. But statutory maximum sentences are often very high, and certainly much higher than most proportionality theorists (including Tonry's looser approach to limits) would accept. It is also countered that desert-based critics are not paying attention to the difference between the usual run of consequentialist theories based on ('passive') deterrence and incapacitation, and the meaning of those strategies within a 'republican' framework which respects the dominion of each individual (Braithwaite and Pettit 1990). We should not find these aspects of Braithwaite's restorative justice theory threatening, it is contended, if we looked at the practical meaning of the pyramid of enforcement and took account of the emphasis on penal parsimony in a republican system. But it is not enough to proclaim penal parsimony and yet to give such prominence, even in a 'background system', to deterrent and incapacitative strategies. What types of deterrent strategy are permissible, within what kinds of limits? What forms of incapacitation? To what extent does the background system permit, nay encourage, sentencing on the basis of previous record rather than present offence? The answers to these questions about restorative justice and recalcitrant offenders remain unclear (see von Hirsch and Ashworth 1998: 317–35), but the need for firm safeguards against undue severity does not disappear if a system is labelled 'restorative'. Penal history yields plenty of examples of apparently benign policies resulting in repressive controls.

Conclusions

It has been argued that, despite the decline of statism and the rise of neo-liberal and 'advanced liberal' programmes for the responsibilization of other agencies of security, it should still be acknowledged to be a fundamental role of the state to maintain a system for the administration of justice and to ensure that proper standards of procedural protection are applied. It is recognized that there have been and are failures of state-led criminal justice, just as there have been and are manifest failures of states to deliver security (Garland 2001: ch. 5). The growth of restorative justice schemes is encouraged by both these phenomena. However, it should remain the responsibility of the state towards its citizens to ensure that justice is administered by independent and impartial tribunals, and that there are proportionality limits which should not only constrain the measures agreed at restorative justice conferences etc. but also ensure some similarity in the treatment of equally situated offenders. If the state does delegate certain spheres of criminal justice to some form of community-based conference, the importance of insisting on the protection of basic rights for defendants is not diminished.

Many of the innovations urged by restorative justice advocates ought to be tested and evaluated—the effect on victims and on offenders of face-to-face meetings, the value of apologies, the effect on victims and offenders of reparation agreements, the effect on victims and offenders of victim partici-pation in conferences, and so forth. Too often, however, enthusiasm for such processes leads proponents either to overlook the need for safeguards, or to imply that they are not relevant. The steps being taken to develop standards for restorative justice processes are important in this respect (see UN 2000; Braithwaite, this issue), but they must be accompanied by a re-examination of deeper issues. In order to ensure that there is no deficit of procedural justice or human rights, it was argued above that governments must retain a primary role, that community-based processes and outcomes should be scru-tinized closely, and that the proper role of the victim in criminal justice processes should be reappraised. Thus any restorative justice processes for offenders who might otherwise go to court should (a) be led by an independ-ent and impartial person;[4] (b) be required to submit its decisions for court approval; (c) allow the participation of the victim, the offender, and their families or significant others; (d) make provision for access to legal advice before and after any restorative justice processes, at a minimum (Council of Europe 2000, para. 8; cf. UN 2000: para. 12); (e) focus on apology and on the appropriate reparation and/or compensation for the offence; and (f) be required to respect relevant principles, such as not imposing on the offender a financial burden that is not means-related. If, contrary to the argument here, a restorative justice conference is permitted to make proposals for community restoration or other responses going beyond reparation to the individual victim(s), there should be clear and circumscribed proportionality limits for those measures. However, the practical implications of 'restoration of the community' call for closer examination than they have hitherto received.

Criticisms of this kind seem to leave many restorative justice practi-tioners baffled, however. They may protest that restorative justice processes are not about punishment anyway; that all the safeguards are about offenders, not victims; and that in practice restorative justice encounters no problems about undue severity, etc. On the first point, Kathleen Daly (2000) rightly calls for caution among those restorative justice advocates who claim not to be in the punishment business but to be engaged in constructive and non-punitive responses to wrongdoing. Even if one were to adopt a narrow defin-ition (that only measures intended to be punitive count as punishment), many restorative justice outcomes satisfy that definition inasmuch as they are known to impose obligations or deprivations on offenders: Johnstone 2001: 106–10; cf. Walgrave 2001. The argument that such obligations or depriv-ations proceed from full consent is, as we have seen, unconvincing. So far as the bias of rights towards offenders is concerned, it must be conceded that most human rights documents do not incorporate victims' rights into their framework—although there are well-known (separate) declarations of victims' rights. This imbalance ought to be rectified, but only after focusing on the arguments presented above. The third point (the absence of severity) may be generally true, since most of those interested in promoting restorative justice seem to oppose penal severity; but attention was drawn above to Braithwaite's 'background system', and even within restorative justice clear limits are important to prevent violations of rights behind a mask of benevolence. Once it is conceded that restorative justice cannot deal with absolutely all criminal cases, the relationship between the formal system and any restorative justice processes must be carefully crafted so as to avoid inequities. This third point is particularly important where enthusiasm for restorative justice leads a government to 'parachute' elements of restorative justice into a system suffused with rather different principles and practices, as has been done with youth justice in England and Wales (Morris and Gelsthorpe 2000; Ball 2000).

Notes

1   This is an inevitably crude and truncated discussion of political theory. For another approach, see e.g. Raz (1986: ch. 3).
2   The *Nunn* case also points to the practical problem arising where two or more victims have different views on the proper response to the crime. A further complication would be where there is a disagreement between the victim and the community representatives over outcome (cf. Law Commission of Canada 1999: 38), although this should be resolved on the basis that the victim's interest lies in reparation and compensation whereas the state's (or community's) interest lies in measures going beyond that.
3   Some RJ schemes are prepared to proceed with a conference in the absence of the victim, which expands the role of the facilitator or coordinator: see, e.g. Daly (2001) on South Australia.
4   This raises the question of police-led conferences, used in England in certain types of case (Young 2001). Braithwaite asks 'whether there is something wrong in principle with the police facilitating a conference. Does it make the police investigator, prosecutor, judge and jury?' (1999:99). He never answers the question of principle, and instead points out the need to have someone assume the role of facilitator, and suggests that police involvement might have beneficial effects on police culture. But the question of principle must surely be answered by stating that this is wrong. It is not appropriate for the police to take on what is a quasi-judicial role, when they are so heavily involved in investigations. More strongly, it is inappropriate for the police to be involved

in any 'shaming' of offenders (cf. Cunneen 1997 and Blagg 1997 with Braithwaite 1997). It is insufficient to reply that offenders who have misgivings can withdraw their consent: as stated above, the 'consent' in these situations may take a severely diluted form. This critique is, of course, no less applicable to the ongoing practice of police cautioning of adults.

5.3

Victim impact statements and sentencing outcomes and processes: the perspectives of legal professionals

by Edna Erez and Linda Rogers

[. . .]

One of the most far reaching legal reforms accomplished by the victims' movement has been laws mandating victim input into criminal justice proceedings. This legislation was the culmination of a long campaign by victim advocates to improve the treatment of crime victims by the system, restore their dignity and provide them with a voice in proceedings (Kelly and Erez 1997). Victim input reforms have also been controversial and most resisted in countries with adversarial criminal justice systems. The legal profession mobilized to oppose reform measures that were imposed from the outside, challenged established legal traditions about the victims' role in criminal justice, and threatened routine court practices (Australian Law Reform Commission 1987; Victorian Sentencing Committee 1988). Legal scholars were quick to point out the regressive ideological underpinning of the reform (Henderson 1985), its inherent legal contradictions (Ashworth 1993) and the limits of the reform in many jurisdictions (Hellerstein 1989).

Despite the high hopes of victim rights advocates, and the misgivings of the opponents of victim participation, the inclusion of victim input has had little or no effect on the processing or outcomes of criminal cases. The research on the subject (reviewed below) suggests that the reform failed to transform court practices in ways prophesied by both its critics and supporters.

The current study sheds light on these findings by utilizing qualitative strategies which provide grounded databased accounts (Glaser and Strauss 1967) from the perspective of those most intimately connected with the implementation of the law—judges, prosecutors, and defence attorneys. This study was conducted in Adelaide, South Australia, where victim input was legislated less than a decade ago. South Australia is one of the least populous states of Australia's six states. The capital city, Adelaide, its major urban setting, comprises 95 per cent of the state population of approximately one million. South Australia has an active modern economy but relative to large cities the crime rate is low.[1] The state has a self contained criminal justice system with a clear division of labour and well-defined roles for agencies. The system is not too overburdened with the processing of cases and is small enough to allow easy access to information and participants in the system.

The current study

Concerned with the paucity of qualitative evidence on the way victim input enters into the 'commonsense reasoning practices' or 'conceptions of justice' (Feeley 1979: 284; Maynard 1982: 347) of court personnel, and how victim impact materials mediate criminal justice outcomes and procedures, we interviewed members of the legal profession who were directly involved in the implementation of the reform: judges, prosecutors and defence counsels. The purpose of the interviews was to illuminate legal professionals' handling of victim input: how they assessed, processed, weighed, listened to or incorporated victim impact information in their decisions, and the kind of experiences they reported regarding the effect of victim input on court processes and outcomes.

The data reported here overcome prior research problems in two ways: first, court officials were interviewed at length, with detailed questions about their experiences, not merely impressions. Professionals were also asked to provide specific examples describing the ways in which they considered victim input. Secondly, the interviewees included officers of the higher courts, where VIS are routinely tendered and considered, and those of the lower courts, where police prosecutors may report victim harm, but rarely tender the VIS forms to the court. The interviews reveal the workings of a hitherto invisible process and offer a textured context for the negligible effects of the reform reported in quantitative studies. The research also highlights the strength of narratives (Daly 1991; Linde 1993) in explaining how victim input influences conceptions of blameworthiness, crime seriousness and complex court decisions concerning offenders' 'just desert'.

Methodology and data collection

As part of a larger study of the effects of VIS on the criminal justice system in South Australia (see Erez *et al.* 1994), members of the legal profession in Adelaide were interviewed concerning their experiences with the VIS. The interviews took place from February through April 1994, approximately five years after the law mandating the VIS for sentencing purposes (section 7 Sentencing Act 1988) became operational. In South Australia impact statements are collected by the police,[2] on a special form, during the initial stage of the crime investigation. South Australia allows only statements concerning the impact of the crime on the victim, but not victim statement of opinion concerning the penalty. The VIS includes special sections for property or financial loss, physical injury and mental harm. It allows annexation of medical or other professional reports which support and elaborate the crime impact.

Participants

The study, conducted under the auspices of the South Australia Attorney General's Department, received official support from the higher echelons of the judiciary, Crown Prosecutor's office and the police.[3] The legal professionals selected for the study included representatives of all of the groups involved in the implementation of the VIS in South Australia: police prosecutors (appearing before magistrates in misdemeanour cases), Crown prosecutors (appearing in felony cases before judges of the District and Supreme courts), defence lawyers (working in all courts), magistrates (who try misdemeanour cases in the lower magistrate's court) judges (who try felony cases in the District Court) and justices (who try felony cases in the Supreme Court). These professionals have to present, receive, challenge, or consider VIS information for sentencing.

The judges and magistrates who were interviewed included all court officials who worked over half of their time in the criminal law area. The sample of prosecutors includes the majority (85 per cent) of the prosecutors who worked in that jurisdiction. The defence lawyers interviewed were recommended to the research team by the South Australian Bar ('Law Society') as attorneys who have extensive experience in criminal defence. Table 5.3.1 presents the legal professionals interviewed and their court assignments.

Interview schedule

The interviews were structured (Spradley 1979) and lasted between 1 hr and 1 hr 50 min, with only two interviews of about 30 min. The interview

Table 5.3.1 Legal professionals interviewed and their court assignments

	Magistrates Court	District Court	Supreme Court	Total
Judges	–	8	7	15
Magistrates	7	–	–	7
Police prosecutors	6	–	–	6
Crown prosecutors	–	Work in District and Supreme Courts		8
Defence attorneys		Work in all courts		6
Total				42

schedule included open-ended questions about the content and quality of victim impact information the professionals have seen, whether information on victim harm has increased since VIS were introduced, and their perceptions of VIS effects on sentencing and on the criminal justice process. The instrument also sought the professionals' opinions about the role of victims in the criminal justice process and the need for VIS. Throughout the interview, respondents were asked to provide specific examples and reasons for their answers. Respondents were asked questions about their professional background, length of experience, views on victims and their penological philosophy.

The bulk of the questions presented to the professionals were identical (e.g. in your experience, has the introduction of VIS resulted in changes in sentencing patterns? What are your concerns about the information presented in the VIS?) However, some of the interview items were tailored to the specific roles, concerns or agenda of these three groups of court officials. For instance, prosecutors were asked about the importance of VIS in the cases that they prosecuted, defence attorneys about VIS in cases that they defended, and judges about the importance of VIS in their sentencing decisions. All of the interviews ended with the question, 'Are there any things about VIS that I overlooked?'

Data coding

The data were coded following Glaser and Strauss (1967) guidelines for constant comparative methodology analyses. All data were first read as individual interviews, and from the analyses of the interviews common themes naturally emerged. We then cross coded the themes according to the roles of the interviewees in the criminal justice system, i.e., the responses of all the judges, prosecutors or defence lawyers, as they fit into the emergent themes. Each group was then separately analysed as to its specific experience and understanding of VIS according to the theme that was being examined.

Results

The interviews reveal variation in respondents' definitions of work, their philosophy of punishment, views on criminal justice aims and on victims' participation in it. Differences appeared to derive from professional experiences and the role the interviewees played in the system, but were also evident within occupational groups.

The finding requiring closer analysis, however, is the significant agreement amongst all three groups about the minimal impact of victim-centred legislation. The across case similarities or 'replication' (Yin 1984) of practices and attitudes of these professionals toward victims and the VIS illustrate the degree of consistency and cohesion between the key players constituting the main 'work group' of the court system (Eisenstein and Jacob 1977).

Victim input and severity of court outcomes

There is agreement among the legal professionals in South Australia that victim input has not increased sentence severity. Practitioners from all groups thought that the reform has not changed sentencing patterns and dispositions substantially, or at best, only marginally. Examination of their responses reveals the way organizational forces, legal occupational culture, and work group dynamics operating in the court militate against individualization of victims.

Typification or the 'normal' victim

The processing of victim harm, as are other criminal case elements (e.g. Sudnow 1965; Emerson 1983, Frohmann 1992), is subject to typification. In the course of routinely adjudicating cases with victims who suffer various types of harm, prosecutors and judges become acquainted with the typical features of cases and their associated impact. Professionals accumulate knowledge and expectations of the typical attributes of cases, classifying them into known categories of 'normal cases' (Sudnow 1965). As a class of a case becomes typified, it is treated in more routine ways. In general, a 'sliding scale of severity' which is based on a 'case stream' (Emerson 1983: 430) is created. The frequently encountered harm, even if initially acknowledged to be inherently serious, loses some of its aura of seriousness over time, as other similar cases are encountered. Consequently, serious harm becomes routinized, institutionalized, built into the typification rather than standing as a feature of the case for the professional (Emerson 1983: 433).

Legal practitioners not only acquire knowledge about the typical manner in which various offences affect victims, they also begin to expect it. Practitioners learn the lay, medical, and forensic discourse about physical and psychological injuries, and short and long-term effects of various crimes. 'Normal victims' are those whose typical features of harm are known and expected by professionals when they invoke specific laws defining the appropriate sentence. The victim of a crime ceases to be an individual, with idiosyncratic responses to his/her experience, but is reduced to the victim of the specific crime category with its concomitant injuries. The focus is not on particular individuals but on offence types; for instance, the kinds of harm rape victims suffer, symptoms characteristic of abused children, or the way burglary victims react. Several interviewees volunteered to cite the 'normal' effects of various offences in the cases that they have tried. This example was provided by a judge:

Rape causes depression, sense of guilt, and fear of strangers. Incest crimes cause long term effects on children, they are fearful of men and sometimes try to commit suicide. Burglary victims also suffer mental effects because of the intrusion on their privacy.

Even magistrates, who were less exposed to victim impact statements when compared to judges and justices, demonstrated an expert knowledge of the effects of crime, as one magistrate stated:

> Most serious long term effects will arise from crimes of violence, but our experience with violence is limited by jurisdiction. Only now do we get some aggravated assault and grievous bodily harm. Intimidatory offences, for instance, wielding a weapon, can have very significant effects. The way some people become distraught if their houses are destroyed is another example for unanticipated harm, as it takes them a long time to get over it. Invasion of privacy and security are very traumatic to victims.

Not only were typical crime effects recognized, but also typical categories of victims were identified. Rape victims, for example, are commonly young women; the typical injuries associated with this offence for this category of victims become familiar. The professionals anticipate and expect these features of physical and psychological harm, and can 'screen out' the human suffering involved, by utilizing common courtroom rhetoric.

We found that knowledge of the properties of 'normal' victim harm, i.e., the typical or familiar victim reactions to crime categories, constituted the mark of any given attorney's or judge's competence. A judge offered a specific example:

> In most rape cases I assume a profound effect on the victim, whether or not there is a VIS. Once a defence attorney said, 'There is no evidence for that.' 'But,' I said, 'This is common sense; we judges know what are the normal expected consequences of crimes.'

Another judge, in response to a question about the parts of the VIS which provide useful information, commented:

> Rarely do I get any useful information. For instance in a rape case which actually included 10 counts on 2 girls, the VIS said no injury. The judge knows what sort of effect such a crime will have on a victim.

Another judge stated:

> In breaking and entering the victim is upset for a long time, but all it (the VIS) says is x dollars covered by insurance. We judges know the effects on the victim and tell that to the prisoner.

Some variations in 'normal' victim reactions were noted by highly experienced judges and prosecutors. Several judges with extensive records on the bench reflected on assessing various victim reactions. One justice commented that:

> Harm varies by offence, by the injury suffered and the resilience of the victim. In armed robbery which could be very frightening, some stand it better than others. For some people any person that resembles the robber will cause them to startle. If there is a severe impact it must receive a lot of weight. At the end of the day you put together all these considerations, including deterrence, rehabilitation and then sentence.

Judges who were less experienced, commented on how much they learned from reading impact statements about victims' reactions, feelings and harm. As one magistrate stated:

> If it was not for the VIS I would have thought he (the victim) could just take a shower and get the whole thing behind him. The VIS makes us, in individual cases, more educated.

As judges and prosecutors become integrated into the local legal culture and get accustomed to the cases they adjudicate, they come to see and treat victim harm that had earlier struck them as 'outrageous' in more neutral routine and 'lenient' ways (see Emerson 1983: 434).

The translation of typical and familiar victim reactions into the 'normal' victim, and the way this construct is used in sentencing practices, is evident in the way legal professionals distinguish between the 'normal' and exceptional characteristics of the case. In a 'normal' crime, harm is viewed as built into sentencing. It is commonly not noticed; it is assumed. As one Crown prosecutor, in response to a question about the relative importance of harm compared to other factors that are considered in sentencing, stated:

> Harm suffered by the victim is built into the sentencing, for instance, rape—life, common assault—lower punishment. I don't think VIS is the biggest thing, it is important but other factors are also important. Harm is a significant consideration but the effect of the crime is built into the sentence. If a rape victim is wrecked it is nothing more than you will expect.

Only in a minority of cases, labelled by one Crown prosecutor as the 'celebrity cases'—those that receive high media coverage and public attention—does the harm suffered by the victim receive special recognition. As another prosecutor commented in response to our question whether the VIS affects sentencing outcomes:

In a standard rape case hardly ever is the harm considered. But in horrible crimes, young child or grandmommy or male rape—then yes. Otherwise, things have not changed, nothing has really changed.

The appearance of atypical crime victims—those not included among the 'normal' victims of their crime category, such as grandmother or baby rape victims—and their reactions, causes legal professionals some level of distress, even abhorrence, in contrast to the matter-of-fact response to typical victims. This differential response emerges as there are no familiar categories of harm, and it is more difficult, indeed impossible, to reduce these individuals to the typical victims of a specific offence category.

Yet the 'normal' victim constitutes an important measure against which judges and other legal professionals evaluate victims and the veracity of their impact statement. In the routine handling of felonies, legal practitioners use their knowledge regarding typification of harm in assessing the truthfulness of victims' input, and the credibility of their testimony. Prosecutors and judges (much more than defence lawyers) develop a repertoire of knowledge about the features of victim harm, the way particular crimes affect victims, and 'normal' victims' emotional and psychological reactions to violations of property and person. Victim reactions that are not perceived as typical are often viewed as exaggerated, illogical, and unbelievable by all groups, and particularly by defence attorneys.

Statutory definitions, charges, or offence levels, however, do not always capture the 'gestalt of the harm' (Daly 1991, 1994). Although many victim injuries tend to cluster around 'normal' harm—their extent is assumed or expressed in the charge—others tend to deviate from the acceptable range. These cases often spark off a disagreement between the prosecution and the defence about the veracity of the input. The disagreement is acute in relation to emotional or mental harm,[4] as the following example given by a defence attorney suggests:

> A middle-aged man was charged with oral rape on a 14-year old, and was found guilty of indecent assault. They knew each other. The VIS stated that the young man's life was almost ruined. I could not accept that his life was ruined; he coped quite well. He probably was embarrassed.

Although a few judges seemed to be more willing to hear or tolerate a victim's apparently extreme or excessive reaction to a crime, the bulk of the accumulated 'typical' victim experiences served to reduce prosecutors' and judges' preparedness to accept as genuine and truthful a reaction that was out of the 'normal' or expected range of experience. This typification phenomenon has contributed significantly to the compression of victim harm reflected in court decision making and outcomes.

Objectivity vs subjectivity in assessing crime impact

'Objectivity' is another occupational feature practitioners used to explain how they approach victim impact materials. Objectivity is the legal apologetic that defends against the use or acknowledgement of affect or standpoint in the perception and construction of legal events or decisions. Objectivity is a normative ideal in law (as well as in other pursuits of 'truth', such as journalism, see Creedon 1993). It is both a strategic presumption and ritual that protects judges from charges of bias toward a particular party interest. Judges claim, and are presumed, to examine cases that come before them objectively, in a 'clinical' fashion, detached from any 'emotional baggage' and subjectivity, the human stories in the criminal cases they try often carry. The legal literature is filled with exaltations of judges' ability to be objective in everyday practice, and thereby produce correct law and 'just' legal decisions (e.g. Naffine 1990: ch. 1).

Despite a growing recognition that objectivity is elusive and problematic in the interpretation and application of legal rules to cases (for gender, see for instance, Naffine 1990; for race, Higginbotham 1978; see also Rogers and Erez 1997), interviewees of all the groups described the routine disposition of cases as 'objective'. The belief in professionals' ability to exercise 'objectivity' in their deliberation allows them to define unusual victims' stories of crime impact as 'subjective', hence irrelevant to sentencing decisions. The classification of input as subjective allows total disregard of crime impact narratives.

In the present study, members of all groups reiterated the importance of 'objectivity' in assessing the VIS. They claimed that although victim input may be useful for therapeutic considerations related to victims, to be considered in sentencing it needs to be carefully scrutinized, as one judge maintained:

> You call on your life experiences and expertise, which may not be an easy task. I ignore them if I think they are exaggerated. If we use it for the victim to work out some anger then it is OK, but to use it for penalty purposes it needs to be more objective.

Invoking the principle of 'objectivity' allows judges to ignore consciously victim input which appears to them 'out of the ordinary', exaggerated, unbelievable, or outside the legal professionals' routine experience with the crime. One magistrate, who tried the case of a person who bit the arresting officer and told him that he (the defendant) had AIDS, explained:

> Sometimes, like in the police assault case I told you [about], people appear unreasonable, though not too often. But it shows only how concerned the victim is, and how upset he or she is. If they are very annoyed it should be there and we can discount this if we think it not

necessary. It's hard to know whether people exaggerate. You sometimes suspect it. I suspected with the police officer that he overstated his concerns, but we don't know. All the medical evidence said he will not get AIDS but he was so concerned. You do your best in assessing human behaviour.

Practitioners who juxtaposed decision makers' objectivity with victims' subjectivity often explained that victims have various motives, or built in incentives, to lie or exaggerate. One motive was the penalty that the offender could receive (victims were presumed to be vindictive). As one magistrate stated:

Victims have the wrong perspective. Most victims will see the sentencing as purely punitive, with retribution as the predominant factor. They do not understand the criminological purpose of sentencing.

Another motive for lying or exaggerating was financial gain, or the size of a compensation order a victim would be awarded (victims were presumed greedy). As one magistrate suggested: 'I think victims will really exaggerate if there is a coin for them in it'. Defence lawyers in particular were sceptical about the veracity of victim input, particularly regarding mental harm. However, these attorneys expressed confidence in judges' ability to see through the input and to ignore what they perceived as exaggerated or unbelievable crime impact. As one defence attorney summarized:

I suspect that some judges may pay lip service to VIS but in fact ignore it, whereas they do not ignore the commonsense injury.

Another defence attorney, in response to a question about inflammatory statements in the VIS minimized the risk subjective input will have on the defendant:

Occasionally we receive inflammatory comments but they are equally obvious to the judge; they are not very damaging to us but to the agency that did the report. I do not believe that a victim of sexual assault has exaggerated the impact but the assimilation of all of the facts are sometimes suspect. In most cases I tend to trust my own view and almost invariably trust the judges' view of the likely effect. I am generally not bothered that the VIS has reported psychological effects. Judges, I suspect, don't give a great deal of weight to it in the majority of the cases. In one case I remember a report done by someone objectively doing it. The judge gave weight to it and I agreed with the weight.

Respondents also ranked, or assigned various levels of objectivity to the different occupational groups whose reports are sometimes annexed to the VIS. One defence attorney suggested that:

> Professional reports prepared by social workers, in contrast to psychiatrists, tend to lack objectivity; indeed they are fairly consistently non-objective in my view.

Another defence attorney concluded that:

> Professional reports are always coloured. I think it is best for judges to stick out to their own views of injury.

The VIS as a practice of 'retelling' victim harm

The effect of the professional preference for objectivity is that it sanitizes the 'retelling' (Abrams 1992) of facts for legal consumption. Victim harm is recast to make it acceptable to the court. The quest for an objective account affects the preparation of impact materials by the police, and judges' readings of the input. Many interviewees emphasized the need to approach victim input in a 'clinical' manner, analogous to the way physicians examine and diagnose patients and their physical illness. The clinical approach to victim harm, according to one police prosecutor, flattens the report and takes the power out of the victims' stories:

> Magistrates take it (the harm) into account on a technical level, but view it in clinical terms. I don't think magistrates have truly human appreciation of the harm that victims suffer. If they are told in court that someone suffered a broken bone it's only words for them.

Professionals acknowledged that the 'retelling' of victim harm in impact statements by reporters other than the actual victim often 'sterilizes' (see Delgado 1989) the event. A judge related the following:

> In breaking and entering offences we always assumed an effect on the victim, but in the VIS I see for breaking and entering I do not find any information on the victim. A typical VIS in breaking and entering is the thief gained entry through the window and the estimate for repairing the window is X dollars and the amount stolen is Y dollars.

Judges mentioned that they often expected the VIS to state more injury based on the offence committed. One judge commented: 'VIS are often too mild compared to what I would expect. A Crown prosecutor complained: 'Some VIS are appalling, for instance, in a rape case the VIS only stated that the victim was upset.'

Downstream consequences

Another factor that explains the minimal impact of the reform is the organizational concern with 'downstream consequences' (Emerson and Paley 1994: 14), with avoiding appeals of sentences. Judges tend to ignore, or assign little weight, to victim harm because they fear that penalties higher than the tariff will attract appeals. For judges, a reversal or modification of a sentence is not a desirable career event; they do not routinely risk a reversal. As one judge, in response to whether victims are satisfied with the sentences meted out by the court, stated:

> We usually get no feedback from victims. But the general reaction is that the sentences are not severe enough. Most people and victims don't think they are enough. Even I know it, but if I give more than the tariff it will attract an appeal.

Defence attorneys know that judges are concerned about the appeals and reversal of sentences. These attorneys use this knowledge to benefit their clients, a practice to which judges respond and keep sentences 'in line'. This organizational concern has contributed to sentence compression and kept disparity in check.

Managerial justice and resource allocation problems

Resource allocation issues are critical in the categorization processes; they affect how various duties are prioritized and handled (Emerson 1983). For judges and prosecutors, 'managerial justice' considerations, and the ubiquitous bureaucratic need to move the cases along accelerated the typification tendencies. In the words of one Crown prosecutor:

> The court will not take a lot of notice of VIS unless it's a very aggravated offence. The court has no time; we have to push the cases through. We don't plea bargain as they do in the USA.

Practitioners admitted that the current practice of VIS constituted, in their words, 'only lip service'. For them, the VIS—collecting, presenting or considering it—was just another formality added to their already busy work schedule and heavy caseload. Complaints about the deficient implementation of this requirement were common: 'these police on the road are lazy or disinterested and we prosecutors have to clean after them.' The effect of limited court resources compounded the problem, as one judge described:

> Some VIS don't tell you anything about the harm, although, when the offence is serious you end up asking for more information. If the offence is not serious, time will not always permit receiving more information. It will cause further delay.

Several professionals noted that in current criminal justice practices victims' input is either not heard or ignored, particularly in less serious offences. Organizational concerns with efficiency, speed and productivity have led students of court reform to note that crime victims suffer yet another 'secondary victimization'—they become 'victims of efficiency' (Douglas *et al.* 1994). Our study supports this observation. The effect of meagre resources on impact statements was described by one justice:

> They (VIS) are variable in the amount of information they provide from none to a lot. VIS are filled out by police investigators at the time of the investigation, when long effects are not known. The big problem is that many VIS provide inadequate information, information which is at best indirect hearsay, often after a phone call by a police officer to the victim. There is no direct information from the victim, and it is often coming from someone who has no qualification to report it. The VIS are probably never seen by the victims and certainly not signed by them.

The impact of these forces on sentencing in the higher court was described by one judge:

> It has been my experience that the VIS is often silent. We are not told why a VIS is missing information or why it says 'effect on victim unknown'. The effect of this is to assume little or no effect and therefore treat the offender more leniently than he would otherwise be treated.

The combined effect of these factors on the presentation of victim harm in the lower court was summarized by one magistrate:

> In today's practice, defendants get a generous understatement of their criminal acts and the harm they inflicted on victims. And because in the Magistrate Courts victims are often not present, this understatement of harm is never challenged.

VIS as a symbolic gesture, political ploy or therapeutic measure

In an effort to justify their views and practices, professionals were quick to offer multiple reasons to overlook victim input in the decision-making process. A small minority claimed that 'the VIS legislation was only formalizing what has always been a practice of the courts', or as one magistrate related:

> When the criminal law (sentencing) came into effect it set out the considerations for sentencing. But these were factors we were taking into account anyway.

The majority of the practitioners, however, engaged in second guessing the 'true' intent of the reform and noted that changes in court practices were not among its purposes. They suggested that impact statements were meant to be merely 'a symbolic gesture for victims', 'a recognition of their interest in the proceedings', 'just a formal mechanism to present crime impact in court', or 'provide victims with a therapeutic occasion for airing their feelings concerning the crime'.

Professionals of all groups viewed the reform as a 'political ploy', or an attempt by government to gain public support. A police prosecutor related: 'Government jumped on it before the previous election and the police department got stuck with it.' A Crown prosecutor intimated: 'government was succumbing to demands or pressures by victim groups'. A judge relayed: 'I think the VIS is a political gimmick, maybe because I do not need re-emphasizing the harm'. One judge, responding to a question concerning the way VIS are structured, proclaimed:

> To me it is a political thing to appease the feminist lobby in rape cases. I cannot help you with this question because I never bother to read them.

Victim input and sentence uniformity or disparity

The explanations offered for the stability in sentence severity also accounted for the reform's negligible impact on sentence uniformity. For instance, one police prosecutor stated that:

> Most judges are fairly commonsensical about the effect of crime on victims. If there is VIS then it amplifies the impact, but I do not think it leads to marked disparity.

One Crown prosecutor explained why disparity is not a likely result due to variations in VIS:

> I don't think it happens often, perhaps sometimes; but in the more serious cases you get VIS, and in the less serious ones, where the effect is not as great, the VIS does not matter as much.

Only four practitioners thought that the lack of impact details could cause disparity. But as one magistrate, who regularly travelled long distances once a month to adjudicate cases in the hinterland, noted, this problem is not unique to the VIS.[5]

> I have no doubt that some victims decline to give statements or that some police do not elicit it. I agree that it may contribute to disparity; if material was not provided you may give harsh or lenient sentence as the case may call. This problem is not peculiar to VIS but to all material

provided in cases. Sometimes we also should have pre-sentence reports but if you are 300 km away there is no way you can ask for it.

Changes in sentencing outcomes and their explanations

The legal professionals we interviewed thought that the reform has resulted in a few changes. Some changes were merely cosmetic. For instance, the impact statements provided for judges a source for sentencing remarks—a narrative from which some phrases can be lifted and incorporated in the court decision. In the words of one judge:

> Now I can say directly as the VIS reports the impact of the crime on the victim and this way you bring home the effect of the crime to offenders.

Practitioners from all groups agreed that judges often cite the VIS in their sentencing remarks. Three practitioners, however, speculated whether citing phrases from the document was not so benign. As one judge stated:

> The introduction of VIS has changed my remarks on the sentence. Insofar as my remarks include comments on the ongoing harm then it has affected the actual sentence as well, by increasing it where there is harm or reducing it where there is no harm or at least, in taking it as a mitigating factor.

About one-eighth of the interviewees claimed that sentence severity has also changed, either due to the increased attention to victims over the last decade, or because changes are inevitable when details on victim harm are available to judges. As one Crown prosecutor stated:

> The focus in the last ten years on victim has impacted sentencing, but not specifically the VIS. Attention to rape and sex offences increased and the VIS itself is the result of focusing on victims.

When legal professionals were asked to provide specific instances in which they thought a sentence was changed or reconsidered based exclusively on the information provided in the VIS, the overwhelming majority could think of a suitable example. The examples they provided, however, illustrate changes for both more severe and more lenient sentences. One justice, who was asked about the importance of VIS in determining sentencing decisions, stated that:

> In trial cases VIS is not that important as I form my own impressions of the victim. On a plea of guilt it's important. One example is a man who was hit in a hotel. The VIS changed my opinion, as I learned from the

VIS that victim was permanently impaired and I did not know it from other sources.

A Crown prosecutor speculated about the likely outcome of a case he prosecuted at the time:

> Judges often point to the effect of the crime on the victim and this may be a reason they impose heavier than normal sentences. I have a case at the moment which is a domestic violence case, that I think the effect on the victim where the husband held a gun to his wife for two hours will make a difference. I think it will influence the sentence and he will probably get prison sentence, or it may influence the length of sentence or whether the judge will suspend the sentence.

A police prosecutor gave the following example:

> I recall a case where a young girl (21) was assaulted by a 42-year-old offender wielding broken glass. He was without prior record and got four years, 18 months non-parole. I think he is appealing it now. Because she suffered scars and emotionally was a wreck the sentence was so severe. She thanked us after the case went through.

A defence attorney provided another example:

> I had a case of a fraudulent conversion by a land broker. There were many victims involved and the pile of VIS was so high on the bar that the prosecutor used the pile to make his point and to get a more severe sentence.

The legal professionals also provided examples for a more lenient sentence as a result of the VIS. This example was provided by a police prosecutor:

> In one case I handled the victim recovered well, was coping with situation and felt no hatred toward his attacker. This caused the court to give a lower sentence.

A Crown prosecutor was discussing the following case:

> I had a situation where a 15-year-old girl was sexually abused by a friend of the family. Through the VIS it became clear that the girl was in counselling because she was grieving for her abuser and the loss of his friendship. It actually reduced the abuser's sentence.

The variable effect of the VIS on sentencing was best exemplified by the following judge's response:

VIS plays an important part in sentencing for crimes of violence, sex offences and culpable driving. However, it makes a direct impact on only a handful of cases, five to six cases altogether so far, or one or two per year. I can remember a nasty sex offender with whom I was more lenient when VIS showed a desire for reconciliation within the family. In another example I imposed a more stern penalty in a culpable driving case, when the VIS showed or emphasized the wide varieties and extent of the trauma for several members of the surviving relatives.

These examples demonstrate that statistical analyses examining aggregate sentencing data are not likely to capture subtle nuances of change in court outcomes, as those detected in the present study.

Victim impact and criminal justice processes

Professionals of all groups did not report any adverse effects of the reform on criminal justice schedules and procedures. Victim input has neither called for longer trials, nor did it lead to challenges of that input, or mini trials on the content of impact materials. At most, respondents agreed, the reform had added few minutes to sentencing: 'it takes only few minutes to read the impact materials' or 'it takes two to three minutes to digest the statements'.

Practitioners stated that victim impact materials are rarely challenged by the defence in court. Even though defence attorneys had serious doubts about the veracity of victim input and highly suspected the truthfulness of most harm statements, particularly psychological injury, none challenged impact statements concerning mental harm. The same professionals did mention challenges of input concerning financial loss caused by the crime, because it is relatively easy to verify the extent of material damage: 'You have receipts, quotes or estimates of item costs etc.'

The professionals explained avoiding challenges of mental harm as 'not a good move for tactical reasons': challenging a statement requires that the victim be called to testify and be crossed examined about his or her input. This is a risk that defence attorneys are generally not willing to take, because of its likely effect on the sentence. As one defence attorney stated:

> My problem with professional reports and VIS is that it's impossible to test their accuracy without incredible disservice to the client.

A Crown prosecutor related his experience:

> I had a case of death by dangerous driving. The accused in this case was not a criminal, but retrieved from a party drunk. The mother and the sister of the victim commented in the impact statement and defence challenged and they were called to give evidence. It was not a smart move

by the defence. It does not happen very often though. Defence in my opinion are best not to draw the judges' attention to the VIS.

Practically all professionals agreed to one judge's observation that:

> A good defence counsel does not challenge it directly, only indirectly. What they do is in submission they will make statements inconsistent with VIS . . . I never held a hearing about VIS content except in one case.

Or in the words of one defence attorney:

> Once the conviction is in, it is impossible to put the victim on the stand again for a sentencing hearing without much harm to the defendant.

One prosecutor provided an example of such 'harm':

> I once had a very articulate victim who was a journalist, and the defence put him on the witness stand because they did not believe that he suffered such injuries as were presented in this impact statement. His testimony was so devastating to the defence and the jury imposed a more severe sentence.[6]

Defence attorneys also avoided challenges because they 'trusted judges' ability to see through' impact statements and ignore exaggerated input. They expressed confidence in judges' ability to impose sentences based on the 'right' considerations, and to 'sentence offenders objectively, as it should be done.'

Challenges of monetary issues were usually settled by counsels' agreement that the inflated claim be withdrawn. Costs and efficiency are omnipresent concerns in criminal justice proceedings, as one judge stated:

> It is not worth it to have a couple of hours evidence about the value of property stolen or damaged. In a direct challenge of impact materials about such things the Crown usually backs off.

In short, the data suggest that courtroom processes have not changed in a significant way. The reform has caused only minor, mostly ritualistic adjustments in courtroom procedures and time schedules.

Conclusion

Attempts to balance conflicting ideologies and paradoxical expectations to redefine victims' role in the criminal justice system cohabit legal practitioners' discourse. Practitioners resist reform initiatives which are inconsistent with their own world views and institutional priorities. They manage to maintain routine established practices by orienting themselves to traditional occupational culture and organizational concerns. The data uncover forces and dynamics embedded in legal culture, which in interaction with organizational concerns, exert a homogenizing effect on sentencing.

The interviews of the practitioners highlight the way mundane and dramatic victim harm enters sentencing considerations, and the manner in which they mediate case presentation, argumentation and defence tactics. The study illuminates the logic behind invoking the 'normal' victim and the dynamics of overlooking 'exceptional' victim harm, which obviate the need to individualize sentences. This handling of victim input in case presentations results in compressed versions of victim harm available for sentence deliberation.

The 'retelling' of injuries, by professionals who approach harm in a 'clinical' fashion, produces impact materials which flatten the harm and takes the power out of victims' stories. The illusion of 'objectivity', combined with typification—the categorization of victim harm as 'normal'—lead to court presentations and readings of VIS which leave minute variations in the distribution of harm within offence categories. The conceptual equipment with which legal representation is played out (for instance, rules of an adversarial legal system) and the organizational concern with 'downstream consequences,' productivity and efficiency, all result in court 'business as usual', and in court outcomes and proceedings which deviate very little from those prevailing prior to the reform.

Resisting change, the legal professionals could provide numerous justifications to reject the idea that the reform intended to modify sentencing practices or proceedings. They offered a variety of interpretations for the reform's 'true' purpose in legislating input rights to victims: political motives to gain public support or win election; government giving in to pressures by vocal victim movements or feminist groups; granting victims a symbolic status in the trial of their offender, or merely a therapeutic opportunity for airing their feelings.

The study reveals a rich and varied repertoire of strategies used by the legal profession to maintain their autonomous status, circumvent external demands to consider victim input, and justify overlooking concrete presentations of harm. Built-in organizational incentives to exclude victims, or proceed with minimal input from them, maintain and reinforce the traditional criminal justice approach to victims as an 'extraneous party' (Erez 1994), if not sheer 'troublemakers' (Kury *et al.* 1994).

Nevertheless, the reform has had a small impact on court outcomes. Practitioners could provide a few examples of cases they tried in which a VIS led to a sentence that otherwise would have not been imposed. They recalled a small number of cases with an equal number of instances in which victim input led to a more severe or more lenient disposition. In a statistical aggregate this phenomenon would not appear as an effect. The use of qualitative methods provides a closer lens to peer into decisions which may be idiosyncratic, uncommon, or indeed, unexpected. Employing this methodology, our study confirms previously unsubstantiated hypotheses (Erez 1990; Sebba 1996) that the small effect VIS reform has had on sentencing is in enhancing sentence accuracy and proportionality rather than increasing punitiveness.

Judges and prosecutors (and to a limited extent defence attorneys) reported that they have become more informed about the way in which crime victims experience harm and react to victimization. Proximity to victims via their input inevitably provides practitioners with an acute sensitivity to the scope of human costs associated with crime. Yet, it is naive to expect that increased exposure to VIS will transform court practices, even if it expands the parameters of 'normal' victim harm to incorporate a few 'atypical' reactions occasionally encountered by legal professionals. This study supports other research findings (e.g. Fromann 1996) that to alter routine court practices to frame and support a broader range of sentencing decisions, the organizational logic, structure, goals and rewards need to change. Top-down reforms, which graft changes into existing court routines by legislative fiat, have only limited success if they do not address legal occupational culture, organizational structure and priorities, and dynamics of courtroom group work (see Feeley 1997).

Knowledge of the full range of victim harm also becomes irrelevant when penalty options are perceived as limited, and more importantly, when organizational goals exert pressures for sentence uniformity, as this study well documents. The reform's mandate to recognize victim impact is reduced to a ritual as other justice concerns—expressed by the movement to increase uniformity in sentencing—become salient. This study illuminates the ubiquitous tension between reconciling victims' and offenders' rights, expressed in the shift away from individualization of punishment.

The findings of this study suggest that victim input provisions created in order to hear victims have also served to silence them. The stability in court outcomes and processes documents the argument (Erez and Roeger 1995a) that current uses of impact statements constitute an acceptable compromise to both camps in the debate concerning victim input rights: contemporary VIS practices in courts in Australia (Erez *et al.* 1994) and elsewhere (e.g. Henley *et al.* 1994) are successful in maintaining the time-honoured tradition of excluding victims from criminal justice with a thin veneer of being part of it.

Notes

1   For instance, in Adelaide the courts process around 600 felonies per year. Yet, from the interviews it emerges that legal professionals in

Adelaide view their system as burdened with a large number of cases, particularly in the magistrates' court.

2   In Canada, VIS are also prepared by the police. In the USA, VIS are usually prepared by the victim/witness programme at the prosecutor's office or by the probation department. The same dynamics and processes revealed by this study would most likely apply to all agencies involved in preparation of VIS.

3   The justices, judges, magistrates and Crown prosecutors were informed about the study by a letter from the Attorney-General to the Chief of Justice, Chief Judge, Chief Magistrate, or the Director of Public Prosecution (DPP). The letter explained the purpose of the study as an evaluation of VIS in South Australia and stated that its purpose was to study the officials' experiences with VIS. The letter emphasized the importance of their input for the study and requested their cooperation. The legal practitioners were then contracted by the research team to schedule and interview. The police prosecutors were informed about the study by the South Australian Police coordinator of VIS, who also scheduled the interviews.

4   Research suggests that victims display a wide and varied array of psychological symptoms and reactions to criminal victimization (Kilpatrick *et al.* 1985; Lurigio 1987; Norris *et al.* 1990; Resick 1993; see summaries by Frieze *et al.* 1987; Lurigio and Resick 1990; Koss 1993). These studies suggest that moderate to acute psychological reactions in the form of distress, fear, alienation, loss of trust and self esteem are common among victims of all types of crime. The extent of these reactions varies according to victims' social, cultural and demographic attributes, prior life experiences including mental health, and the number and extent of current and prior victimization. Yet, whether many of these reactions were genuine was often questioned by the legal professionals, particularly the defence counsels.

5   A similar point was made by Justice White in *Booth* v. *Maryland*, arguing against the majority decision to outlaw the use of VIS in capital cases.

6   This example is in line with the literature on the impact of victim assessment, particularly attributes such as class and gender, on court outcomes (Stanko 1981–82; Cooney 1994).

5.4

Fiefs and peasants: accomplishing change for victims in the criminal justice system
by Joanna Shapland

The results of research into victims' reactions to their victimization and sub-sequent treatment by the criminal justice system now read almost like a litany, so universal are the findings. The studies emphasize the need for support and help to get over the effects of the offence, and for information from and consultation with the agencies of the criminal justice system, notably the police and prosecution. It has been shown consistently that throughout the Anglo-American system of adversarial criminal justice – in England, Scotland, the United States and Canada – victims who are bewildered, angry or fearful, turn to the police and other officials for comfort and guidance, only to find them operating according to different priorities which place concern for victims low on the list (Shapland *et al.* 1985; Chambers and Millar 1983, 1986; Elias 1983c; Holmstrom and Burgess 1978; Kelly 1982; Baril *et al.* 1984; Canadian Federal-Provincial Task Force 1983). There are fewer research findings concerning the more inquisitorial systems of continental Europe, but questionnaire returns from member states of the Council of Europe – on which the Council's proposals for reform are substantially based – show little difference there (Council of Europe 1983, 1985, 1987).

Ideas and strategies to alleviate the plight of victims have come thick and fast over the last few years and, in contrast to the consistent way the problem has been defined, the response presents a varied picture. Victimologists in the United States have largely followed a 'rights'-based strategy – encouraging the passing of state and federal legislation to allow victims greater parti-cipation in the criminal justice process (see, for example, NOVA 1985). Legislation is also in train in Canada (Waller 1986b), and here it has been accompanied by significant funding of pilot and demonstration programmes for victim assistance, based within various agencies of the criminal justice system (Bragg 1986). These initiatives have seemed slightly alien to European eyes. In Europe, by contrast, the emphasis has been on training and/or com-manding parts of the criminal justice system to take on duties relating to the provision of victim services (for example, van Dijk 1986a; Council of Europe 1985). In Britain, official action has been particularly low-key, and has been based on a perceived need to persuade agencies to devise their own responses and actions on behalf of victims.

These differences are unsurprising. Where action on behalf of victims has to involve the criminal justice system, it will tend to follow the criminal justice tradition of that country. Indeed, victims themselves will expect action within their own tradition. In complete contrast, however, the provision of *victim support* varies relatively little between different countries. If one looks through the summary of questionnaire returns made by member states of the Council of Europe, it is clear that the pattern of support and assistance is extremely similar throughout (Council of Europe 1987). State provision of social and medical services of course varies, but many countries also have generalist victim support services similar to those provided by VSS in the UK, as well as RCC and shelter homes for battered women.

The development of these services has been essentially a process of parallel evolution. Though there are personal and, on occasion, more formal links between those running services in different countries, these have tended to occur after the different services have become established. The trend towards cross-national associations, meetings and conferences is growing in strength now, mainly because quite a few countries have formed the kinds of networks or formal associations which make it easier to take part.

Does this similarity of organization, then, repudiate the assertion above that criminal justice traditions will compel different solutions to victim needs? I think not. The interesting fact about these victim support and assistance programmes is that they seem everywhere to have developed outside the realm of government and largely outside the ambit of the criminal justice agencies. They have their roots in the community or in voluntary associations, and rely heavily on voluntary workers and support. Governments have been hastening to try to catch up with and understand these mushrooming and popular voluntary bodies, not helped by their localization and hence the lack of central information about them. The problems of the associations are those of the voluntary sector: underfunding, lack of publicity about their services, inconsistency of approach in different parts of the same country, untrained personnel and shortage of specialist advice and support (see Maguire and Corbett 1987 for a comprehensive review of the position in England and Wales). The relative similarity of victims' services in different countries has resulted, I would argue, from their independence from criminal justice systems and governments.

The above exception is clearly of great importance and merits exploration elsewhere. However, in the remainder of this paper I shall concentrate upon those victim services which have had to involve the criminal justice system. The main task will be to use the experiences of different countries to assess the likely outcomes and relative success of different approaches to instituting change. This is problematic, given the lack of evaluation of initiatives in many countries, and it will be necessary to fall back on occasions upon theoretical analysis of the likely results of each approach.

Victim services involving the criminal justice system

Where the response to victim need has had to involve the criminal justice system, it has tended to be different in different countries. In North America, as mentioned above, it has often taken the form of legislated rights for individual victims or the drawing up of charters of such rights. These are essentially expressions of opinion or statements of values as to what the position of victims should be in a particular jurisdiction. They derive their strength from the future developments they may produce in concrete practices – through individual victims claiming and using those rights, or from the inspiration that practitioners in the system may derive from those statements of values to change their own practices. There is, however, very little *coercion* on either victim or practitioner to improve the lot of victims.

This is the problem with the use of a rights strategy to accomplish change. Success depends crucially on the willingness of individuals to institute legal action which will lead to judgments that enforce change. It has proved relatively successful in the field of prisoners' rights in England, where cases taken to the European Court of Human Rights in Strasbourg have led to a few changes in practices in prisons (see Maguire *et al.* 1985). However, even these changes have been patchy: an approach to change based on individual action cannot accomplish a wide-ranging review of current assumptions and practices. Moreover, individuals are often only successful in such cases if they are supported by a dynamic pressure group of their fellows, entirely committed to that strategy. This was the case, for example, with the campaign based upon legal action taken by MIND in England to change the 1959 Mental Health Act (cf. Gostin 1977).

While the national association in North America, NOVA, strongly supports the passing of legislation improving victim rights, the same is not true of its English counterpart, NAVSS. In England and Wales until recently, the language of individual rights has generally been seen as alien to the historical tradition of the criminal justice system (though one exception has been the right of the offender not to be unlawfully detained). In order to explore how change might be accomplished here, we need to digress in order to explore the nature of the English criminal justice system.

There has been considerable talk recently about interdependence and the benefits of cooperation among the various agencies of the criminal justice system (for example, Moxon 1985). By agencies, I am referring not only to those commonly seen as separate parts of the system – police, prosecution, judiciary, court administration, probation, prisons, and so on – but also to the various branches of the executive: the Home Office, the Lord Chancellor's

Office and, now, the Attorney General's Department. Despite the obvious links between the agencies in terms of the numbers of offenders passing through from one to the other, I feel it is more apt to characterize the agencies not as part of an interconnected system, but as independent 'fiefs' under a feudal system. Each fief retains power over its own jurisdiction and is jealous of its own workload and of its independence. It will not easily tolerate (or in some cases even permit) comments from other agencies about the way it conducts its business. This tendency is exacerbated and continued by the separate education and training of the professional workers for each fief, by their separate housing and by the hierarchical structure of promotion within fiefs, with little or no transfer between them. Negotiations between adjacent fiefs do occur over boundary disputes (for example, in the form of Court User Groups), but these tend to be confined to the agencies directly affected which see themselves as entering the negotiations as equally powerful parties (Feeney 1985). Nor is there any 'Round Table' (such as a sentencing commission – see Ashworth 1983; Shapland 1981).

It is interesting that the recent construction of a new system of prosecution was accomplished by the production of yet another separate fief in the form of the Crown Prosecution Service, whose workers, premises and philosophy will again be separate from all the others, and which will be responsible to a different Minister (the Attorney General). This new fief, charged with producing a statement of its working practices, has responded naturally enough with one that concentrates almost entirely upon the central task – that of deciding upon prosecution. Its *Code of Conduct for Crown Prosecutors* appears to ignore the need to discuss and regulate relations with other fiefs and with those not represented by fiefs at all – victims and defendants (Crown Prosecution Service 1986).

This type of criminal justice system has the advantage that the necessary independence of its different parts is built into the structure. The structure does not need careful tending, since the natural tendencies of the fiefs will reinforce it in its current state. However, their separateness and pride in their independence are also likely to lead – and in my view have already led to a very great degree – to failures to perceive the need for control of the whole system and to an overall lack of consistency. The system breeds a reliance on individual decision making and on discretion by the fief's workers, which has been elevated by some into an absolute virtue. There is no corresponding stress upon the needs of the consumers of the fief's services, whether other fiefs or individuals. When individuals seriously question what is happening, as those espousing the needs of victims have done, their challenge is likely to be taken as a challenge to the autonomy and authority of the fief, rather than as a comment on its ways of working.

Taking again the advent of the Crown Prosecution System as an example, the negotiations that have taken place on the needs of victims – for information, for consultation and for the effective collection and presentation to the courts of information related to claims for compensation – seem to have been fraught with difficulty and demarcation disputes. The difficulty with victims is that their needs span several fiefs. For example, the police are the agency that will have both the most contact and the most ready contact with victims to ascertain losses and injuries; but with responsibility passing to the Crown Prosecution Service they can no longer ensure that this information is made available to the court. Again, as the police are now often not told the results of cases, they cannot notify victims of the outcome, even should they be willing to do so. In fact, the relatively simple and uncontroversial needs of victims in relation to the criminal justice system (advice, information, consultation, witness expenses, compensation – see Shapland *et al.* 1985) cannot be the subject of an instruction such as a Home Office Circular without negotiations taking place with at least six fiefs (three ministries and three other agencies).

The problem of producing change in such a system is one of either persuading an agency that its own view of its mandate and of the way it operates must change, or of imposing change from without. In other parts of Europe, the sectors of the criminal justice system are fewer in number and there is an acceptance that some are subordinate to others. For example, in the Netherlands, the police are under the direction of the prosecutors, who in turn are part of the Ministry of Justice. Changes in policy can be accomplished through convincing just one agency – the Ministry of Justice – of the need for them. For example, the Ministry has issued instructions to other agencies to support victim assistance schemes and to inform victims of the results of cases, and has affected sentencing levels by asking prosecutors to advocate different sentence lengths in court. Opposition from other, independent parts of the system, such as the judiciary, has been muted, owing partly to the similarity of outlook and frequency of communication between them. Another example is to be found in Scotland, where prosecutors have the power to influence police investigations and to talk directly to witnesses.

Even in these more co-ordinated systems, there are those who advocate a still greater degree of consistency and central co-ordination and communication (for example, Steenhuis 1986). In England and Wales, people have always railed at the criminal justice system for its inconsistencies and its diffusion of power. They have usually been answered with incantations about the need for independence of the various fiefs. It is not my purpose to advocate a centrally controlled, uniform system. Clearly, the separateness of its parts is one of its main strengths. On the other hand, there is also the danger that the checks and balances will become so 'perfectly' adjusted that stasis sets in. At that point, one which I think we have reached now, change becomes extremely difficult to produce without coercion (or popular revolt from those not enfranchised in a fief). Persuasion may not work because agencies see no need to change their current positions.

Legislation or persuasion?

There is little detailed information about how agencies in England and Wales have responded to the pressure for change to meet victims' needs. At the central government level, Rock (1987) has documented how the Home Office, in contrast to the relevant government agencies in Canada, has been slow to change its view. He shows how it has tended to follow belatedly, rather than produce policy to lead, on such issues as victim support. We still have no co-ordinated government policy on all matters affecting victims in the criminal justice system. Even where there have been relevant international documents, such as the Council of Europe Convention on state compensation for victims of violent crime (1983), these have not formed a central pivot of policy. Indeed, the Convention has not yet been ratified. This lack of a central policy lead for agencies, one suspects, partly reflects the division into fiefs at government, as well as at practitioner, level.

Nevertheless, certain agencies have become convinced of the need for change to take account of the problems of victims. Senior police officers have changed their attitudes markedly over the last ten years and, in certain cases, this has led to local initiatives to improve the lot of victims in practice. The most notable examples are the part played by the police in the rise of VSS (Maguire and Corbett 1987) and the provision of facilities for victims of sexual assault (Shapland and Cohen 1987). The police have not, however, been able to pass on this enthusiasm to other fiefs (and indeed would not see it as appropriate that they should exert such an influence).

We have already addressed the problems in respect of the Crown Prosecution Service. (In case it may be thought that this inactivity is an inevitable feature of the prosecutorial role, it is pertinent to mention initiatives involving prosecutors in other countries. These include the guidelines of South Australia (1985) promoted by the Attorney General and the right of victims in the Netherlands to appeal to an ombudsman – who may award damages – against the decision of the prosecutor). Shapland and Cohen's (1987) survey also covered the administration of justice, in the form of justices' clerks from England and Wales. Here, it was apparent that a substantial minority of clerks were not only not trying to improve the lot of victims, but did not agree that to do so was part of their job. In other words, it may be concluded that where there is no agreement within a fief that a particular task, such as providing for victims, is part of its mandate, then persuasion will not work. Nor will guidelines or other manifestations of the service model be produced from within the profession. Pressure from without can be resisted.

Would legislated rights for individual victims, on the American model, break the deadlock? The problem is that, in order to claim them, victims have to be acknowledged as parties to the criminal justice system. If they are not, then again pressure can be ignored. A potential right of this kind was embodied in the Criminal Justice Bill 1986, although it was not legislated because of the intervention of the general election. This was a proposed requirement upon sentencers to give reasons if they decided not to make a compensation order. It is interesting to compare this with the obligation put upon magistrates under the Criminal Justice Act 1982 to give reasons before passing a custodial sentence upon a young adult. Burney's (1985) finding, that as many as 14 per cent of custodial disposals were not accompanied by a statement of reasons, does not lead one to believe that all judges and magistrates would comply with the comparable obligation proposed in the Criminal Justice Bill. Furthermore, an important difference between the two measures is that, while young adult defendants have a definite right of appeal in such cases, the position of victims is less clear. Could victims appeal if no reasons were given? What would then happen to the sentence if any appeal was allowed – would the defendant be re-sentenced? Would the victim obtain damages (on the Dutch model)?

More pertinently, even if these kinds of difficulties could be overcome, it appears that few, if any, young adult defendants have exercised their right of appeal in connection with the provisions of the 1982 Criminal Justice Act. Would victims exercise any equivalent right of appeal?

As a means of imposing change, then, such legislative provisions do not seem to be very effective. (They may be stimulating changes in attitudes, of course, but that is a long-term and stealthy process, not susceptible to research.) Given the lack of acknowledgement of the legal status of victims and the lack of a legally-inclined pressure group for victims, it is unlikely that this path will produce much change in the short term.

This is not to decry the need for individual, justiciable rights in some circumstances for victims. I have argued elsewhere (Shapland and Cohen 1987) that procedural duties backed up by victims' rights of appeal may well need to be enacted, for example, to ensure that details of victim injuries are placed before the court at the time of sentence (to allow the court to consider a compensation order). The need for rights as remedies, however limited the circumstances in which they apply, is a token of the difficulty of producing change in an unwilling system – a system which is unwilling both because parts of it do not appreciate the need for change and because it is unsufficiently coherent to be able to produce change between its separate fiefs. The difficulty is that rights, by themselves, will be insufficient – they will need backing up by training and by codes of practice which bridge the gaps between the fiefs involved.

In essence, a package of measures is required to accomplish the changes in the criminal justice system that are necessary to ensure that victims are informed and consulted and that information about their losses and injuries is placed before the court at the appropriate time. To be effective, this package will need to contain some justiciable rights for individual victims and/or some legally enforceable duties upon particular fiefs of the criminal justice system. That implies new legislation. More pertinently, the package should

include directives, codes of practice or circulars from Government departments to different fiefs and the promotion of training and different attitudes
within fiefs.

There is only one body that can encourage the development of such
a package – the same body that is able to enact its legislative elements –
Parliament. But even Parliament cannot put together its own package with
no other resources. There is a prior step to be taken: to produce a policy
which attempts to address all the needs of victims in the context of a discussion of the balance to be struck between the needs of the various fiefs and
of defendants and victims in the criminal justice system. Even the initiation
of this policy will be difficult. The medieval solution to a plethora of
independent fiefs was a Round Table committed to the pursuit of justice.
Such a standing convention of fiefs could discuss relevant policy and likely
practicalities before legislation is drafted.

The continued non-development of policy by the 'fiefs' raises another
spectre: that of growing unrest by the 'peasants' – the victims – or by those
who represent their interests. This unrest may, indeed, lead to the subsequent
adoption of the only apparently successful formula for action within the
system: in other words, the current stasis may be leading to the birth and
growth of another small fief – that of victims, or of associations and people
pressing on their behalf. Such a fief will have to distinguish its interests from
those of other fiefs. It will become more adversarial in respect to other parties,
including offenders, than the current groupings have been. The overall question is whether the English criminal justice system has within itself the ability
and determination to discuss, and if necessary legislate, a package of rights,
duties and services in respect of victims before such a fief is created.

Part 6

Mainstream victimology

by Sandra Walklate

It is possible to identify several competing theoretical strands within victimology work. These have been variously labelled positive, radical and critical victimology. (For a fuller discussion of each of these different strands of thought see Walklate, 2007). What both Walklate (1989, 2007) and Miers (1990) have differently referred to as conventional or positivist victimology is here referred to as 'mainstream victimology'. Mainstream victimology can be defined as that which is concerned with the everyday, ordinary experience of crime and, importantly, the policy implications that flow from this concern. Miers (1989: 3) defined positivist victimology as being concerned with 'the identification of factors which contribute to a non-random pattern of victimisation, a focus on interpersonal crimes of violence, and a concern to identify victims who may have contributed to their own victimisation'. So the parallels with mainstream victimological work are fairly clear. Mainstream (read positivist) victimology has had as its primary concern the need to measure the nature and extent of criminal victimization understood for the most part to be the kind of crime that people most readily define as being criminal: street crime, crimes of violence, and crimes against property. One of the key drivers for mainstream victimological work has been the criminal victimization survey. First used in the late 1960s in the United States, this method took a sample survey of the general population and asked them about their experiences of crime in order to establish a much more complete picture of the nature and extent of criminal victimization. Since that time criminal victimization survey data has become an established part of measuring crime not only nationally, with the development of the highly influential British Crime Survey first conducted in 1982 and now conducted annually, but also internationally through the periodic use of the International Criminal Victimization Survey.

This version of victimological work, while fairly narrow in its focus and methodological orientation has played an influential role in ensuring that issues relating to criminal victimization, in many different jurisdictions and settings, are now not only better understood but at the forefront of policy concerns. As other sections of this *Reader* illustrate the world of victimology is peopled by academics, policy makers, practitioners and campaigners, all of whom make claims on, and for, the victim of crime. The readings in this section illustrate both the diversity of the influences on mainstream victimological work, and despite its focus on the relatively everyday experiences of crime in different settings, that focus illustrates not only the widespread nature of victimisation but also the potential for policy agendas to flow from this.

Our last reading, while set in the context of the prison, relies on a methodological data base very similar to that used by positivist victimology: the criminal victimization survey. O'Donnell and Edgar used this mainstream victimological method with inmates in two prisons (a young offender institution and an adult male prison) and their article discusses their findings. While this work has all the trappings of mainstream victimological work, its findings have significant radical implications in the current penal climate. Their work documents the mundane, ordinary and routine patterns of victimization that occur in prison. The incidents they document are not sensational or headline grabbing, but they are nevertheless rather chilling in their consequences. In their view the routine experience of victimization in prison from assault, robbery, threats of violence, thefts from cells, exclusion, verbal abuse, 'taxing' of inmates by other inmates for their offences, shape the nature of prison life. The nature of these interactions support and serve prison culture and its associated hierarchy; a hierarchy in which violence and abuse is normal. As Sim (1994) commented, men in prison need to be 'tougher than the rest' in order to do their time thus lending weight to those critical of what is actually achieved by the prison regime and for whom.

The findings reported by O'Donnell and Edgar in this section raise all kinds of policy questions not only for the prison service (on which the authors comment) but for penal policy in general. It is significant that such findings emanate not from prisoners' stories, or radical campaign groups but from mainstream victimological work using highly conventional methodology. These findings are clearly suggestive that the routine relationships in which ordinary crimes flourish outside of the prison are replicated within the prison thus seriously challenging any rehabilitative aspirations associated with such institutions. Of course, it is useful to observe that this article relates to data gathered in the mid-1990s and the reader might like to consider the extent to which the processes discussed by O'Donnell and Edgar have undergone, if at all, any transformation. It is also useful to note that in the last decade the prison population has increased considerably. This fact alone, alongside the findings discussed by O'Donnell and Edgar, should encourage the reader to think quite critically about what might have changed or remained the same in those intervening years. Moreover the routine nature of victimization that this article presents to us should also encourage the reader to think about the bigger question: what are prisons for? In thinking about this question it may also be worth reflecting upon whether or not it is individual risk-averse or risk-seeking behaviour that we need to consider or whether it is also worth thinking about institutional settings that in and of themselves may be risk-averse or risk-seeking.

The other two readings in this section extend our understanding of mainstream victimological work in a different direction. These readings take us into the realm of policy and support and illustrate the extent to which victims who were previously hidden from the policy gaze are now less marginal to it. Both readings extend out understanding of who can be understood as a victim and what might be put in place for them in different ways. Goodey considers some of the issues relating to sex trafficking and Howarth and Rock consider the role of an organization called 'Aftermath' in their endeavours to support families dealing with the effects of one of their relatives being found guilty of a serious offence. Goodey considers the potential for different legal systems to respond to sex trafficking. Howarth and Rock look to facilitate an understanding of a voluntary organization in supporting a 'victim' very hidden from the legal system. Consequently these papers serve to remind us of a continuum of responses potentially available to the victim of crime and their efficacy. It will be useful to say a little about each of these papers in turn.

Goodey in this section considers the extent to which it is possible to promote 'good practice' between different jurisdictions in respect of managing cases of sex trafficking. As an issue this has certainly risen up the policy and political agenda over the last decade as cross-border regulations have relaxed, especially in Europe, and economic migration has increasingly become a feature of associated social movements. In these circumstances women and children appear to have become increasingly vulnerable to and become part of the sex-trafficking market. Goodey considers what might be understood as 'good practice' in such cases and charts the problems and possibilities of witness protection schemes in different European jurisdictions, and reminds us of the likelihood of victims who become witnesses in such cases being subjected to the secondary victimization of the criminal justice process. She offers her own good practice checklist and suggests that it is of crucial importance for there to be cross-national comparative studies to ensure that the safety of the victim remains at the centre of criminal justice responses in cases of this kind.

If Goodey's paper addresses issues of concern relating to victims that have attained some considerable visibility within contemporary criminal justice policy, Howarth and Rock chart a concern with a 'victim' still invisible to such processes: the families of serious offenders. Serious offenders are defined as those who have committed murder, manslaughter, rape, and other violent and sex offences who are serving a long term prison sentence. As Howarth and Rock state, 'those families may be deeply affected by the repercussions of crime, and their plight documents the capacity of certain crimes to lay waste to a wide range of social worlds in a way hitherto neglected'. It is certainly the case that despite increasing interest in and policy attention to the victim of crime generally, the group of people supported by Aftermath, founded in 1997, has not featured in day-to-day understandings of who counts as a victim. Yet in the story that Howarth and Rock document, family members of a serious offender become guilty by association and are often embroiled in a world of moral ambiguity in which they may care about their guilty family member, disapprove of what they have done, and be subjected to the disapproval and blame of others despite having committed no offence themselves. In comparison with the family of the murder victim or the rape victim as Howarth and Rock state, 'both have lost control. Both point to the catastrophically invasive knowledge that is impossible to absorb, accept or integrate. Both point to a disintegration of meaning; to feelings of oppression, vulnerability, guilt, stigma, isolation and to a profound sense of bereavement and loss'. Of course, in stretching our understanding of the concept of victim this way, this reading challenges the hidden agenda that lies behind the term itself. As Christie (1986) pointed out, the term 'victim' more often than not conjures an 'ideal' victim. This victim has a legitimate claim to the victim status and is deserving of our sympathetic response: Little Red Riding Hood out minding her own business, doing good deeds. In encouraging us to think about a victim largely hidden from public view but nevertheless sharing in the same reaction to events that had little, if anything, to do with them, the families of serious offenders, from an experiential point of view, have a claim to victim status. It is a moot point, however, as to the extent to which social and cultural processes are yet ready to recognize this.

In conclusion, while all of these readings tap into different aspects of mainstream victimological work from research methodology, to the role of criminal justice responses to the importance of work done by campaign and support groups, each of them also challenges our notion of who counts as a victim in different ways. Wiles et. al. (2002) hint at the role of human agency in exposure to victimisation and O'Donnell and Edgar (1998) point to the importance of the institutional context in setting an agenda for exposure to victimization. Each in their own way encourages us to think more critically about what the concept of victim means in relation to exposure to risk. Goodey, and Howarth and Rock hint at different victim stories from the increasing visibility of sex trafficking victims and the appropriateness of criminal justice responses to them, to the sustained invisibility of the families of serious offenders as 'other' victims of such crimes. These readings also encourage a critical thinking around the concept of victim but perhaps pointing to the importance of appreciating the cultural processes that encourage us to see some victims and not others. So while taken together all these papers support the comment made by Zedner (2002) that the victim can now no longer be considered the forgotten party of the criminal justice system, and illustrate the role that mainstream victimology has played in changing that status of the victim. All of these readings also point to the work that remains to be done, and the policy implications that might flow from taking on board the issues that they each address.

Recommended further reading

Christie, N. (1986) 'The ideal victim', in E.A. Fattah (ed.), *From Crime Policy to Victim Policy*. London: Macmillan.

Walklate, S. (2007) *Imagining the Victim of Crime*. Maidenhead: Open University Press.

Zedner, L. (2002) 'Victims', in M. Maguire, R. Morgan and R. Reiner (eds), *The Oxford Handbook of Criminology*. Oxford: Oxford University Press.

6.1

Promoting 'good practice' in sex trafficking cases
by Jo Goodey

[. . .]

Introduction: developing 'good practice' for victims of sex trafficking

There are a number of publications and policy guidelines offering recommendations in consideration of criminal justice and human rights responses to victims of sex trafficking (for example: Apap, 2002; Kelly and Regan, 2000; Sjolinder, 2002).[1] These recommendations are often introduced as 'good' or 'best' practice models for application in different contexts. Reports by Kartusch (2001) and Pearson (2002), singled out in this article, present two of the most recent comprehensive comparative accounts of legislation in different jurisdictions. They offer an excellent oversight of the extent of the trafficking problem in Europe, and the range of legislative and criminal justice responses to it. But, as this article attempts to highlight, their accounts, alongside others, are usually undertaken without sufficient understanding of what exists in practice for victims of crime, in general, and what exists, in particular, for other categories of vulnerable and at risk victims. In turn, suggestions for 'good practice' are often made without this concept being defined.

Recommendations for legislative and criminal justice practice concerning sex trafficking victims need to re-think the generalised responses that are currently on offer. When attempting to build 'good practice' guidelines, and offering examples from different jurisdictions of current legislation and practice, due regard must be given to three central points:

1. What is good practice?

   The basic premises of 'good practice' need definition and clarification with respect to their goals, 'success' rate, and possibilities for replication in different contexts. 'Good practice' should be offered with reference to how existing or similar practices currently work for other victim categories and, in this regard, whether they can be considered as a viable option for victims of sex trafficking as a particularly vulnerable victim category.

2. Cross-national and comparative issues

    Cross-national comparative examples of criminal justice 'good practice' demand sensitivity to different judicial–legal practices. For example, at a basic level, can ideas be transferred from a common law system of justice to an inquisitorial system?

3. The place of the victim

    Consideration needs to be given to how different criminal justice systems assign relative importance to victims of crime, in general, and different categories of vulnerable and at risk victims, in particular, when suggesting a range of victim-centred 'good practice' for trafficking victims.

Working to these three guidelines it should be the case that 'good practice' is offered with greater knowledge of, and, therefore, sensitivity to, the problems and promises of transferring 'good practice' ideas from one set of victims to another, and from one jurisdiction to another. Lists of recommendations are best offered with substantive knowledge of what currently works in practice for other categories of victims, and, in particular, vulnerable and at risk victims. Evidence based research from victimology should be at the forefront of critiques exploring how jurisdictions might adopt and adapt 'good practice' initiatives.

The 2000 UN Convention Against Transnational Organised Crime and its accompanying Trafficking Protocol are frequently referred to in papers that address the development of 'good practice' in consideration of trafficking victims.[2] However, these international instruments can only, at present, be regarded as guideline recommendations for States to aspire to when attempting to combat and respond to the problem of trafficking in human beings. Given that most of the Convention's recommendations for protection and assistance to trafficking victims are not reflected in many countries' current treatment of victims of crime, let alone the specific category of trafficking victims, it is remiss simply to reiterate these recommendations without providing a way forward to recommend the practical application of 'good practice' initiatives.

This article addresses the development of 'good practice' models for victims of sex trafficking with a critical eye to the three points raised at the beginning. Examples from recent cross-national reports on the problem of and responses to sex trafficking, alongside insights from the author's research in selected EU member states, will serve to illustrate the problems and promises of attempting to develop 'good practice'. The article does not adopt the common method of describing existing criminal justice practices, and assigning them the label of 'good/best practice' (Pearson, 2002), but offers a more critical reading of what is meant by 'good practice'. As criminal justice and civil responses to sex trafficking typically encompass the three broad themes of prevention, prosecution, and protection and assistance, the article will limit its discussion to selected points in relation to victim/witness protection and assistance.

Research in EU member states

This article is part of a wider research project undertaken by the author on the criminalisation of migrants in the context of 'Fortress Europe'.[3] Specifically, the research has focused on policy and criminal justice responses to some of the most marginalised migrants, such as trafficked women, who have, until recently, been typecast as 'offenders' under the terms of an EU 'migration-crime-security' continuum. In response to this negative stereotyping, the author's research explores how 'victims' of sex trafficking fare in selected EU member states. The 'place' of sex trafficking victims, in criminal justice, is compared with other victim categories in an effort to clarify the practice behind the political rhetoric. While other papers by the author have examined the above issues in more depth (for example: Goodey, 2000; Goodey, 2002; Goodey, 2003a; Goodey, 2003b), this article explores the problems faced when developing 'good practice' for victims of sex trafficking in light of the three points identified for discussion at the beginning of the paper.

The mainstay of the author's research is focused on theoretical and policy discussions of governmental and inter-governmental responses to crime, migrants, and the particular case of organised crime and human trafficking. The remainder of the research examines evidence collected from experts in the fields of victim-centred criminal justice, and, specifically, sex trafficking. As the research was based in the Crime Programme at the United Nations in Vienna, the author was able to identify international experts using the Secretariat's established contacts with criminal justice agencies and NGOs in different EU member states. Attendance at expert group meetings and international conferences, over a period of months, also helped to identify potential experts who were approached in person and asked to participate in the research. These introductory meetings were followed up with a letter, and oftentimes a second letter, requesting their participation.[4] In turn, questionnaire respondents and interviewees were asked to recommend other experts who might be in a position to assist the research. Correspondence, including the research questionnaire, was variously distributed in English, French and German to maximise respondents' willingness to participate in the project.

A detailed questionnaire was distributed to experts from the police, prosecutors' offices, government ministries, victim support groups, NGOs, and academics. The questionnaire at 33 pages long provided ample scope for qualitative responses to open-ended questions. It comprises six sections: (1) recognising 'vulnerable' and 'at risk' victims/witnesses; (2) legislation and guidelines for victims of crime, in general; (3) specific criminal justice provisions/services for 'vulnerable' and/or 'at risk' victims/witnesses; (4) special programmes: victims/witnesses and organised crime; (5) organised crime; most significant victim/witness programme; (6) comparing programmes for 'vulnerable' and 'at risk' victims/witnesses.

The questionnaire was distributed either in whole or in part to respondents according to their particular area of expertise. While the original questionnaire was developed with the potential for quantitative analysis, statistical analysis has not been adopted for the following reasons: first, the number of responses per country were insufficient for a meaningful statistical comparison between member states; secondly, ambiguous responses to pre-ordained response categories did not lend themselves to definite answers for statistical analysis; and, thirdly, respondents often submitted anecdotal and additional evidence that did not comply with the questionnaire's response categories. To some extent this reflects inherent problems encountered when trying to get respondents from different working and disciplinary backgrounds, and different judicial cultures, to reply to pre-determined response categories that might not necessarily apply to or reflect their particular socio-legal experiences. In turn, it is often very difficult to categorise legal and criminal justice practice as there are many exceptions under which certain laws and provisions can be applied. However, with provision for respondents to reply to open-ended questions, the questionnaire received some interesting qualitative responses.

In addition to the research questionnaire, the author also conducted a number of research interviews with representatives from the police, government, and NGOs, and attended meetings addressing the problem of organised crime and human trafficking.[5] Interview schedules asked interviewees to elaborate on any special programmes for victims of sex trafficking that they had referred to in parts four and five of the questionnaire. Interviewees were asked to describe any existing witness protection programmes and associated provisions for victim assistance in relation to trafficking cases. Interviews took place in the following countries: Austria, Germany, the Netherlands, and the U.K. While research findings from the questionnaire encompass all fifteen EU states, the research analysis has focused on eight countries due, primarily, to the number and detail of responses from these jurisdictions.[6]

Together, the research questionnaire and interviews offer a rich descriptive account of criminal justice responses to vulnerable and at risk victims of crime, including victims of sex trafficking, in different EU member states. Research results are utilised in the article as a means of illustrating the problem of suggesting 'good practice' interventions for victims of sex trafficking. The questionnaire and the research interviews did not ask respondents to specifically address the subject of 'good practice' in criminal justice interventions with victims of crime, in general, and trafficking victims, in particular. Consideration of 'good practice', and the transferability of ideas within and between jurisdictions, emerged during the course of the research. The central remit of the article is to critique what is meant by 'good practice' with respect to the three points set out at the beginning. With this in mind, the following section offers a discussion of 'good practice' as it impacts on suggestions for and responses to victims of crime and sex trafficking victims.

1. What is good practice?

'Good practice', or 'best practice' as it is often interchangeably referred to, in criminal justice intervention against traffickers, and for trafficking victims, is difficult to define. While 'practice' refers to the plans and activities formulated and carried out by criminal justice agencies, it is difficult to determine what is meant by 'good' or 'best'. These are subjective labels assigned to practices by their instigators and critics, because they are deemed to be 'successful'. In turn, the meaning of 'successful' is highly subjective. What might be considered to be a 'successful' criminal justice intervention by the police might not be regarded as a 'success' by trafficked women.[7] And, while the UN Convention and Trafficking Protocol can be promoted as the 'gold standard' of internationally agreed 'good practice', each jurisdiction can present a range of 'good practice' initiatives that partially agree with and challenge the standards set out in the Convention and Trafficking Protocol.

According to the authors of an unpublished preliminary report by the Home Office, Europol, and partners from the Swedish Crime Prevention College (2000),[8] 'good practice' for reducing organised crime should be cost effective and should satisfy one or more of the following criteria: '(1) Innovative; encapsulate new or creative solutions to recurring problems relating to organised crime; (2) Make a difference; demonstrates a positive and tangible impact (disruption) on one or more groups of organised criminals, or reduces their influence; (3) Are sustainable and socially and ethically acceptable; have an on-going influence on the operation or impact of organised criminals; (4) Can be replicated; are generalisable to situations outside those in which they have been shown to work [sic].[9]

These four principles for 'good practice' can be transferred to initiatives that set out to protect and assist victims of sex trafficking, as the victims of organised criminal networks. Here, the author has adjusted the above list, and added to it, to offer a 'good practice' checklist:

1. Positive Results: Identify projects, through results, with a positive and tangible impact on and for victims of sex trafficking. Results must clearly define what is meant by 'successful' and 'unsuccessful' practice

according to the instigators and users of projects. Results must take account of the opinions of sex trafficking victims.

2. Innovation: Employ new and/or innovative solutions that aim to protect and assist victims of sex trafficking. Identify and reject established practices that have not served the interests of trafficking victims.

3. Sustainability: Look for projects with long-term and durable protection and assistance to sex trafficking victims, their families, and endangered NGO/criminal justice employees, beyond, and in addition to, the setting of a criminal trial. Only promote projects that take into consideration their long-term social and ethical impact.

4. Replication: Given that sex trafficking involves the exploitation of women in and between countries, seek practical solutions that can be replicated in other settings. Encourage information exchange regarding successful and unsuccessful practices in an effort to replicate success stories.

5. Co-coperation: Foster co-operation between agencies from criminal justice and civil society, including NGOs, both nationally and, in appropriate cases, internationally, in an effort to formulate working partnerships primarily for the protection and assistance of trafficked women. Avoid competition between agencies working to protect and assist trafficked women.

6. Ethical: Only promote projects that prioritise the safety and welfare of trafficking victims, and other social groups affected by sex trafficking. Consider the opinions and concerns of trafficking victims at different stages of criminal justice and social intervention.

This revised six point checklist of 'good practice' guidelines, for consideration in relation to sex trafficking projects, should be read alongside the generic three point criteria laid out at the beginning of the article. The six point checklist suggests a 'good practice' course of action for agencies that set out to protect and assist trafficking victims. What it does not provide is a list of prescriptive criteria specifying what is meant by 'successful' and 'positive' results that should follow this course of action. The first point asks that projects identify what is meant by 'successful' and 'unsuccessful' practice according to project instigators and users, and, in this regard, definitions are left open. However, the following can be considered as an additional checklist of 'good practice' results:

7. More trafficking victims are offered protection and/or assistance as a result of the project. Based on resources, projects should specify how many victims they intend to help in the course of a fixed time period.

8. Trafficking victims indicate they are satisfied with the protection and/or assistance offered by the project. 'Satisfaction' criteria should be defined

by the project organisers and, in turn, clarified by trafficked women as project users.

9. Co-operation and working partnerships are fostered and improved within and between agencies running projects. As a result, more 'successful' cases of victim support pass through projects.

Fundamentally, these good practice descriptors demand one essential factor: that knowledge about successful and unsuccessful interventions be shared between practitioners and policy makers both abroad and at home. While one project might be considered as 'successful' under the terms of its particular remit, it cannot be offered up as a 'good practice' solution for other jurisdictions without due consideration being given to the context in which sex trafficking occurs and is responded to.

One of the greatest hurdles to address, when suggesting good/best prac-tice initiatives for sex trafficking victims, is the willingness of organisations to exchange information about their successful and unsuccessful experiences. Examples of accessible on-line 'good practice' databases exist, but these have a limited applicability when it comes to the specifics of criminal justice interventions in trafficking cases as they are usually targeted at other users.[10] Given the nature of organised crime and human trafficking, it is unlikely that criminal justice agencies will provide detailed accounts of their successful initiatives in an open public forum such as the internet. Limiting exchange of details about criminal justice intervention against traffickers, using an extranet provider or in the course of closed meetings, is one means of attempting to avoid the problem of information getting into the wrong hands. Having said this, publicly available general guidelines of what good/best prac-tice can be, as indicated above, can assist organisations needing to establish good practice initiatives, whilst avoiding any leakage of reserved information, and preserving the security of criminal justice agencies, NGOs, and trafficked women.

At present, discussion about the development of 'good practice', in response to the problem of sex trafficking, tends to rest with generalised guidelines about what should be done in consideration of the three themes of: prevention, prosecution, and protection and assistance. Where reference is made to international and national legislation and practice, this is usually made minus the three considerations offered at the beginning of this chapter; although great emphasis is usually placed on the need for inter-agency co-operation in an effort to combat trafficking.[11] In this regard, there are two recent reports that exemplify efforts at cross-national comparison of legal, criminal justice, and NGO practice concerning trafficking. One is Kartusch's (2001) 'Reference Guide for Anti-Trafficking Legislative Review' for the Ludwig Boltzmann Institute of Human Rights and the Organisation for Security and Cooperation in Europe (OSCE). The other is Pearson's (2002) publication 'Human Traffic, Human Rights: Redefining Witness Protection' for Anti-Slavery International. While the two publications are very different in style, both work towards recommendations for harmonisation of legal and criminal justice practice concerning sex trafficking victims, and the central role that NGOs can play in this process. Both texts emphasise harmonisation of 'good practice' recommendations within and between countries in an effort to promote co-ordinated responses with 'successful' results; however, at no point is 'good practice' clarified as a concept.[12]

Kartusch's publication focuses on legislation and criminal justice practice with respect to south eastern Europe; namely, the former Yugoslavia. From a legalistic comparativist perspective, Kartusch's report compares the wording and application of national and international legal instruments with respect to their relative 'usefulness' against traffickers and on behalf of trafficking victims. Employing case studies of legislation in different countries in an effort to promote 'good practice', Kartusch's report is divided into three broad categories: prevention of trafficking; prosecution of offenders; and protection and assistance for victims. Pearson's report covers much the same area as Kartusch's with respect to legislation and practice in ten countries around the world, and makes 45 recommendations, or 'good practice' suggestions, under ten thematic headings ranging from investigation and prosecution of traffickers, through to return and repatriation of trafficked women. Pearson's report does not offer the legislative depth provided in Kartusch's report, but it does provide an insight into the experiences of trafficked women with extracts from 30 case studies.

In addition to these two reports, the recent 'Brussels Declaration' on Preventing and Combating Trafficking in Human Beings,[13] that emerged from an IOM organised conference on trafficking,[14] includes nineteen 'draft recommendations, standards and best practices' in consideration of the following broad themes: mechanisms for co-operation and co-ordination at the level of the EU; prevention of trafficking in human beings; victim protection and assistance; police and judicial co-operation. The Brussels Declaration, following the initiative of the Greek Presidency of the EU, has been presented by the EU Directorate General for Justice and Home Affairs to the Multidisciplinary Group of the Council of the EU for discussion and action. The Declaration presents another comprehensive and wide-ranging checklist for 'good practice' initiatives at an international level. It reiterates a number of points made by other international instruments, notably the 2000 UN Convention and Trafficking Protocol, without any sense of progress regarding a specific plan of action for agencies to follow on the ground. And, once again, recommendations are made with no reference to what exists and doesn't exist in practice for other victim categories, or to what 'good practice' means.

Together, the publications by Kartusch and Pearson, and the Brussels Declaration, present a comprehensive and unified response to the problem of sex trafficking that focuses on the human rights of trafficking victims.

However, these publications critique legislation and criminal justice practice for trafficking victims, and go on to suggest 'good practice' initiatives, without a thorough understanding of current criminal justice practice concerning other categories of vulnerable and intimidated victims/witnesses.

2. Cross-national and comparative issues

Reference to international 'good practice' standards for victims of crime, including victims of trafficking, tend to mean one of two things. Either international legislation and guidelines are employed as the starting point from which to assess 'good practice'; for example, the UN Convention Against Transnational Organised Crime and its accompanying Trafficking Protocol (van Dijk, 2002). Or, existing criminal justice practices are described and assigned the label of 'good' or 'best' practice, often without recourse to comparison of practices in similar settings, with similar populations, or concerning similar experiences of victimisation. For example, the British Home Office's list of exemplary interventions in cases of violence against women, while providing a wide-ranging database, does not explain how each project might be considered as 'good practice'.[15] In turn, such examples leave us with context specific case studies that do not necessarily lend themselves to relocation.

The author's research in fifteen EU member states highlighted the problems of attempting to undertake a cross-national comparative study of victim-centred practice between jurisdictions. Each state responds differently to victims' needs, with some affording victims more rights than others. With the Justice and Home Affairs pillar of the EC moving increasingly towards the unification of criminal justice across the EU, in an effort to stem the tide of unwanted immigration, we can expect a more coherent response towards legal and illegal immigration, asylum seekers, refugees, and, in turn, trafficked women. While the latest Brussels Declaration on Trafficking reflects moves towards standardisation of criminal justice responses to trafficking, it will be some time yet before criminal justice practice is harmonised across the EU's courtrooms. Differences in procedural practices, and the admissibility of evidence, prevent the straightforward transfer of criminal justice practice between jurisdictions. And, as my own research has shown, the scant availability of basic victim/witness protection measures across the EU, such as video-links and use of screens, means that these provisions are not readily available for vulnerable and at risk victims of crime in general, let alone trafficking victims.

If 'good practice' suggestions for trafficking victims are to be made without resorting to generalisable 'gold standards' of practice ideals, consideration should be given to the reality and possibilities for criminal justice practice in different jurisdictions. A list of 'good practice' standards, such as those offered by Kartusch and Pearson, can be critically examined against an exploration of the reality of practice in selected jurisdictions. Each 'good practice' can be tested against basic criteria that explore its application and possibilities for adoption. For example, taking a basic standard of victim/ witness protection, such as use of video-links, we can start by asking whether this provision exists in a selected jurisdiction.

Table 6.1.1 presents a series of basic steps to follow when looking to adopt 'good practice guidelines in sex trafficking cases. The table utilises one particular example, use of video links, as an illustration. Although the list appears to offer no more than 'common sense' guidelines, there is no reference in the literature on trafficking as to how lessons can be learned and transferred from one jurisdiction to the next. The table offers a series of guidelines to build on existing practice in a particular jurisdiction, or to borrow examples of 'good practice' from other jurisdictions. The steps, or questions, attempt to explore 'good practice' for sex trafficking victims with due consideration for what exists and does not exist for other victim categories. In turn, when borrowing 'good practice' examples from other jurisdictions, careful consideration should be given to matching jurisdictions with: (1) similar legal structures and criminal justice set-ups; (2) similar levels of development with regard to victim-centred justice; and (3) comparable levels of sex trafficking. In this regard, rather than all jurisdictions aspiring to the same UN goals or EC directives in the first instance, it might be more effective and realistic for countries to adopt a graded system of 'good practice'. What this would mean in practice is that countries critically assess their own response to crime victims, in general, and trafficking victims, in particular, relative to a country at a similar level of criminal justice development. Having done so, practical suggestions can be made with respect to specific areas in need of improvement. In turn, countries need to look outside collective suggestions for 'good practice' that do not reflect their own experiences of trafficking. For example, the adoption of a witness protection programme modelled on US practice is, in most EU jurisdictions, inappropriate.

The following section critiques suggestions for 'good practice' in sex trafficking cases for their lack of insight in consideration of the 'place' of victim-centred justice in different jurisdictions. This critique is made using evidence from the author's research in selected EU member states, to this end, the evidence presented here reflects respondents' collective knowledge, and not that of the author, about their own country's criminal justice practice.

[. . .]

Concluding comments: challenges to 'good practice' in sex trafficking cases

It is unwise and impractical to offer 'good practice' recommendations for sex trafficking victims that currently are not on offer to other victim categories. Promotion of various standards for trafficking victims should not be made

Table 6.1.1

IDENTIFY A 'GOOD PRACTICE' STANDARD *Are video-links available in the selected jurisdiction?*			
IF YES		**IF NO**	
What exists locally/nationally as: Legislation Guidelines Examples of practice		*What exists in other jurisdictions as:* Legislation Guidelines Examples of practice	
Are video-links available to all crime victims or particular categories?		Could international examples of video-link use be adapted for use in your jurisdiction?	
Are video-links currently used in cases involving trafficking victims?		Could video-link be used in cases involving trafficking victims?	
IF YES Have video-links been used successfully?	**IF NO** What barriers exist against application of video-links in sex trafficking cases?	**IF YES** What action plan could be adopted for application of video-links in the selected jurisdiction?	**IF NO** What barriers exist against the use of video-links in sex trafficking cases?
How is 'success' defined? Are trafficking victims involved?	• Lack of knowledge about the problem • Lack of resources	• New legislation and/or guidelines • Police and judicial training	• Lack of knowledge about the problem • Lack of resources
Can lessons be learnt from adoption of video-links to improve application of other measures to sex trafficking victims?	• Absence of victim-centred justice • Prejudicial treatment against trafficked women • Other	• Bring NGO expertise on board • Work in partnership with other agencies • Draw on expertise from other jurisdictions	• Absence of victim-centred justice • Prejudicial treatment against trafficked women • Other

without knowledge of current provisions on offer to other vulnerable and at risk victims in the same jurisdiction; for example, victims of domestic violence, victims of rape, and child victims of sexual abuse. Having explored what exists for victims of crime, in general, and vulnerable and at risk victims, in particular, such as trafficking victims, examples of 'good practice' can also be drawn from other jurisdictions. Careful consideration should be given to matching jurisdictions to ease the transfer of 'good practice' between countries.

This paper has gone some way to developing a discussion about what 'good practice' should take into account with respect to criminal justice responses to sex trafficking victims in different jurisdictions. The paper suggests three core themes for consideration. What the research cannot offer, given the fact that respondents were not asked to comment on 'good practice', is a set of 'good practice' guidelines according to respondents from different working backgrounds, and from different jurisdictions. This is the work of another paper. What the research has pointed to is the gap between the law in the books, as forwarded through 'good practice' checklists, and the reality of criminal justice practice as it impacts on victims of crime and trafficking victims.

General recommendations for 'good practice' should more accurately be viewed, alongside the UN Convention Against Transnational Organised Crime and the Trafficking Protocol, as standards to aspire to. As the research has illustrated, there is a great difference between what can be offered 'on paper' for sex trafficking victims, and what exists in reality for victims as criminal justice practice. Suggestions for 'good practice' should more critically explore the reality of transferring ideas with respect to the three points highlighted at the beginning of this article. In critiquing the response of international organisations, governments, criminal justice authorities and NGOs to the problem of sex trafficking, it is hoped that this article has shed some light on what is meant by 'good practice' for victims, and sex trafficking victims, in a comparative, cross-national context.

Notes

1 For the purpose of this article, discussion of trafficking will be limited to trafficking in women for sexual exploitation; hereafter referred to as 'sex trafficking' or 'trafficking'. Under the terms of the Protocol to Prevent, Suppress and Punish Trafficking in Persons, Especially Women and Children (supplementing the 2000 UN Convention Against Transnational Organised Crime), Article 3(a) states: ' "Trafficking in persons" shall mean the recruitment, transportation, transfer, harbouring or receipt of persons, by means of the threat or use of force or other forms of coercion, of abduction, of fraud, of deception, of the abuse of power or of a position of vulnerability or of the giving or receiving of payments or benefits to achieve the consent of a person having control over another person, for the purpose of exploitation. Exploitation shall include, at a minimum, the exploitation of the prostitution of others or other forms of sexual exploitation, forced labour or services, slavery or practices similar

to slavery, servitude or the removal or organs' (A/55/383). See also Bales (2000) and IOM (1995) for a general introduction to the nature and scale of trafficking in a global context.

2 See: *www.unvienna.org* – for full Convention and Protocol.

3 The author's research was funded by the European Commission: Marie Curie Research Programme; individual fellowship (HPMF-CT-1999-0383); funded from September 2000 to May 2003 (with a break of nine months duration). The research was based in the Crime Programme at the United Nations in Vienna; since October 2002, the Centre for International Crime Prevention has been renamed the Crime Programme. Prior to the start of the research, Vienna hosted the Tenth UN Congress on the Prevention of Crime and Treatment of Offenders. The Congress laid the foundations for the 2000 UN Convention Against Transnational Organised Crime (TOC), and its accompanying Protocol to Prevent, Suppress and Punish Trafficking in Persons; especially women and children (hereafter referred to as the Trafficking Protocol). In addition, since 1999, the Vienna UN has been running the UN's Global Programme Against Trafficking. The UN's work has formed a backdrop to the author's research on the 'place' of trafficking victims in the context of broader discussions and international action focusing on organised crime, and the prosecution of organised criminals.

4 Meetings and conference attended included, for example: Tenth UN Congress on the Prevention of Crime and Treatment of Offenders, Vienna, April 2000; British Society of Criminology Conference, Leicester, July 2000; Tenth International Symposium on Victimology, Montreal, August 2000; Expert Meeting on State Compensation to Crime Victims in the EU, Sweden, October 2000; American Society of Criminology Conference, San Francisco, November 2000.

5 For example: Economic and Social Council organised meeting on Transnational Organised Crime, Home Office, London, December 2000; Europol Expert Meeting on Trafficking in Human Beings for the Purpose of Sexual Exploitation, The Hague, March 2001 – closed meeting; Meeting with representatives from the Dutch Rapporteur's Office on Trafficking, The Hague, March 2001; Meeting with Anti-Trafficking Team of the Federal Bundeskriminalamt, Wiesbaden, March 2001; see BKA (1999); International Organisation for Migration meeting on trafficking, European Parliament, Brussels, September 2002; Organisation for Security and Co-operation in Europe, Expert Meeting on Development of an Anti-Trafficking Training Module for Judges and Prosecutors, Sofia, April 2003 – closed meeting.

6 In total, about 130 research questionnaires were distributed within the EU. This resulted in a 50 per cent response rate; with some countries returning eight completed questionnaires (Austria; Belgium; England

and Wales; Finland; France; Germany; Italy; the Netherlands – selected for detailed research), and others only one or two (Denmark; Greece; Ireland; Luxembourg; Portugal; Spain; Sweden).

7   See: *www.iom.int* – The International Organisation for Migration's website contains direct quotes from trafficked women regarding their experiences of trafficking and criminal justice responses. Pearson's report (2002) contains quotes from 30 case studies of trafficked women's experiences of trafficking and criminal justice interventions.

8   Falcone, Home Office, Europol and Swedish Study on the Exchange of Good Practice for Reducing Organised Crime; preliminary report on findings by Levy, M., Maguire, M., Sutton, M., Browne, D., Oldfield, D., Korsell, L., Dekker, B. and Ekblom, P., December 2000, London: Home Office.

9   Ibid. The unpublished preliminary report contains no page numbers; this quote was taken from Part 1, titled: An examination of the feasibility of setting up a European Database for Good Practice in Organised Crime Prevention.

10 *www.mjin.net* – world justice information network; *www.marchmont.ac.uk* – Marchmont observatory; *www.cabinet-office.gov.uk/servicefirst/2000/ guidance* – British government cabinet office best practice database.

11 Holmes (2002) presents an exemplary checklist for police and NGO co-operation in trafficking cases that is both concise and informative. His checklist requires introspection on the part of the police and NGOs regarding their current practices and the need for reform. The checklist is based on his extensive experience as a police officer, originally based with the Metropolitan Police in London, working in the field of counter-trafficking and law enforcement co-ordination.

12 A comprehensive publication by Brienen and Hoegen (2000) compares victim-centred criminal justice practice between 22 European jurisdictions, and attempts to identify those States with 'good practice'; however, once again 'good practice' is not defined.

13 See: *http://register.consilium.eu.int/pdf/en/02/st14/14981en2.pdf* – to access the document of the Council of the European Union of 29 November 2002 entitled 'Brussels Declaration on Preventing and Combating Trafficking in Human Beings'.

14 'The Conference on Preventing and Combating Trafficking in Human Beings: A Global Challenge for the 21st Century' was organised by IOM (International Organisation for Migration) in collaboration with the European Commission, European Parliament, and EU member states. The Conference took place in the European Parliament in Brussels on 18–21 September 2002.

15 *www.homeoffice.gov.uk/domesticviolence/crpguide.htm.*

6.2

Aftermath and the construction of victimisation: 'the other victims of crime'

by Glennys Howarth and Paul Rock

Aftermath, a self-help and counselling organisation established by and for the families of serious offenders, defines its members as 'the other victims of crime'. That is a claim which raises important and interesting questions not only about procedures for *establishing moral identity* but also about the reach and impact of crime.

[. . .]

Aftermath

The big foundational idea of Aftermath is that offences have many victims, and that in several important senses the family of a serous offender must also be regarded as his victim. It was conceived in March 1988 when Shirl Marshall, a victim support volunteer based in Sheffield, accompanying the mother of a murder victim to trial, came to an understanding of how very widely-ramifying the consequences of a serious crime could be:

> . . . it was really very, very harrowing indeed, and every day, coming into the court we saw this stricken-face woman, and my friend and I realised that she was the mother of the man in the dock. . . . There was one of those interminable adjournments where the judges cleared the court and we went out for a coffee, and I looked round for ____ and she wasn't there. . . . She returned a few minutes later and I said 'where have you been?' and I was so worried because she was in such a state, and she said 'I've been to see her'. I said 'not her?' 'Yes', she said, 'I saw her across the court and I went to see her'. I said, '____ whatever did you find to say?' . . . She said, 'I told her that I love my son very much, and I knew that she must love her son very much', and, she said, 'I just wanted her to know that I had no hatred for her . . . we just spoke, burst into tears and hugged one another'. I was so moved because [she] later on that

day said to me, 'Shirley there are so many victims!' and 'I thought that's it!'.

Shirl Marshall was one of those formidably powerful and energetic matri-archal figures who may be discovered founding and running voluntary organisations in distressed communities (Campbell 1993; Rock 1988b). Indeed, she has chosen to describe herself variously as a 'mum' and a grandmother figure. Although she had no formal qualifications in counselling she had had abundant experience of voluntary work with Victim Support, probation and self-help groups for alcoholics, the mentally ill and drug abusers; in befriending the families of prisoners and prisoners themselves on death row in Georgia; and in visiting prisoners in England. She came to conclude that the problems of serious crime could be challenged only by enabling offenders to gain a better understanding of themselves and their family, and conversely, by enabling families to gain a better understanding of themselves and the offender in their midst:

> The men are part of the family and unless we can get to understand what it's all about, we can't help the family. . . . It began to dawn on me that the only way to really deal with the family of a serious offender was to know the offender. [Otherwise] it was incomplete . . . you've got to have a whole picture to fit the jigsaw together.

Shirl Marshall was to be advised by Geoffrey Pollit, a former prison psych-iatrist and medical officer, whose professional maxim had been 'you listen to the offender, because in Wakefield, certainly, I learned that by listening one can find out very much more than [from] any other source'. Pollit had long held the view that those whom he called 'emotional' rather than 'acquisitive' offenders were particularly disturbed in the earlier stages of their sentence about:

> . . . how their relatives were being treated and received in the outside world, not only by neighbours but by parents, uncles, aunts, relatives, anybody like that, and they found that a lot of these people who should have been supportive were in fact rejecting them. . . . There was nobody to whom these people in the outside world could turn. One evening I was in the kitchen, I turned Radio 4 on, and I heard a programme [about Aftermath] which was three mums of young murderers talking. . . . I thought this is just the sort of thing these people have been talking about!

Aftermath came originally to work through an extended exploration of the motives, patterns, meanings and consequences of offending. On the one hand, ex-offenders would be groomed as counsellors, forming what was to be called the offenders team or 'therapy team', and, in Shirl Marshall's phrase, 'shaping their remorse and putting it to practical use' by talking about themselves and their transgressions to families, helping families to make sense of the offending of their own members.[1] On the other hand, families would be encouraged to constitute 'a loving family network' (Aftermath nd(b), p. 2) linked by telephone; newsletter (after 1996); and monthly 'Aftermath lunches' that were to meet first in Sheffield and London and then in Portsmouth, Chester and elsewhere. At those lunches, attended by ten or so people bringing food to create a 'warm and welcome atmosphere', families could be guided not only towards a clearer comprehension of the genesis and development of offenders and offending, but also towards a greater mastery over their own distress and bewilderment. Their world, it was said, had been turned upside down. Unbearable consequences flowed from the abrupt revelation that one's son, father, husband, nephew or brother had been arrested for murder, manslaughter, rape or sexual assault, and the families found it hard to contend with what had befallen them.

Aftermath offered not only support to families but also a programme of individual counselling to prisoners and their relatives in which Shirl Marshall was vigorously involved until she quit the organisation in February 1996. After Shirl Marshall's resignation, Aftermath came to concentrate more squarely on mutual aid,[2] it being the view of later members of the Aftermath committee that there had been an imbalance and an excessive concentration on the offender.

Turning more markedly towards the standard pattern of a self-help group (see Wilson nd), Aftermath has sought to normalise the abnormal, rebuild self-respect, reduce alienation, and reassure the afflicted that there are others like them, that their responses and problems are not untoward. It 'provides [a] network of those who have been there, who know the pain, and the guilt, and the relief of being listened to, believed and accepted' Pollit was to tell Aftermath in Sheffield in 1995. Pollit concluded later that:

> The nub of Aftermath, certainly in my opinion, is a number of people, the hidden victims, the mothers and the wives of the offenders, coming together with the same experiences, with the same understanding and being able to listen to each other and exchange their experiences and support each other and, particularly, to reassure each other that the way they are behaving is perfectly normal ('I must be going mad') and, if they are, reassure that everybody else has felt the same . . . this helps them a great deal.

Aftermath was launched formally in September 1988, and like many another self-help group, its existence was publicised haphazardly through sporadic reports in the mass media and in information circulating in professional and lay referral networks. An increasing number of families approached it for help (it is claimed that some 1,000 families have done so since its inception and that 200–300 families are active at any one time), and it may be seen in Figure 6.2.1 that the relatives of murderers and sex offenders were in a preponderance from the first.

Those who came to Aftermath meetings talked about their rank disbelief, confusion and dismay at what they had learned about the offence and the offender. 'In many of these cases', Aftermath stated, 'the offence and subsequent trial and imprisonment came as a complete shock – literally a bolt from the blue – to the families concerned. They had no idea that a close relative could commit such a crime, particularly in cases where the offender is a child' (Aftermath nd(a), p. 5). One woman said: 'I felt sick . . . I didn't think for one moment that my son was involved'.

The two main groups of crimes touching Aftermath are held to be 'emotional' and 'sexual', and their etiology and effects are quite distinct. 'Emotional' crimes of violence are represented as untoward events that could not readily have been anticipated by the naive onlooker. They are percussive discharges of anger and pain that may have accumulated unseen and virtually unrecognised in the offender over long periods (Shirl Marshall reflected in 1995; 'the motive is in the heart of the man who did it and the build-up of damage in him gets to such a point that he vomits it out . . .', and an ex-offender member of the therapy team, a close associate of Marshall, a man

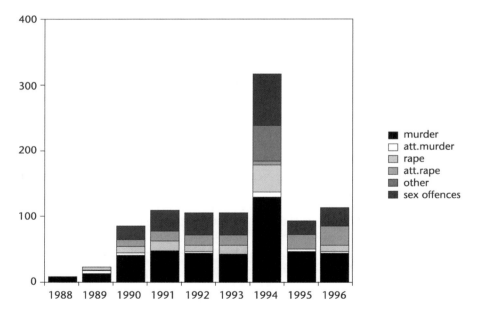

Figure 6.2.1 Yearly Breakdown of Cases Referred to Aftermath: 1988 to 1996.

(*Source:* Taken from Aftermath (1997a). 'Other cases' were defined as 'Drugs, armed robbery, fraud, GBH, arson, burglary etc')

who had been imprisoned for rape, said: 'it all builds up and all builds up until it comes out like a volcano . . .').

Sexual crimes, by contrast, may be known to some members of the family but they are represented as so shameful that the guilty knowledge of one person might not be divulged to others for years. Not only had many victims sensed that they must somehow have deserved what had befallen them, but the manipulation of guilt is a common enough technique deployed by many paedophiles and, indeed, other sex offenders. Stephen Will, Chairman of Aftermath in 1997, said:

> For the most part, from the people I've spoken to . . . and I guess we're talking primarily about sexual behaviour here, it's not even a suspicion of something happening for the most part. It's something that's come out of the blue, where the daughter, the son, whoever has turned round and said 'my father, my brother, my uncle, whoever, offended against me'. And sometimes it's years past, many years past, and so, yes, for the most part, it isn't something that they've been aware of.

A family might be riven by pluralistic ignorance in which each knew about his or her victimisation but not the victimisation of others:

> . . . let's say Jill and Jenny. Jill sits there knowing that she's been abused but Jenny doesn't know she's been abused, and Jill hasn't been able to share it with her. Jenny sits there knowing that she's been abused, and exactly the same thing – can't share it with her sister, can't share it with anybody. Why? Because the abuser has probably said 'Nobody's going to believe you. I'll always love you. I don't do this to hurt you'. Whatever. Things like that.

The disclosures about offence and offender that accompanied an arrest or public exposure were consequently defined as shocking, as something for which there could have been no effective preparation. The mother of a rapist said at a meeting: 'You go through the stage of disbelief. That's the first one. And I think in all honesty that's the best. That sounds strange, but you don't feel anything. The shock was so great that I didn't feel anything'.

Some part of those professions of ignorance and incredulity may quite possibly have been *faux naif*. they are, after all, a powerful method of exculpating and distancing the family. Some part may have been shaped by the narratives that were rehearsed again and again in Aftermath meetings, narratives that gave raw, confused experience a conventional form with which to 'rewrite the soul' of those who recited and heard them (Hacking 1995). But the incredulity and hurt which were so frequently displayed could not easily have been feigned, and much more seems to have been entailed.

It really did appear as if the family had been abruptly presented with a mass of appalling knowledge which it could not assimilate.

If that were indeed the case, one wonders how the portents of such a calamitous occurrence could have been so successfully concealed or disregarded until the moment of its traumatic revelation.[3] On many occasions, no doubt, the onset of offences such as murder, sexual abuse and rape might not actually have been presaged by intelligible signs that would have alerted a person in his or her natural attitude. Even had the person been so alerted, it may have been difficult to imagine that one's own son, brother or father could actually commit such a monstrous crime. It would have been easier by far to overlook or award a benign interpretation to portents that were perhaps only barely heeded at the time. Many families survive by not talking or thinking too much about disagreeable matters[4] and there is a profound phenomenological gulf between the confusing mass of ambiguities, underdeveloped suspicions, uncertainties and dimly-noticed events that constitutes everyday life, on the one hand, and, on the other, the brutally stark realisation that a dreadful act has indeed been committed by one who is very close. It is often necessary that that should be so: in Stan Cohen's (1995) words: ' "vital lies" [are] sustained by family members about violence, incest, sexual abuse, adultery, unhappiness. Lies [can] continue unrevealed, covered up by family's silence, alibis and conspiracies' (p. 22).

It is quite probable that awareness contexts were indeed sometimes manipulated in the past (Glaser and Strauss 1965), families having tacitly collaborated not to reveal, scrutinise or confront areas of behaviour that might have disquieted them (Hughes 1984), and the boundaries between those awareness contexts would have been strengthened by the gendered organisation of space. After all, in Steffensmeier's (1983) phrase, there is 'institutionalized sexism in the underworld' just as there is in the 'overworld' (p. 1010). Much offending (but not all) is committed by males in public places away from the home and the domestic gaze of women and families (Hagan and McCarthy 1992; Hagan, Simpson and Gillis 1979; Thrasher 1927). And there is certainly some sparse evidence to suggest that the public delinquencies of men tend not to be reported in the private recesses of the home. Woman, children and other relatives are often relieved of the burden of guilty knowledge about what males do (Decker and Van Winkle 1996, p. 236; Taylor 1984, p. 162). Such is the physical, emotional and economic dependence of many women on men that they cannot afford to know too much. In any event, even if family members *did* ask too many questions, they might well have not received a reply (Riley and Shaw 1985): Stephen Will, Chairman of Aftermath, observed: 'I think that quite often parents, if they suspect something may have been going on, they tend to say: "What has been going on? I'm here. Talk to me". But they don't get the answers'.

Not only may there then be good reasons to accept the dominant accounts of Aftermath members but it is always a useful precept to assume that what people define as real is real enough in its consequences (Thomas 1932, p. 572). Whether there had indeed been discreditable information available in the past, and however families may have dealt with that information, members of Aftermath *had* come to agree upon a discursive reality that seemed to be coherent, compelling and consequential, and it is instructive to pursue its logic. What follows will be a brief and simplified ideal-type that captures a few of its principal themes.

Aftermath members were to argue that the events surrounding the disclosure of a serious crime was a 'devastating experience' (Aftermath nd(a), p. 5) that can throw the family into a turmoil which is itself quite unintelligible except to those who have been similarly afflicted. It leaves the family at a loss for explanation. It can incite feelings of bereavement, families talking about the physical loss of an offender consigned to prison and the symbolic loss of their own collective innocence. It would be easier to bear a death, some parents say, than the imprisonment of a son for so outrageous a crime. Shirl Marshall claimed that a number of families evince the competitive grief of the bereaved to protest that having a murderer for a son was worse than having a child murdered because there are no temporal limits to the grief which must be borne ('when you've lost somebody, when somebody has died, you go through the stages, you go and visit the grave, it's final . . .'). Others would as vehemently disagree (and it should be noted that all these assumptions about the nature of loss and grief for other individuals and groups are necessarily based on a lack of direct experience of those particular forms of trauma).

The experience of disclosure and its aftermath can re-awaken memories of past crises (one mother whose son had been convicted of rape was to be beset by images of her own former husband who had raped her: 'I felt that my nightmares of what had happened to me in the past . . . were still there where I thought I had got rid of it. . . . My first husband brutally raped me over and over again, and my son was a rapist . . .'). It can bring about bad dreams, anger, sleeplessness, isolation, alienation, confusion, fears and insecurities. It may lead to breathing difficulties, palpitations and bodily disorders. There may be guilt about what has occurred, prompting people to argue that 'if only' they had been more vigilant or more attentive they might have prevented the offence. They may wonder whether they are being punished for some wrong they themselves have committed ('it might be "What did I do to deserve this?" ' commented Stephen Will).

The experience may precipitate a rush of new and discrediting information about the offender and the offender's life that makes the process of assimilating knowledge about his crime even harder to bear. Police inquiries, press reports, the trial and the collapse of pluralistic ignorance can bring about a rush of unpalatable news. 'All the sludge from the years comes up all at once so you're dealing with fifty thousand things at once', said Shirl Marshall. In one instance, a woman informed an Aftermath lunch that her brother had killed his wife because their daughter, whom he had abused sexually, had warned her about the possible further abuse of their grand-children: 'as time went on, we found out more and more of what he had done, and bit by bit, we all admitted that he had abused us all in the past, every single female in the family, each of us thinking we were the only one'.

The outcome could be *anomie*, a collapse of structure, meaning and purpose. It could make members of the family fear for their very reason. One member, a psychiatric nurse, recalled: 'I had the horrible feeling I was going to be destroyed because of the sheer intensity of the trauma . . .'. After all, what scripts for public behaviour are available to those who have suddenly and unexpectedly become the father of a murderer or the brother of a rapist? How is one to make sense of the family's history now that it must be so profoundly and unheroically reconstructed? It is as if the families had never really known the offender and needed to rework their biographies within the frame of new knowledge. What mentors exist to guide the family through such experiential disorder?

There is an urgent need for information, comprehension and a practic-able analysis that will restore a measure of organisation, control and direction to confused lives, and every sign will be repeatedly perused for the meaning it might convey about what happened. One mother observed at a meeting: 'we go through the part where you're reading statements over and over again and you're going over it in your head . . .'. Pollit remarked:

> Relatives need to know *why* they did what they did and *when* they did it and the when is always very important in finding out the why. The problem of knowing why causes great distress to the offenders as well as to the relatives. If you do not know why, you do not know whether it will happen again, that's the thing that bothers them.

Part of the Aftermath project was to offer a new comprehension which could identify the patterns and symptoms that explained the past and predicted the future, and 'help [. . .] the family understand why the crime was committed – the background, the motivations and the causes' (Aftermath nd(b), p. 5). Instead of receiving 'bolts out of the blue', ex-offenders and their families would be schooled to read the world with intelligent eyes. The explosive emo-tional crime is heralded by alarm signals, Marshall said: 'it's like pus building up in a boil. It's like a pressure cooker. . . . He's been revving and revving and revving so that, when he did this, it wasn't out of the blue. It was because he was ready to do it, because he'd been building up from the day he was born'.

Aftermath and traumatic stress

It may be seen that, in effect, and in common with many other self-help groups in the broad area of crime and victimisation, Aftermath members made sense of their changed lives by invoking the language of post-traumatic stress disorder, and that their self-portraits are made up of the standard clinical components of the traumatised personality (American Psychiatric Association 1980). There is recurrent reference to trauma in their talk and writing. For instance, one woman wrote to other members of Aftermath: 'I'm sure you are all familiar with the trauma that I, and my family went through . . . shock, horror, disbelief, shame, anger, fear, sadness, despair and pain' (Aftermath *Newsletter*, April 1997, vol. 2.2, p. 2). And on 18–19 October 1997, a weekend seminar was conducted by Aftermath on 'Trauma – The Family Sentence': 'we will be trying to understand the TRAUMA (and its effects) that is experienced when becoming a Family Member of a Serious Offender'.

Members define themselves in part as that new entity, a 'survivor', and like other survivors, they may contend with a special form of guilt. It was their relative that committed the crime, and they should not only have known but also should have done something to stop him. Guilt is at the very heart of the practical criminogenics of criminologists, politicians, practitioners and policy makers which, instigated by Freud, and echoed in vernacular theorising, blames the family. In childhood, it is held, are to be found the roots of evil, and the mother as primary carer may well feel the force of a public expectation that she should take responsibility for the sins of the son. A question addressed to a panel of criminal justice practitioners at an Aftermath seminar in October 1997 asked poignantly: 'To follow the view that criminality is a family phenomenon is in my opinion wholly wrong. To do so is to add further insult to the already sustained injury. How do you foresee Society's unjust intolerance towards Aftermath members?'.

Indeed, so central were trauma and its treatment to become that it was one of the issues which brought about the resignation of Shirl Marshall and her associates from the organisation which she had founded. Charismatic authority gave way to rational-legal authority,[5] experienced intuition was to be complemented by technical expertise, as a new generation of members asserted that Aftermath counsellors had to be professionally trained, qualified and accredited to cope with so serious a condition as the symptoms of post-traumatic stress disorder ('the difference now is that . . . we do not hurt people by ignoring or disregarding their feelings or what they say'). The Secretary of Aftermath reported in April of that year, two months after the exodus of its founder:

> It was recognised that much emotional damage can be done to individuals if they are not treated carefully and enabled to cope with the trauma that beset them. This often takes a long time. Patience is required . . . It was with this in mind that the proposal was put forward that formal training should be received by some counsellors and it was this, apparently, which caused Shirl to resign and others to follow. (Aftermath 1996, p. 1)

The post-traumatic stress of Aftermath members was held to have been shaped by some very special features of the experience which they had endured. First, members would have undergone a radical, reductive and undignified transformation of identity. Their offending relatives had been reified into monsters, and it is to monsters that they were now tied. They were redefined and contaminated (a mother recalled that she had felt 'soiled, dirty').

Stephen Will said: 'they're given a new identity, one they'd rather not have, and that is . . . guilty by association, in other words, "you're a member of his family" '. They themselves would no longer be people with moral and social attributes independently acquired but merely a 'rapist's mother' or a 'murderer's son'. One wrote: 'Five years ago I was a mother, child-minder; an ordinary person living an ordinary life. Today I'm _____ wife, mother, child-minder and sister to a killer!' and another said: 'My name is _____ and I'm the mother of a killer and sex offender'. Shirl Marshall reflected:

> This is the worst devastation of the lot. Mrs Brown ceases to be Mrs Brown. She becomes that rapist's mother, a different identity, the siblings, husband, the same. And then that awful compounding of the issue where the one inside has got a different identity, the one we are horrified of – I can't go and see him because he is a murderer!

Members of the family would become defined by a crime they had not them-selves committed, and they would share the opprobrium which is heaped upon the offence and the offender ('Judged guilty as the offender by associ-ation, the only 'crime' these families have committed is being related to the offender. Yet they often receive a strongly hostile reaction from Society' (Aftermath nd(b))). They might lose their jobs or experience other forms of exclusion (a former usher in a magistrates' court remembered: 'I was no longer me but the mother of _____ and I was no longer to be trusted . . . At work, I was treated as an outsider'). Suffering, they receive little under-standing or pity (Shirl Marshall said: 'it is worse than being on the other side, because if you have someone who is in your family and then murdered, then the horror in unspeakable, but you know that the whole world is with you, and that is a strength, but our side haven't even got that . . .'). Unlike other victims, they are not considered to be morally deserving, and they cannot effect a clear moral divide between themselves and the offender. To the con-trary, they are ineluctably entangled with the phenomenology of the crime and the criminal. One said: 'somehow you're stained with the blood of the perpetrator . . .'.

Theirs has become a grey world of moral ambiguities and contra-dictions, a world in which they are enjoined to 'hate the sin and love the sinner' (an Aftermath leaflet was prefaced by the anonymous statement: 'He's a murderer but he's still my son'), and in which they may themselves be simultaneously bound to the victim *and* to the offender, and quite unable to resolve a satisfactory relation or identity (one woman said: 'I've been brought up as a black and white person and suddenly it's all greys').

Stephen Will, Aftermath's chairman, talked about the situation of one member: 'the offender is within her family. The murdered person is within her family. She is a victim in every respect of the word . . .'. And his predecessor, Shirl Marshall, talked about the situation of another member, related to a 'sexual offender who's ravaged his way right through the family for many years'. What are the dominant moral identities to which people can adhere? There can only be confusion. So it was that a woman said at an Aftermath lunch: 'people say "I know how you must feel", and you say, "no you don't, because *I* don't know how *I* feel". I've got the difficult situation that, although he is my brother, he has killed my sister-in-law, a good friend'. How are children to establish who they are or where to repose their loyalties and affections when their father has killed their mother? (Hendricks, Black and Kaplan 1993). The very idea of self can be thrown into disarray. One woman, the daughter of a murderer and sister-in-law of the victim, said: 'your own identity as a person, as a daughter, as a female [is affected] which has clouded my sense of who I am in life and where I'm going'. Members may indeed feel ambivalent both about the murderer and the victim, although convention forbids such ambivalence.

Aftermath members may become anxious about the 'bad blood' that has been shown to flow in the family, and wonder whether others might not also prove themselves capable of offending in the same way: 'am I going to turn out like him? Am I going to be a murderer? . . . You're really terrified that it's all your fault . . . or . . . you're going to do the same thing . . . or that it's your badness that's come out in your son' said Shirl Marshall. The schizophrenia of a son or brother may induce fears about their own sanity and the sanity of other members of the family. They may wish not only to aid the offender but also protect the family from the offender when he is released (see Aftermath *Newsletter*, April 1997, vol. 2.2, p. 1)

Unlike many other traumatised people, they can resort to no neat resolution of confusion. They cannot distance themselves from the other and align themselves morally in a newly polarised world. On the contrary. They are stuck between the offender whom they may not have renounced and his victim for whom they may well feel compassion: a committee member wrote there is the: 'ongoing agony over the pain or suffering caused to the victim or their family. *We do not condone the offence*. This pain is forever with us. It is like a double bereavement' (italics in original).

The families of serious offenders may suffer physical and symbolic attack: Stephen Will talked of: 'fire bombs [and] paint daubed on walls 'Murderer lives here'. There's a situation in Scotland at the moment where this chap lives on an estate, who was accused of a sexual offence by his daughter, and it got round at the estate and arrows were painted on all these walls pointing to his house'. They will suffer stigma, shame, ostracism and vilification, some part of which will be self-directed. Shirl Marshall put the matter graphically at an Aftermath meeting:

> We are the scum of society and, as you get to know people in Aftermath, you will know that there couldn't be a lovelier group of balanced, compassionate, courageous and wonderful people and I'm proud to be one of them, and the world looks on and thinks that we're scum and I find that really very sad.

[. . .]

Some implications

Even if the members of Aftermath are not necessary 'typical' of all families of serious offenders (and there is no reason to assume they are not), even if they are saying no more than what they believe it is formally appropriate to say about an egregious event (and that would still give a special interest and effect to what they say), even if there is some exaggeration in what is said (after all, not every family of a serious offender will have been a stranger to crime), their narratives of crime and victimisation do raise some telling questions. Let us review a number of their implications for criminology.

It is clear that serious crime affects and disturbs almost all those whom it touches: victims and survivors proper; secondary victims and witnesses; and, it is being claimed with increasing frequency, police officers, court officers, prison officers, jurors and even offenders themselves. Aftermath represents yet a further addition to that roll. The offender's own immediate social circle, including his family, can become deeply embroiled in the havoc which crime leaves behind.

It is clear too that the effects of serious crime are importantly phenomenological and moral, and that those effects are remarkably similar across different worlds. They fan out, in the words of Stephen Will, from the criminal event at their centre to 'brothers, sisters, mothers, fathers, sons and daughters [and thence to] the extended family – aunts, uncles . . . grandparents, grandchildren, because the ripple effect of crime spreads that far and even further'. And the effects touch offenders' families in very much the same way as they do victims and victims' families, although it would be otiose and difficult to attempt a precise comparison of the depth and extent of the suffering endured. The effects alter identities and relations. They threaten the very meaning which people attach to themselves and their world. They act as a grave affront to embedded notions of pattern and purpose, and for a while they may throw those whom they influence into chaos and confusion.

If serious crime can indeed induce confusion, one of its prime consequences will be an urgent need to regain meaning and control, and we have shown that the recourse adopted by the members of Aftermath is to claim the title of 'victim'. 'Victim' is a recognised and serviceable status, more or less to hand, which captures something of the feelings of suffering, loss, and deprivation of agency and innocence, that can beset the members of an offender's family. It is eminently appropriate to those troubled by the effects of crime, it distances them from the immorality of the act and actor, it excites compassion and it unites the family firmly with others who have also been harmed.

Acknowledgement as a morally deserving victim is not easily won by any group, and its attainment and retention have become the political goal of a succession of charitable and campaigning organisations. Their project makes evident what structuralists and phenomenologists have long argued, that the significance of serious crime is enmeshed in structures of classification: first, in the essentialising work that defines and separates perpetrators and victims; and then in the construction and patrolling of the boundaries that maintain those separations against attack (Ben-Yehuda 1990; Douglas 1970; Durkheim 1960; Erikson 1966).

Yet serious crime has a profound power to colour and even to contaminate anyone or anything within its reach, and not even its victims may be exempt. The very presence of the seemingly blameless victim can endanger the bystander's belief in a just world, in the powerful presupposition that there must be an overarching moral agency in human affairs which rewards and protects the virtuous and punishes and restrains the wrongdoer. It is tempting always to find fault with those who suffer, to argue, in effect, that they must somehow have deserved their own misfortune, that the universe is not, after all, a disquietingly amoral or wicked place where the innocent can be allowed to suffer (Lerner 1980).

'Victim-blaming' exonerates the offender (Lamb 1996), allays fears and conflates categories, and it will meet with a bitter resistance that underscores quite how much moral store campaigners set on the unambiguous bifurcation of victim and offender. Victims' political champions are prone to dispute any allegation that serious crime could possibly be a transaction in which victim and offender are both complicit (see Clark and Lewis 1977). Indeed, writing about the politics of victimisation, Fattah has pointed to 'the paranoid attitude generated by the concepts of victim-precipitation and victim-participation' (Fattah nd, p. 14).

The boundary-maintaining programme of victims' groups has met with varying success. It has been most successful when the victim is one whom Nils Christie (1986) would call stereotypically 'ideal', and he offers the example of the 'little old lady' who is transparently innocent, bears no conceivable relation to the offender, and is utterly undeserving of her fate. It has been less successful where the victim was himself an offender in the past (and that was a problem which was to bedevil a new Criminal Injuries Compensation Scheme determined to make awards only to the 'innocent victims of violent crime' (Criminal Injuries Compensation Board 1964, p. 9);

where the victim and offender have known one another (and, again, the Criminal Injuries Compensation Scheme was at first to deny compensation in cases of domestic violence); and where they have shared a history of joint activity. In short, moral separations are difficult to sustain where, as is so often the case, the victimology of social relations and criminal causality seems most sensibly cast in greys rather than in blacks and whites (Antilla 1974, p. 8). The programme will be least successful of all where the very standing of the victim *as* victim has yet to be publicly conceded;[6] where the connection with the offender is intimate, ascribed and indelible; and where, hating the sin but loving the sinner, the victim herself or himself may be loath utterly to disown the offender but remains in ambivalent relation with him. How are separations to be enforced then?

It is evident that the members of Aftermath are caught in a double bind from which they cannot easily extricate themselves, and their plight illumin-ates most poignantly the power of crime simultaneously to threaten and to bestow identity. It is a moral plight that has discernible consequences not only on the personal plane but also for the politics and organisation of Aftermath. Unlike groups of rape survivors, Vietnam veterans and the fam-ilies of homicide victims, for instance, the members of Aftermath do not readily disclose the nature of their meetings to the wider world (one weekend seminar in a semi-public building was warily described to curious outsiders simply as a 'private meeting'). The group is not driven by the black and white politics of a Manichaean *Weltanschauung*, and it has little of the righteous anger, vociferous campaigning and denunciation of outsiders that so beset the politics of other survivors' groups.[7]

Notes

1 On their release from prison, Aftermath maintains, offenders may well resume their place as members of a family and are to be so treated for purposes of mutual aid and counselling.

2 One critical issue was the assertion made by Pollit, and acted upon by Marshall, that all violent offenders manifested a history of childhood abuse. The outcome, remarked members of a new generation of After-math members, was the trading of allegations and counter-allegations, extensive blaming of families as part of a larger pattern of victim-blaming, and the estrangement of offenders from their families, which ran quite contrary to Aftermath's professed aims. One was to write to us in 1997: 'this [assertion] is not a proven fact, it was SM's belief and her view was the not the view of Aftermath'. After the change of leadership in the group, Aftermath members ceased visiting prisoners expressly as Aftermath counsellors, 'particularly when the probation service are really paid to take on that role . . . I like to think that actually we've gone back to what the original ethos was. The ethos of Aftermath

was to support families. I think that we lost our way . . . and now we're getting back on track'.

3 Farrington (1997) observed: 'criminal behaviour does not generally appear without warning; it is commonly preceded by childhood antisocial behaviour (such as bullying, lying, truanting, and cruelty to animals) and followed by adult anti-social behaviour (such as spouse assault, child abuse and neglect, excessive drinking and sexual promiscuity)' (p. 361.) One problem, Aftermath members would say, is that even when those early signs are visible and heeded, there is little that they can do to inhibit offending in their families: 'those in Aftermath who have asked for help for their loved one, having observed themselves that something is not quite right, the help . . . was not forthcoming. The police cannot act until an offence has been committed . . .'.

4 Denial can be very strong in families with a discredited past. There are, for example, a number of revealing studies of Nazis and the children of Nazis (see Bar-On 1989; Sereny 1996).

5 Stephen Will remarked: 'we've written all the policies. There were no policies in place. The only thing we had was a constitution which we felt needed revision . . .'.

6 That reluctance was starkly evident in the observations of two criminal justice practitioners who addressed the October 1997 Aftermath seminar on 'Trauma – The Family Sentence'. One, a woman police inspector, would not recognise the general claims made by Aftermath to be the victims of their own family members' offending. Families became victims, she said, only when they were subject to an identifiable crime, such as an offence linked to harassment, that was committed by their relatives or by some other person. To Stephen Will's comment that: 'three times you stressed "*if* you become victims", we believe in Aftermath that because of the situation we are in we are *already* victims', she replied: 'I would repeat that if you are victims of crime, through harassment, then that is how we would respond. You will become victims of crime if you have harassment. We will respond because we have to respond'. The other, the governor of an open prison, replying to remonstrations about the repeated humiliation of strip searches of visiting relations, said: 'we tend to get rammed down our throats [by the prisoners] that the families are innocent victims. We sometimes get a little sceptical. Are you sure you didn't notice that your son was out burgling all night? The other thing is drugs. Where do they come from? Visitors'.

7 *Acknowledgements.* We are most grateful to Janet Becham, Elaine Meagher and Seeta Persaud for transcribing interviews and to Rachel Condry, David Downes, Stephen Will and members of the committee of Aftermath for their comments on an earlier draft of this article.

Update note

We thought it appropriate to include an update of the work of Shirl Marshall.

Since October 1996, the original version which inspired Shirl Marshall to found 'Aftermath' has been revitalised and sustained by her creation of a new charity, 'Consequences'. The Trustees and colleagues who stand with her are convinced that the founding premise of the charity must be that the offender be viewed, not as a single entity, but as part of a family unit. An effective rehabilitation process cannot be offered if one part of the unit is considered alone, without the balanced consideration of the other.

'Consequences' offers a more holistic approach which works towards changing attitudes so that offenders, together with their families, aim to deal with the consequences of the crime on a continuous basis. Everyone is encouraged to try to make sense of what happened, and to work together to avoid recidivism thus sustaining a more comprehending, supportive quality of life.

All in 'Consequences' believe that an essential criterion for their success is their being separate from all the professional services which are involved as a result of the crime. They have to establish credibility with the offenders' families who are devasted by coming to terms with the crime and the responsibility of guilt of someone they love. They consider that people in this position need the empathy of those who have trodden the path they now face. Families tend to feel alienated by the many official approaches at a time when they feel vulnerable and uncertain.

'Consequences' offers compassionate support from those who have experienced all the emotions which follow the crime and have come to terms with the new identities imposed on the family and their offender. Moreover, ongoing open access is there for them all. The offender and his family can turn to the group at any time during the sentence and through to the later years. By then the original crime will have been accommodated into their lives, but they are then all faced with the emotional pressures surrounding release and the changing roles they again have to adopt.

For effective rehabilitation, the emphasis must be on the offender finding the motivation to develop a purposeful future, the likelihood of which is greatly enhanced if he has the support of the people who care about him. 'Consequences' feel they have to balance their attention between the offender and his loved ones – and are conscious that this approach evokes less under-standing and sympathy than that experienced by most families' support groups.

They do believe, however, that they concur with Robert Frost: 'I chose the path less well trod – and that has made all the difference'. They have the faith that their choice of path will make the difference in the lives of many offenders and their families.

6.3

Routine victimisation in prisons
by Ian O'Donnell and Kimmett Edgar

[. . .]

This paper aims to provide a snapshot of the extent and nature of victimisation and violence in prisons and young offender institutions. It is not a study of the sensational acts of violence and disorder which sometimes occur in penal institutions, although some of the incidents described are certainly shocking. Rather, it is an examination of the more mundane victimisation to which inmates are exposed and which defines the prison experience. It is an attempt to explore the consequences for inmates of exposure to a regular threat of minor harm. This risk exists in addition to the distant threat of serious harm which is so often the focus of concern.

However, the work reported here is more than just a victim survey. It is an analysis of the functions which victimisation serves, the guises in which it appears, and the meanings ascribed to it by those involved. It is an exploration of the social relationships within which victimisation flourishes.

The effects of routine victimisation in prisons have rarely been considered in the academic literature. From the classic works of prison sociology we can learn something of the nature of inmate hierarchies and the processes of socialisation and prisonisation, particularly the defining features of the inmate 'code'. Sykes (1958), for example, described how prisoners maintained an uneasy balance between solidarity and mutual exploitation. However, his analyses of inmate-on-inmate predation gave no indication of the scope of the problem.

Others saw inmates as a cohesive and stable group, united in opposition to their captors (for example, Clemmer 1940; Garabedian 1963; Irwin and Cressey 1962). Breaches of the code which governed their behaviour (for example by passing information to staff) were met with violence. The primary focus of such work was on conformity to the code rather than the social dynamics of prisoner–prisoner interactions. It is possible that interactions between inmates received little attention because of the assumption that they were determined by a sense of solidarity and shared values, which meant that their outcome was predictable and as such not worthy of study.

Some scholars have investigated the most extreme forms which inmate–inmate victimisation can take, such as homicide (Porporino *et al.* 1987), sexual assault (Davis 1968; Dumond 1992; Lockwood 1980), riots (Adams 1994), and hostage-taking (Davies 1982). We also know something about the correlates of prison violence and how it may be related to factors such as overcrowding or population density (Farrington and Nuttale 1980; Gaes and McGuire 1985), defensible space (Atlas 1983), penal reform (Engel and Rothman 1983), increased security (Bidna 1975), the activities of inmate gangs (Fong 1990), prisoner characteristics such as psychiatric impairment (Baskin *et al.* 1991) or age and time in custody (Cooley 1993), and regime factors such as staff morale and training (Cooke 1991).

More recent work has attempted to untangle the extent to which inmates' behaviour in custody is an extension of the 'criminal subculture' more generally (the 'importation hypothesis') or is a mode of adaptation to the pains of confinement (the 'deprivation hypothesis'). For examples of studies in this tradition see Grapendaal (1990), McCorkle *et al.* (1995) and Wooldredge (1994). Others have examined the structures and processes which generate and maintain 'order' within the prison community (Sparks *et al.* 1996).

In addition, there is growing interest in the related subject of 'bullying', a special form of predatory victimisation which is characterised by an enduring and exploitative dominance relationship. The nature and consequences of bullying have recently become a source of concern, particularly in schools (Besag 1989; Byrne 1994; Olweus 1993), and young offender institutions (Beck 1995; Howard League 1995; Prison Service 1993; Tattum and Herdman 1995). For an authoritative and comprehensive review of this literature see Farrington (1993).

The work reported here is novel in several ways. First, rather than examining how inmates relate to the prison code, it homes in upon interactions between inmates. Second, rather than attempting to identify the factors associated with major disorder, it focuses upon the routine victimisation which shapes prison life. Third, it is not limited to bullying, but is much more inclusive, taking as the starting point inmates' experiences of six discrete forms of victimisation: assault, robbery, threats of violence, cell theft, exclusion and hurtful verbal abuse.

Sources of data

The fieldwork for this research was carried out between April 1994 and December 1995 in two adult male prisons and two male young offender institutions.[1] Data were collected by means of a victim survey. Every inmate in each institution was approached in person by one of the authors and asked to complete a twelve page questionnaire which dealt primarily with his personal experience of victimisation in the past month.

The response rate was very satisfactory – 92% of the young offenders agreed to take part and filled out a questionnaire (820/892). In the adult institutions, 87% did so (722/827). Thus the overall response rate was 90%. In addition to the survey, structured interviews were carried out with 92 prisoners, 61 of whom were interviewed as victims and 31 as victimisers.

The extent and dynamics of prison victimisation

The results presented here are based on the questionnaires returned by inmates who had been at the institution where the fieldwork was being carried out for at least one month, the reference period for this study (n = 1,182). Table 6.3.1 summarises the main findings about the extent of victimisation. This table is based upon the number of individuals who reported having been victimised rather than the number of incidents of victimisation.

The rates of victimisation were broadly similar in the young offender institutions. There was a similar degree of consistency in the adult prisons. Overall however the rates for young offenders were much higher than those for adults. Five of the six types of victimisation were reported by greater proportions of young offenders than adults. For verbal abuse and exclusion the rates were over twice as high. Cell theft was the only type of victimisation which was more commonly reported by adult prisoners. Amongst young offenders verbal abuse was most common, followed by threats and assaults. Amongst adults cell theft was most common, followed by threats and verbal abuse. The lowest rates in each institution were for exclusion and robbery.

Table 6.3.1 Percentage of Inmates Victimised on One or More Occasions in the Previous Month

	YOI_1 (n = 436)	YOI_2 (n = 152)	All YOs (n = 588)	Adult_1 (n = 408)	Adult_2 (n = 186)	All adults (n = 594)
Assault	32	26	30	20	17	19
Threat	46	40	44	27	25	26
Robbery	11	8	10	5	2	4
Theft	28	26	27	30	42	34
Verbal abuse	58	51	56	26	26	26
Exclusion	20	12	18	7	7	7

Assaults

Assault in prison serves diverse functions and arises from a variety of circumstances, just as it does in the outside world. Inmates described a wide range of physical attacks: from minor slaps to life-threatening woundings; from spontaneous aggression to chronic beatings. The interviews carried out for this study revealed that the motivations for assaults typically followed one of several patterns. These included the wish to settle a conflict with force, the nature of an individual's offence, the desire to enhance one's status, simple retaliation, the lure of material gain, or the relief of boredom. Assaults sometimes also occurred in the context of a trading relationship.

A key function of assault was conflict-management. Crudely speaking, prison conflicts were sometimes dealt with through force. Occasionally, as in the following example, the victim believed he merited the attack. This inmate respected the attacker's motives and was confident that the assault had resolved the dispute:

> I found phonecards at the telephone. There was no name on them so I took them. He found out, came to my cell. 'Have you got my cards?' I said no. He found out that I did, though, and came back and hit me a number of times. I gave him back the cards. Afterwards he apologised. We shook hands, had a cigarette and no more problems. I asked for it myself. He didn't want to do it but I lied to him.

It was sometimes the view of participants that fights which were mutually initiated relieved tension and restored the *status quo*. In some of these cases, far from initiating a cycle of retaliation, a fight established a bond between the two foes:

> He was winding me up about my work, throwing plates at me. Been boiling up for a few days. I said: 'If you want to start something, then start something'. I got hit over the head three times with a kitchen ladle. He got worse after he done that. I went mad and busted him up. I got the ladle off him and whacked him. We get on better now 'cause he knows he can't take the piss. It's usually that way – you get on better after you've had a fight.

Some assaults were directly related to the victim's offence. One young offender's problems began following the disclosure of his case in a newspaper. Until this point he had managed to survive on normal location, but a series of increasingly vicious attacks eventually wore down his resistance and he requested a move to the Vulnerable Prisoner Unit:

No one on the wing would associate with me. Three or four guys were saying that I was in for rape. I said I wasn't. They'd read the newspaper account of the trial. They said: 'You're in for rape you nonce. I'm going to kill you'. One went to hit me in the face which I blocked. One hit me on the face. Next thing I knew I was banged on the head and blacked out. Then another day during association 30 guys – everybody on that side of the wing – came around and beat me up, shouting, spitting etc. They left me on the floor where a few minutes later officers found me. I was cut and bruised all over. This led to my moving off the wing.

Other attacks were motivated by status. One inmate was explicit about how he used assaults to establish his position, particularly in a situation where he was unknown:

In prison, you've got to prove yourself. When I go on a wing I look, and I pick out a respected person. And not right away but if he says something to me I tell him: 'Let's go in the showers'. And we fight. And then the pressure's off me.

Another interviewee felt insecure about his status, and believed that his credibility had been compromised by the allocation to his cell of an inmate he considered inferior. In order to force the other prisoner to move out of the cell he attacked him viciously:

I was in a double cell. They brought in some geezer who said he was in for begging. I told him he was a fraggle and to get out of my cell. But he wouldn't. Plus he smelled. So I beat him up. He said: 'You could kill me but I'm not going'. I hit him with batteries in a pillow case, mostly hit his body. I took a sharpened tooth brush to him. He wasn't fighting back. He was going: 'Go on, kill me. I got nothing to live for', enticing me to do it.

Some inmates espoused the principle that if one is wronged there is a duty to retaliate. These retaliatory strikes were among the most serious of the assaults. It was widely believed that an inmate who failed to take revenge might signal vulnerability to others. Furthermore, it was accepted that personal retribution for wrong-doing was entirely legitimate. Hence, those who described assaults involving retaliation did not seem to feel that their motivation required any further explanation:

At night someone told me to suck my mother, to perform oral sex. When I came out in the morning I told one of the officers what he said and that I wanted to fight him. The officer said: 'Yeah', because it was a fair story. So then we had a fight. He didn't want to fight but I hit him. One of the officers bent the rules. They let me hit him and stopped it when it got serious. They just took him back in his cell. They didn't nick us for fighting.

In other cases the violence was used in self-defence. Sometimes the victim played a very active role and it was an open question who victimised whom:

I was called to my window by my next-door neighbour. I was called names. He said my dad was a beast. He said my mum was a bitch and a slag. I couldn't get to him then because we were locked up. Next day at work he pushed me. I punched him in the face and he ran straight to one of the officers on his hands and knees, crying, bleeding from his nose, saying I hit him.

Assault was also used to enforce debts. It was generally understood that being beaten for failing to repay a debt did not settle the debt. The assault was considered to be a way of persuading the person to repay:

Someone owed me an ounce of burn [tobacco]. I got him in a corner on association, and told him: 'Give me burn or I'll slap you'. I hit him. He had bruises to his arms and legs. I told him if he grassed me up I would do him.

Some incidents began as games designed to pass the time. It should be noted that both of the incidents reported next took place in four-man dormitories, which seemed to provide an ideal setting for such harmful behaviour. The first episode shows that prisoners can be assaulted regularly and suffer significant emotional harm despite a lack of serious physical injuries:

They used to have pillow fights and I used to get battered. It would turn from fun into all three on me. They would turn off the light. I was getting headaches from all the pillows. Happened twice, three times a week.

The second episode shows how serious assaults could emerge with explosive speed from minor play-fighting. A small number of victimisers said that they enjoyed such violence. In the following example drug use and the dormitory setting clearly aggravated the seriousness of the offence, leading the attackers to behave in increasingly damaging ways. It is important to point out that although there was a sexual element in this case, sexual assaults were rarely reported in the institutions studied:

There were four of us in one dorm. One come off his visit with some cannabis. He shared it out. We started pillow fighting. He showed he was the weakest. All three of us set on him. We had books stuffed in the pillows. It turned nasty and we were punching him. It started as a joke, but it got serious. My friend held him down on the bed and I put a pillow over his head and held it. And he was crying and we started hitting him. I said: 'If you don't stop crying we will do it for real'. I put the pillow back on and held it for longer. My friend got a broomstick and put it up his boxer shorts. If he had done something to resist it would have ended right there. If he had tried to stand up for himself, then things might have been different. But he just stayed still and the other boy shoved it up his arsehole. I don't know why we did it. In the dorms, people get bored and look for entertainment and fun. Unfortunately, it is the weak who are the entertainment.

Threats of violence

All threats aim to force someone to do something against their will. In the interviews, adults and young offenders described threats as a tool used in conjunction with some other form of victimisation, either to coerce a person into surrendering his goods, or to invite another to fight, or to secure some service, or to put an end to an escalating round of insults.

By definition, of course, attempts at robbery must involve a threat:

One or two say: 'I'm going to batter your head in the shower'. They want my canteen. They pick on me because I'm black and weak.

Sometimes threats were a means to enforce debts:

Someone owed me something. So I threatened to beat him up. He was banged up and I threatened him through the door. I said: 'Where's my stuff you owe me?' He said he hasn't got it. I said: 'Well, we'll meet in a cell and sort it out'.

Threats had two opposing functions when used in situations of conflict. First, they could be used to force the other to back down in order to win the dispute without having to resort to physical violence. Second, threats sometimes functioned to 'wind up' the other person, to provoke a fight which the perpetrator could justify:

This geezer was waiting to play pool. It was my turn and he said it was his turn next, not mine. I told him I'd hit him round the head with a pool ball if he took me for a cunt. He backed off so I invited him up to my cell and he wouldn't come up and fight.

A young offender described how threats were sometimes issued in a specula-tive attempt to obtain drugs:

> If someone comes in with drugs everyone shouts out the window: 'Give me some or I'll get you tomorrow'.

Occasionally pressure was brought to bear on inmates in order to persuade them to bring drugs into the prison after a visit. This is an example of coercing services from other prisoners, a technique known as 'tasking':

> They wanted me to bring in Class A drugs. They would arrange a visitor for me. They knew I had a habit in the past so they said I could have half of what I brought in. I refused point blank, said that if they wanted it, they could bring it in themselves.

In another example of 'tasking' an inmate was threatened with a beating if he did not bring in money. He tried to do so, was caught and ended up in the segregation unit for his own protection:

> Someone came up to me and said that this guy was going to do me in unless I brought in some money. I got money at a visit but was strip searched after the visit and it was found. I can't risk going back onto any wing here. I don't know what would happen. Someone could slash me with a razor blade.

One of the adults described having received written threats. This was highly unusual in that it gave the victim documentary evidence which staff could use as proof if they elected to charge the perpetrator. Clearly inmates believed that they could act with impunity against this particular individual.

In a final example, a young offender who was interviewed minutes after he had been attacked described a complex web of victimisation, of which threats were an integral part, but which also included insults, 'tasking' and assault:

> Today, working in the kitchens, someone said: 'Your mother's a slag'. Someone else came up and put a sharp knife against my throat. Everyday I get pushed and slapped around by some black guys. They want me to steal things from the kitchen for them. This time I went to an officer and said: 'I ain't going to say why but I've got problems and I want out'. The officer said: 'You can wait'. I went to walk out the gate and somebody head-butted me from behind. As soon as I started walking I was jumped from behind and bang I was on the floor. They were kicking my body and the back of my neck. They walked off. I just laid there for a few seconds then walked down the corridor punching a few windows. I broke my wrist in here already punching my cell wall out of frustration. They know I won't fight back. They try to push me to my limit so that I'll lose it.

Robbery

The act of taking possessions by force is robbery. 'Taxing' is the term used to describe such behaviour in English prisons. The use of such language legitimises and trivialises the behaviour by drawing a parallel with revenue collection by the State. This offence is often thought to be the essence of victimisation in prisons, although in reality it occurs relatively infrequently (see Table 6.3.1). By definition it involves both a threat and an attempt to steal. It is often accompanied by verbal abuse and in its more serious form can also involve an assault. It is a complex form of victimisation.

Victims and victimisers described a range of techniques. Sometimes robbery was carried out by an inmate with the support of others, sometimes inmates acted alone. The target goods varied from the trivial, for example cigarettes or biscuits, to valuable possessions such as radios or cannabis. Tobacco, drugs, radios or phonecards could be desirable objects in their own right or used as currency to purchase something else.

As a 'taxing' relationship develops between inmates it may intensify. The following example shows how trivial requests were replaced by more serious demands, coupled with an expectation that the victim would routinely surrender his goods:

> Every week I would get parcels in the post. Four boys would come on to me. First they asked me for a loan. So I was giving them ½ oz here and there. Then they started demanding it. They threatened to slash me. I started blaming myself for giving in, in the first place.

In another case an attempt at robbery built up over several days. The prisoner being victimised was fully aware that the sole objective was to take his radio from him. Assault featured as a part of the perpetrator's method:

> For three or four days he was trying to get me to lend him my radio. I wasn't having it, 'cause I knew he wasn't planning on giving it back. He started threatening: 'If you don't you will be knocked out'. It's all prison talk. Only one per cent really happens. I told him no. He whacked me on the jaw; started saying: 'You still think you're brave?'. I got away. He wasn't trying to injure me, he was trying to frighten me.

This victim knew that the assault was purely a means of reinforcing the attempted robbery. The slaps on the face were unpleasant, but the victim was able to neutralise their seriousness by accurately interpreting their purpose. He knew he was engaged in a war of nerves and that he was unlikely to be seriously harmed if he continued to resist. As the perpetrator had only a few days left to serve, the victim resolved to wait it out.

It is interesting to trace the development of 'taxing' relationships over time. The following extract shows how the victim's resistance gradually increased to the extent that he threatened his victimisers:

> These black boys come into my cell and say: 'Right I'm taking your radio'. I didn't want to get in a fight, so I said: 'Take it'. One said: 'If you grass me up I'm gonna do you'. This other boy said: 'I want all your canteen'. I told him: 'Go suck out your girl'. I told an officer. He went and got my radio back. Later the same three took my phonecards and matches and Rizzlas. I put a razor blade up to his throat and told him: 'Give me that phonecard back before I cut your throat'. And he gave the phonecard back.

Phonecards were a popular target. They were simple to take, easily hidden, in plentiful supply, and could be kept for personal use or traded for tobacco or drugs at standard, reliable rates. Some felt they had no choice but to change their routine activities in order to minimise the risk of further victimisation.

> I was talking to my wife. When I put the phone down, he took my card from me. 'I want to use that' he said. I said: 'Give it back'. But he wouldn't. There were 38 units left on it. Now I'm frightened to go upstairs and use the phone if they're there. I phone now in the morning before they get up.

For many prisoners illicit drugs were the ideal item to steal because victims would be unlikely to report their loss to staff. Indeed, the purpose of taking other goods was often to trade them for drugs. The remote probability of an official response encouraged robbers to act without fear of the consequences. Young offenders were particularly forthcoming about situations in which they robbed others of their drugs. There was no doubt that the most systematic and serious 'taxing' was drug related:

> A little boy came back from a visit with cannabis. I pushed him into my cell and shoved a pencil against his throat. I said I would stab him if he didn't give me the cannabis. Then I punched him and he got frightened and handed it over. I target his kind because I know he will give it up without problems. I find most people prefer to take the easy way and give it up instead of fight.

Another described how successful he was at maintaining a heavy use of cannabis while in custody, at the expense of many others. Indeed he welcomed the opportunity which his forthcoming promotion to red-band (trusted prisoner) would give him to move outside his wing and find new victims so that he could increase his consumption:

> No one refuses me. I wouldn't take no one's biscuits, just drugs. If I know someone has a £20 draw and they won't give it, I'm taking it man. They can't report it 'cause it's drugs. When I'm made a red band next week I'll have about £40 worth every day. I can't wait!

Cell theft

Cell theft was sometimes purely opportunistic – the perpetrator saw an open cell door and quickly took what he could:

> Once in a blue moon – when there's an easy opportunity. Door ajar. Looked in. Saw the watch on the table. Thought: 'I haven't got one. I can have one for myself. If you see something, take it. Just like a burglar.

One young offender made a sport of the behaviour:

> If a cell is open I nip in, thieve things out: biscuits, edible stuff, smoking stuff – everything I could get. I do it for a laugh – see if I can get away with it. If I get caught I just laugh it off.

Sometimes cell theft did appear to be a petty type of victimisation:

> I was going to work one morning. I thought my door was shut but the bolt was on. After work I came back. Some stuff was gone. Juice, stamps, burn, Just because my door was open.

In another case the loss was not trivial. The victim's interpretation of the episode, based on his suspicions about the identity of the perpetrator, suggested it was not coincidental that he had been the victim of theft:

> I was cleaning. When I come back someone had been in and took every-thing. All my canteen, burn, bikkies, the lot. £28 worth. They also took my medicine. It is out of order. He's the same one has been trying to tax me.

However, prisoners generally felt fatalistic about cell theft because the identity of the perpetrator was usually unknown. Furthermore they were largely dependent on staff to defend their property and keep their cell doors locked. For these reasons many simply resigned themselves to the inevitability of such losses, which were seen as part of the hazards of prison life:

When I went down for meals I had stuff stolen. Very vulnerable because officers are not patrolling the landings during meal times. You can't lock your doors every minute.

Verbal abuse

Following the usual pattern, hurtful insulting language was much more common in YOIs than in adult establishments. In the previous month, over half (56%) of all young offenders had borne the brunt of comments which they felt to be offensive and upsetting, compared with a quarter (26%) of adults (Table 6.3.1).

Insults were frequently used as a tool in the first stages of building a relationship of dominance. Three types of malicious insults emerged from the victims' descriptions. These were manipulative insults, slander, and racist abuse.

Insults which were manipulative were intended to break the inmate's spirit. The person making the remarks goaded the victim, playing on any perceived weakness:

> Only thing that really annoys me is when they make comments about my girlfriend. She's just lost my baby. They say she's a whore and all that. They know it winds me up.

Common terms of abuse included 'nonce' or 'beast' (sex offender), 'fraggle' (mentally disordered offender), 'muppet' (vulnerable prisoner; inadequate), and 'grass' (informer). The purpose of such labelling is to damage the prisoner's reputation. Unless the victim can demonstrate that he does not fit the label, the rest of the wing may accept its validity and ostracise him.

One type of insult which carried great force amongst adults was to be accused of being a sex offender:

> Even if I just step out my door I get called a child molester, dirty nonce bastard and so on. Even when I walk down to get my dinner at night they're always shouting their mouths off. 'We know what you're in for. You had intercourse with a fifteen year-old girl. Here comes the child-snatcher'.

Given the widespread antipathy towards sex offenders and informers, to be identified as such – even without foundation – put an inmate at risk of attack (both physical and verbal) from other prisoners:

> On the wing in the evening, while we were locked up, this guy started shouting I was a rapist. He was shouting, wanting everyone to hear. He wanted to turn people against me.

The final form is racist abuse:

> Outside they don't say those things to me, but here they call me Paki. It don't bother me 'cause I'm not from Pakistan. I could say: 'You white bastard, you black cunt'. But what good would it do? I ignore it and they go quiet.

Verbal abuse may also function as a tool of victimisation by isolating the victim from his support base. Prisoners who are successfully isolated are confirmed in their vulnerability. This use of insults resembles the sixth form of victimisation studied, exclusion, to which we turn next.

Exclusion

The exclusion of one inmate by another often involved threats, and sometimes physical assaults. On occasion it was no more than avoidance of a despised prisoner. Exclusion arose in conflicts over control of shared equipment such as games or television. Two equals could argue about who was next to play table tennis or pool, but exclusion was used to prevent someone considered to be of lower status from their right to take a turn. Exclusion sometimes inflicted profound wide-ranging harm as victims could face threats if they even attempted to enter the television room or use the telephone.

Like robbery, rates of exclusion were comparatively low. As shown in Table 6.3.1, 18% of young offenders and 7% of adults reported that they had been excluded at least once during the preceding month.

The interviews revealed that some instances of excluding another inmate were attempts to establish dominance:

> Playing table tennis, this geezer who didn't like me came in with his friend and tried to take over the table. He goes: 'It's my game now'. He tried to take my bat and I carried on playing. Then he hit me on the face with his fist. I put the bat on the table and walked out. His friend tried to stop me going out the door so they could continue hitting me but I pushed past and got out.

A pattern of exclusion over time could lead to an inmate being cut off from all possible allies. Many of those who had been excluded once or twice changed their behaviour so that they did not put themselves in situations where they could be ostracised. If someone knows that their attempts to play pool or table tennis will be rebuffed, it is futile even to try to do so. As such, one experience of exclusion could have long-lasting effects on the victim, forcing him to change his lifestyle in order to avoid situations of potential conflict.

Those who have been excluded resigned themselves to their lower status. One man described how exclusion had affected many aspects of his life on the Vulnerable Prisoner Unit:

> I don't get a chance to play games. Get pushed off it. At evening meal time, we were standing at the gate, first in the queue. We got pushed out of the way. I've been told not to use the phone, but I've got to keep in touch so I risk it. Now I've been told not to use the shower.

Another inmate described how he had been isolated from the potential support of his peers. This situation was engineered over a considerable period of time by one prisoner who gradually brought others around to his point of view. Once social support has been withdrawn the victim becomes progressively more vulnerable:

> Another prisoner put round the rumour that I was nonce. It took me quite a long time to know what he was doing. I became aware of the vibes from former friends. People started moving away from me. When I come on the landing they all duck behind their doors. When I was becoming isolated from others the rest of the harassment began.

Like verbal abuse, exclusion could be very damaging to the victim's self-esteem. Unlike insults, however, there was little possibility that the victim of exclusion could retaliate in kind. Like robbery, exclusion was accomplished by a show of superior strength, proving to the victim his insignificance. But exclusion was a demonstration of power and influence as distinct from robbery with its primary goal of material gain. As stated above, incidents of exclusion often arose over access to resources, just as assaults were sometimes the result of such conflicts. It could be argued that, where conflict arose over a shared resource, those who gave way rather than resisting through negotiation or force, were by definition victims of exclusion.

Conclusion

Self-reports showed victimisation to be frequent, particularly among young offenders, of whom 30% had been assaulted and 44% threatened with violence on at least one occasion in the previous month. For adults the respective figures were 19% and 26%. Although many of these incidents were undoubtedly minor, the fact that a third of young offenders and a fifth of adult male prisoners had been assaulted in one month demonstrates a level of harmful activity which is frustrating for staff, frightening for inmates and potentially destabilising for regimes.

The routine victimisation which we have described shapes the social ethos of prisons and young offender institutions. The potential for assault, theft and verbal abuse grinds down prisoners and shifts their attitudes about the boundaries of acceptable behaviour. Hence, custody can be damaging in gradual, subtle ways which are all the more pernicious for being intangible and difficult to quantify.

One finding of this study, which is reported in detail elsewhere (O'Donnell and Edgar 1996a) was that previous experience of custody did not reduce the risk of being victimised. Although first-time prisoners may complain more about their victimisation this could reflect not increased risk, but rather a lower threshold of tolerance for such behaviour, and perhaps a degree of naivety regarding how informing staff is viewed by other inmates. However, prior custodial experience did increase the probability that a prisoner would victimise others. The capacity to assault, threaten and rob was in this sense acquired, and was a likely consequence of having been assaulted, threatened or robbed by others. Thus, not only do prisons allow for the transmission of specific criminal techniques, but they also de-sensitise people to the effects of their actions on others.

The pervasiveness of victimisation makes clear the scale of the challenges facing the Prison Service as it strives to fulfil its statement of purpose, that is: '. . . to serve the public by keeping in custody those committed by the courts . . . to look after them with humanity and help them lead law-abiding and useful lives in custody and after release'.

In recent years the Prison Service has risen to meet these challenges. A national strategy on bullying has been formulated (Prison Service 1993) and a variety of imaginative approaches have been developed at individual establishments. These are characterised by a shift away from the traditional focus on providing shelter for victims and potential victims to the creation of a whole prison approach, which recognises the widespread impact of victimisation and calls upon everyone in the institution to take personal responsibility for reducing the problem. For a description of the major components of any strategy to tackle victimisation see Edgar and O'Donnell (1997) and O'Donnell and Edgar (1996b, 1998).

It is clearly difficult to provide prison environments which are safe all of the time. The findings reported here demonstrate the need for the Prison Service to continue to build on the initiatives already in place for reducing the risks of victimisation. By shedding light on some of the reasons for this harmful behaviour and on the circumstances in which it occurs, this study will hopefully contribute to the process of finding an effective response to a problem which has too often been dismissed as intractable.[2]

Notes

1   The institutions studied were a Category B local/training prison for adult males which held 625 inmates at the mid-point of the fieldwork period; a Category C prison which held 302 men; a closed YOI/remand centre

with 825 young offenders and juveniles; and a closed YOI with a population of 224 young offenders.

2   During the course of this research, Ian O'Donnell was a Research Officer at the Oxford Centre for Criminological Research and a Fellow of Linacre College. We are indebted to Diane Caddle and John Ditchfield of the Home Office Research and Statistics Directorate and Pam Wilson from Prison Service Security Group (Order and Control Unit). As always, Roger Hood, Director of the Oxford Centre for Criminological Research, was a constant source of support, encouragement and advice. Thanks are also due to the prisoners whose thoughts and experiences form the basis of this study.

Conclusion

The pieces included in this *Reader* span the history and development of work within the field of victimology. The pieces contained in the first chapter highlight how in its infancy the discipline aimed to identify who might be likely to become a victim of crime, but in effect then labelled people as being responsible for their own victimization. These pieces are an interesting introduction to victimology, though they are very much a product of their time. The way in which they discuss victims of crime, and female victims in particular may cause anger among those reading them with modern sensibilities. They remain important however because debates around victim blaming are still evident when discussing victimization today, particularly with regard to certain crimes, for example recent research carried out by Amnesty International (2005) which has shown how widespread opinions continue to be held that women who experience sexual violence are held responsible for what has happened to them.

Despite this, much has changed for female victims of crime, since the second wave of feminism in the 1970s in particular. As demonstrated in Chapter 2, critical victimologists have helped to put certain crimes, such as domestic violence and sexual violence on the mainstream agenda. This has led to the creation of services for victims of crime such as refuges, but also improved treatment for these victims within the criminal justice system. Issues remain such as high attrition rates in cases of sexual and domestic violence, but victimologists also continue to highlight and challenge these.

Victimologists have also helped raise awareness of the impact of crimes on vulnerable people, and to challenge commonly held beliefs about who should be seen as a victim of crime. Williams, in a piece originally written in 1993 raises issues around the treatment of victims with learning difficulties by the criminal justice system. These issues are only now starting to be tackled with the introduction of victim advocates to the court system. Bowling challenges us to not take a simplistic view of the effects of racial harassment on victims as this can be affected by gender and ethnicity. These issues tie into topics considered in Part 3 which goes on to discuss further the impact of religion on victims and victimology. Spalek discusses the importance of religion to female victims of crime, and outlines the impact the religious writings and academics have played in the development of victimology, and restorative justice in particular.

Alternatives to the traditional criminal justice system, such as those proposed by restorative justice practitioners are well discussed these days but have failed to make into mainstream criminal justice provision for victims of adult offenders in the UK (as discussed in Stout and Goodman Chong, 2008). The field of victimization continues to develop however, and this is a particularly interesting time to be involved in these debates. The government in the UK has released a number of developments in recent years aimed at 'placing victims at the heart of the criminal justice system', including the Domestic Violence, Crime and Victims Act of 2004, and introductions of practical moves including witness care units.

New services introduced by the government are often brought in with funding limited in both its extent and timescale. Support services for victims of crime continue to be located very much within the voluntary sector in the UK, existing on short-term funding and subject to much uncertainty.

There also continues to be limits on who can access services, for example the *Code of Practice for Victims of Crime* (Home Office, 2006) states that services are only offered through a named person on behalf of a business, placing that person in the role of gatekeeper to services. As discussed in Part 4, this affects huge numbers of people who could also be seen as victims. Walklate makes this point in her section introduction by highlighting the number of people killed in the course of business each year. This has led victimology to develop a radical branch aimed at challenging again our perception of who is a victim of crime, and adding a human rights perspective.

Shapland raised the question of whether developments which have been introduced aim to improve the lot of victims of crime, or whether they have been brought in to improve the working of the Criminal Justice System. Whatever the reason for these changes, if they continue to be brought in with piecemeal funding, their effectiveness will always be limited.

Research into the experiences of victims of crime continues to add to our understanding of what people want and need following victimization. Part six discussed new methodologies which have been used by victimologists to broaden our understanding of victimization. Victimization surveys were first introduced in the 1960s and these form an integral part of our understanding about the extent of crime. These have also become an established research tool, with the British Crime Survey now being carried out every year.

This reader has aimed to introduce you to a variety of sources which trace the development of victimological theory and practice from its earliest beginnings to the present day. During this time the terminology of victimology has changed, and victimological theory has developed, as our understanding of who experiences crime and the effects that this might have on people has grown. We are in a better position to understand what support victims of crime are likely to need in order to carry on with their lives following victimization, and also to progress with their case through the Criminal Justice System. There remain issues to be tackled and gaps in service provision for victims of crime which need to be filled. There continues to be a place for victimologists to further our knowledge, improve services for victims, and challenge the system where it is found to be wanting.

Recommended reading

If you are interested in further reading, the following are very accessible sources of information and debate on victimology:

Spalek, B. (2006) *Crime Victims: Theory, Policy and Practice.* Basingstoke: Palgrave Macmillan.

Walklate, S. (2007) *Imagining the Victim of Crime.* Maidenhead: Open University Press.

Walklate S. (ed.) (2007) *The Handbook of Victims and Victimology.* Cullompton: Willan.

Williams, B. (1999) *Working with Victims of Crime: Policies, Politics and Practice.* London: Jessica Kingsley.

Bibliography

Abram, S. (2002) All that fuss over 100 houses: identities and moralities of building on land, in M. Saltman (ed.) *Land and Territoriality*. Oxford: Berg.

Abrams, K. (1992) Hearing the call of stories, *California Law Review*, 79: 971–1052.

Adams, R. (1994) *Prison Riots in Britain and the USA*. London: Macmillan.

Adler, Z. (1987) *Rape on Trial*. London: Routledge and Kegan Paul.

Adler, Z. (1991) Picking up the pieces, *Police Review*, 31 May, 1114–15.

Advisory Committee on Human Radiation Experiments (1995) *Final Report*. Washington, DC: USGPO.

Aftermath (1996) *Secretary's AGM Report, 27 April*. Sheffield: Aftermath.

Aftermath (1997a) *Training and Education Strategy 1997–2000*. Sheffield: Aftermath.

Aftermath (1997b) *Chairman's Report, Aftermath Annual Report, 26 April*. Sheffield: Aftermath.

Aftermath (nd a) *Aftermath*. Sheffield: Aftermath.

Aftermath (nd b) *Information Notes*. Sheffield: Aftermath.

Alder, C. and Wundersitz, J. (1994) *Family Conferencing and Juvenile Justice*. Canberra: Australian Institute of Criminology.

Allard, P. and Northey, W. (2001) Christianity: the rediscovery of restorative justice, in M. Hadley (ed.) *The Spiritual Roots of Restorative Justice*. Albany, NY: SUNY Press.

Alvazzi del Frate, A. (1998) *Victims of Crime in the Developing World*, UNICRI publication No. 57. Rome: UNICRI.

Alvazzi del Frate, A. (2002) Criminal victimisation in Latin America, in P. Nieuwbeerta (ed.) *Crime Victimization in Comparative Perspective*. The Hague: Boom Juridische Uitgevers.

Alvazzi del Frate, A. (2003) The future of the International Crime Victim Survey, *International Journal of Comparative Criminology*, 2(1).

Alvazzi del Frate, A. and van Kesteren, J. (2002) Criminal victimization in Eastern-Central Europe, in P. Nieuwbeerta (ed.) *Crime Victimization in Comparative Perspective*. The Hague: Boom Juridische Uitgevers.

Alvazzi del Frate and J. van Kesteren, J. (2003) The ICVS in the developing world, *International Journal of Comparative Criminology*, 2(1)57–76.

330 VICTIMS AND VICTIMIZATION

Alvazzi del Frate, A., Zvekic, U. and van Dijk, J. J. (eds) (1993) *Understanding Crime: Experiences of Crime and Crime Control*, UNICRI publication No. 57. Rome: UNICRI.

American Association for World Health (1997) *Denial of Food and Medicine: The Impact of the U.S. Embargo on Health and Nutrition in Cuba.* Washington, DC: American Association for World Health.

American Friends' Service Committee (1971) *Struggle for Justice.* New York: Hill and Wang.

American Psychiatric Association (1980) *Diagnostic and Statistical Manual of Mental Disorders* (3rd edn). Washington, DC: American Psychiatric Association.

American Psychiatric Association (2000) *Diagnostic and Statistical Manual of Mental Disorders* (DSM-IV R). Washington, DC: American Psychiatric Association.

Amnesty International (2002) *United Kingdom: Failing Children and Young People in Detention.* Available at: http://web.amnesty.org/library/Index/ENGEUR4500 42002?open&of=ENG-360.

Amnesty International (2005) *UK: New Poll Finds a Third of People Believe Women Who Flirt Partially Responsible for Being Raped.* Available at: http://www. amnesty.org.uk/news details.asp?NewsID=16618

Anderson, C. (1982) *Teaching People with Mental Retardation About Sexual Abuse Prevention.* Santa Cruz, CA: Network Publications.

Antilla, I. (1964) Victimology: a new territory in criminology, *Scandinavian Studies in Criminology*, 5.

Apap, J. (2002). *Counteracting Human Trafficking: Protecting the Victims of Trafficking.* European Conference on Preventing and Combating Trafficking in Human Beings: Global Challenge for the 21st Century, Brussels: European Parliament, 18–20 September.

Araki, C. T. (1990) Dispute management in the schools, *Mediation Quarterly*, 8(1): 51–62.

Ashworth, A. (1986) Punishment and compensation: state, victim and offender, *Oxford Journal of Legal Studies*, 6: 86–122.

Ashworth, A. (1993) Victim impact statements and sentencing, *Criminal Law Review*, 498–509.

Ashworth, A. (1998) *The Criminal Process.* Oxford: Oxford University Press.

Ashworth, A. (2000) *Sentencing and Criminal Justice.* London: Butterworths.

Ashworth, H. (2004) Racism drives man out of county, *Eastern Daily Press*, 22 April.

Asthana, A. (2003) Martin: I'll go home despite death threats, *Observer*, 13 July.

Atlas, R. (1983) Crime site selection for assaults in four Florida prisons, *Prison Journal*, 53: 59–71.

Aulette, J. R. and Michalowski, R. (1993) Fire in Hamlet: a case study of state-corporate crime, in K. Tunnell (ed.) *Political Crime in Contemporary America.* New York: Garland.

Australian Law Reform Commission (1987), *Sentencing*, Report No. 44, AGPS, Canberra.

Ayres, J. and Braithwaite, J. (1992) *Responsive Regulation: Transcending the Deregulation Debate.* New York: Oxford University Press.

Bagley, C. and King, K. (1991) *Child Sexual Abuse: The Search for Healing.* London: Routledge.

Bales, K. (2000). *Disposable People: New Slavery in the Global Economy.* Berkeley, CA: University of California Press.

Balkin, S. (1981) Toward victimisation research on the mentally retarded, *Victimology: An International Journal,* 6 (1–4): 331–7.

Ball, C. (2000), The Youth Justice and Criminal Evidence Act 1999: a significant move towards restorative justice, or a recipe for unintended consequences?, *Criminal Law Review,* 211–22.

Barak, G. (1991) *Crimes by the Capitalist State.* Albany, NY: State University of New York Press.

Barak. G. (1993) Crime, criminology, and human rights: toward an understanding of state criminality, in K. Tunnell (ed.) *Political Crime in Contemporary America.* New York: Garland.

Barclay, G. and Tavares, C. (2003) *International Comparisons of Criminal Justice Statistics 2001.* Home Office Statistical Bulletin 12/03. London: Home Office.

Barlow, H. D. and Kauzlarich, D. (2002) *Introduction to Criminology.* Upper Saddle River, NJ: Prentice Hall.

Bar-On, D. (1989) *Legacy of Silence: Encounters with Children of the Third Reich.* Cambridge, MA: Harvard University Press.

Baskin, D. R., Sommers, I. and Steadman, H. J. (1991) Assessing the impact of psychiatric impairment on prison violence, *Journal of Criminal Justice,* 19: 271–80.

Bayley, D. (1988) Community policing: a report from the devil's advocate, in J. R. Greene and S. Mastrofski (eds) *Community Policing: Rhetoric and Reality.* New York: Praeger.

Bayley, D. (2001) Security and justice for all, in H. Strang and J. Braithwaite (eds) *Restorative Justice and Civil Society.* Cambridge: Cambridge University Press.

Beck, G. (1995) Bullying among young offenders in custody, in N. K. Clark and G. M. Stephenson (eds) *Criminal Behaviour: Perceptions, Attributions and Rationality.* Leicester: British Psychological Society.

Beirne, P. and Messerschmidt, J. (1995) *Criminology* (2nd edn). Orlando, FL: Harcourt Brace.

Beirne, P. and Messerschmidt, J. (2000) *Criminology* (3rd edn). Boulder, CO: Westview.

Ben-Yehuda, N. (1990) *The Politics and Morality of Deviance.* New York: State University of New York Press.

Bergen, R. K. (1998). *Issues in Intimate Violence.* Thousand Oaks, CA: SAGE.

Berger, R. J., Searles, P. and Neuman, W. L. (1988) The dimensions of rape reform legislation, *Law and Society Review,* 22: 329–57.

Besag, V. E. (1989) *Bullies and Victims in Schools.* Milton Keynes: Open University Press.

Bichard, Sir Michael (2004) *An Independent Inquiry Arising from the Soham Murders.* London: The Stationery Office.

Bidna, H. (1975) Effects of increased security on prison violence, *Journal of Criminal Justice,* 3, 33–46.

BKA (1999) *Trafficking in Human Beings, Situation Report 1999.* Wiesbaden: Bundeskirminalamt.

Blagg, H. (1997) A just measure of shame? Aboriginal youth and conferencing in Australia, *British Journal of Criminology,* 37(4): 481–501.

Blake, J. (1990) *Sentenced by Association: The Needs of Prisoners' Families*, London: Save the Children.

Blom-Cooper, L. (1985) *A Child in Trust: The Report of the Panel of Inquiry into the Circumstances Surrounding the Death of Jasmine Beckford*. Wembley: London Borough of Brent.

Bnenen, M. and Hoegen, E. (2000) *Victims of Crime in Twenty-Two European Jurisdiction*. PhD Thesis, Katholieke Universitcit Brabant, Nijmegen.

Bohm, R. (1993) Social relationships that arguably should be criminal although they are not: on the political economy of crime, in K. Tunnell (ed.) *Political Crime in Contemporary America*. New York: Garland.

Boswell, G. (1995) *Violent Victims*. London: The Prince's Trust.

Boswell, G. (1996) *Young and Dangerous: The Backgrounds and Careers of Section 53 Offenders*. Aldershot: Avebury.

Boswell, G. (1999) Young offenders who commit grave crimes: the criminal justice response, in H. Kemshall and J. Pritchard (eds) *Good Practice in Working with Violence*. London: Jessica Kingsley.

Boswell, G. (2000) *Violent Children and Adolescents: Asking the Question Why*. London: Whurr.

Boswell, G., Fisher, D., Flaxington, F. and Loughlin, M. (2002) Working with young adults sentenced to life, *British Journal of Community Justice* 1(2): 77–89.

Bowers, L., Smith, P. K. and Binney, V. (1992) Cohesion and power in the families of children involved in bully/victim problems at school, *Journal of Family Therapy* 14(4): 371–87.

Bowling, B. (1998) *Violent Racism: Victimisation, Policing and Social Context*. Oxford: Clarendon Press.

Box, S. (1971) *Deviance, Reality and Society*. London: Holt, Rinehart and Winston.

Box, S. (1983) *Power, Crime and Mystification*. London: Routledge.

Bradshaw, W. (1995) Mediation and therapy, in M. S. Umbreit (ed.) *Mediating Interpersonal Conflicts: A Pathway to Peace*. West Concord, MN: CPI.

Braithwaite, J. (1989) *Crime, Shame and Reintegration*. Cambridge: Cambridge University Press.

Braithwaite, J. (1993) Shame and modernity, *British Journal of Criminology*, 33(1): 1–18.

Braithwaite, J. (1997) Conferencing and Plurality: Reply to Blagg, *British Journal of Criminology*, 37(4): 502–6.

Braithwaite, J. (1999) Restorative justice: assessing optimistic and pessimistic accounts, *Crime and Justice: A Review of Research*, 25: 1–127.

Braithwaite, J. and Pettit, P. (1990) *Not Just Deserts*. Oxford: Oxford University Press.

Braithwaite, S. (2002) *Restorative Justice and Responsive Regulation*. Oxford: Oxford University Press.

Brown, H. (1991) Facing facts, *Nursing Times*, 87(6): 65–6.

Brown, H. and Craft, A. (1992) *Working with the 'Unthinkable': A Trainers' Manual on the Sexual Abuse of Adults with Learning Difficulties*. London: Family Planning Association.

Brownmiller, S. (1975) *Against Our Will: Men, Women and Rape*. Harmondsworth: Penguin.

Bull, R. and Davies, G. (1996) The effect of child witness research on legislation in Great Britain, in B. Bottoms and G. Goodman (eds) *International Perspectives on Child Abuse and Children's Testimony*. London: SAGE.

Bureau of International Labor Affairs (1996) *Forced Labor: The Prostitution of Children*. Washington, DC: US Department of Labor.

Bureau of International Labor Affairs (1998) *By the Sweat and Toil of Children*. Washington, DC: US Department of Labor.

Bureau of Justice Statistics (1991) *Female Victims of Violent Crime*. Washington, DC: Department of Justice.

Bureau of Justice Statistics (1992) *Criminal Victimization in the United States, 1991*. Washington, DC: US Department of Justice.

Burgess, A. and Holmstrom, L. (1974) Rape trauma syndrome, *American Journal of Psychiatry*, September: 981–6.

Burney, E. (2002) The uses and limits of prosecuting racially aggravated offences, in P. Iganski (ed.) *The Hate Debate: Should Hate Be Punished as a Crime?*. London: Institute for Jewish Policy Research.

Burney, E. and Rose, G. (2002) *Racist Offences: How Is the Law Working? The Implementation of the Legislation on Racially Aggravated Offences in the Crime and Disorder Act 1998*. Research Study 244. London: Home Office.

Bush, R. A. B. and Folger, J. P. (1994) *The Promise of Mediation: Responding to Conflict Through Empowerment and Recognition*. San Francisco, CA: Jossey-Bass.

Butler-Sloss, Dame Elizabeth (1988) *Report of the Inquiry into Child Abuse in Cleveland 1987*. London: HMSO.

Byrne, B. (1994) Bullies and victims in a school setting with reference to some Dublin schools, *Irish Journal of Psychology*, 15: 574–86.

Calouste Gulbenkian Foundation (1995) *Children and Violence*. London: Calouste Gulbenkian Foundation.

Cameron, C. (2000) *Resolving Childhood Trauma: A Long-term Study of Abuse Survivors*. London: SAGE.

Campbell, B. (1993) *Goliath: Britain's Dangerous Places*. London: Methuen.

Campbell, C., Devlin, R., O'Mahony, D., Doak, J., Jackson, J., Corrigan, T. and McEvoy, K. (2006) *Evaluation of the Northern Ireland Youth Conference Service*. NIO Research and Statistics Series: Report No. 12. Belfast: Northern Ireland Office.

Caulfield, S. (1991) The perpetuation of violence through criminological theory: the ideological role of subculture theory, in H. E. Pepinsky and R. Quinney (eds) *Criminology as Peacemaking*. Bloomington, IN: Indiana University Press.

Caulfield, S. and Wonders, N. (1993) Personal AND political: violence against women and the role of the state, in K. Tunnell (ed.) *Political Crime in Contemporary America*. New York: Garland.

Cavadino, M. and Dignan, J. (1997) Reparation, retribution and rights, *International Review of Victimology*, 4: 233–71.

Cervi, R. (1992a) The time has come, *Community Care*, 25 June: 14–15.

Cervi, R. (1992b) Inquiry seeks action over alleged abuser, *Community Care*, 14 May: 4.

Chahal, K. and Julienne, L. (1999) *'We Can't All Be White': Racist Victimisation in the UK*. York: York Publishing Services.

Chakraborti, N. and Garland, J. (2004a) *Meeting the Challenge? Understanding the Needs and Experiences of Minority Ethnic Households in North Warwickshire and Stratford-on-Avon.* Department of Criminology, University of Leicester.

Chakraborti, N. and Garland, J. (2004b) England's green and pleasant land? Examining racist prejudice in a rural context. *Patterns of Prejudice*, 38(4): 383–398.

Chakraborti, N., Garland, J. and Keetley, K. (2003) *Responding to Racist Incidents in Wellingborough and East Northamptonshire: An Assesment of Agency Practice and Victim Satisfaction – Final Report.* Leicester: PRCI.

Chakraborti, N., Garland, J. and Spalek, B. (2004) Out of sight, out of mind? Towards developing an understanding of the needs of 'hidden' minority ethnic communities, *Criminal Justice Matters*, 57: 34–5.

Chambers, G. and Millar, A. (1986) *Prosecuting Sexual Assault.* Edinburgh: Scottish Office Central Research Unit.

Chambliss, W. J. (1989) State-organized crime, *Criminology*, 27: 183–208.

Chambliss, W. J. (1995) Commentary, *Society For the Study of Social Problems Newsletter*, Winter.

Chan, J. (1997) *Changing Police Culture: Policing in a Multicultural Society.* Cambridge: Cambridge University Press.

Chomsky, N. (1985) *Turning the Tide: U.S. Intervention in Central America and the Struggle for Peace* Boston, MA: South End Press.

Chomsky, N. (1992) *Deterring Democracy.* New York: Hill & Wang.

Chomsky, N. (1993) *Year 501: The Conquest Continues.* Boston, MA: South End Press.

Chomsky, N. and Herman, E. S. (1979) The United States versus human rights in the third world., *The Monthly Review*, 29: 22–45.

Christie, N. (1977) Conflicts as property, *British Journal of Criminology*, 17(1): 1–15.

Christie, N. (1986) The ideal victim, in E. A. Fattah (ed.) *From Crime Policy to Victim Policy.* London: Macmillan.

Churchill, W. (1995) *Since Predator Came: Notes from the Struggle for American Indian Liberation.* Littleton, CO: Aigis.

Churchill, W. and Vander Wall, J. (1990) *The Cointelpro Papers.* Boston, MA: South End Press.

Clancy, A., Hough, M., Aust, R. and Kershaw, C. (2001) *Crime, Policing and Justice: The Experience of Ethnic Minorities. Findings from the 2000 British Crime Survey.* London: Home Office.

Clark, L. and Lewis, D. (1977) *Rape: The Price of Coercive Sexuality.* Toronto: The Women's Press.

Clark, S., Valente, E. and Mace, R. R. (1992) *Mediation of Interpersonal Disputes: An Evaluation of North Carolina's Programs.* Chapel Hill, NC: Institute of Government, University of North Carolina.

Clemmer, D. (1940) *The Prison Community.* New York: Rinehart.

Clinard, M. and Quinney, R. (1973) *Criminal Behavior Systems: A Typology.* New York: Holt, Rinehart, and Winston.

Clinard. M. and Yeager, P. C. (1980) *Corporate Crime.* New York: The Free Press.

Cloke, P. (1997) Poor country: marginalisation, poverty and rurality, in P. Cloke and J. Little (eds) *Contested Countryside Cultures: Otherness, Marginalisation and Rurality.* London: Routledge.

Cloke, P. (2004) Rurality and racialised others: out of place in the countryside?, in N. Chakraborti and J. Garland (eds) *Rural Racism*. Cullompton: Willan.

Coates, R. B. and Gehm, J. (1989) An empirical assessment, in M. Wright and B. Galaway (eds) *Mediation and Criminal Justice*. London: SAGE.

Cohen, S. (1993) Human rights and crimes of the state: the culture of denial, *Australian and New Zealand Journal of Criminology*, 26: 97–115.

Cohen, S. (1995) *Denial and Acknowledgement*. Jerusalem: Centre for Human Rights, Hebrew University of Jerusalem.

Cohen, S. (1996) Government responses to human rights reports, *Human Rights Quarterly*, 18: 517–43.

Comfort, M. (1998) Language and experience: the construction and consequences of a narrative for prisoners' families. MSc Criminology dissertation, London School of Economics, unpublished.

Community Care (1991a) Client accused of murder after fire in special unit, 16 January.

Community Care (1991b) An ordeal shared, 4 July.

Community Security Trust (CST) (2006) *Anti-Semitic Incidents Report 2005*. London: Community Security Trust.

Conley, R. W., Luckasson, R. and Bouthilet, G. (1992) *The Criminal Justice System and Mental Retardation: Defendants and Victims*. New York: Paul H. Brookes.

Cook, R., Roehl, J. and Sheppard, D. (1980) *Neighborhood Justice Centers Field Test: Final Evaluation Report*. Washington, DC: Government Printing Office.

Cooke, D. J. (1991) Violence in prisons: the influence of regime factors, *Howard Journal*, 30: 95–109.

Cooley, D. (1993) Criminal victimization in male federal prisons, *Canadian Journal of Criminology*, 35: 479–95.

Cooney, M. (1994) Evidence as partisanship, *Law and Society Review*, 28(4): 833–58.

Cooper, J. (1992) Catalogue of neglect at unit, *Evening Gazette* (Colchester), 8 January.

Coote, A. (ed.) (nd) *Families, Children and Crime*. London: Institute for Public Policy Research.

Council of Europe (1993) *Consistency in Sentencing*. Recommendation R (92) 18. Strasbourg: Council of Europe.

Council of Europe (1999) *European Sourcebook of Crime and Criminal Justice Statistics*. Strasbourg: Council of Europe.

Council of Europe (2000) *Mediation in Penal Matters*. Recommendation R (99) 19. Strasbourg: Council of Europe.

Craine, L. S., Henson, C. E., Colliver, J. A. and Maclean, D. G. (1988) Prevalence of a history of sexual abuse among female psychiatric patients in a state hospital system, *Hospital and Community Psychiatry*, 39: 300–4.

Crawford, A. (2000) Salient themes towards a victim perspective and the limitations of restorative justice, in A. Crawford and J. Goodey (eds) *Integrating a Victim Perspective within Criminal Justice*. Aldershot: Ashgate.

Crawford, A. and Goodey, J (eds) (2000) *Integrating a Victim Perspective within Criminal Justice*. Aldershot: Ashgate.

Creedon, P. (1993) *Women in Mass Communication*. Newbury Park, CA: SAGE.

Creighton, S. J. (2004) *Prevalence and Incidence of Child Abuse: International Comparisons*. London: NSPCC.

Creighton, S. J. and Tissier, G. (2003) *Child Killings in England and Wales*. London: NSPCC.

Cretney, A., Davis, G., Clarkson, C. and Shepherd, J. (1994) Criminalizing assault: the failure of the 'offence against society' model, *British Journal of Criminology*, 34(1): 15–29.

Criminal Injuries Compensation Board (1964) *Compensation for Victims of Crimes of Violence*, Cmnd. 2323.

Cuffe, J. (1991) Why Caroline's mother cried in court, *Independent*, 29 November.

Cullen, F. T. and Gilbert, K. E. (1982) *Reaffirming Rehabilitation*. Cincinnati, OH: W. H. Anderson.

Cunneen, C. (1997) Community conferencing and the fiction of indigenous control, *Australia and New Zealand Journal of Criminology*, 30: 297–320.

Daly, K. (1991) Of numbers and narrative, paper presented at the Law and Society Annual Meeting, Amsterdam, The Netherlands, June.

Daly, K. (1994) *Gender, Crime and Punishment*. New Haven, CT: Yale University Press.

Daly, K. (1999) *Does Punishment Have a Place in Restorative Justice?*, unpublished paper presented to the ANZ Criminology conference.

Daly, K. (2000) *Restorative Justice: The Real Story*, unpublished paper presented to Scottish Criminology Conference.

Daly, K. (2001) Conferencing in Australia and New Zealand: variations, research findings and prospects, in A. Morris and C. Maxwell (eds) *Restorative Justice for Juveniles: Conferencing, Mediation and Circles*. Oxford: Hart.

Davis, A. J. (1968) Sexual assaults in the Philadelphia prison system and sheriff's vans, *Transaction*, 6: 8–16.

Davis, J. K. (1992) *Spying on America*. Westport, CT: Praeger.

Davis, R. C. and Smith, B. (1994) The effect of victim impact statements on sentencing decisions: a test in an urban setting, *Justice Quarterly*, 11(3): 453–69.

Davis, R., Tichane, M. and Grayson, D. (1980) *Mediation and Arbitration as Alternative to Prosecution in Felony Arrest Cases: An Evaluation of the Brooklyn Dispute Resolution Center*. New York: VERA Institute of Justice.

Davis, W. (1982) Violence in prisons, in P. Feldman (ed.) *Developments in the Study of Criminal Behaviour*. Chichester: John Wiley and Sons.

Decker, S. and van Winkle, B. (1996) *Life in the Gang: Family, Friends, and Violence*. Cambridge: Cambridge University Press.

De Lima, P. (2001) *Needs Not Numbers: An Exploration of Minority Ethnic Communities in Scotland*. London: Commission for Racial Equality and Community Development Foundation.

del Frate, A., Zvekic, U. and van Dijk, J. (1993) *Understanding Crime: Experiences of Crime and Crime Control*. Rome: UNICRI.

Delgado, R. (1989) Storytelling for oppositionists and others: a plea for narrative, *Michigan Law Review*, 87: 2411–41.

Department of Health, Home Office and Department for Education & Employment (1999) *Working Together to Safeguard Children*. London: The Stationery Office.

Depner, C. E. Cannata, K. V. and Simon, M. N. (1992) Building a uniform statistical reporting system: a snapshot of California family court services, *Family and Conciliation Courts Review*, 30(2): 185–206.

Derbyshire, H. (1994) *Not in Norfolk: Tackling the Invisibility of Racism.* Norwich: Norwich and Norfolk Racial Equality Council.

Dingwall, G. and Moody, S. R. (eds) (1999) *Crime and Conflict in the Countryside.* Cardiff: University of Wales Press.

Doak, J. and O'Mahony, D. (2006) The vengeful victim? Assessing the attitudes of victims participating in restorative youth conferencing, *International Review of Victimology*, 13: 157–78.

Donat, P. L. N. and D'Emilio, J. (1992) A feminist redefinition of rape and sexual assault: historical foundations and change, *Journal of Social Issues*, 48(1): 9–22.

Douglas, M. (1970) *Natural Symbols.* Harmondsworth: Penguin.

Douglas, R., Laster, K. and Inglis, N. (1994) Victims of efficiency: tracking victim information through the system in Victoria, Australia, *International Review of Victimology*, 3: 95–110.

Downes, D. and Morgan, R. (1997) Dumping the 'hostages to fortune'? The politics of law and order in post-war Britain, in M. Maguire et al. (eds) *The Oxford Handbook of Criminology.* Oxford: Clarendon.

Downey, R. (1992) Open to abuse, *Social Work Today*, 4 June.

Drapkin, I. and Viano, E. (1974) *Victimology.* New York: Hanson.

Duff, R. A. (2000) *Punishment, Communication and Community.* New York: Oxford University Press.

Dumond, R. W. (1992) The sexual assault of male inmates in incarcerated settings, *International Journal of the Sociology of Law*, 20: 135–57.

Dunn, P. (1991) How missing Jo failed to make the headlines, *Independent*, 5 May.

Dunne, T. and Power, A. (1990) Sexual abuse and mental handicap: preliminary findings of a community-based study, *Mental Handicap Research*, 3: 111–25.

Durkheim, E. (1960) *The Division of Labor in Society.* Glencoe, IL: Free Press.

Duryee, M. (1992) Mandatory court mediation: demographic summary and consumer evaluation of one court service, *Family and Conciliation Courts Review*, 30(2): 260–7.

Dyer, C. (1991) Outdated legal rules 'shielding criminals', *Guardian*, 9 May.

Edgar, K. and O'Donnell, I. (1997) Responding to victimisation, *Prison Service Journal*, 109: 15–19.

Edwards, I. (2001) Victim participation in sentencing: the problems of incoherence, *Howard Journal of Criminal Justice*, 40: 39–54.

Eisenstein, J. and Jacob, H. (1977), *Felony Justice.* Boston: Little Brown and Company.

Elias, R. (1985) Transcending our social reality of victimisation: towards a new victimology of human rights, *Victimology*, 10: 6–25.

Elias, R. (1986) *The Politics of Victimisation.* Oxford: Oxford University Press.

Elias, R. (1993) *Victims Still.* London: SAGE.

Emerson, R. M. (1983) Holistic effects of social control decision making, *Law and Society Review*, 17: 425–55.

Emerson, R. M. and Paley, B. (1994) Organizational horizons and complaint filing, in K. Hawkins (ed.) *The Use of Discretion.* Oxford: Oxford University Press.

Emery, R. E, and Jackson, J. A. (1989) The Charlottesville mediation project: mediated and litigated child custody disputes, *Mediation Quarterly*, 24: 3–18.

Engel, K. and Rothman, S. (1983) Prison violence and the paradox of reform, *The Public Interest*, 73: 91–105.

Epstein, J. and Langenbahn, S. (1994) *The Criminal Justice and Community Response to Rape*. Washington, DC: US Department of Justice.

Erez, E. (1989) The impact of victimology on criminal justice policy, *Criminal Justice Policy Review*, 3(3): 236–56.

Erez, E. (1990) Victim participation in sentencing: rhetoric and reality, *Journal of Criminal Justice*, 18: 19–31.

Erez, E. (1994) Victim participation in sentencing: and the debate goes on, *International Review of Victimology*, 3: 17–32.

Erez, E. (1999) Who's afraid of the big bad victim? Victim impact statements as empowerment and enhancement of justice, *Criminal Law Review*, 545–56.

Erez, E. and Roeger, L. (1995a) Crime impact v. victim impact: victim impact statements in South Australia, *Criminology Australia*, 6(3): 3–8.

Erez, E. and Roeger, L. (1995b) The effect of victim impact statements on sentencing outcomes and dispositions, *Journal of Criminal Justice*, 23: 363–75.

Erez, E. and Rogers, L. (1999) victim impact statements and sentencing outcomes and processes: the perspectives of legal professionals, *British Journal of Criminology*, 39(2): 216–39.

Erez, E. and Sebba, L. (forthcoming) From individualization of the offender to individualization of the victim, in W. Laufer and F. Adler (eds) *Advances in Criminological Theory*.

Erez, E. and Tontodonato, P. (1990) The effect of victim participation in sentencing on sentence outcome, *Criminology*, 28(3): 451–74.

Erez, E. and Tontodonato, P. (1992) Victim participation in sentencing and satisfaction with justice, *Justice Quarterly*, 9: 393–427.

Erez, E., Roeger, L. and Morgan, F. (1994) *Victim Impact Statements in South Australia: An Evaluation*, Series C No. 6. Adelaide: Office of Crime Statistics, South Australian Attorney-General's Department.

Erikson, E. (1968) *Identity: Youth and Crisis*. London: Faber.

Erikson, K. (1966) *Wayward Puritans*. New York: John Wiley.

Ermann, M. D. and Lundman, R. J. (1996) *Corporate and Governmental Deviance*. New York: Oxford University Press.

Estrich, S. (1987) *Real Rape*. Cambridge, MA: Harvard University Press.

European Monitoring Centre on Racism and Xenophobia (2005) *The Impact of 7 July 2005 London Bomb Attacks on Muslim Communities in the EU*. Vienna: EUMC

European Monitoring Centre on Racism and Xenophobia (2006) *Muslims in the European Union: Discrimination and Islamophobia*. Vienna: EUMC

Everett, B. and Gallop, R. (2001) *The Link between Childhood and Mental Illness: Effective Interventions for Mental Health Professionals*. Thousand Oaks, CA: SAGE.

Falk, R., Kolko, G. and Lifton, R. J. (1971) *Crimes of War*. New York: Vintage.

Fancourt, R., Shand, C., Broadmore, J. and Milford, R. (1994) *The Medical Management of Sexual Abuse*. Auckland: Doctors for Sexual Abuse Care (DSAC).

Farrington, D. (1993) Understanding and preventing bullying, in M. Tonry (ed.) *Crime and Justice: A Review of Research*. Chicago, IL: University of Chicago Press.

Farrington, D. (1997) Human development and criminal careers, in M. Maguire et al. (eds) *The Oxford Handbook of Criminology*. Oxford: Clarendon.

Farrington, D. and Nuttall, C. (1980) 'Prison size, overcrowding, prison violence and recidivism', *Journal of Criminal Justice, 8,* 221–31.

Farrington, D. and West, D. (1990) The Cambridge study in delinquent development, in H. Kerner and G. Kaiser (eds) *Criminality, Personality, Behaviour and Life History.* Berlin: Springer-Verlag.

Fattah, E. (nd) Becoming a victim: the victimization experience and its aftermath. (unpublished paper).

Feeley, M. (1979) *The Process is the Punishment.* New York: Russell Sage.

Feeley, M. (1997) two models of the criminal justice system: an organizational perspective, in B. Hancock and P. Sharp (eds) *Public Policy: Crime and Criminal Justice.* Upper Saddle River, NJ: Prentice Hall.

Feldman-Summers, S. and Norris, J. (1984) Differences between rape victims who report and those who do not report to a public agency, *Journal of Applied Social Psychology,* 14: 562–73.

Feley, M, and Simon, J. (1992) The new penology: notes on the emerging strategy of corrections and its implications, *Criminology,* 30: 449–74.

Finkelhor, D. (1997) The victimization of children and youth, in R. C. Davis, A. J. Lurigio and W. G. Skogan (eds) *Victims of Crime.* London: SAGE.

Fitzgerald, M. and Hale, C. (1996) *Ethnic Minorities: Victimisation and Racial Harassment: Findings from the 1988 and 1992 British Crime Surveys.* Home Office Research Study No. 154. London: HMSO.

Flynn, M. C. (1989) *Independent Living for Adults with Mental Handicap: A Place of My Own.* London: Cassell.

Fogel, D. (1975) *We Are Living Proof . . .: The Justice Model for Corrections.* Cincinnati, OH: W. H. Anderson.

Fong, R. S. (1990) The organizational structure of prison gangs: a Texas case study, *Federal Probation,* 54: 36–43.

Ford, R. (2003) Unrepentant Tony Martin refused early release, *The Times,* 17 January.

Fox, J. and Szockyj, E. (1996) *Corporate Victimization of Women.* Boston, MA: Northeastern University Press.

Francis, D. and Henderson, P. (1992) *Working With Rural Communities.* Basingstoke: Macmillan.

Friedrichs, D. O. (1983). Victimology: A consideration of the radical critique. *Crime and Delinquency,* April, 283–294.

Friedrichs, D. O. (1996a) *Trusted Criminals: White Collar Crime in Contemporary Society.* New York: Wadsworth.

Friedrichs, D. O. (1996b) Governmental crime, Hitler, and white collar crime: a problematic relationship, *Caribbean Journal of Criminology and Social Psychology,* 1: 44–63.

Friedrichs, D. O. (1998) *State Crime: Volumes I and II.* Aldershot: Ashgate/Dartmouth.

Frieze, I., Hymer S. and Greenberg, M. (1987) Describing the crime victim: psychological reactions to victimization, *Professional Psychology: Research and Practice,* 18: 299–315.

Frohmann, L. (1992) Discrediting victims' allegations of sexual assault: prosecutorial accounts of case rejections, *Social Problems,* 38(2): 213–26.

Frohmann, L. (1996) Hard cases: prosecutorial accounts for filing unconvictable sexual assaults complaints, *Current Research on Occupations and Professions*, 9: 189–209.

Furedi, F. (2002) *Culture of Fear: Risk Taking and the Morality of Low Expectation*. London: Continuum.

Gaes, G. G. and McGuire, W. J. (1985) Prison violence: the contribution of crowding versus other determinants of prison assault rates, *Journal of Research in Crime and Delinquency*, 22(1): 41–65.

Garabedian, P. G. (1963) Social roles and processes of socialisation in the prison community, *Social Problems*, 11: 139–52.

Gardner, J. (1998) Crime: in proportion and in perspective, in A. Ashworth and M. Wasik (eds) *Fundamentals of Sentencing Theory*. Oxford: Oxford University Press.

Garland, D. (2001) *The Culture of Control: Crime and Social Order in Contemporary Society*. Oxford: Oxford University Press.

Garland, D. (2002) Of crimes and criminals: the development of criminology in Britain, in M. Maguire, R. Morgan and R. Reiner (eds) *The Oxford Handbook of Criminology*. Oxford: Oxford University Press.

Garland, J. (2004) The same old story? Englishness, the tabloid press and the 2002 Football World Cup, *Leisure Studies*, 23(1): 79–92.

Garland, J. and Chakraborti, N. (2002) *Tackling the Invisible Problem? An Examination of the Provision of Services to Victims of Racial Harassment in Rural Suffolk*. Leicester: Scarman Centre, University of Leicester.

Garland, J. and Chakraborti, N. (2004a) Racist victimisation, community safety and the rural: issues and challenges, *British Journal of Community Justice*, 2(3): 21–32.

Garland, J. and Chakraborti, N. (2004b) Another country? Community, belonging and exclusion in rural England, in N. Chakraborti and J. Garland (eds) *Rural Racism*. Cullompton: Willan.

Geis, G. (1973) Victimisation patterns in white collar crime, in L. Drapkin and E. Viano (eds) *Victimology: A New Focus*. Lexington, MA: D. C. Heath.

Gelernter, D. (1997) *Surviving the Unabomber*. New York: Free Press.

Gelles, R. J. and Straus, M. A. (1988) *Intimate Violence*. New York: Simon and Schuster.

Getzel, G. and Masters, R. (1984) Serving families who survive homicide victims, *Social Casework*, 65(3): 138–44.

Ghate, D., Hazel, N., Creighton, S. J., Finch, S. and Field, J. (2003) *The National Study of Parents, Children and Discipline in Britain: Key Findings*. ESRC Violence Research Programme.

Giddens, A. (1994) Living in a post-traditional society, in U. Beck, A. Giddens and S. Lash (eds) *Reflexive Postmodernisation*. Cambridge: Polity.

Gill, M. and Pease, K. (1998) Repeat robbers: are they different?, in M. Gill (ed.) *Crime at Work: Increasing the Risk for Offenders*. Leicester: Perpetuity.

Gilmore, K. and Pittman, L. (1993) *To Report or Not To Report: A Study of Victim/ Survivors of Sexual Assault and Their Experience of Making an Initial Report to the Police*. Melbourne: Centre Against Sexual Assault (CASA House) and Royal Women's Hospital.

Glaser, B. G. and Strauss, A. L. (1965) *Awareness of Dying*. Chicago, IL: Aldine.

Glaser, B. G. and Strauss, A. L. (1967) *The Discovery of Grounded Theory: Strategies for Qualitative Research*. Chicago, IL: Aldine.

Glendenning, F. (1999) The abuse of older people in institutional settings, in N. Stanley, J. Manthorpe and B. Penhale (eds) *Institutional Abuse: Perspectives Across the Life Course*. London: Routledge.

Goddard, C. R. and Stanley, J. R. (1994) Viewing the abusive parent and the abused child as captor and hostage: the application of hostage theory to the effects of child abuse, *Journal of Interpersonal Violence*, 9(2): 258–69.

Gold, L. (1993) Influencing unconscious influences: the healing dimension of mediation, *Mediation Quarterly*, 11(1): 55–66.

Goldson, B. (2002) *Vulnerable Inside: Children in Secure and Penal Settings*. London: The Children's Society.

Goldstein, A. S. (1984) The victim and prosecutorial discretion: the Federal Victim and Witness Protection Act of 1982, *Law and Contemporary Problems*, 47: 225–48.

Goodey, J. (2000) Non-EU citizens: experiences of offending and victimisation: the case for comparative European research, *The European Journal of Crime, Criminal Law and Criminal Justice*, 8(1): 13–34.

Goodey, J. (2002) Whose insecurity? Organised crime, its victims and the EU, in A. Crawford (ed.) *Crime and Insecurity: The Governance of Safety in Europe*. Cullompton: Willan.

Goodey, J. (2003a) Organised crime, its victims and the EU: the case of human trafficking, in A. Edwards and P. Gill (eds) *Transnational Organised Crime: Perspectives on Global Security*. London: Routledge.

Goodey, J. (2003b) Migration, crime and victimhood: responses to sex trafficking in the EU, *Journal of Punishment and Society*, 5(4): 415–32.

Goodey, J. (2005) *Victims and Victimology: Research, Policy and Practice*. Edinburgh: Pearson Longman.

Gottfredson, M. and Hirschi, T. (1990) *A General Theory of Crime*, Stanford, CA: Stanford University Press.

Gove, M. (2005) You don't have to be a redneck to see red at travellers flouting the law, *The Times*, 22 March.

Grabosky, P. N. (1987) Victims, in G. Zdenkowski et al. (eds) *The Criminal Injustice Systems*. Sydney: Pluto Press.

Grapendaal, M. (1990) The inmate subculture in Dutch prisons, *British Journal of Criminology*, 30: 341–57.

Green, P. J. and T. Ward (2000) State crime, human rights, and the limits of criminology, *Social Justice*, 27: 101–20.

Greene, J. R. and Mastrofski, S. (eds) (1988) *Community Policing: Rhetoric and Reality*. New York: Praeger.

Gregory, J. and Lees, S. (1996) Attrition in rape and sexual assault cases, *The British Journal of Criminology*, 36(1): 1–17.

Griffiths, C. T. and Belleau, C. (1993) *Restoration, Reconciliation and Healing: The Revitalization of Culture and Tradition in Addressing Crime and Victimization in Aboriginal Communities*. Paper presented at the 11th International Congress on Criminology, Budapest, Hungary.

Gross, H. (1979) *A Theory of Criminal Justice*. New York: Oxford University Press.

Gross, H. and von Hirsch, A. (eds) (1981) *Sentencing*. New York: Oxford University Press.

Guardian (1991a) Odd-job man had sex with girl after being made social worker, 31 August.

Guardian (1991b) Disabled boy forces *Sun* to pay for 'worst brat' libel, 24 May.

Gunn, M. J. (1990) The law and learning disability, *International Review of Psychiatry*, 2: 13–22.

Haass, R. (1998). *Economic Sanctions and American Diplomacy*. New York: Council on Foreign Relations.

Hacking, I. (1995) *Rewriting the Soul*. Princeton, NJ: Princeton University Press.

Hagan, F. (1997) *Political Crime: Ideology and Criminology*. Boston, MA: Allyn and Bacon.

Hagan, J. and McCarthy, B. (1992) Streetlife and delinquency, *British Journal of Sociology*, 43(4): 533–61.

Hagan, J., Simpson, J. and Gillis, A. (1979) The sexual stratification of social control, *British Journal of Sociology*, 30(1): 25–38.

Halfacree, K. (1993) Locality and social representation: space, discourse and alternative definitions of the rural, *Journal of Rural Studies*, 9(1): 23–37.

Hall, D. J. (1991) Victim voices in criminal court: the need for restraint, *American Criminal Law Review*, 28(2): 233–66.

Hall, R. (1985), *Ask Any Woman: A London Inquiry into Rape and Sexual Assault*. Bristol: Falling Wall Press.

Hall, S. et al. (1978) *Policing the Crisis*. London: Macmillan.

Hamber, B. (2002) 'Ere their story die': truth, justice and reconciliation in South Africa, *Race and Class*, 44(1): 61–79

Hamlyn, B., Phelps, A. and Sattar, G. (2004) *Key Findings from the Surveys of Vulnerable and Intimidated Witnesses 2000/01 and 2003*. Home Office Research Findings 240. London: Home Office.

Hamm, M. S. (1993) State-organized homicide: a study of seven CIA plans to assassinate Fidel Castro, in W. Chambliss (ed.) *Making Law: The State, the Law, and Structural Contradictions*. Bloomington, IN: Indiana University Press.

Hamm, M. S. (1995) *The Abandoned Ones: The Imprisonment and Uprising of the Mariel Boat People*. Boston, MA: Northeastern University Press.

Harland, A. (1981) *Monetary Remedies for the Victims of Crime: Assessing the Role of the Criminal Courts*. Working Paper 16. Albany, NY: Criminal Justice Research Center.

Harris, J. and Grace, S. (1999) *A Question of Evidence? Investigating and Prosecuting Rape in the 1990s*. London: Home Office.

Haseltine, B. and Miltenberger, R. G. (1990) Teaching self-protection skills to persons with mental retardation, *American Journal on Mental Retardation*, 95: 188–97.

Hatalak, O., Alvazzi del Frate, A. and Zvekic, U. (eds) (2000) *The International Crime Victim Survey in Countries in Transition: National Reports*. UNICRI publication No. 62. Rome: UNICRI.

Hazlehurst, K. (1991) Passion and policy: Aboriginal deaths in custody in Australia 1980–1989, in G. Barak (ed.) *Crimes by the Capitalist State*. Albany, NY: State University of New York Press.

Hellerstein, D. R. (1989) Victim impact statement: reform or reprisal?, *American Criminal Law Review*, 27: 391–430.

Henderson, J. H. and Simon, D. R. (1994) *Crimes of the Criminal Justice System*. Cincinnati, OH: Anderson.

Henderson, L. N. (1985) The wrongs of victims' rights, *Stanford Law Review*, 37: 937–1021.

Hendricks, J., Black, D. and Kaplan, T. (1993) *When Father Kills Mother: Guiding Children Through Trauma and Grief*. London: Routledge.

Henley, M., Davis, R. C. and Smith, B. E. (1994) The reactions of prosecutors and judges to victim impact statements, *International Review of Victimology*, 3: 83–93.

Herman, E. S. (1982) *The Real Terror Network: Terrorism in Fact and Propaganda*. Boston, MA: South End Press.

Herman, E. S. (1987) U.S. sponsorship of international terrorism: an overview, *Crime and Social Justice*, 27/28: 1–31.

Hewitt, S. E. K. (1987) The abuse of deinstitutionalised persons with mental handicaps, *Disability, Handicap & Society*, 2: 127–35.

Heydebrand, W. and Seron, C. (1990) *Rationalizing Justice: The Political Economy of Federal District Courts*. New York: State University of New York Press.

Higginbotham, A. L. Jr (1978) *In the Matter of Color: Race and the American Legal Process*. New York: Oxford University Press.

Hillenbrand, S. W. and Smith, B. E. (1989) *Victim Rights Legislation: An Assessment of Its Impact on Criminal Justice Practitioners and Victims*. Report of the American Bar Association to the National Institute of Justice. See www.ncjrs.gov/app/publications/abstract.aspx?id=124014

Hindelang, M. J., Gottfredson, M. R. and Garofolo, J. (1978) *Victims of Personal Crime: An Empirical Foundation for a Theory of Personal Victimization*. Cambridge, MA: Ballinger.

Hinsliff, G. (2005) Howard lashes out at gypsy 'squatters', *Observer*, 20 March.

Holmes, P. (2002) *Law Enforcement Co-operation with Non-Governmental Organisations, with Reference to the Protection of Victims and Victims as Witnesses*. Paper presented at the European Conference on Preventing and Combating Trafficking in Human Beings: Global Challenge for the 21st Century. European Parliament, 18–20 September, Brussels.

Holmstrgm, L. L. and Burgess, A. W. (1978) *The Victim of Rape: Institutional Reactions*. New York: John Wiley.

Holmstrgm, L. L. and Burgess, A. W. (1991) *The Victim of Rape*. New Brunswick: Transaction.

Home Office (1990) *Victims' Charter*. London: Home Office.

Home Office (1991) *A Digest of Information on the Criminal Justice System*. London: Home Office.

Home Office (2003). *A New Deal for Victims and Witnesses: National Strategy to Deliver Improved Services*. London: Home Office.

Home Office (2004) *2003 Home Office Citizenship Survey: People, Families and Communities*. London: Home Office.

Home Office (2006) *Code of Practice for Victims of Crime*. Available at http://www.homeoffice.gov.uk/documents/victims-code-of-practice?view=Binary

Hough, M. and Roberts, J. (1999) Sentencing trends in Britain: public knowledge and public opinion, *Punishment and Society*, 1(1).

Howard League (1995) *Banged Up, Beaten Up, Cutting Up: Report of the Howard League Commission of Enquiry into Violence in Penal Institutions for Teenagers under 18.* London: The Howard League for Penal Reform.

Hubbard, P. (2005) Inappropriate and incongruous: opposition to asylum centres in the english countryside, *Journal of Rural Studies*, 21: 3–17.

Huber, M. (1993) Mediation around the medicine wheel, *Mediation Quarterly*, 10(4): 355–66.

Hufbauer, G., Schott, J. and Elliot, A. (1990) *Economic Sanctions Reconsidered.* Washington, DC: Institute for International Economics.

Hughes, E. (ed.) (1984) *The Sociological Eye.* New Brunswick, NJ: Transaction.

Humphries, D. (1999) *Crack Mothers: Pregnancy, Drugs, and the Media.* Columbus, OH: Ohio State University Press.

Hurst, G. (2005) Tories reject racism accusation over plans to curb travellers, *The Times*, 22 March.

Iganski, P. and Kosmin, B. (2003) Globalised Judeophobia and its ramifications for British society, in P. Iganski and B. Kosmin (eds) *A New Antisemitism? Debating Judeophobia in 21st-century Britain.* London: Profile Books.

IOM (1995) *Trafficking and Prostitution: The Growing Exploitation of Migrant Women from Central and Eastern Europe.* Geneva: IOM.

IOM (1996) *Trafficking in Women to Austria for Sexual Exploitation.* Geneva: IOM.

Irwin, J. and Cressey, D. R. (1962) Thieves, convicts and the inmate culture, *Social Problems*, 10, 142–55.

Jalota, S. (2004) Supporting victims of rural racism: learning lessons from a dedicated racial harassment project, in N. Chakraborti and J. Garland (eds) *Rural Racism.* Cullompton: Willan.

Jay, E. (1992) *Keep Them in Birmingham: Challenging Racism in South West England.* London: Commission for Racial Equality.

John, M. (2003) *Children's Rights and Power: Charging up for a New Century.* London: Jessica Kingsley.

Johnson, R. and Leighton, P. (1999) American genocide: the destruction of the black underclass, in C. Summers and E. Markusen (eds) *Collective Violence: Harmful Behavior in Groups and Governments.* New York: Rowman & Littlefield.

Johnstone, G. (2001) *Restorative Justice.* Cullompton: Willan.

Jones, J. (2002) The cultural symbolisation of disordered and deviant behaviour: young people's experiences in a Welsh rural market town, *Journal of Rural Studies*, 18: 213–17.

Jordan, J (1998a) *Reporting Rape: Women's Experiences with the Police, Doctors and Support Agencies.* Wellington: Institute of Criminology.

Jordan, J. (1998b) 'There's not a lot of justice in the system': rape victims' views and the police response', in R. Du Plessis and G. Fougere (eds) *Politics, Policy and Practice: Essays in Honour of Bill Willmott.* Christchurch: University of Canterbury.

Kangaspunta, K., Joutsen, M. and Ollus, N. (1998) *Crime and Criminal Justice Systems in Europe and North America 1990–1994.* Helsinki: HEUNI.

Kartusch, A. (2001) *Reference Guide for Anti-trafficking Legislative Review: With*

Particular Emphasis on South Eastern Europe. Vienna: Ludwig Boltzmann Institute of Human Rights/OSCE.

Kaufhold, M. &and VanderLaan, R. (1988) Evaluating developmentally disabled victims of sexual abuse. Paper presented at the *National Symposium on Child Abuse*, San Diego, CA.

Kauzlarich, D. (1995) A criminology of the nuclear state, *Humanity and Society*, 19: 37–57.

Kauzlarich, D. and Kramer, R. C. (1993) State-corporate crime in the U.S. nuclear weapons production complex, *The Journal of Human Justice*, 5: 4–28.

Kauzlarich, D. and Kramer, R. C. (1998) *Crimes of the Nuclear State: At Home and Abroad.* Boston, MA: Northeastern University Press.

Kauzlarich, D., Kramer, R. C. and Smith, B. (1992) Toward the study of governmental crime: nuclear weapons, foreign intervention, and international law. *Humanity and Society* 16: 543–63.

Kauzlarich, D., Matthews, R. A. and Miller, W. J. (2001) Toward a victimology of state crime, *Critical Criminology*, 10(3): 173–94.

Kelly, D. P. (1987) Victims, *Wayne Law Review*, 34: 69–86.

Kelly, D. P. and Erez, E. (1997) Victim participation in the criminal justice system, in R. C. Davis, A. J. Lurigio and W. Skogan (eds) *Victims of Crime.* Thousand Oaks, CA: SAGE.

Kelly, J. B. (1983) Mediation and psychotherapy: distinguishing the difference, *Mediation Quarterly*, 1(1): 33–4.

Kelly, J. B. (1989) Mediated and adversarial divorce: respondents' perceptions of their process and outcomes, *Mediation Quarterly*, 24, 71–88.

Kelly, J. B. (1990) *Final Report. Mediated and Adversarial Divorce Resolution Processes: An Analysis of Post-divorce Outcomes.* Washington, DC: National Institute for Dispute Resolution.

Kelly, L. and Regan, L. (2000) *Stopping Traffic: Exploring the Extent of, and Responses to, Trafficking in Women for Sexual Exploitation in the UK.* Police Research Series, paper 125. London: Home Office.

Kempe, C. H. (1978) *Child Abuse.* Cambridge, MA: Harvard University Press.

Kennedy, J., Davis, R. and Taylor, B. (1998) Changes in spirituality and well-being among victims of sexual assault, *Journal of the Scientific Study of Religion*, 37(2): 322–8.

Kershaw, C., Chivite-Matthews, N., Thomas, C. and Aust, R. (2001) *The 2001 British Crime Survey: First Results, England and Wales.* Home Office Statistical Bulletin 18/01. London: Home Office.

Kilpatrick, D., Best, C., Veronen, L., Amick, A., Villeponteaux, L. and Ruff, G. (1985) Mental health correlates of victimization: a random community survey, *Journal of Consulting and Clinical Psychology*, 53: 866–73.

Kirkey, K. and Forsyth, A. (2001) Men in the valley: gay male life on the suburban-rural fringe. *Journal of Rural Studies*, 17(4): 421–41.

Klockars, C. B. (1988) The rhetoric of community policing, in J. R. Greene and S. Mastrofski (eds) *Community Policing: Rhetoric and Reality.* New York: Praeger.

Kohut, H. (1985) *Self Psychology and the Humanities: Reflections on a New Psychoanalytic Approach.* New York: W. W. Norton.

Kolb, D. M. and Rubin, J. Z. (1989) Mediation through a disciplinary kaleidoscope: a summary of empirical research, in *Dispute Resolution Forum*. Washington, DC: National Institute for Dispute Resolution.

Koss, M. (1993) Rape: scope, impact, interventions, and public policy responses, *American Psychologist*, 48: 1062–9.

Koss, M. P., Dinero, T. E., Seibel, C. and Cox, S. (1988) Stranger and acquaintance rape: are there differences in the victim's experience? *Psychology of Women Quarterly*, 12: 1–23.

Kramer, R. C. (1992) The space shuttle *Challenger* explosion: a case study of state-corporate crime, in K. Schlegel and D. Weisburd (eds) *White Collar Crime Reconsidered*. Boston, MA: Northeastern University Press.

Kramer, R. C. and Kauzlarich, D. (1999) The world court's decision on nuclear weapons: implications for criminology, *Contemporary Justice Review*, 2(4): 395–413.

Kramer, R. C. and Michalowski, R. (1990) *State-corporate Crime*. Paper presented at the Annual Society of Criminology Meeting, Baltimore, MD.

Krinsky, M. and Golove, D. (1993) *United States Economic Measures Against Cuba: Proceedings in the United Nations and International Law Issues*. Northampton, MA: Aletheia Press.

Kury, H., Kaiser, M. and Teske, R. (1994) The position of the victim in criminal procedure: results of a German study, *International Review of Victimology*, 3: 69–81.

Lacey, N. (1988) *State Punishment*. London: Routledge.

Lacey, N. (1998) *Unspeakable Subjects*. Oxford: Hart.

Lamb, S. (1996) *The Trouble with Blaming: Victims, Perpetrators, and Responsibility*, Cambridge, MA: Harvard University Press.

Laming, H. (2003) *The Victoria Climbié Inquiry: Report of an Inquiry by Lord Laming, Presented to Parliament by the Secretary of State for Health and the Secretary of State for the Home Dept*. London: The Stationery Office.

Lau, E. (1988) Sex abusers of disabled 'often get away with it', *Hong Kong Standard*, 1 May.

Law Commission (1991) *Mentally Incapacitated Adults and Decision-making: An Overview*. London: HMSO.

Law Commission of Canada (1999) *From Restorative Justice to Transformative Justice*, discussion paper. Ottawa: Law Commission.

Lea, J. and Young J. (1984) *What Is to Be Done About Law and Order?* Harmondsworth: Penguin.

Lees, S (1996) *Carnal Knowledge: Rape on Trial*. London: Hamish Hamilton.

Lees, S. (1997) *Ruling Passions: Sexual Violence, Reputation and the Law*. Buckingham: Open University Press.

Lees, S. and Gregory, J. (1993) *Rape and Sexual Assault: A Study of Attrition*. London: Islington Council.

Lees, S. and Gregory, J. (1997) In search of gender justice, in S. Lees (ed.) *Ruling Passions: Sexual Violence, Reputation and the Law*. Buckingham: Open University Press.

LeResche, D. (1993) Native American perspectives on peacemaking, editor's notes, *Mediation Quarterly*, 10(4): 321–5.

Lerner, M. (1980) *The Belief in a Just World*. New York: Plenum Press.

Levy, A., and Kahan, B. (1991) *The Pindown Experience and the Protection of Children:*

The Report of the Staffordshire Child Care Inquiry. Stafford: Staffordshire County Council.

Light, R. (1993) Why support prisoners' family-tie groups, *Howard Journal*, 34: 322–9.

Linde, C. (1993) *Life Stories: The Creation of Coherence.* New York: Oxford University Press.

Little, L. (2004) Victimisation of Children with Disabilities, in A. Kendall-Tackett (ed.) *Health Consequences of Abuse in the Family: A Clinical Guide for Evidence-based Practice.* Washington, DC: American Psychological Association.

Llewellyn, J. J. and Howse, R. (1998) *Restorative Justice: A Conceptual Framework.* Ottawa: Law Commission of Canada.

Lockwood, D. (1980) *Prison Sexual Violence.* New York: Elsevier.

London Borough of Hammersmith and Fulham (LBH) (1992) *The Needs of People with Disabilities: A Survey of the Needs of People with Disabilities and Long-term Illnesses: Stage 1.* London: LBH.

London Rape Crisis Centre (1984) *Sexual Violence: The Reality for Women.* London: Women's Press.

Los, M. (1990) Feminism and rape law reform, in L. Gelsthorpe and A. Morris (eds) *Feminist Perspectives in Criminology.* Milton Keynes: Open University Press.

Lovett, J., Regan, L. and Kelly, L. (2004) Sexual assault referral centres: developing good practice and maximising potentials. Available from http://www.home-office.gov.uk/rds/pdfs04/hors285.pdf

Loy, D. (2001) Healing justice: a buddhist perspective, in M. Hadley (ed.) *The Spiritual Roots of Restorative Justice.* Albany, NY: SUNY Press.

Lurigio, A. (1987) Are all victims alike? The adverse, generalized and differential impact of crime, *Crime and Delinquency*, 33: 452–67.

Lurigio, A. and Resick, P. (1990) Healing the psychological wounds of criminal victimization: predicting post-crime distress and recover, in A. Lurigio, W. Skogan, and R. Davis (eds) *Victims of Crime: Problems, Policies and Programs.* Newbury Park, CA: SAGE.

MacCormick, N. and Garland, D. (1998) Sovereign states and vengeful victims: the problem of the right to punish, in A. Ashworth and M. Wasik (eds) *Fundamentals of Sentencing Theory.* Oxford: Oxford University Press.

McCorkle, R. C., Miethe, T. D. and Drass, K. A. (1995) The roots of prison violence: a test of the deprivation, management, and 'not-so-total' institution models, *Crime and Delinquency*, 41: 317–31.

McCormack, B. (1991) Sexual abuse and learning disabilities, *British Medical Journal*, 303: 143–4.

McDonald, E. (1997) 'Real rape' in New Zealand: women complainants' experience of the court process, *Yearbook of New Zealand Jurisprudence*, 1(1): 59–80.

McEvoy, K. and Mika, H. (2001) Punishment, policing and praxis: restorative justice and non-violent alternatives to paramilitary punishments in Northern Ireland, *Policing and Society*, 11.

McKay, C. (1991) *Sex, Laws and Red Tape: Scots Law, Personal Relationships and People with Learning Difficulties.* Glasgow: Scottish Society for the Mentally Handicapped.

McLeod, M. (1986) Victim participation at sentencing, *Criminal Law Bulletin*, 22: 501–17.

Macpherson, Sir W. (1999) *The Stephen Lawrence Inquiry: Report of an Inquiry by Sir William Macpherson of Cluny*. London: HMSO.

Madsen, L. N. and Adriansen, H. K. (2004) Understanding the use of rural space: the need for multi-methods, *Journal of Rural Studies*, 20: 485–97.

Magne, S. (2003) *Multi-ethnic Devon: A Rural Handbook – The Report of the Devon and Exeter Racial Equality Council's Rural Outreach Project*. Exeter: Devon and Exeter Racial Equality Council.

Maguire, M. and Pointing, J. (eds) (1988). *Victims of Crime: A New Deal?* Milton Keynes: Open University Press.

Malcolm, D. (2004) Outsiders within: the reality of rural racism, in N. Chakraborti, J. Garland (eds) *Rural Racism*. Willan; Cullompton.

Marchetti, A. G. and McCartney, R. (1990) Abuse of persons with mental retardation: characteristics of the abused, the abusers, and the informers, *Mental Retardation*, 28: 367–71.

Markey Report (1986). *American Nuclear Guinea Pigs: Three Decades of Radiation Experiments on U.S. Citizens*. Washington, DC: USGPO.

Marshall, T. F. (1999) *Restorative Justice: An Overview*. London: Home Office Research, Development and Statistics Directorate.

Matthews, J. (1983) *Forgotten Victims: How Prison Affects the Family*. London: NACRO.

Matthews, R. and Kauzlarich, D. (2000) The crash of ValuJet Flight 592: a case study in state-corporate crime, *Sociological Focus*, 3(3): 281–98.

Mauer, M. (1999) *The Crisis of the Young African American Male and the Criminal Justice System*. Washington, DC: Sentencing Project.

Mawby, R. I. and Walklate, S. (1994) *Critical Victimology*. Thousand Oaks, CA: SAGE.

Mayhew, P. and van Dijk, J. J. M. (1997) *Criminal Victimisation in Eleven Industrialised Countries: Key Findings from the 1996 International Crime Victims Survey, No. 162*. The Hague: Ministry of Justice.

Maynard, D. W. (1982) Defendant attributes in plea bargaining: notes on the modeling of sentencing decisions, *Social Problems*, 46: 347–60.

Medea, A. and Thompson, K. (1974) *Against Rape*. New York: Farrar, Straus and Giroux.

Meier, B.-D. (1998) Restorative justice? A new paradigm in criminal law? *European Journal of Crime, Criminal Law and Criminal Justice*, 6: 125–36.

Mendelsohn, B. (1956) Une nouvelle branche de la science bio-psycho-sociale: Victimogie, *Revue Internationale de Criminologie et de Police Technique*, 10–31.

Michalowski, R. J. (1985) *Order, Law, and Power*. New York: Random House.

Midlands Probation Training Consortium (MPTC) in Collaboration with Midlands Region ACOP (1998) *From Murmur to Murder: Working with Racist Offenders*. Birmingham: MPTC

Miers, D. (1989) Positivist victimology: a critique, *International Review of Victimology*, 1: 3–22.

Miers, D. (1990) Positivist victimology: a critique, part two *International Review of Victimology*, 1 (3): 219–30.

Miers, D. (1992) The Responsibilities and Rights of Victims, *Comparative Law Review*, 55.

Miers, D. (1997) *State Compensation for Criminal Injuries*. London: Blackstone.

Miers, D. (2001) *An International Review of Restorative Justice*. London: Home Office.

Miller, A. (1987) *For Your Own Good: Hidden Cruelty in Child-rearing and the Roots of Violence*. London: Virago.

Miller, J. (1996). *Search and Destroy*. Cambridge: Cambridge University Press.

Molhan, S. (1996) *A Mother's Mission: The Sue Molhan Story*. South Bend, IN: Diamond Communications.

Moore, P. and Whipple, C. (1988) *Project Start: A School-based Mediation Program*. New York: Victim Services Agency.

Morgan, J. and Zedner, L. (1992) *Child Victims*. Oxford: Oxford University Press.

Morris, A. and Gelsthorpe, L. (2000) Something old, something borrowed, something blue, but something new? Comment on the prospects for restorative justice under the crime and disorder act, *Criminal Law Review*, 18–30.

Morris, A. and Maxwell, G. (2000) The practice of family group conferences in New Zealand: assessing the place, potential and pitfalls of restorative justice, in A. Crawford and J Goodey (eds) *Integrating a Victim Perspective within Criminal Justice*. Aldershot: Ashgate.

Morris, P. (1965) *Prisoners and Their Families*. London: Routledge and Kegan Paul.

Murray, L. (2007) *Inventing Fear of Crime*. Cullompton: Willan.

Naffine, N. (1990) *The Law and the Sexes: Exploration in Feminist Jurisprudence*. Boston, MA: Allen and Unwin.

National Victim Center and Crime Victims' Research and Treatment Center (1992) *Rape in America*. Fort Worth: National Victim Center.

Naudé, B. and J. Prinsloo (2002) Crime victimization in Southern Africa, in P. Nieuwbeerta (ed.) *Crime Victimization in Comparative Perspective*. The Hague: Boom Juridische Uitgevers.

Neergaard (1997) 50s Fallout posed threat to thyroids. *Philadelphia Enquirer*, August 2.

Neufeldt, R. (2001) Justice in Hinduism in M. Hadley (ed.) *The Spiritual Roots of Restorative Justice*. Albany, NY: SUNY Press.

New Zealand Police (2000) *Report of the New Zealand Police for the Year Ended 30 June 2000*. Wellington: New Zealand Police.

Newburn, T. (2003) *Crime and Criminal Justice Policy*. Edinburgh: Pearson Longman.

Newey, G. (2005) Home alone mum's vile secret, *Birmingham Evening Mail*. 25 February.

Newiss, G. and Fairbrother, L. (2004) *Child Abduction: Understanding Police Recorded Crime Statistics*. Home Office Findings 225. London: Home Office Research Development and Statistics Directorate.

Newsbreak (1991) People with a mental handicap have their say in court, Summer.

Nottingham Health Authority and Nottinghamshire Social Services Department (1992) *Abuse of Adults with a Mental Handicap/Learning Disability: Procedural Guidelines*. Nottingham: Nottingham Health Authority.

Nova Scotia (1991) *Protocol for Investigation and Prosecution of Cases Involving Persons with Special Communication Needs*. Halifax: Department of the Attorney General Department of Solicitor General.

O'Day, B. (1983) *Preventing Sexual Abuse in Persons with Disabilities*. Santa Cruz, CA: Network Publications.

O'Donnell, I. and Edgar, K. (1996a) *The Extent and Dynamics of Victimization in Prisons*. Unpublished report to the Home Office Research and Statistics Directorate.

O'Donnell, I. and Edgar, K. (1996b) *Victimisation in Prisons*. Research Findings No. 37. London: Home Office Research and Statistics Directorate.

O'Donnell, I. and Edgar, K. (1998) *Bullying in Prisons*. Occasional Paper No. 18. Oxford: Centre for Criminological Research, University of Oxford.

O'Malley, P. (1984) Technocratic justice in Australia, *Law in Context: A Socio-Legal Journal*, 2: 31–49.

Ofshe, R. and Watters, E. (1994) *Making Monsters: False Memories, Psychotherapy, and Sexual Hysteria*. New York: Scribner's.

Olweus, D. (1993) *Bullying at School: What We Know and What We Can Do*. Oxford: Blackwell.

Pavligh, G. (2001) The Force of Community, in H. Strang and J. Braithwaite (eds) *Restorative Justice and Civil Society*. Cambridge: Cambridge University Press.

Pearson, E. (2002) *Human Traffic: Human Rights*. London: Anti-slavery.

Pendergast, M. (1996) *Victims of Memory: Sex Abuse Accusations and Shattered Lives*. Hinesburg, VT: Upper Access.

Pettit, P. with Braithwaite, J. (1993) Not just deserts, even in sentencing, *Current Issues in Criminal Justice*, 4: 222–32.

Porporino, F., Doherty, P. and Sawatsky, T. (1987) Characteristics of homicide victims and victimizations in prisons: a Canadian historical perspective, *International Journal of Offender Therapy and Comparative Criminology*, 31: 125–35.

President's Task Force on Victims of Crime (1982) *Final Report*. Washington, DC: US Government Printing Office.

Prison Service (1993) *Bullying in Prison: A Strategy to Beat It*. London: Prison Service.

Pugh, R. (2004) Responding to rural racism: delivering local services, in N. Chakraborti and J. Garland (eds) *Rural Racism*. Cullompton: Willan.

Quinney, R. (1972) Who is the victim? *Criminology*, 10(3): 314–23.

Quinney, R. (1980) *Criminology*. Boston, MA: Little, Brown Company.

Ratcliffe, P. (2004) *'Race', Ethnicity and Difference: Imagining the Inclusive Society*. Maidenhead: Open University Press.

Ray, L., Smith, D. and Wastell, L. (2004) Shame, rage and racist violence. *British Journal of Criminology*, 44(3): 350–68.

Rayner, J. (2005) Chance of racist attack increase fourfold, *Observer*, 27 March.

Reckless, W. (1957) The good boy in a high delinquency area, *Journal of Criminal Law, Criminology and Police Science*, 48: 18–26.

Reeves, H. and Mulley, K. (2000) The new status of victims in the UK: opportunities and threats, in A. Crawford and J Coodey (eds) *Integrating a Victim Perspective within Criminal Justice*. Aldershot: Ashgate.

Reiman, J. (1979) *The Rich Get Rich and the Poor Get Prison*. New York: Allyn and Bacon.

Reiner, R. (1992) *The Politics of the Police*. New York: Harvester Wheatsheaf.

Resick, P. (1993) The Psychological Impact of Rape, *Journal of Interpersonal Violence*, 8: 223–55.

Riley, D. and Shaw, M. (1985) *Parental Supervision and Juvenile Delinquency*. Home Office Research Study No. 83. London: HMSO.

Roach, K. (1999) *Due Process and Victims' Rights: The New Law and Politics of Criminal Justice*. Toronto: University of Toronto Press.

Robinson, V. and Gardner, H. (2004) Unravelling a stereotype: the lived experience of black and minority ethnic people in rural Wales, in N. Chakraborti and J. Garland (eds) *Rural Racism*. Cullompton: Willan.

Rock, P. (1988a) The birth of organizations, *Canadian Journal of Sociology*, 13(4): 359–84.

Rock, P. (1988a) Crime reduction initiatives on problem estates, in T. Hope and M. Shaw (eds) *Communities and Crime Reduction*. London: HMSO.

Rock, P. (1998b) *After Homicide: Practical and Political Responses to Bereavement*. Oxford: Clarendon.

Rogers, C. (1961) *On Becoming a Person*. Boston, MA: Houghton Mifflin.

Rogers, L. and Erez, E. (1997) *The Contextuality of Objectivity in Sentencing Among Legal Professionals in South Australia*, paper presented at the Annual Meeting of the American Society of Criminology in San Diego, November.

Rose, N. (2000) Government and control, *British Journal of Criminology*, 40(2): 321–39.

Rose, V. M. (1977) Rape as a social problem: a by-product of the feminist movement, *Social Problems*, 25: 75–89.

Rosoff, S., Pontell, H. and Tillman, R. (1998) *Profit Without Honor*. Upper Saddle River, NJ: Prentice-Hall.

Ross, J.I . (1995) *Controlling State Crime*. New York: Garland.

Ross, J. I. (1998) Situating the academic study of controlling state crime, *Crime, Law and Social Change*, 29: 331–40.

Ross, J. I. (2000) *Varieties of State Crime and Its Control*. Monsey, NY: Criminal Justice Press.

Ross, J. I., Barak, G., Ferrell, J., Kauzlarich, D., Hamm, M., Friedrichs, D., Matthews, R., Pickering, S., Presdee, M., Kraska, P. and Kappeler, V. (1999) The state of state crime research: a commentary, *Humanity and Society*, 23: 273–81.

Rowe, M. (2004) *Policing, Race and Racism*. Cullompton: Willan.

Rubel, H. C. (1986) Victim participation in sentencing proceedings, *Criminal Law Quarterly*, 28: 226–50.

Rumgay, J. (2004) *When Victims Become Offenders: In Search of Coherence in Policy and Practice*. London: Fawcett Society.

Russell, D. (1990) *Rape in Marriage*. Indianapolis, IN: Indiana University Press.

Rutter, M. and Smith, D. (eds) (1995) *Psychosocial Disorders in Young People*, Chichester: Wiley.

Sage, A. (1991) Who cares about Alex, *Independent*, 19 May.

Sanders, A., Hoyle, C., Morgan, R. and Cape, E. (2001) Victim impact statements: can't work, won't work, *Criminal Law Review*, 447–58. VOLUME NUMBER?

Sanderson, C. (1992) *Counselling Adult Survivors of Child Sexual Abuse*. London: Jessica Kingsley.

Sarat, A. (1997) Vengeance, victims and the identities of law, *Social & Legal Studies*, 6: 163–84.

Satir, V. (1976) *Making Contact*. Berkeley, CA: Celestial Arts.

Saunders, B. E. (2003) Understanding children exposed to violence: toward an integration of overlapping fields, *Journal of Interpersonal Violence*, 18(4): 331–7.

Schur, E. (1965) *Crimes Without Victims: Deviant Behavior and Public Policy*, Englewood Cliffs, NJ: Prentice-Hall.

Scottish Executive (2004) *Vulnerable and Intimidated Witnesses: Review of Provisions in Other Jurisdictions*. Available from:http://www.scotland.gov.uk/Publications/ Recent.

Sebba, L. (1994), 'Sentencing and the Victim: The Aftermath of Payne', *International Review of Victimology*, 3: 141–65.

Sebba, L. (1996) *'Third Parties': Victims and the Criminal Justice System*. Columbus, OH: Ohio State University Press.

Segal, E. (2001) Jewish perspectives on restorative justice, in M. Hadley (ed.) *The Spiritual Roots of Restorative Justice*. Albany, NY: SUNY Press.

Senn, C. (1988) *Vulnerable: Sexual Abuse and People with an Intellectual Handicap*. Toronto: Rocher Institute.

Sereny, G. (1996) *Albert Speer: His Battle with Truth*. London: Picador.

Shapland, J. (1995) Preventing retail-sector crimes, in M. Tonry and D. Farrington (eds) *Building a Safer Society: Strategic Approaches to Crime Prevention*. Chicago, IL: University of Chicago Press.

Shapland, J., Atkinson, A., Atkinson, H., Chapman, B., Colledge, E., Dignan, J., Howes, M., Johnstone, J., Robinson, G. and Sorsby, A. (2006) Situating restorative justice within criminal justice, *Theoretical Criminology*, 10: 505–32.

Shapland, J., Willmore, J. and Duff, P. (1985) *Victims in the Criminal Justice System*. Aldershot: Gower.

Shaw, M., van Dijk, J. and Rhomberg, W. (2003) Determining trends in global crime and justice, *Forum on Crime and Society*, 3(1/2) 35–64.

Shearing, C. (2000) Punishment and the changing face of governance, *Punishment and Society*, 3(2) 203–20.

Shearing, C. (2001) Transforming security: a South African experiment, in H. Strang and J. Braithwaite (eds) *Restorative Justice and Civil Society*. Cambridge: Cambridge University Press.

Shook, E. V. (1989) *Ho'oponopono*. Honolulu, HI: University of Hawaii Press.

Shorter-Gooden, K. (2004) Multiple resistance strategies: how African American women cope with racism and sexism, *Journal of Black Psychology*, 30(3): 406–25.

Siegel, L. (1998) *Criminology*. Boston, MA: West/Wadsorth.

Simon, D. R. (2002) *Elite Deviance*. Boston, MA: Allyn and Bacon.

Sim, J. (1994) Tougher than the rest, in T. Newburn and B. Stanko (eds) *Just Boys Doing Business*. London: Routledge.

Simon, D. R. and Eitzen, S. D. (1982) *Elite Deviance*. Needham Heights, MA: Allyn and Bacon.

Simon, D. R. and Hagan, F. (1998) *White Collar Deviance*. Boston, MA: Allyn and Bacon.

Sinason, V. (1992) *Mental Handicap and the Human Condition: New Approaches*. London: Tavistock.

Singh, P. (2001) Sikhism and restorative justice: theory and practice, in M Hadley (ed.) *The Spiritual Roots of Restorative Justice*. Albany, NY: SUNY Press.

Sjolinder, N. H. (2002) *Trafficking in Human Beings: European Response*. DG Justice and Home Affairs, European Commission, European Conference on Preventing and Combating Trafficking in Human Beings: Global Challenge for the 21st Century. 18–20 September 2002. European Parliament; Brussels.

Slater. A., Shaw, J. A. and Duquesnel, J. (1992) Client Satisfaction survey: a consumer evaluation of mediation and investigative services, *Family and Conciliation Courts Review*, 30(2): 207–21.

Smith, L. (1989) *Concerns About Rape*. Home Office Research Study 106. London: HMSO.

Smith, L. (2004) Villagers bristle at accusation of rural prejudice, *Guardian Unlimited*, 9 October.

Sobsey, D. and Varnhagen, C. (1989) Sexual abuse and exploitation of people with disabilities: towards prevention and treatment, in M. Csapo and L. Gougen (eds) *Special Education Across Canada*. Vancouver: Centre for Human Development & Research.

Sparks, R., Bottoms, A. E. and Hay, W. (1996) *Prisons and the Problem of Order*. Oxford: Clarendon Press.

Spradley, J. P. (1979) *The Ethnographic Interview*. New York: John Wiley.

Stanko, E. A. (1981–2) The impact of victim assessment on prosecutors' screening decisions: the case of the New York County District Attorney's Office, *Law and Society Review*, 16(2): 225–39.

Steffensmeier, D. (1983) Organization properties and sex-segregation in the underworld: building a sociological theory of sex differences in crime, *Social Forces*, 61(4): 1010–32.

Stephens, B. J. and Sinden, P. G. (2000) Victims' voices: domestic assault victims' perceptions of police demeanor, *Journal of Interpersonal Violence*, 15(5): 435–47

Stern, M., Van Slyck, M. and Valvo, S. (1986) *Enhancing Adolescents' Self Image: Implications of a Peer Mediation Program*. Paper presented at the Annual Meeting of the American Psychological Association, Washington, D.C., 1986.

Stitt, B. G. and Giacopassi, D. (1995) Assessing victimization from corporate harms, in M. Blankenship (ed.) *Understanding Corporate Criminality*. New York: Garland.

Stone, J., Barrington, R. and Bevan, C. (1983) The victim survey, in *Rape Study, Vol. 2: Research Reports*. Wellington: Department of Justice and Institute of Criminology.

Stout, B. and Goodman Chong, H. (2008) Restorative justice: theory, policy and practice in B. Stout, J. Yates and B. Williams (eds) *Applied Criminology*. London: SAGE.

Sudnow, D. (1965) Normal crimes: sociological features of the penal code in a public defender office, *Social Problems*, 12: 255–77.

Sumner, C. J. (1987) Victim participation in the criminal justice system, *Australian and New Zealand Journal of Criminology*, 20: 195–217.

Sumner, C. J. and Sutton, A. C. (1990) Implementing victims' rights: an Australian perspective, *Journal of the Australian Society of Victimology*, 1(2): 4–10.

Sutherland, E. H. (1945) Is 'white-collar crime' crime? *American Sociological Review*, 10: 132–9.

Sutherland, E. H. (1949) *White-collar Crime*. New York: Holt, Rinehart and Winston.

Sykes, C. (1992) *A Nation of Victims: The Decay of the American Character*. New York: St. Martin's Press.

Sykes, G. M. (1958) *The Society of Captives: A Study of a Maximum Security Prison.* Princeton, NJ: Princeton University Press.

Sykes, G. M. and Matza, D. (1957). Techniques of neutralization: A theory of delinquency. *American Sociological Review*, 22: 664–70.

Talbert, P. A. (1988) The relevance of victim impact statements to the criminal sentencing decisions, *UCLA Law Review*, 36: 199–232.

Tattum, D. and Herdman, G. (1995) *Bullying: A Whole-prison Response.* Cardiff: Institute of Higher Education.

Tauri, J. (1999) Exploring recent innovations in New Zealand's criminal justice system: empowering Maori or biculturising the state? *Australia and New Zealand Journal of Criminology*, 32: 153–70.

Tavuchis, N. (1991) *Mea Culpa: A Sociology of Apology and Reconciliation.* Stanford, CA: Stanford University Press.

Taylor, I., Walton, P. and Young, J. (1973) *The New Criminology.* London: Routledge and Kegan Paul.

Taylor, L. (1984) *In the Underworld.* London: Unwin.

Taylor, M. and Quayle, E. (2003) *Child Pornography: An Internet Crime.* Hove: Brunner-Routledge.

Temkin, J. (1987) *Rape and the Legal Process.* London: Sweet & Maxwell.

Temkin, J. (1997) Plus ça change: reporting rape in the 1990s, *British Journal of Criminology*, 37(4): 507–28.

Temkin, J. (1999) Reporting Rape in London: A Qualitative Study, *The Howard Journal of Criminal Justice*, 38(1): 17–41.

Tendler, S. (2003) Tony Martin 'wants a return to simple life', *The Times*, 28 July.

Teurfs, L. and Gerard, G. (1993) *Reflections on Building Blocks and Guidelines for Dialogue.* Laguna Beach, CA: Dialogue Group.

Tharinger, D., Horton, C. B. and Millea, S. (1990) Sexual abuse and exploitation of children and adults with mental retardation and other handicaps, *Child Abuse & Neglect*, 14: 301–12.

The Times (1984) Mentally handicapped man jumps to death, 9 January.

The Times (2005). Swastika vandals, 14 March.

Thomas, B. and Mundy, P. (1991) Speaking out, *Nursing Times*, 87(6): 67–8.

Thomas, W. (1932) *The Child in America.* New York: Alfred Knopf.

Thrasher, F. (1927) *The Gang.* Chicago, IL: University of Chicago Press.

Tifft, L. and Markham, L. (1991) Battering women and battering Central Americans: A peacemaking synthesis, in R. Quinney and H. E. Pepinsky (eds) *Criminology as Peacemaking.* Bloomington, IN: Indiana University Press.

Titus, R. M. and Gover, A. R. (2001) Personal fraud: the victims and the scams, in G. Farrell and K. Pease (eds) *Repeat Victimization.* Monsey, NY: Criminal Justice Press.

Tizard, B. and Phoenix, A. (2002) *Black, White or Mixed Race? Race and Racism in the Lives of Young People of Mixed Parentage.* London: Routledge.

Tonry, M. (1994) Proportionality, parsimony and interchangeability of punishments, in A. Duff, S. Marshall, R. E. Dobash and R. P. Dobash (eds) *Penal Theory and Practice.* Manchester: Manchester University Press.

Tonry, M. (1995) *Malign Neglect: Race, Crime, and Punishment in America.* Oxford: Oxford University Press.

Transparency International (2001) *Global Corruption Report 2001*. Berlin: Transparency International.

Travis, A. (2005) Rape conviction rate falls to all-time low, *Guardian*. Available from http://www.guardian.co.uk/uk_news/story/0,,1424915,00.html.

Tunnell, K. D. (1993) *Political Crime in Contemporary America*. New York: Garland.

Turk, A. T. (1969) *Criminality and Legal Order*. Chicago, IL: Rand McNally.

Turk, V. (1991) Research confirms high prevalence of sexual abuse, *Community Living*, 5(2): 18–19.

Umbreit, M. S. (1991) Minnesota mediation center gets positive results, *Corrections Today Journal*, August: 194–7.

Umbreit, M. S. (1993) Juvenile offenders meet their victims: the impact of mediation in Albuquerque, NM, *Family and Conciliation Courts Review*, 31(1): 90–100.

Umbreit, M. S. (1994) *Victim Meets Offender: The Impact of Restorative Justice and Mediation*. Monsey, NY: Criminal Justice Press.

Umbreit, M. S. (1995a) *Mediation of Criminal Conflict: An Assessment of Programs in Four Canadian Provinces*. St. Paul, MN: Center for Restorative Justice and Mediation, University of Minnesota.

Umbreit, M. S. (1995b) The development and impact of victim–offender mediation in the United States, *Mediation Quarterly*, 12(3): 263–76.

Umbreit, M. S. (1995c) *Mediating Interpersonal Conflicts: A Pathway to Peace*. West Concord, MN: CPI.

Umbreit, M. S., and Kruk, E. 'Parent-Child Mediation.' In E. Kruk (ed.), *Mediation and Conflict Resolution in Social Work and the Human Services*. Chicago: Nelson Hall, 1997.

Umbreit, M. S. and Roberts, A. W. (1996) *Mediation of Criminal Conflict in England: An Assessment of Services in Coventry and Leeds*. St. Paul, MN: Center for Restorative Justice and Mediation, University of Minnesota.

United Nations (2000) *Basic Principles on the Use of Restorative Justice Programmes in Criminal Matters*. Available from www.restorativejustice.org/.ents/UNDec BasicPrinciplesofRJ.htm.

United Nations General Assembly (1989) *Convention on the Rights of the Child*. New York: United Nations.

United Nations, Office for Drug Control and Crime Prevention (1999) *Global Report on Crime and Justice*. New York: Oxford University Press.

US Sentencing Commission (1987) *Sentencing Guidelines and Policy Statements*. Washington, DC: US Sentencing Commission.

Utting, Sir William (1997) *People Like Us: The Report of the Review of Safeguards for Children Living Away from Home*. London: The Stationery Office

Utting, Sir William (2004) *Progress on Safeguards for Children Living Away from Home*. York: Joseph Rowntree Foundation.

Van Dijk, J. J. M. (2002) Empowering victims of organized crime: On the concurrence of the Palermo Convention with the UN Declaration on Basic Principles of Justice for Victims. *International Review of Victimology*, 9: 15–30.

Van Dijk, J. J. M., Mayhew, P. and M. Killias (1990) *Experiences of Crime across the World: Key Findings from the 1989 International Crime Survey*. Deventer: Kluwer.

van Kesteren, J., Mayhew, P. and Nieuwbeerta, P. (2000) *Criminal Victimisation in Seventeen Industrialised Countries: Key Findings from the 2000 International Crime Victims Survey, No. 187*. The Hague: Ministry of Justice.

van Ness, D. W. (1993) New wine and old wineskins: four challenges of restorative justice, *Criminal Law Forum*, 4: 251–76.

van Zyl Smit, D. (1999) Criminological ideas and the South African transition, *British Journal of Criminology*, 39(2): 198–215.

Victorian Sentencing Committee (1988) *Sentencing: Report of the Committee.* Melbourne: Attorney-General's Department.

VOICE (1991) Private correspondence.

von Hentig, H. (1941) The limits of penal treatment, *American Journal of Criminal Law and Criminology*, Nov/Dec: 408.

Von Hentig, H. (1942/2005) The criminality of the colored woman, in S. L. Gabbidon and H. T. Greene (eds) *Race, Crime, and Justice: A Reader.* London: Routledge.

Von Hentig, H. (1948/1967) *The Criminal and His Victim: Studies in the Sociobiology of Crime.* Yale, CT: Yale University.

Von Hirsch, A. (1993) *Censure and Sanctions.* Oxford: Oxford University Press.

Von Hirsch, A. and Ashworth, A. (eds) (1992) *Principled Sentencing.* Boston, MA: Northeastern University Press.

Von Hirsch, A. and Ashworth, A. (eds) (1998) *Principled Sentencing: Readings on Theory and Policy.* Oxford: Hart.

Wachtel, T. and McCold, P. (2001) Restorative justice in everyday life, in H. Strang and J. Braithwaite (eds) *Restorative Justice and Civil Society.* Cambridge: Cambridge University Press.

Walgrave, L. (1995) Restorative justice for juveniles, *Howard Journal of Criminal Justice*, 34: 228–49.

Walgrave, L. (2001) On restoration and punishment, in A. Morris and G. Maxwell (eds) *Restorative Justice for Juveniles.* Oxford: Hart.

Walklate, S. (1989) *Victimology: The Victim and the Criminal Justice Process.* London: Unwin Hyman.

Walklate, S. (1995) *Gender and Crime: An Introduction.* London: Prentice Hall.

Walklate, S. (2007) *Imagining the Victim of Crime.* Maidenhead: Open University Press.

Waterhouse, Sir Ronald (2000) *Lost in Care: Report of the Tribunal of Inquiry into the Abuse of Children in the Former County Council Areas of Gwynedd and Clwyd since 1974.* London: The Stationery Office.

Wedge, P., Boswell, G. and Dissel, A. (2000) Violent victims in South Africa: key factors in the backgrounds of young, serious offenders. *Acta Criminologica* 13(1) and 13(2) 31–38.

Weiss, T. G. (1997) *Political Gain and Civilian Pain: Humanitarian Impacts of Economic Sanctions.* Lanham, MD: Rowman & Littlefield.

Western Telegraph (1991) Former manager cleared of attacking handicapped man, 27 March.

Whine, M. (2003) Anti-Semitism on the streets, in P. Iganski and B. Kosmin (eds) *A New Antisemitism? Debating Judeophobia in 21st-Century Britain.* London: Profile Books.

Whitehaven News (2005). Gang in race attack on moor takeaway, 14 March.

Whitfield, D. (1998) *Introduction to the Probation Service.* Winchester: Waterside Press

Whyte, D. (2007) Victims of corporate crime, in S. Walklate (ed.) *Handbook of Victims and Victimology*. Cullompton: Willan.

Widom, C. and White, H. (1997) Problem behaviour in abused and neglected children grown up: prevalence and co-occurrence of substance abuse, crime and violence, *Criminal Behaviour and Mental Health* 7: 287–310.

Williams, B. (1999) *Working with Victims of Crime: Policies, Politics and Practice.* London: Jessica Kingsley.

Williams, L. S. (1984) The classic rape: when do victims report? *Social Problems,* 31: 459–67.

Wilson, J. C. and Davies, G. M. (1999) An evaluation of the use of videotaped evidence for juvenile witnesses in criminal courts in England and Wales, *European Journal on Criminal Policy and Research,* 7(1): 81–96.

Wilson, J. P. and Raphael, B. (eds) (1993) *International Handbook of Traumatic Stress Syndromes.* New York: Plenum Press.

Wolf, E. S. (1988) *Treating the Self: Elements of Clinical Self Psychology.* New York: Guildford Press.

Wolfgang, M. E. (1958) *Patterns of Criminal Homicide.* Philadelphia, PA: University of Pennsylvania Press.

Wolfgang, M. E. (1982) Basic concepts in victimology theory: individualization of the victim, in H-J. Schneider (ed.) *The Victim in International Perspective.*

Wooldredge, J. D. (1994) Inmate crime and victimization in a southwestern correctional facility, *Journal of Criminal Justice,* 22: 367–81.

World Health Organization (WHO) *World Report on Violence and Health.* Geneva: WHO.

Wright, M. (1996) *Justice for Victims and Offenders.* Winchester: Waterside.

Wright, R. (1984) A note on attrition of rape cases, *British Journal of Criminology,* 24(4): 399–400.

Yin, R. K. (1984) *Case Studies Research.* Beverly Hills, CA: SAGE.

Young, R. (2001) Just cops doing 'shameful' business: police-led restorative justice and the lessons of research, in A. Morris and G. Maxwell (eds) *Restorative Justice for Juveniles.* Oxford: Hart.

Young, W. (1983) *Rape Study, Vol. 1: A Discussion of Law and Practice.* Wellington: Department of Justice and Institute of Criminology.

Yule, W. (1993) Children as victims and survivors, in P. J. Taylor (ed.) *Violence in Society.* London: Royal College of Physicians.

Zedner, L. (1994) Reparation and retribution: are they reconcilable?, *Modern Law Review,* 57: 228.

Zedner, L. (2002) Victims, in M. Maguire, R. Morgan and R. Reiner (eds) *The Oxford Handbook of Criminology.* Oxford: Oxford University Press.

Zehr, H. (1990) *Changing Lenses: A New Focus for Criminal Justice.* Scottsdale, PA: Herald Press.

Zimring, F. E. (1981) Making the punishment fit the crime: a consumer's guide to sentencing reform, in H. Gross and A. von Hirsch (eds) *Sentencing.* New York: Oxford University Press.

Zubenko, W. N. (2002) Developmental issues in stress and crisis, in W. N. Zubenko and J. A. Capozzoli (eds) *Children and Disasters: a Practical Guide to Healing and Recovery.* Oxford: Oxford University Press.

Zvekic, U. (1998) *Criminal Victimisation in Countries in Transition*, UNICRI publication No. 61. Rome: UNICRI.

Zvekic, U. and Alvazzi del Frate, A. (eds) (1995) *Criminal Victimisation in the
Developing World*, UNICRI publication No. 55. Rome: UNICRI.

Zvekic, U. and Camerer, L. (2002) Corruption in Southern Africa: a surveys-based
overview, in U. Zvekic (ed.) *Corruption and Anti-Corruption in Southern Africa*.
United Nations Office on Drugs and Crime, Regional Office for Southern
Africa.

Index

cross-national issues on good practice,
    287–8
Crown Prosecution Service, 50, 86, 127,
    268–70
cruelty, 5, 48
Cuba, 201–3
culpability, 163, 233–4, 260
cult of victimhood, 166
Currie, Edwina, 120

data about child victims, 45–7
data analysis of ICVS, 216–21
    crime count, 217–21
data collection in sentencing outcomes
    study, 245–7
    interview schedule, 246–7
    participants, 246
data on victimisation, 26–30
DDGC see domestic–domestic
    governmental crime
death row, 294
death threats, 200
deaths from corporate crime, 167–77
decline of statism, 240–42
decoys, 8, 188, 193
decremental strategy, 240
definitions
    child, 45
    good practice, 283–7
    state crime, 196–8
    victim, 208–9
delinquency, 8, 10
delinquent subculture, 29
demarcation disputes, 269
demographic characteristics of
    offenders, 35
denial, 5
depressed people, 12
deprivation hypothesis, 310
deranged people, 9–10
description of incidents of racism, 63–4
desire for companionship, 15
deterrence, 181–5, 192
deterrence trap, 181
developing effective responses to rural
    racist incidents, 89–92
developing good practice for sex
    trafficking victims, 279–81

development of criminology as
    discipline, 1–40
    criminal and victim, 5–25
    theory of personal victimisation,
        26–40
DIGC see domestic–international
    governmental crime
dignity, 244
disparity of sentencing, 257–8
displacement activity, 54
dissatisfaction with overall police
    response, 109–112
distressed communities, 294
doctor's gender in post-rape medical
    examination, 102–3
Doctors for Sexual Abuse Care, 102,
    104
doli incapax, 47
domestic violence, 43, 47, 136, 207,
    226–7, 239, 259, 306
Domestic Violence, Crime and Victims
    Act 2004, 57
domestic–domestic governmental crime,
    200–201
domestic–international governmental
    crime, 198–200
domination/submission continuum,
    53–4
Down's Syndrome, 124
downstream consequences of VIS, 255,
    262
'Driving While Black', 199
drunk driving, 232, 260
DSAC see Doctors for Sexual Abuse
    Care
dull normals, 10–12
Durkheim, Émile, 137
dynamics of prison victimisation,
    311–22
dysfunction, 157

economic costs of corporate crime,
    169–77
effects of victimisation, 74–6, 122–3
    people with learning disabilities,
        122–3
elements of responsive regulation,
    192

Related books from Open University Press
Purchase from www.openup.co.uk or order through your local bookseller

---

ETHNICITY AND CRIME
A READER

Basia Spalek

> Basia Spalek has compiled an excellent reader about a much researched and highly sensitive subject. Crucially, she contextualises ethnicity and crime within broadly defined social and intellectual contexts, avoiding the limitation of all too frequently repeated research based solely on statistical measures and policy evaluations.
>
> *Simon Holdaway, Professor of Criminology and Sociology, Sheffield University*

Issues in relation to race and ethnicity have generated substantial and ever-growing interest from, and within, a multitude of academic, research and policy contexts. This book brings together important material in race and ethnic studies and provides different ways of thinking about race and ethnicity in relation to crime and the criminal justice system.

Ethnicity and Crime: A Reader consists of a collection of works that capture the main themes that arise from within this vast area of work. It is divided into five sections:

- 'Race and crime', racial discrimination and criminal justice
- The racialisation of crime: Social, political and cultural contexts
- Race, ethnicity and victimisation
- Self and discipline reflexivity: Ethnic identities and crime
- Ethnic identities, institutional reflexivity and crime

Each section contains recurring and overlapping themes and includes many different ways of thinking about race and ethnicity in relation to crime. It spans theoretical approaches that might be labelled as positivist, critical race analyses, left realist approaches, feminist, as well as post-modern perspectives.

This is the first title in the new series Readings in Criminology and Criminal Justice and follows the series format of thematic sections, together with an editor's introduction to the complete volume and an introduction to each section.

Contents
Part One: 'Race and crime', racial discrimination and criminal justice – Part Two: The racialisation of crime: Social, political and cultural contexts – Part Three: Race, ethnicity and victimisation – Part Four: Self and discipline reflexivity: Ethnic identities and crime – Part Five: Ethnic identities, institutional reflexivity and crime.

2008   352pp
978–0–335–22379–4 (Paperback)   978–0–335–22378–7 (Hardback)